DATE DUE

FEB 2 3 1991	DEC - 5 1994
MAR 1 5 1991	
MAR 1 5 1991	DEC 1 1 1995
JUL 3 1 1991	DEC 3 2001
NOV 2 5 1991	MAR 3 0 2002
JAN 2 4 1992	
FEB 2 4 1992	
MAR 2 6 1992	
APR 2 1 1992	
NOV 7 1992	
NOV 1 8 1992	
DEC 1 6 1992	
FEB 4 1993	
APR - 8 1993	
OCT 2 1 1993	
NOV 1 2 1993	
APR 1 1 1994	
APR 2 5 1994	

Aging, Stress and Health

Aging, Stress and Health

Edited by

Kyriakos S. Markides
University of Texas Medical Branch,
USA

and

Cary L. Cooper
University of Manchester Institute of Science and Technology,
UK

JOHN WILEY & SONS
Chichester · New York · Brisbane · Toronto · Singapore

Library of Congress Cataloging-in-Publication Data

Aging, stress, and health.

  Includes bibliographies and index.
  1. Aged—Health and hygiene. 2. Stress (Psychology)
I. Markides, Kyriakos S. II. Cooper, Cary L.
  [DNLM: 1. Aged—psychology. 2. Life Change
Events. 3. Social Environment. 4. Stress, Psychological
—in old age. WM 172 A267]
RA564.8.A43 1989   155.67′2   88–37841
ISBN 0 471 92157 2

British Library Cataloguing in Publication Data

Aging, stress and health. –
  1. Man. Stress
I. Markides, Kyriakos S. II. Cooper,
Cary L. (Cary Lynn), *1940 –*
155.9

ISBN 0 471 92157 2

Typeset by Woodfield Graphics, Fontwell, Sussex, England.
Printed and bound in Great Britain by Courier International Ltd, Tiptree, Essex

List of contributors

A. J. BAGLIONI, JR

Colgate Darden Graduate School of Business Administration, University of Virginia, Box 6550, Charlottesville, VA 22906, USA

NEENA L. CHAPPELL

Centre on Aging, 338 Isbister Building, University of Manitoba, Winnipeg, Manitoba, Canada R3T 2N2

DAVID A. CHIRIBOGA

School of Allied Health Sciences, University of Texas Medical Branch, Galveston, TX 77550, USA

CARY L. COOPER

Manchester School of Management, University of Manchester Institute of Science and Technology, PO Box 88, Manchester M60 1QD, UK

PAUL T. COSTA, JR

Gerontology Research Center, National Institute on Aging, National Institutes of Health, USA

KENNETH F. FERRARO

Department of Sociology, Northern Illinois University, De Kalb, IL 60115, USA

LINDA K. GEORGE

Duke Medical Center, PO Box 3003, Durham, NC 27710, USA

LORNA W. GUSE

School of Nursing, 171 Bison Building, University of Manitoba, Winnipeg, Canada

GILCHRIST L. JACKSON

Kelsey-Seybold Foundation, Cancer Prevention Center, Houston, Texas, USA

NEAL KRAUSE

Health Gerontology, School of Public Health, The University of Michigan, Ann Arbor, MI 48103, USA

KYRIAKOS S. MARKIDES   *Department of Preventive Medicine and
                           Community Health, Division of Sociomedical
                           Sciences, Room 202 Gail Borden (D–13), Univer-
                           sity of Texas Medical Branch, Galveston, TX
                           77550, USA*

ROBERT R. MCCRAE   *Gerontology Research Center, National Institute
                           on Aging, National Institutes of Health, USA*

ANN E. MCGOLDRICK   *Department of Management, Manchester
                           Polytechnic, Aytoun St., Manchester, M1 3GH,
                           UK*

RHONDA J. V. MONTGOMERY   *Institute of Gerontology, Wayne State University,
                           Detroit, MI 48202, USA*

SHELDON S. TOBIN   *Ringel Institute of Gerontology, SUNY Albany,
                           Albany, NY 12222, USA*

SALLY W. VERNON   *University of Texas, School of Public Health,
                           Houston, TX 77025, USA*

Contents

INFORMAL AND FORMAL SUPPORTS

PSYCHOLOGICAL FACTORS AND OUTCOMES

Preface

Much theory and research on aging follows what has been called a 'social stress' paradigm. This is particularly the case in studies focusing on health, both physical and mental. Aging is seen as being accompanied by a number of 'role transitions' that are stressful for the individual and, in some cases, for significant others. The cumulative effect of these transitions, role losses, and other life events is a negative effect on the health of people as they grow old.

A social stress paradigm has also been prominent in social, behavioral, and epidemiologic research on health in the general population. Recent literature in these fields has paid particular attention to the role of social support in moderating or 'buffering' the negative influence of stressful experiences on physical and mental health. The related concepts of social support, 'social networks', 'social integration', or 'social connectedness' are rapidly achieving high prominence in psychosocial approaches to health and illness. A related literature has focused on how personality factors modify the influence of stress on health. All this literature is only now beginning to be applied to older people and we are witnessing a gradual fusing of this approach with those of social gerontologists and other social scientists interested in lifecourse transitions.

This volume is an attempt to bring together scholars from the various perspectives discussed above to assess and synthesize the emerging literature on how social stress, social support, as well as personality factors interact to influence health along the lifecourse. In addition to covering major transitions, the volume includes chapters on the measurement of stress and social support, formal and informal support systems, caregiver burden, depression, personality factors, and outcomes of breast cancer in elderly women.

We express our gratitude and appreciation to our contributors who individually and collectively have written this book. Many thanks go to Anne Winkler who has read and commented on most chapters. Her insights and suggestions have been invaluable to us in preparing the introductory chapter. Finally, we acknowledge the expert typing assistance provided by Kandy Burke.

KSM and CLC

Chapter 1

Aging, Stress, Social Support and Health: An Overview

Kyriakos S. Markides
and Cary L. Cooper

INTRODUCTION

Over the past several decades what has given the social and behavioral sciences legitimacy as important disciplines in the study of health in human populations, has been the repeated finding that 'stress' is causally related to health outcomes (Cooper, Cooper and Eaker, 1988). Stress is, of course, a vague concept, that has been defined and operationalized in a variety of ways (see Chapter 2 by Chiriboga), but primarily in terms of life events. During the 1960s we see the first major attempt to develop a scale measuring life events (Holmes and Rahe, 1987) which became the instrument of choice during the late 1960's and in the 1970s.

As we will see below, stress research has a long history going back to the work of Cannon (1935), Selye (1956), Lazarus (1966), and others. Recent developments in the stress field owe a great deal to the pioneer work of these scholars. During the 1960s when behavioral, social and medical scientists were beginning systematic investigations of the effects of stress on health and mental health, social gerontologists were engaged in a lively debate about the merits of two theoretical perspectives, disengagement and activity theories, both of which aimed at explaining 'successful' adaptation in old age (Maddox and Campbell, 1985). The issue of successful adaptation, which has dominated gerontology for the last three decades, was couched in a social stress perspective. Adaptation has been considered a key task in old age primarily because of the major role losses older people experience (George, 1980) which are thought to be accompanied by a considerable amount of stress. It is safe to say the 'activity' has emerged as the key formula to successful adaptation (Lee, 1985).

Although the body of work surrounding the concept of activity is vast, few studies have attempted to formalize and test the theory. One exception is the study by Lemon, Bengtson and Peterson (1972), which defined activity as 'any regularized or patterned action or pursuit that is regarded as beyond routine physical or personal maintenance' (p. 513). A major activity type outlined by these authors is social activity involving interactions with other human beings.

Aging, Stress and Health Edited by K.S. Markides and C.L. Cooper
© 1989 John Wiley & Sons Ltd

Thus, the concept of activity so central to gerontological theory, is akin to the concepts of social support, social networks, social integration, etc., which are so central in the more general social stress field. Increasingly, however, gerontologists are embracing these concepts and are linking them to health, mental health, and psychological well-being outcomes in older people or across the life-course. A key challenge in this work is the documentation of the extent to which social support and related concepts are useful in predicting health and mental health outcomes in older people directly, or indirectly by 'buffering' the effects of stress. An even greater challenge, which is only now beginning to be addressed, is how social support and stress operate at different stages in the life-course.

This book is an attempt to bring together information bearing on the relationship between stress, social support and health in aging studies. We have asked scholars to address both methodological and substantive issues. As it will be clear, the challenges outlined in the previous paragraph have not yet been met by the literature. Gaps in our knowledge remain vast. Much remains to be learned by gerontologists from the more general field of stress. However, it should also become apparent after reading this book, that the gerontological perspective has much to offer the general stress field because it is sensitive to age and life-course differences with respect to the relationship between stress, social support and health.

STRESS, AGING AND HEALTH

It was earlier said that, at least implicitly, social and behavioral gerontology has always followed a social stress approach. However, it is only recently that the concept of stress has become part of the gerontological vocabulary. Perhaps this is the case because gerontologists have only recently begun to engage in systematic studies of the health of populations (see Ward and Tobin, 1987). At the same time, it is only recently that social epidemiologists, who have long embraced a stress perspective, have begun to study older people. Many of these epidemiologic studies have focused on predictors of mortality in older people (e.g. Blazer, 1982; Seeman *et al.*, 1987). This new marriage of gerontologists and epidemiologists is likely to help improve our understanding of the mortality and health of older people (Markides, 1987).

Although the concept of stress is a recent addition to the social gerontological vocabulary, Chiriboga's chapter points out that stress research in gerontology has a relatively long history operating under assumptions of what may be called a 'Catastrophe Model'. He explains that subjects having undergone what was commonly thought to be a stressful experience, such as relocation, were studied to ascertain its outcome. No particular attention was paid to measuring the stressful experience itself and how it was perceived by different subjects. The assumption that stressful experiences affected people similarly was indeed naive as modern research has shown repeatedly.

However, even more modern research has made naive assumptions about the influence of stress. For example, as Chiriboga points out, Holmes and Rahe (1967) initially assumed that their life events instrument had universal applicability to all subjects regardless of age. Although adjustments to this and other measures of stress have been made to account for age differences, many researchers continue to use old versions of the instruments.

Even though we have made some progress in developing general instruments to measure stress in older people, gerontologists have, over the years, focused on particular major single stressors such as widowhood, retirement, relocation and institutionalization. Ferraro's chapter (Chapter 4) notes that widowhood was considered the most significant event in the life events instrument of Holmes and Rahe (1967). It is indeed a major event in the lives of older people, particularly women. However, gerontologists are beginning to conceptualize widowhood as a life-course transition that has implications far beyond the event of death of one's spouse.

Ferraro makes clear that our approach to studying the effects of the transition to widowhood has followed a stress perspective. And even though a variety of health outcomes have been studied, most studies of the health effects of widowhood have linked it to mortality. Ferraro asks: 'Can the stress of losing a spouse be so severe that it can kill the survivor?' (p.74). The answer is not simple. Yet some interesting patterns have emerged. For example, there is a suggestion that widowhood is not associated with mortality among older widows, perhaps because older women are more psychologically prepared to lose their spouse. To use Pearlin's term (e.g. Pearlin *et al.*, 1981), widowhood is a normative transition for older women in modern society and, therefore, it should not be as stressful as in younger age groups. There is also a suggestion that widowhood is likely to lead to greater mortality among men for whom it is not a normative transition.

With regard to morbidity, Ferraro concludes that health declines have been observed in many studies, but only in the short term. Long-term effects are non-existent or modest at best. Again, early and unexpected widowhood is more likely to have negative consequences.

Retirement is another major life-course transition that has dominated gerontological thinking and research for several decades, much of it following a social stress perspective. As our volume on retirement in ten industrialized societies (Markides and Cooper, 1987) has shown, however, there is little evidence that retirement has negative health outcomes for the individual, perhaps because it has increasingly become an expected and normative transition for most people (see also Ekerdt, Baden, Bosse and Dibbs, 1983). McGoldrick (Chapter 5) shows that data from the United Kingdom even show that early retirees report improved health after retirement (see also Parker, 1987). Similarly, no negative effects are observed on the mental and psychological well-being of early retirees, although people retiring early because of poor health must be treated separately. McGoldrick concludes: 'Evidence does suggest that early retirement on a financially viable basis may, in fact, represent a "double-edged strategy" for many older workers, providing both a basis for coping and an opportunity for personal development outside the work role. (p.101).

A life event or transition that has been studied from a social stress perspective has been residential relocation. As Baglioni (Chapter 6) clearly shows, the extent to which residential relocation, both interinstitutional and voluntary residential moves, is associated with greater mortality or other negative health outcomes, has been the subject of considerable debate in the literature. As in other research, there are problems with research designs and the ability to separate the effect of relocation from that of other factors. Also, the health consequences of relocation appear to be dependent on a number of factors such as pre-relocation orientation and preparation, age, sex, and length of hospitalization as well as characteristics of both original and receiving environments. As in other areas of research the association between relocation and health among the elderly is complex and requires a more complex approach if useful results are to be obtained.

One special type of relocation that has been the topic of considerable research, has been institutionalization. Tobin (Chapter 7) shows that the entry from a community setting into a long-term care setting can be conceptualized as a life-course transition that takes place over a period of time. For example, there is an anticipatory stage that can have psychological effects such as feelings of abandonment and redefinition of one's self. After admission, there is a brief period of adjustment referred to by Tobin as the 'first-month syndrome'. During this period, many residents deteriorate rapidly, others become severely depressed, others become disoriented and still others exhibit bizarre behaviors. According to Tobin there is no question that institutionalization is a highly stressful experience. His research, and that of others, has shown that it is accompanied by increased morbidity and often by increased mortality. However, as in other research, there are problems of obtaining adequate control in order to isolate the effect of institutionalization from the effects of other factors.

Another category of stressors in the lives of many older people includes the various life-threatening chronic diseases so common in old age. Being diagnosed with a major disease can be quite stressful and can lead to further health deterioration. With regard to physical health outcomes, the issue here is less one of the effect of stress than it is of the direct effect on a person's health and survival. Cancer, for example, is common in old age and often leads to death. Breast cancer, in particular, is a major cause of death in older women. However, breast cancer can be arrested through early screening and can be managed successfully. For many, however, diagnosis comes late with death a direct outcome. As we will see later, social factors can be important in postponing death from breast cancer. From a stress perspective, however, breast cancer can be seen as having major psychological consequences on the afflicted individuals. Vernon and Jackson (Chapter 8) demonstrate, however, that diagnosis of breast cancer does not always translate into more psychological or psychiatric problems and poorer self-concept.

There is some suggestion in the literature that younger women may have greater adjustment problems than older women, possibly because the diagnosis of a chronic disease in old age is more expected than in younger years.

Thus far, we have focused on the effects of stressful events or experiences on the individual older person. One area of increasing importance in gerontology has examined the outcomes of the stress associated with the caregiver role when taking care of older people, what is commonly referred to as caregiver burden or caregiver strain. Here the situation is not one of a single stressful event and its outcomes but the continual strain involved in caring for an elderly family member. Montgomery's chapter (Chapter 9) attempts to conceptualize and clarify the concept of caregiver burden. She makes clear that the literature investigating the effects of caregiver burden on the caregiver as well as the elderly person cared for, is at its infancy. The caregiver situation is quite complex, she argues. In addition to understanding the caregiving situation for its immediate effects, Montgomery feels that such understanding can help us predict future outcomes such as future caregiving behavior and institutionalization. Much remains to be done, however, with respect to both conceptualizing and measuring caregiver burden (see also, Deimling, Bass, Townsend and Noelker, 1989; Romeis, 1989).

No book on the outcomes of stress on health could ignore mental and psychological effects. As Monroe and Peterman recently noted, 'The idea that adverse life experiences cause psychological distress is neither new nor profound.' (1988, p.31). Yet a vast amount of research has been conducted on this topic (see, for example, the recent volume by Cohen, 1988). And as George points out, this research has provided the strongest evidence regarding the effect of stress on well-being. Specifically with regard to depression, George points out that literally hundreds of studies have examined the effects of stress on depression or depressive symptoms including a number of studies of older people. Although a relationship between the two has been found consistently, the effect appears to be stronger in the case of chronic stress than in the case of life events.

SOCIAL SUPPORT, AGING AND HEALTH

The concept of 'social support' is rapidly approaching the status of the concept of stress in social and behavioral research of health and illness. Like stress, the concept of social support is vague and has been approached from a variety of perspectives. Most definitions of the concept focus on supportive social interactions that enable individuals to meet their goals and deal with the demands of their environment (Antonucci, 1985).

Although the notion that social relationships have beneficial effects on people's health and psychological well-being is not new, it was not until the 1970s before a significant number of studies documented the association in a variety of settings, samples and with various measures of health and well-being. Recent studies have also documented associations between social support measures and mortality with samples of older people (e.g. Blazer, 1982; Seeman *et al.*, 1987), even though there is reason to believe that social factors should be less predictive of the health and mortality of older than of middle-aged people because of selective survival factors (Markides and Machalek, 1984).

Despite the enthusiasm surrounding the concept of social support during the 1970s, it has become apparent that it is related to health and mental health in rather complex ways (Thoits, 1982). And although it can be argued that support influences health directly, most research has focused on its indirect influence in interaction with stress. As Krause's chapter (Chapter 3) outlines, this 'stress-buffering' hypothesis can take a variety of forms. The 'moderator' model is the most common and is usually evaluated by examining the interaction of stress and social support in a multiple regression analysis format. Other models include the 'suppressor' and 'distress-deterrent' models (see also Barrera, 1988; Wheaton, 1985).

Although the above models are normally stated explicitly in studies utilizing extensive measures of stress, they are equally applicable to studies examining the effects of single stressors on health. As Ferraro's chapter (Chapter 4) shows, for example, there is widespread agreement that supportive social networks are important in helping people deal with the crisis of widowhood and accompanying period of bereavement. Yet systematic studies of how social support buffers the negative effects of widowhood and bereavement on health are few. Widowhood itself may constitute removal of important social support. Ferraro notes, however, that social networks sometimes increase after widowhood. With regard to older people, according to Ferraro, evidence shows that: 'Widowhood is an intense struggle for most, but older adults seem no less able to wage the fight, especially if they are able to draw upon the resources known to help in the process' (p.80). While this conclusion sounds plausible, much remains to be done to document how and what types of supports buffer the stress associated with widowhood and bereavement in different age groups.

With respect to retirement, it may very well be inappropriate to speak of the 'buffering' effect of social support on the effect of retirement on health when no effect is generally observed. Yet, as McGoldrick (Chapter 5) shows, certain types of retirees are more likely to be negatively affected as in the case of those forced to retire early against their will. Studying the beneficial effects of support networks on such individuals would be more fruitful than studying average effects in general samples.

As with widowhood, there is no question among researchers that social support helps people cope with chronic disease such as breast cancer. As Vernon and Jackson show (Chapter 8), social support may even prolong survival. As in other research, however, measures of social support are often crude. For example, several studies have limited themselves to marital status or marital quality as measures of support. The question regarding the effect of social support on survival of breast cancer patients in different age groups has not been resolved with the limited available evidence being contradictory. Contradictory evidence also exists with respect to the effect of social support on psychiatric and other psychological outcomes in breast cancer patients.

As with stress, it is with mental health and psychological well-being measures that social support has shown its greatest association. George (Chapter 11) shows that there is substantial evidence documenting a significant direct effect on depression including among older people. She also notes that the literature is beginning to document how specific types of support buffer specific stressors. For example, instrumental supports have been found to buffer material deficits while emotional supports buffer the effects of bereavement.

George also discusses the rapidly growing literature on the mediators of the effects of stress on depression. She notes that in addition to social support, a number of psychological mediators have been identified including measures of mastery, self-efficacy, internal locus of control and high self-esteem. These mediators, however, have rarely been studied with regard to older people. Yet there are problems with psychological mediators, many of which, according to George, may be seen as components rather than antecedents of depression. Specifically, with respect to the association between social support and depression, there is the added issue of the correct causal ordering of variables. As George points out, while some research has suggested that social support reduces the effect of stress on depression by bolstering self-esteem (e.g. Krause, 1987), other research has suggested self-efficacy reduces depression by mobilizing support networks in the face of stress (Holahan and Holahan, 1987). Perhaps both types of effects can be simultaneously at work, although more appropriate longitudinal data would certainly help clarify such complex associations.

Despite the above issues, it is becoming increasingly apparent that stress research has a long way to go in examining the coping effectiveness of social support vis-a-vis that of individual psychological attributes. Costa and McCrae (Chapter 12) outline an additional complication in stress research that is rarely addressed by researchers focusing on social support. This complication becomes evident when scholars attempt to distinguish conceptually, as well as empirically, between such concepts as 'personality', 'stress' and 'coping'. As an example, they ask: 'Is venting frustration on others a sign of stress, or a form of coping, or a personality trait, or perhaps an outcome indicating a failure of coping?' (p.270). These authors feel that progress has been made in sorting out these concepts conceptually and in developing instruments aimed at avoiding overlap among measures of these concepts. For example, Costa and MaCrae define coping as a 'set of concrete responses to a stressful situation or event that are intended to resolve the problem or reduce distress.' (p.271). Thus, measures should elicit actual responses to particular stressors rather than the characteristic style of how individuals usually or typically respond to stress. Such operational distinctions between personality and coping, according to Costa and McCrae, permit meaningful questions about how the two are interrelated.

Costa and McCrae point out that recent studies employing appropriate controls for types of stress have found little evidence of significant age differences in coping. They conclude that the association between age and coping resembles that between age and personality traits, where stability is the rule in the adult years. Longitudinal studies, however, are necessary to give more credence to this hypothesis.

An area receiving increased attention in gerontology, has to do with the relationship between informal and formal support systems. Chappell and Guse (Chapter 10) note that the emerging social stress and aging literature has almost exclusively concentrated on the role of informal supports as buffers against stress. Another tradition in gerontology has long focused on documenting the existence of strong informal (primarily family) supports for most elderly. These authors point out formal supports are becoming increasingly important for most elderly in modern society. However, it is secondary to informal ties and support and complements the latter instead of substituting for it. Neither the literature on formal, nor the literature on informal support, however, has examined adequately the negative and stressful effects of receiving support nor the linkages between the two.

CONCLUDING REMARKS

It is our hope that individually and collectively the chapters in this volume demonstrate that social gerontological research is more systematically embracing a social stress perspective that better enables the understanding of what happens to the health and mental health of people as they get older. Key concepts of stress, social support and coping are increasingly becoming part of our vocabulary. Much remains to be done, however, in better conceptualization of and measurement of these concepts at different stages in the life-course.

A life-course perspective on the interrelationship among stress, social support and health has obviously a great deal to offer. Key life events are becoming conceptualized as life-course transitions that differentially affect individuals depending on their demographic, social and psychological characteristics as well as social resources and life circumstances. Although we have made much progress in conceptualizing the life-course, our empirical verifications lag behind our conceptualizations. For example, a life-course perspective demands longitudinal data. The chapters in this volume demonstrate that even cross-sectional studies of age differences in the interplay among stress, social support and health have not been many. Clearly, longitudinal analyses provide many opportunities but at the same time present serious methodological challenges. We hope that these rather diverse chapters will provide a springboard for future research that is likely to lead to a better understanding of what happens to the health and mental health of people as they grow older.

REFERENCES

Antonucci, T.C. (1985). Personal characteristics, social support, and social behavior. In R.H. Binstock and E. Shanas (eds.) *Handbook of Aging and the Social Sciences*, 2nd edn, Van Nostrand Reinhold, New York, pp. 94–128.

Barrera, M. (1988). Models of social support and life stress. In L.H. Cohen (ed.) *Life Events and Psychological Functioning: Theoretical and Methodological Issues*, Sage Publications, Newbury Park, CA, pp. 211–36.

Blazer, D.G. (1982). Social support and mortality in an elderly community population. *American Journal of Epidemiology*, **115**, 684–94.

Cannon, W.B. (1935). Stress and strain of homeostasis. *American Journal of Medical Science*, **189**, 1.

Cohen, L.H. (ed.) (1988). *Life Events and Psychological Functioning: Theoretical and Methodological Issues*, Sage Publications, Newbury Park, CA.

Cooper, C.L., Cooper, R.D. and Eaker, L. (1988). *Living with Stress*. Penguin Books, New York, London.

Deimling, G.T., Bass, D.M., Townsend, A.L. and Noelker, L.S. (1989). Care-related stress: A comparison of spouse and adult-child caregivers in shared and separate households. *Journal of Aging and Health*, **1**, (Feb).

Ekerdt, D.J., Baden, L., Bosse, R. and Dibbs, E. (1983). The effect of retirement on physical health. *American Journal of Public Health*, **73**, 779–83.

George, L.K. (1980). *Role Transitions in Later Life*, Brooks/Cole, Monterey, CA.

Holahan, C.K. and Holahan C.J. (1987). Self-efficacy, social support, and depression in aging: A longitudinal analysis. *Journal of Gerontology*, **42**, 65–8.

Holmes, T. and Rahe, R. (1967). The social readjustment rating scales. *Journal of Psychosomatic Research*, **11**, 213–18.

Krause, N. (1987). Life stress, social support, and self-esteem in an elderly population. *Psychology and Aging*, **2**, 349–56.

Lazarus, R.S. (1966). Some principles of psychological stress and their relation to dentistry. *Journal of Dentistry Research*, **45**, 1620–6.

Lee, G.R. (1985). Theoretical perspectives on social networks. In W.J. Sauer and R.T. Coward (eds.) *Social Support Networks and the care of the Elderly*, Springer, New York, pp. 21–37.

Lemon, B.W., Bengtson, V.L. and Peterson, J.A. (1972). An exploration of the activity theory of aging: Activity types and life satisfaction among in-movers to a retirement community. *Journal of Gerontology*, **27**, 511–23.

Maddox, G.L. and Campbell, R.T. (1985). Scope, concepts, and methods in the study of aging. In R.H. Binstock and E. Shanas (eds.) *Handbook of Aging and the Social Sciences*, 2nd edn, Van Nostrand Reinhold, New York, pp. 3–31.

Markides, K.S. (1987). Characteristics of dropouts and the prediction of mortality in a longitudinal study of older Mexican Americans and Anglos. In R.A. Ward and S.S. Tobin (eds.) *Health in Aging: Sociological Issues and Policy Directions*, Springer, New York, pp. 86–97.

Markides, K.S. and Cooper, C.L. (eds.) (1987). *Retirement in Industrialized Societies: Social, Psychological and Health Factors*, John Wiley & Sons, Chichester.

Markides, K.S. and Machalek, R. (1984). Selective survival, aging and society. *Archives of Gerontology and Geriatrics*, **3**, 207–22.

Monroe, S.M. and Peterman, A.M. (1988). Life stress and psychopathology. In L.H. Cohen (ed.) *Life Events and Psychological Functioning: Theoretical and Methodological Issues*, Sage Publications, Newbury Park, CA, pp. 31–63.

Parker, S.R. (1987). Retirement in Britain. In K.S. Markides and C.L. Cooper (eds.) *Retirement in Industrialized Societies: Social, Psychological and Health Factors*, John Wiley & Sons, Chichester, pp. 77–102.

Pearlin, L.I., Lieberman, M.A., Menaghan, E.G. and Mullan J.T. (1981). The stress process. *Journal of Health and Social Behavior*, **22**, 337–56.

Romeis, J.C. (1989). Caregiver strain: Toward an enlarged perspective. *Journal of Aging and Health*, **1**, (May).

Seeman, T.E., Kaplan, G.A., Knudsen, L., Cohen, R. and Guralnick, J. (1987). Social network ties and mortality among the elderly in the Alameda County Study. *American Journal of Epidemiology*, **126**, 714–23.

Selye, H. (1956). *The Stress of Life*, McGraw-Hill, New York.

Thoits, P.A. (1982). Conceptual, methodological, and theoretical problems in studying social support as a buffer against life stress. *Journal of Health and Social Behavior*, **23**, 145–59.

Ward, R.A. and Tobin, S.S. (eds.) (1987). *Health in Aging: Sociological Issues and Policy Directions*, Springer, New York.

Wheaton, B. (1985). Models of the stress-buffering functions of coping and social support. *Journal of Health and Social Behavior*, **26**, 352–64.

Methodological Issues

Chapter 2

The Measurement of Stress Exposure in Later Life

David A. Chiriboga

Research on the stressors faced by older people has a relatively long history. As was the case with stress research in general, many of the earliest studies followed what might be called a 'Catastrophe Model.' In these studies, subjects were identified who had experienced, or might experience, some condition that most would agree was stressful. The goal was generally to examine what actually happened to the subjects: how they coped with the situation, and how they ultimately fared. An example is the study of relocation. From the early research on relocation, such as Pollack's (1925) investigation of hospitalized patients, to those in more recent times (e.g. Tobin and Lieberman, 1978; Pruchno and Resch, 1988), the focus of research has been on mediating factors and outcomes, rather than on how to assess the actual stress context.

One of the obvious problems with using the Catastrophe Model is that it assumes that the stress experience is essentially equivalent across subjects. In other words, all individuals who have been through the same crisis situation, whether it be a flood, bereavement or relocation, are faced with a similar context and perceive the situation in the same way. This assumption stands in contrast to a common adage in modern stress research that what represents a crisis to one individual may simply be a challenge to another. For reasons such as this, in the 1960s gerontologists began to address ways of actually measuring the stress context. An empirical approach offered at least two critical advantages over the approach of selecting people in crisis: (1) degree of stress exposure could be quantified and therefore compared; and (2) samples could be drawn from the general population, and not just from those suffering from comparatively rare 'major' stress conditions.

Although no one would probably go so far as to say that gerontologists have been successful in identifying and developing effective ways of measuring the stressors of later life, a number of vigorous and promising avenues of research and instrumentation have been developed. In the remainder of this chapter, our attention will turn to these avenues. The next section documents why gerontologists are interested in studying stress and generally where the field stands at present. The next section presents some basic definitional and

Aging, Stress and Health Edited by K.S. Markides and C.L. Cooper
© 1989 John Wiley & Sons Ltd

conceptual issues, while the remaining sections focus on specific research efforts that hold promise.

STRESS: WHY STUDY IT?

As illustrated in the other chapters of this volume, exposure to stress has multiple implications for well-being. Theorists and researchers have traditionally viewed stress in terms of its relevance for short-term deterioration in physical, psychological and social function. In study after study of bereavement, amputation, relocation, divorce and other social traumas, the typical investigation evaluates respondents, at the most, from one to two years after the stress event. Although the results generally have demonstrated an important, and possibly causal, link between stress exposure and a variety of indicators of physical and psychological well-being, it should be emphasized that the verdict, especially for older populations, is not in. For example, after reviewing a variety of studies using life events in older populations, Murrell, Norris and Grote (1988; see also Rabkin and Streuning, 1976; Tausig, 1986) conclude that life events have shown only minor associations with outcome criteria, and go on to suggest that the current focus on life events may be too narrow.

The short-term impact of stress experiences, however, is not the only reason why gerontologists are studying stressors such as life events. Students of adult development and aging have begun to pay attention to the long-term implications of stress, especially life events (e.g. Chiriboga and Cutler, 1980; Neugarten, 1977; Whitbourne, 1985). For example Wallerstein (1986) has found many of her adult respondents still to be suffering from divorce well into the tenth year of her longitudinal study. And in a longitudinal study of ordinary, community-living younger and older adults, life events at all ages were found to exert a major influence on levels of well-being not only shortly after the events but 11 to 12 years later as well (Chiriboga, 1984).

Because of their long-term implications, stressors such as life events are now seen as critical elements in the study of adult development. According to Brim and Ryff (1980, p. 368), for example, 'life events are as integral to life-span development theory as are atoms and other lesser particles to physical theory.' The importance of stress conditions is also emphasized when subjects themselves are asked what has influenced their lives. Lowenthal, Thurnher and Chiriboga (1975) had subjects draw graphs of their life course and then describe what had caused the up-and downswings. Almost without exception the ascribed causes were what could broadly be defined as stressors. Perhaps of more importance, these stressors included not only life events, but expected events, nonnormative transitions such as divorce, chronic problems and even events, such as marriage or graduation, that failed to happen. In other words, the importance of stressors to development in adulthood and aging is not limited to life events but covers a broad range of impinging agents.

The need for a review of measurement in stress

Despite the general acceptance of stressors as factors influencing the well-being of men and women, and partly because of the variety of stressful conditions that could be influential, there are at present no generally accepted instruments to measure stressors. In consequence, it is difficult to make any kind of generalization concerning the impact of stressors.

This kind of confusion was not always the case. At one point there was a single instrument, the Schedule of Recent Events (SRE), that was widely used with all age groups. For a period of approximately 10 to 15 years after its introduction, the SRE (Rahe *et al.*, 1964; Holmes and Rahe, 1967) was the instrument of choice for stress research. A 42 item inventory of life events, the SRE included a sophisticated weighting system based on the assumption that each life event imposed upon people a more or less standard demand for readjustment. The SRE was also readily comprehensible to both researchers and subjects, and quick to administer. Although it had much to offer, by the mid to late 1970s a number of researchers began publishing evidence suggesting that the SRE manifested multiple problems in content validity, predictive validity and generalizability. The practice of combining positive and negative items into a single Life Change Unit (LCU) score was also questioned, as research demonstrated rather conclusively that positive and negative events had differing implications for at least psychological well-being (e.g. Chiriboga and Cutler, 1980).

One of the most telling problems with the SRE weighting system was that it yielded results that were correlated in the 0.70 to 0.90 range with simple counts of events reported (Chiriboga, 1977; Rahe, 1978). It was also found that the LCU scores assigned each event, far from representing a weight generalizable across all socio-demographic groups and even across nations, were significantly different. For example, younger and older subjects in the original sample used by Holmes and Rahe (1967) to arrive at their LCU scores, differed in assigned LCU on approximately two-thirds of the life events (Masuda and Holmes, 1978).

From the mid-1970s onward, a number of instruments have been developed as replacements for the SRE. These included alternative life inventories, usually including either an expanded number of items or a different approach to weighting events, and alternatives to life events themselves. The latter approach has focused on measures of conditions such as hassles and the more durable or chronic stressors. Non-events and anticipated events have also been suggested as relevant to persons of all ages, and there is evidence that for persons in the middle and later years, stressful experiences happening to one's children and friends play an increasingly important role (Lowenthal *et al.*, 1975).

Current drawbacks in stress measurement

Letting go of the Schedule of Recent Events as the standard 'tool' of the trade has had the advantage of freeing researchers to explore more innovative and diverse approaches to stress measurements. A host of alternative instruments have resulted. One drawback to the rapid proliferation and evolution of stress indices over the past decade has been that there are now, in a sense, too many choices. Another, less obvious problem is that many of the existing instruments are undergoing continuous evolution. In consequence, those who adopt the instruments are often using instruments that are months to years out of date, or are using them in ways that the original authors have now abandoned.

For example, Holmes and Rahe (1967) originally thought that their stand-ardized weighting system had universal applicability and that findings were generalizable across extremely diverse samples. In later work, Holmes and Rahe independently arrived at the conclusion that there were major and significant differences, for example, in the weights that older and younger people would apply to the same event (e.g. Masuda and Holmes, 1978; Rahe, 1978). Therefore, while the originators of the SRE warned against generalizing across age groups, numerous research projects have continued to use the SRE in its original form.

In much the same way, Lazarus and his colleagues at UC Berkeley developed several instruments to tap dimensions of stress, including measures of hassles and uplifts and coping (Lazarus and Launier, 1978). However, while several of these indices were modified in later work (e.g. Lazarus and Folkman, 1984), many researchers and practitioners continue to use the original version. Similarly, the geriatric life events inventory developed by Eva Kahana and her colleagues (Kahana, Fairchild and Kahana, 1982; Kiyak, Liang and Kahana, 1976) has undergone considerable revision since its initial development. While Kahana (personal communication, 1988) feels the resulting instruments are much improved, others continue to use an older version that represents work conducted up to 10 years in the past.

Sometimes of course it may be necessary to continue using older versions. For example, in longitudinal research where the focus is on test and retest over considerable periods of time, the researcher may quite rightly be unwilling to modify or change an instrument. And when replicating or expanding on existing research, an investigator may decide to use an older instrument that has been used in the previous work.

The particular problems in measuring stress among older persons

If serious measurement problems exist in the general field of stress, those associated with the study of stress in later life must be considered nothing short of overwhelming.

1. Many researchers persist in using standard instruments that were originally developed and standardized on relatively young populations. A resulting issue has been content validity, since many of the items have little relevance to persons in middle or later life. For example, Ander, Lindstrom and Tibblin (1974) reported that only about half of the items included in the SRE are likely to be experienced even by middle-aged subjects, let alone the elderly.

2. Although a number of instruments have been developed for use with older populations, few have received serious attention from a psychometric point of view.

3. The majority of instruments are limited by their operational definition of stress. For example, much of the focus in developmental research on stress has been on life events, which reflect acute conditions. In contrast, the more durable or chronic conditions of life have only just begun to receive attention. According to theorists such as Len Pearlin (1980; Pearlin, Menaghan, Lieberman and Mullins, 1981) in fact, chronic stressors may have a greater impact on an individual's functional state than acute stressors—which may seem bad, but whose effects tend to dissipate in time. This is actually a debatable point since many life events, such as bereavement, are especially devastating to those who experience them. Moreover, life events sometimes chain to other events, over a period of time, and hence supposedly temporary life events may extend in impact for considerable lengths of time.

4. In part because it is relatively easy to put together life event inventories, it is rare for gerontologists to use instruments developed by others. More common is for researchers and their students to employ the instrument they themselves have developed. For this reason, there are at least 20 different life event inventories for older adults currently available, and the only finding that seems generalizable across studies is that older subjects probably experience fewer life events than do younger (e.g. Lin, Ensel and Dean 1986, Horowitz and Wilner, 1980).

DIFFERENT PERSPECTIVES ON STRESS EXPERIENCES

Before preceding with the main point of this chapter, a consideration of how to measure stress exposure in older adults, it would seem appropriate to address some basic conceptual and definitional issues. The reason is that there is marked disagreement concerning what the word 'stress' actually means. Stress initially was a term most widely used in engineering. In that discipline, it refers to the load or burden imposed on a structural element, such as a steel girder. Strain, in contrast, is the 'give' or reaction of the element to the load.

In the more human sciences, 'stress' is used in several different ways. One of the first biobehavioral applications of the term was made by Hans Selye, sometimes referred to as the father of modern stress theory. In his book, *The Stress of Life*, Selye (1956) described the physiologic response of an animal to physical trauma.

He developed a stress paradigm, the General Adaptation Syndrome, in which it was proposed that mammals respond in a similar way to most if not all physical (and by extension, psychosocial) trauma. Selye went on to identify three factors he felt to underlie stress and in doing so helped to clarify what researchers and clinicians are actually talking about. The three factors were: stressors, conditioning factors (now often called mediators), and responses. Since people often employ the term 'stress' in referencing any one of these three factors, and sometimes in referencing the whole model, care must be exercised in distinguishing between these factors.

Stressors

Stressors are the impinging conditions, or agents of change, and may represent both one time and chronic problems. The earliest and greatest attention has been focused on this component of the stress paradigm. In the early 1960s, several teams of investigators began putting together checklists of stressors that were used to investigate stress responses such as psychological symptomatology (e.g. Lowenthal, Berkman and Associates, 1967; Antonovsky and Katz, 1967). Stress research really came of age, however, with the publication of the Schedule of Recent Events, an instrument developed by Holmes and Rahe (1967) that was easy to administer in community surveys and appeared to have excellent validity.

Mediators

Mediators are those factors that modulate or buffer against the impact of stressors. They include both internal conditions such as intelligence and well-developed skills in areas relevant to the stress situation; mediators may also include external conditions such as the availability of community service agencies and social supports. Interest in these mediators has followed the dramatic increase in interest in the field of stress generally. Sometimes referred to as coping resources, those that currently receiving the most attention are measures of social supports (e.g. Thoits, 1983; Pearlin, 1980; see Chapter 3 for a review of measurement issues) and coping (e.g. Lazarus and Folkman, 1984; Kahana *et al.*, 1982).

Responses

Stress responses are the various ways, physical, and psychological and social, in which people respond to stressors; they are often subdivided into short- and long-term responses. Stress responses are generally not in themselves an object of intense scrutiny; the instruments generally are borrowed from other fields, such as mental health. Most commonly employed are measures of depression, including the CES-D (Radloff, 1977), anxiety instruments such as the Spielberger, Sorsuch, Lushene and Vagg (1977) State – Trait Anxiety Scale, dimensions of symptomatology tapped by omnibus instruments such as the Hopkins Symptoms Checklist-90 (Derogatis and

Cleary, 1977), or morale indices such as the Lawton (1977) Philadelphia Geriatric Center Morale Scale.

Complexity and diversity within the paradigm

This basic paradigm can be made more complex, by expanding on the basic elements and by adding feedback loops. For example, Pearlin *et al.* (1981) see self-esteem as playing a major role in determining the significance not only of stressors but of mediators. As another example, severe and prolonged depression experienced after the loss of a loved one might well create feedback, becoming an additional stressor since the bereaved person often is fully aware of how dysfunctional he or she currently is. Overall, it would be hard to justify the study of stressors and responses alone, given the relatively advanced level of conceptualization in the mainstream of stress research (e.g. Thoits, 1983; Lin, Dean and Ensel, 1986; Elliott and Eisdorfer, 1982).

In the present chapter we will be concerned principally with the stressor end of the stress paradigm. As mentioned above, stressors have in fact received the most attention, in recent years, due in part to the seminal work of Holmes and Rahe. An advantage of the resulting diversity of instrumentation is that when used in various combinations, they may help us to understand how an individual responds to an immediate or specific problem. Rarely, of course, do individuals experience only one stress at a time; we live in a real world that seethes with change, some good, some bad, some fleeting, some permanent.

One disadvantage of the diversity is that, when trying to evaluate measures of this dimension, there are so many approaches to measurement that it is simply hard to organize the material. Over the years, and as a vehicle for trying to understand the phenomenon of stress, our transitions research team developed a model of the stress experience that has helped to guide our own research, and to interpret our findings. For convenience, we have sometimes referred to the model as 'the three faces of stress,' since it involves a basic categorization of stress situations into three levels. These consist of the micro, mezzo and macro levels.

The micro level

At what we call the micro level, the focus is on the day to day experiences of people: the stressors of everyday life. Examples include running out of toothpaste, getting caught in a traffic jam, or finding your child in the bathroom just when you're in a rush to take a shower. By far the most commonly experienced stressors, they are also the least studied. In one early panel investigation, Holmes and Holmes (1970) reported that such day to day problems were associated with minor physical complaints, including the common cold. In a more recent study, Lazarus and Folkman (1984) found day to day hassles to correlate with the physical and emotional well-being of middle-aged men and women. Several studies conclude that day to day hassles are correlated more strongly with physical and psychosocial outcomes than are life events (e.g. Lazarus and Folkman, 1984; Weinberger, Hiner and Tierney, 1987).

The mezzo level

The most studied of the three levels, mezzo stressors deal with situations that are generally less frequent than micro stressors, but which also apply directly to the individual. The well-known life events type of research (e.g. Holmes and Rahe, 1967) falls into this category, as do studies of the more chronic or durable stressors (e.g. Pearlin, 1980). In studies of older populations, mezzo level stressors have been found to predict all sorts of physical mental and social dysfunction. Everything, in fact, from coronary heart disease (e.g. Lynch, 1977; Preston and Mansfield, 1984) to general psychiatric symptomatology (e.g. Dohrenwend, 1974, Chiriboga, 1984) to depression (e.g. Brown and Harris, 1978; Pearlin, 1980).

The macro level

Stressors at the macro level are those that impact first on society at large. The threat of war, bad economic news, a flurry of near-misses in the air lanes or a spill of environmentally hazardous materials not only make the headlines but can create anxiety and a generally heightened sense of distress on the part of the populace. Perhaps the earliest investigation of macro level events was conducted inadvertently. In the United States, Norman Bradburn and his colleague David Caplovitz were testing a new morale measure in a series of national probability studies conducted before and after the assassination of President John Kennedy. They found a national increase in the experiencing of negative emotions in the wake of the murder (Bradburn and Caplovitz, 1965).

More recently Harvey Brenner (1985) a sociologist at Johns Hopkins University, has reported a very strong linkage between downturns in the United States economy and upturns in admission rates to mental institutions. This linkage was subsequently replicated in a study conducted by Richard Suzman (1980), using longitudinal data from the same study that I have referenced before: the Longitudinal Study of Transitions. In part because of findings such as this, gerontologists are now becoming interested in the role of macro level events, which are viewed as having the potential for creating not only change in the short run but change that may affect the trajectory of the individual's entire life (e.g. Miller, 1980; Birren, 1988). Perhaps the best known macro level study, however, is Glen Elder's (1974, 1981) qualitative analysis of the long-term impact of the Great Depression, developed on the basis of data from the Institute of Human Development, University of California, Berkeley.

In the remainder of this chapter we shall review approaches to stress measurement that fall within the three levels of stressor described above. The goal is not to present an exhaustive list of instruments and interviews, but rather to highlight the research teams and instruments that represent promising approaches to the study of stressors experienced by older populations.

STRESSORS OF THE MICRO LEVEL

In what is probably the first structured approach to studying stressors at the micro level, Holmes and Holmes (1970) gave a stress inventory to subjects every day for one week. Results indicated that common, every day experiences such as running out of coffee were associated with minor health problems, such as feeling tired or having a roughness in the throat. Despite its promise, their inventory, however, received little or no attention from other researchers.

In the field of gerontology there has been little interest in micro level stressors until comparatively recently. Current research tends to be dominated by an instrument, the Hassles Scale, developed by Richard Lazarus and his colleagues. At present, however, a number of alternatives exist. Zautra, Suarnaccia, Reich and Dohrenwend (1988), for example, have spent several years developing an alternative approach that is briefer, and possibly more applicable to older populations.

The hassles scale

Richard Lazarus and his research team originally developed the 117 item Hassles Scale for use in a study of stress among the middle-aged (Lazarus and Launier, 1978; Folkman, Lazarus, Pimley and Novacek, 1987). They define hassles as follows:

> Hassles are the irritating, frustrating, distressing demands that to some degree characterize everyday transactions with the environment. They include annoying practical problems such as losing things or traffic jams and fortuitous occurrences such as inclement weather, as well as arguments, disappointments, and financial and family concerns.
>
> (Kanner, Coyne, Schaeffer and Lazarus, 1981, p. 3)

Areas covered by the Hassles Scale include work, health, family, friends, the general environment, practical considerations such as home maintenance, and 'chance occurrences.' Subjects rate each hassle they have experienced on a three point severity scale, with results generally summated into a single hassles score (Kanner *et al.*, 1981).

In its initial application, a sample of 100 middle-aged men and women filled out the Hassles Scale once a month for nine months. Test–retest reliability averaged 0.79 for the frequency of occurrence and 0.48 for an intensity score obtained by dividing cumulative severity ratings by cumulative frequency (Kanner *et al.*, 1981). Hassles were found to correlate significantly with a measure of positive affect, and to predict psychological symptoms more strongly than did a minimally described modification of the SRE. While the instrument is comprehensive, and has been used with older populations (e.g. Folkman *et al.*, 1987), its length could prove a handicap.

The uplifts scale

In addition to their Hassles Scale, a negatively-oriented instrument, Lazarus and Folkman (1984; Kanner *et al.*, 1981) have also developed a 135 item Uplifts Scale to look at daily occurring positive life changes that might affect behavior. As described in directions to subjects, 'Uplifts are events that make you feel good' (Kanner *et al.*, 1981, p. 30). Content areas covered by the items were the same as those used in the Hassles Scale.

Included in the same panel study described for the hassles measure, the average reliability from month to month was 0.72 for frequency and 0.60 for an intensity rating. In terms of predictive validity, uplift frequency was significantly correlated with positive but not negative affect, and was only minimally related with psychological symptoms (Kanner *et al.*, 1981). Perhaps because of its weaker associations with measures of maladaptation, this instrument is less widely used than the Hassles Scale.

The UCSF hassles scale

In an effort to reduce the time and effort involved in completing the Lazarus Hassles Scale, our transitions research team at the University of California San Francisco developed a shorter version of the Lazarus instrument. This instrument, the UCSF Hassles Scale, contains questions concerning hassles in 12 general domains of life, such as work, marriage and family (Chiriboga and Cutler, 1980; Chiriboga, 1984). Test – retest reliabilities over a two year period were 0.62 for men and 0.64 for women. A recent revision of the scale adds two specific questions concerning hassles involved in providing care to an elderly parent (Chiriboga and Weiler, 1988). In general, both versions demonstrate significant associations with indices of negative affect and psychological symptoms (Chiriboga, 1984; Chiriboga and Weiler, 1988).

The inventory of small life events (ISLE)

The ISLE (Zautra *et al.*, 1988) has been developed as a complement to the PERI Life Events Scale that will be described in the next section. Because it is a companion measure, special care was taken to avoid overlap with items in the more standard event inventory. For example, a standard weighting score (Dohrenwend, Krasnoff, Ashehasy and Dohrenwend, 1978) of 250 units was arbitrarily selected as the maximum allowable score for inclusion in ISLE. Items were taken from existing instruments and other unspecified sources to produce a 178 item inventory that includes content from 13 domains: work, the family, social, household, love and marriage, financial, children, transportation, school, recreation, crime, religious concerns, and health.

Although the ISLE uses a standard weighting system derived from undergraduate raters and experts in stress research, it has been used to study older populations with some success (e.g. Reich *et al.*, 1986; Zautra *et al.*, 1988). However, the instrument given to the older group represents a modification of the basic ISLE: the number of items was expanded to 199 and several of the original items were reworded. At the time this chapter was written, the older adult version of the ISLE was still in the process of review and potential revision (Zautra, personal communication).

Daily hassles

Although most measures of hassles are structured, at least one follows a more open approach similar to that employed by Brown and Harris (1978). Dolan (1986) has developed a semi-structured instrument that is to be filled out at the end of the day, by respondents. Designed to assess 'daily hassles,' the instrument is actually labeled the 'Episode Description' form. Subjects briefly describe the 'most bothersome' experience of the day, categorize it by context (e.g. work or school, health or finances, or family or friends). They rate the situation as to type of cognitive appraisal (e.g. was it something that could be changed, that had to be accepted, etc.), and also evaluate their response to the situation according to degree of effectiveness on a five point scale.

This instrument has been given to college educated, professional women (mean age = 33) and its applicability to older populations is unclear. At the same time, its more open nature should make the instrument relevant to almost any age group.

STRESSORS OF THE MEZZO LEVEL

The original SRE developed by Holmes and Rahe (1967) has received extensive treatment in the literature and will not be reviewed in this chapter. Rather, attention will focus on instruments that seem particularly relevant to studies of older populations.

The recent life changes questionnaire (RLCQ)

The RLCQ was developed by Rahe and Arthur (1978) to address problems associated with the content validity of the original SRE. It differs from the original in three basic ways. First, content validity was improved by increasing the number of items from 42 to 77. Second, instead of responding for a single time period (usually one year in the SRE), the RLCQ asks the subject to note the incidence of life events over a 24 month period that is subdivided into four six month intervals. Third, as a means of avoiding the arbitrary nature of the SRE, subjects themselves are asked to rate the degree of change, using a 100 point range. This latter procedure is a tactic researchers can use with any inventory employing standard weights, even the original SRE, if there is an expectation that the weights might not be applicable.

In the expanded version, the RLCQ covers five basic domains of life: work (17 items), family and home (29 items), personal and social (18 items), financial (7 items) and health (6 items). Although a number of items are of low probability for an elderly population (e.g. wife becomes pregnant, wife has a miscarriage, birth of a child), the majority of items are more or less relevant and the instrument would appear to have reasonable validity as a life span instrument. One source of concern with this and many other SRE-type instruments is the inclusion of items pertaining to the individual's own physical health status. While clearly a major health problem can be a stressor, including such problems in a total Life Change Unit score to predict health status may lead to artificially inflated estimates of association.

Despite potential problems that may arise from the use of this instrument without awareness of its limitations, the RLCQ does meet many of the objectives to the original SRE. The use of subject-provided weights, plus the expanded content, should make it more relevant to older populations. Curiously, however, the SRE remains more commonly used.

SRE-type instruments for specialized samples

One advantage of instruments based on the SRE approach is that they are fairly readily adapted for use with specialized populations, such as surgical patients or graduate students. Kobasa, Maddi and Courington (1981), for example, used a modified version of SRE designed for use with middle and upper level managers. The age range for their sample was 32 to 65, with most subjects falling into the middle years. Kobasa replaced ambiguous items (i.e. 'change in financial condition' was revised to 'improvement of financial condition'). They added 15 items, on the basis of pilot testing, that would be relevant to the lives of management personnel. New items received weights based on the same scaling procedures followed by Holmes and Rahe (1967); the result is an instrument sensitive to life events experienced by middle-aged managers.

SRE-type instruments for older populations

The adaptability of the SRE has led to several revisions designed for use with older populations. In one of the first such revisions, Amster and Krauss (1974) removed a number of items and added several, including reaching the age of 65. Although Amster and Krauss provided little rationale for the new items, and their instrument has received little or no attention, other revisions have fared somewhat better. Mensh (1983), for example, has developed a 27 item modification with promise, while Kahana, Kahana and Young (1987) (see also Kiyak *et al.*, 1976) and George (1980) have developed more comprehensive inventories. Despite efforts to expand the range of items, a major limitation of most of these measuring tools is the adequacy of their content, given the diversity of life events that may be encountered during later life and the general lack of systematic attempts to identify suitable content.

The geriatric life events schedule

This instrument, developed by Kahana *et al.*, (1987), is particularly relevant because it represents the result of a research effort than spans over a decade. In the initial version, Kiyak *et al.*, (1976) modified the original SRE substantially. Twenty-three of the original SRE items were retained; another six, initially vague as to whether the event was positive or negative (i.e. 'change in health of a family member'), were recreated as 12 items with desirability clearly specified; two additional items were collapsed into one. Based on the results of unstructured questions dealing with the stressors experienced by older persons, 19 additional items were added (e.g. 'move to home for the aged'). The new schedule requires 10 to 15 minutes for completion (Kahana *et al.*, 1982); subjects check off those events experienced during the past three years, and indicate (on a scale from 0 to 100) the amount of change that each event would require in their usual way of life.

The psychiatric epidemiology research interview (PERI) life events scale

In what may be the most carefully executed series of developmental studies, Bruce and Barbara Dohrenwend, and their colleagues, have spent over 15 years developing and refining the PERI Life Events Scale. This is one of the more comprehensive or omnibus inventories, in that it includes 102 items and is intended to have life span applicability. Since the PERI scale was not designed specifically for an older population, the number of items could conceivably be reduced substantially. However, after reviewing the scale, the author of this chapter concluded that in fact only three items were probably impossible for an older person to experience: 'entered the Armed Services,' 'became pregnant', and 'abortion.' The remainder varied widely in probability of occurrence, but still were possible. For example, it is possible for an older man to experience 'birth of a first child' or for an older women or man to start working for the first time.

Instrument development

The life events chosen for inclusion in the PERI scale were based on qualitative responses to questions about events that subjects in two New York City samples felt had interrupted or changed their activities. Events included in the SRE, as well as the general prior research experience of the investigators, were also included. Ambiguous phrasing, especially concerning whether the event was desirable or undesirable, was avoided and the instrument includes proportionately more desirable events than either the SRE or the RLCQ. Several alternative standardized weightings are available, although the researchers caution that selection of the appropriate weighting system, or of simple counts as the alternative, must depend on the particular research questions and sample.

The PERI scale has been used in several studies of older populations. While generally employed in its full version, some researchers have shortened the instrument to reduce its time requirement, as well as the negative reaction subjects sometimes have to lengthy inventories. Cohen, Teresi and Holmes (1985), for example, reduced the PERI scale to 15 items. As is often the case with studies that modify existing instruments, no detailed rationale or psychometric justification is provided for the actual items included. However, demonstrating the robustness of the PERI scale, even this small subset of items was found to effectively divide subjects by social network characteristics.

The Krause checklist of stressful life events

Modifications to the PERI scale are not always as drastic as that produced by Cohen *et al.* (1985). In an effort to create a more age-relevant instrument, Krause (1986a, 1986b) reduced the PERI scale, but added items from other scales. The resulting 77 item inventory groups events into categories involving: children, spouse, other relatives, friends, neighborhood, finances, crime, and miscellaneous. Using simple tallies of reported life events, as opposed to the standard weights developed by Dohrenwend *et al.* (1978), Krause has found his modification to have good construct and predictive validity (Krause, 1986a, 1986b, 1986c).

Use with older populations

Overall, the PERI scale seems to represent a reasonable approach to studying life events experienced by any age group. Its length might represent a problem for researchers considering the use of mailed questionnaires or who already have a multitude of lengthy instruments. The fact that the list of life events was derived from an urban sample also raises questions concerning its relevance to rural populations. On the other hand, few investigators have drawn on other than urban samples of convenience, if anything, in selecting items for inclusion.

The Louisville older persons events scale (LOPES)

LOPES was developed by Murrell *et al.* (1984, 1988) as a broad spectrum life events inventory specifically designed for older persons. It includes 54 items, selected on the basis of extensive pretesting with older populations. In addition to its own qualities, a major strength of this instrument is that it has been included in a very carefully designed large scale study. A stratified, multi-stage probability sample was drawn that represented all geographic areas of Kentucky. The sample, moreover, is large enough to permit some confidence in the results: it included 1102 men and 1758 women.

LOPES elicits information on life events experienced over a shorter time period, six months, than is usually the case with event inventories. One consequence of this shorter time span may be greater reliability of recall. The instrument also requests information on more characteristics of each event than is usual or perhaps even necessary for most research needs, including desirability, degree of continued preoccupation, date and novelty.

In one early report using LOPES, Murrell *et al.* (1984) have established the frequency and degree of undesirability of life events experienced by the sample but generalizable at least to the state level. A number of additional reports have come out (e.g. Norris and Murrell, 1984, 1987; Murrel *et al.*, 1988) that continue to show the appropriateness of this instrument to studies of the elderly. As is the case with all geriatric event inventories, however, LOPES lacks content validity when applied to younger populations—a factor that may limit the use of this otherwise excellent scale.

The University of California life events questionnaire (UCSF-LEQ)

The UCSF-LEQ (Chiriboga, 1977, 1984) was given to the same community sample three times over a period of approximately six years. Since data from an earlier version was available for a period six years before its first application, the instrument has provided a relatively unique perspective on stress experiences of younger and older persons.

In the early 1970s, a collaborative team of researchers at the University of California worked at addressing three key problems associated with the SRE of Holmes and Rahe: the lack of content validity for middle-aged and older samples, the confounding of positive and negative events that was created by the mixing of both into a single Life Change Unit score, and the threats to predictive validity created by using a sample of convenience to determine the weighting system. The team consisted of Mardi Horowitz, a psychiatrist, David Chiriboga, a life-span developmental psychologist, Marjorie Fiske Lowenthal, a social psychologist, and Nancy Wilner, a social worker. In addition, Dr Richard Rahe, co-creator of the SRE, was brought in extensively as a consultant.

In creating a new instrument, the team drew on two sources of data. One source consisted of extensive clinical interviews with several hundred troubled individuals who sought therapy from the Center for the Study of Neuroses (Dr Mardi Horowitz, Director). In selecting items for consideration, one decision rule was to rule out any event not mentioned by at least 5% of this admittedly highly selective population.

The second source consisted of semi-structured to unstructured interviews with 216 men and women aged 16 to 65, all participants in the baseline phase of a proposed longitudinal study of transitions (Lowenthal, *et al.*, 1975). Each of these interviews lasted an average of eight hours, usually divided into three interview sessions, and focused on factors influencing people's lives. Again, life events reported in response to open-ended questions about change agents produced a provisional list of items for inclusion in a new inventory.

The UCSF-LEQ

The basic life events instrument developed by the team included 125 items. These items formed the core of what Horowitz and Wilner (1980) subsequently labeled the 'long form' and Chiriboga (1977; Chiriboga and Cutler, 1980) labeled the UCSF-LEQ. While Horowitz utilized averaged ratings by pyschiatrists to serve as weights for each item, Chiriboga and his colleagues incorporated a somewhat different approach. Their version also incorporated 13 items related to childhood stress experiences (Chiriboga, Catron and Weiler, 1987).

The UCSF-LEQ scores were subdivided into 11 dimensions, on the basis of a content analysis: (1) marital and dating (21 items); (2) family (20 items); (3) habits and appearance (6 items); (4)non-family relationships (9 items); (5) personal (23 items); (6) legal (4 items); (7) financial (6 items); (8) work (19 items); (9) home (4 items); (10) school (7 items); and (11) health (6 items). Scores on the health dimension were generally omitted from analyses, to avoid confounding predictions of mental and physical health status (Chiriboga and Cutler, 1980). The information on the 13 item childhood stress dimension was also omitted from general analyses since it did not deal directly with current events.

Test — retest reliability

Measures of positive and negative life events were available at four of the five contacts: baseline, five years, seven years and 12 years, although the baseline instrument was developed on the basis of content analysis and therefore did not constitute a self-report instrument. The basic question was whether desirable and undesirable events demonstrate stability, and to examine this question all the life event measures were correlated with each other at all times. This was done for men and women separately, in analyses computed for this chapter.

The men

For men two basic trends were found. First, positive events correlate at moderately high levels over considerable periods of time, whereas negative events were only minimally correlated. For example, the tally of positive life events at baseline correlated at 0.50 ($p=0.01$) with positive events reported at the five year follow-up, and at 0.33 ($p=0.01$) for positive events reported at the 12 year follow-up. In contrast, the negative event tally at baseline was not significantly associated with negative events at either the five or seven year follow-ups but showed a significant association only at the 12th year contact. Similarly, correlations among positive totals from the Life Events Questionnaire at the fifth year, seventh and 12th year contacts were in the high forties to fifties, whereas correlations among the negative totals were in the high twenties to mid-thirties.

Second, positive and negative event totals were generally uncorrelated with each other. In other words, having a lot of negative events had no bearing on exposure to positive experiences.

The women

For women two basic trends were also found. First, and in contrast to data for the men, negative life events were generally more highly correlated over time than were the positive, even though the differences were generally not substantial. For example, negative events at the five and seven year follow-ups correlated at 0.43 ($p=0.01$), where positive events correlated at 0.32 ($p=0.01$). Negative events at seven years correlated with the 12 year data at 0.58 while the positive correlated at 0.55.

Second, for women there was also an interesting tendency for positive and negative events to be significantly correlated with each other, although the correlations explained only small portions of the variance. For example, negative events at the five year point correlated 0.26 ($p=0.05$) with positive events for the same period, 0.39 ($p=0.01$) with positive events reported at the seven year follow-up and 0.55 with positive events reported at the 12th year follow-up. This kind of finding could mean many things. One explanation is that some people generally experience lots of things, both positive and negative.

The life events survey (LES)

Irwin Sarason and his colleagues (Sarason, Johnson and Siegel, 1978; Sarason, Sarason, Potter and Antoni, 1985) have developed a life events inventory that includes a combined desirability/impact rating that ranges from 'extremely negative' to 'extremely positive.' The LES was designed as a general instrument that would be appropriate to all adult age groups (Sarason *et al.*, 1978). In an effort to increase its sensitivity to aging issues, Davis (1985) modified the LES by deleting events irrelevant to the later stages of life, adding items deemed more relevant to the later stages of life, expanding subject ratings on desirability and impact of each event, and expanding the time frame assessed from the 'previous year' in the original LES to all years since (for persons in middle age) the 40th birthday or (for persons aged 60 and over) since the 60th birthday. The result is two instruments, a 67 item survey form for middle-aged respondents and a 59 item form for respondents aged 60 and over.

While the basic modifications made by Davis (1985) may be of interest to those that deal with middle-aged or older populations, the potentially extensive but also quite variable time span assessed in the instrument would seem to raise major questions concerning accuracy of recall. No test—retest information is provided in this cross-sectional study. Using a sample of 435 midlle-aged subjects and 154 subjects aged 60–79, Davis (1985) reports that the middle-aged reported significantly more events than did the older sample. The five most frequent events for the middle-aged group were: a change in work situation, child leaving home, death of a close family member, major change in economic situation, major change in eating habits. The five most frequently experienced events for the older group included: major changes in eating habits and in economic situation, grandparenthood, major change in church activities, and decrease in physical activity.

The Lewinsohn event inventories

Lewinsohn and his colleagues have developed several stress inventories that are relevant to studies of older populations.

The pleasant events schedule (PES)

The original PES was developed on the basis of reports by college students, as well as an unspecified number of subjects 'of diverse educational and social backgrounds and ranging in age from 35 to 76' (MacPhillamy and Lewinsohn, 1976, p. 2). Subjects rate each event for (1) frequency of occurrence over the past 30 days ('This has not happened..., This has happened a few times (1 to 6)..., This has happened often (7 or more)...') (MacPhillamy and Lewinsohn, 1976, pp. A–1), and (2) pleasantness ('This was not pleasant, This was somewhat pleasant, This was very pleasant'). A number of subscales have been defined on arbitrary (e.g. social, nonsocial and indeterminant) and factorial (e.g. general, masculine versus feminine-related, extroverted and stimulus seeking versus introverted) grounds. Test—retest reliabilities on subscales range from 0.69 to 0.88 over a one month period, and from 0.50 to 0.72 over a three month period (MacPhillamy and Lewinsohn, 1982). Predictive and construct validity has been assessed, and norms have been established for adult males and females.

In studies with younger and older populations, older adults have been found to report fewer pleasant events but to find those that are experienced as enjoyable as younger adults (Lewinsohn and MacPhillamy, 1974). While this age difference may reflect a true difference in the experiencing of pleasant events, as interpreted by Lewinshohn and MacPhillamy (1974), it may also reflect an instrument heavily weighted towards the kinds of events more commonly experienced by younger persons. For this reason, and since the 320 item PES is a relatively lengthy instrument, Teri and Lewinsohn (1982) have revised this instrument by considering impact and frequency of occurrence among subjects ranging in age from 50 to 97. The shorter version, labeled the PES-Elderly (PES-E), contains 114 items but retains the original tally of frequency and ratings on how enjoyable was each event. Sample items included 'being in the country, laughing, kissing, taking a nap, being with my grandchildren, and traveling.' The short form correlates very strongly ($r=0.96$) with the long form. Internal reliability for the PES-E is 0.98.

The unpleasant events schedule (UES)

The UES is designed to assess the frequency and unpleasantness of 320 events reported to be generally aversive in nature (Lewinsohn and Talkington, 1979; Lewinsohn, Mermelstein, Alexander and MacPhillamy, 1983). The instrument has been used extensively in studies of depression, where it has demonstrated worth as a predictor (e.g. Lewinsohn, Mermelstein, Alexander and MacPhillamy, 1985). As was the case in the development of the PES, however, the UES instrument development phase drew largely on undergraduate populations and therefore the bulk of the items are not particularly relevant to middle-aged and older adults.

The UES was subsequently reduced in length to 131 items, using the same procedures followed in shortening the PES. Sample items include 'being alone, receiving junk mail, death of an acquaintance, shopping for daily necessities, owing money, having my pet sicken and die' (Teri and Lewinsohn, 1982, p. 445). The short form correlates very strongly ($r=0.99$) with the long form. Internal reliability for the UES-E is 0.96.

Overlap in stressor categories

The two instruments developed by Lewinsohn and his colleagues include events ranging from the day to day to mezzo level. Hence, events can be expected to vary widely in their separate and cumulative association with indices of physical and mental health. No age differences were reported in the standardization samples, although women found the pleasant events to be less pleasant and the unpleasant events to more unpleasant.

A comment on the use of arbitrary versus individualized weights

An unresolved issue in the use of life events, or any index of stress exposure for that matter, concerns what type of weighting system is most appropriate, and whether a weighting system is in fact appropriate at all. As mentioned earlier, Holmes and

Rahe (1967) in their original instrument incorporated standard weights based on averages obtained from a large but unrepresentative sample.

Not using standard weights

A number of researchers have concluded that (1) weighted inventories correlate quite highly with simple summations of life event frequencies, and (2) individual variations in the perception of events are so great that the use of standardized weighting systems is questionable (e.g. Chiriboga, 1977; Tausig, 1986). Generally, the use of standardized weights would seem contraindicated if the group on which standards are based differs from the sample population on major socio-demographic features. For example, it is clear that older and younger subjects differ significantly on how they weight SRE items (Masuda and Holmes, 1978).

Unweighted scores may also be more appropriate than standard scores when the variability in event weights is minimal. For example, Chiriboga (1977) concluded that the reason two standard weighting systems correlated highly with a simple count was that most of the weights fell into a very restricted range, and that the difference between, for example, a 29 and 30 on the SRE system really is inconsequential in the prediction of adaptation.

Using weights

There definitely are compelling arguments for the use of standard weights. One such argument is that when subjects are asked to evaluate how 'negative' or 'undesirable', etc., are the events in their lives, their responses may be colored by their mental status which may create an artificial or spurious linkage between event ratings and mental status ratings. For example, a depressed widow might weight all recently experienced events more negatively due to her depression, while someone in vibrant health might rate all events more positively. One result might be that self-rated life events would correlate more strongly with mental health scores.

The response of at least some researchers to the above argument is that, while valid in cross-sectional research, the spurious association can be controlled for in panel and longitudinal designs. A perhaps more interesting argument is that by employing standardized weights arrived at from large and representative groups, one can obtain what Kobasa *et al.* (1981) have called the 'culturally-defined stressfulness of events.' In other words, standard weights represent the evaluation of the average member of the society, and therefore may be useful, especially when the focus is on group differences or associations.

If the decision is made to use some weighting system, rather than relying on the simpler total count of events reported, the researcher is faced with the decision of whether or not to use (or develop) some standard weighting system. Here the major issue is whether the available systems are appropriate to older populations similar to those of interest to the investigator. For example, weights based on a sample of white urban elderly may be entirely inappropriate for use with rural black elderly. A frequent recourse of investigators is to have their subjects complete the same standardization procedures employed in the original development of an existing inventory (most often the SRE).

Standard weights: towards a resolution

All the arguments for and against standard weights seem to have some merit. To help define the situation, one issue that should be considered is the homogeneity of the sample, and whether the sample that defined the standard weights would seem generally similar in values and attitudes to the prospective samples.

If the sample does in fact seem different from the standardizing group, then the researcher is faced with a dilemma. First, unless the study follows a repeated measures design there is a possibility of confounding when individual weights are used. Second, if standard weights are used, they may be entirely inappropriate to the sample. As mentioned above, one solution might be to develop standard weights on the basis of the sample, and use these weights instead of the individual ones. A third and perhaps the easiest solution is to forget the whole weighting issue and simply use summary counts of life events experienced. Finally, the researcher may develop a system in which each subject rates the impact or desirability of each event, and therefore the weighting system is tailored to the individual. This last approach would seem most appropriate when used in longitudinal designs that can control for spurious associations (Dohrenwend *et al.*, 1978).

Life events: concluding thoughts

Despite the problems inherent in the SRE, it continues to be the method of choice for many researchers. When used with younger populations, as in a recent study of herpes simplex among men and women aged 20 to 46 (VanderPlate, Aral and Madger, 1988), the SRE may be reasonably appropriate as to content validity and general applicability of weights. When the sample includes individuals at mid-life and beyond, problems can accrue. For example, in Pilisuk, Boylan and Acredolo's (1987) secondary analysis of men and women aged 40 and over who were members of a large HMO system in California, use of the unmodified SRE may be a factor underlying the apparent lack of association of stress with clinic visits during the first year of the study. The mixing of positive and negative events, and the ambiguous wording of several items, are definite liabilities to the SRE and instruments that employ the same weighting system.

Non-event oriented approaches to assessing mezzo level stressors

The interview schedule for events and difficulties

In a number of studies, primarily focused on depression in middle-aged and older subjects, Brown and Harris (1976) have gone against the push towards structured event inventories by employing a guided interview approach. In their major publication, Brown and Harris (1978) found this method to elicit quantifiable data with high content and predictive validity.

Chronic or durable stressors

While much of the focus in developmental research on stress has been on life events, which tape acute conditions, the more durable or chronic conditions of life have also received attention. According to theorists such as Len Pearlin (1980; Pearlin *et al.*, 1981) chronic stressors may, in fact, have a greater impact on an individual's functional state than acute stressors—which may seem bad, but whose effects tend to dissipate in time. This is a debatable point since many life events, such as bereavement, are especially devastating to those who experience them. Moreover, life events sometimes chain to other events over a period of time and hence supposedly temporary life events may extend in impact for considerable lengths of time.

The bottom line is that life events, as viewed at one point in time, may in fact lead to repetitive conditions that many researchers would judge to constitute chronic stress. For example, one surprising finding from the Longitudinal Study of Transitions was that when life events at each of the five contact points were correlated, the magnitude of the correlations approximated those found in personality research (e.g. Chiriboga, 1984). This finding indicated both that life events are not random and that they chain forward in time.

MACRO STRESSORS

Although several investigators (e.g. Miller, 1980) have considered the impact of community and social disruption on the lives of older persons, only one structured instrument is currently available: the Social Problems Scale.

The social problems scale (SPS)

The SPS (Fiske and Chiriboga, 1985) was developed on the basis of content analyses of responses to open-ended questions, given at both the baseline and first follow-up of a five wave longitudinal study. The questions dealt with the respondent's perception of local, national and international affairs, and how they affected his or her life (Lowenthal *et al.*, 1975).

From the content analyses, the 14 item SPS was developed. Respondents are asked to rate how strongly they have been affected by each of the several macro level stressors. Results indicate considerable stability over a two year period. For men ($N=64$), test−retest correlations were 0.67, while for women ($N=75$) they were 0.51. The instrument was found to predict the psychological symptoms and affective well-being of older adults in the sample (Chiriboga, 1984; Fiske and Chiriboga, 1985). However, since the item specifies the macro level stressors, and included items covering the Vietnam War and other topical events, some revisions would be necessary to make the SPS more contemporary.

IMPLICATIONS AND CONCLUSIONS

As was noted earlier in this chapter, the measurement of stressors experienced by persons in later life is both complex conceptually and difficult to assess operationally. The complexity arises from the multiple and poorly specified nature of the stressors. Life events, for example, clearly represent only one component of the experiences faced by older adults. Stressors at all levels should probably be included when the researcher is interested in this domain of experience. And, of course, once the researcher accepts the necessity of a broader definition of stressor, the task has only begun. None of the stress indices extant today that were designed for older populations have very wide acceptance. And, while many appear to have reasonable psychometric properties, none have received extensive use with diverse sampling populations.

Despite these reservations, there are several stress instruments that hold considerable potential in the field of gerontology. For example, Zautra and Lazarus have developed instruments at the micro level that have reasonable psychometric properties and seem to hold predictive validity as well. At the mezzo level, the researcher is faced with a number of reasonable and appropriate instruments, although choice becomes restricted at the macro level.

Stress measures: some general concerns

There seem to be at least five problems with the stress instrument currently available for use with older populations. The first is the lack of any generalizable base of qualitative information from which to determine the kind of stressors to be included. This problem seems to be inherent to stress research. With the possible exception of the instrument developed by Murrell *et al.*, 1988), rarely if ever are potential items developed on the basis of preliminary studies that draw on large and well-developed sampling frames. In consequence, it is hard to judge if the items, as well as standard weights when present, are appropriate to any specific sampling population. Indirectly, the lack of national studies has resulted in a general lack of attempts to determine population norms. Again, the work of Murrell *et al.* (1984) represents a notable exception.

Second, although reasonable measures exist of stressors at the micro and mezzo levels, few if any structured instruments exist for the macro level. The instrument developed by Fiske and Chiriboga (1985), for example, includes items that are outdated for today's populations (regarding impact of the Vietnam War, etc.) but possibly could serve as a model. The literature on ecological psychology might also provide examples of instruments that could be modified for use (e.g. Evans, 1982), since this literature often deals with issues such as crowding, the neighborhood environment, etc.

Third, few if any respresent in themselves a reasonable mix of the variety of stressors that are of potential relevance to elderly populations. That is, most instruments tap either life events or hassles or chronic strains; they do not represent a comprehensive sampling from the array of stressors potentially facing the nation's elderly.

Fourth, as Brim and Ryff (1980) have observed, there are many stressors that are not readily obvious, either because they have not come to the attention of the researcher or because they are in fact 'hidden' or suppressed even from the awareness of subjects. Still others may be difficult to talk about, such as homosexual rape, and child or parent abuse. For such events, Brim and Ryff recommend accessing clinicians and the clinical literature.

Finally, there may be time and historical effects that influence both the distribution and impact of life events. Divorce, for example, may have a greater impact on older than younger people today, and conversely may have less effect on today's older people than it did in the past.

Difficulties in life stage comparisons

Another issue of concern to researchers interested in the stressors of later life is often how these stressors compare in quality and quantity to those experienced by persons in earlier stages of life. For example, while most of the studies that have compared persons of differing ages have concluded that older people experience fewer stressors, several have pointed out that differences in stress content may account for the apparent lack of stress. Instruments such as the original SRE (Holmes and Rahe, 1967) have even been shown to lack content validity for persons in middle age (e.g. Ander *et al.*, 1974).

For those interested in comparing the stress experiences at earlier and younger stages of life, the problems are multiple. Perhaps from an ideal perspective, the more appropriate solution might be to select different inventories for each stage of life, if in fact stress indices were available that focused, say, only on middle age, only on young adulthood, only on the young aged and only on the old old. However, such is not the case: no one in the field of adult development has yet duplicated Coddington's (1972) admirable efforts to develop life event inventories for early childhood, middle childhood, later childhood and adolescence.

In the absence of such life cycle inventories, the researcher may wish to select inventories with fairly extensive lists of items. In the area of micro level stressors, all but the UCSF hassles measure are comprehensive if not exhaustive.

For life events, the PERI Life Events Scale (Dohrenwend *et al.*, 1978) may be the most carefully developed and validated. The RLCQ (Rahe and Arthur, 1978) and the UCSF-LEQ (Chiriboga and Cutler, 1980; Chiriboga, 1984) may also be appropriate. No instrument with proven psychometric properties and applicability yet exists for stressors at the macro level.

If, despite all the problems that have been outlined, the researcher persists in studying the phenomenon of stress exposure in later life, there are bound to be payoffs. One reason is that stressors have been found to predict well-being in elderly populations, even when the measurement tools have been highly suspect. Another is that stress exposure may in fact have a more powerful impact on the lives of elderly populations. Although there is some evidence (e.g. Horowitz and Wilner, 1980) that older people perceive life events as less troublesome because they are more likely to be more experienced, there are competing indications that older people may be more disrupted by stressors (e.g. George, 1980).

REFERENCES

Amster, L.E. and Krauss, H.H. (1974). The relationship between life events and mental deterioration in old age. *International Journal of Aging and Human Development*, **5**, 51–5.

Ander, S., Lindstrom, B. and Tibblin, G. (1974). Life changes in random samples of middle-aged. In E.K. Gunderson and R.H. Rahe (eds.) *Life Stress and Illness*, Charles C. Thomas, Springfield, Ill.

Antonovsky, A. and Katz, R. (1967). The life crisis history as a tool in epidemiological research. *Journal of Health and Social Behavior*, **8**, 15–20.

Birren, J.E. (1988). A contribution to the theory of the psychology of aging: As a counterpart of development. In J.E. Birren and V.L. Bengtson, *Emergent Theories of Aging*, Springer, New York.

Bradburn, N. and Caplovitz, D. (1965). *Reports on Happiness*, Aldine, Chicago.

Brenner, M. Harvey (1985). Economic change and the suicide rate: A population model including loss, separation, illness, and alcohol consumption. In M.R. Zales (ed.) *Stress in Health and Disease*, Brunner/Mazel, New York.

Brim, O.G., Jr and Ryff, C.D. (1980). On the properties of life events. In P.B. Baltes and O.G. Brim Jr *Life-span Development and Behavior Vol. 3*, Academic Press, New York.

Brown, G.W. and Harris, T. (1978). *Social Origins of Depression: A Study of Psychiatric Disorder in Women*, Tavistock Publications, London.

Chiriboga, D.A. (1977). Life event weighting systems: A comparative analysis. *Journal of Psychosomatic Research*, **21**, 415–22.

Chiriboga, D.A. (1984). Social Stressors as antecedents of change. *Journal of Gerontology*, **39** (4), 468–77.

Chiriboga, D.A., Catron, L., and Weiler, P.G. (1987). Precursors of adaptation: a study of marital separation. *Family Relations*, **36**, 164–67.

Chiriboga, D.A. and Cutler, L. (1980). Stress and adaptation: life span perspectives. In L. Poon, (ed.) *Aging in the 1980s: Psychological Issues*, American Psychological Association, Washington, D.C.

Chiriboga, D.A. and Weiler, P.G. (1988). Stress factors in adult child caretakers of Alzheimer's patients. Paper presented at the annual meeting of the American Society on Aging, San Diego, March 22.

Coddington, R. (1972). The significance of life events as etiological factors in the diseases of children. *Journal of Psychosomatic Research*, **16**, 7—18.

Cohen, C.I., Teresi, J. and Holmes, D. (1985). Social networks, stress, and physical health: A longitudinal study of an inner-city elderly population. *Journal of Gerontology*, **40** (4), 478—86.

Davis, G.R. (1985). Developmental patterns of stress and coping: Middle age and older adulthood. Unpublished doctoral thesis, University of Washington. (Dissertation Abstracts International, 46, 10a; University Microfilms No. 85—21, 580).

Derogatis, Leonard R. and Cleary, P.A. (1977). Confirmation of the dimensional structure of the SCL-9-: A study in construct validation. *Journal of Clinical Psychology*, **33**, 981— 89.

Dolan, C.A. (1986). An idiographic and nomothetic assessment of coping with daily stressors. Unpublished doctoral dissertation, University of North Carolina at Greensboro.

Dohrenwend, B.P. (1974). Problems in defining and sampling the relevant population of stressful life events. In B.S. Dohrenwend and B.P. Dohrenwend (eds.) *Stressful Life Events*, Wiley, New York.

Dohrenwend, B.S., Krasnoff, L., Ashehasy, A., and Dohrenwend, B.P. (1978). Exemplification of a method for scaling life events: The PERI life events scale. *Journal of Health and Social Behavior*, **19**, 205—29.

Elder, G.H., Jr. (1974). *Children of the Great Depression* University of Chicago Press, Chicago.

Elder, G.H., Jr. (1981). History and the family: The discovery of complexity. *Journal of Marriages and the Family*, **43**, 489—519.

Elliott, G.R. and Eisdorfer, C. (eds.) (1982). *Stress and Human Health*, Springer, New York.

Evans, G.W. (ed.) (1982). *Environmental Stress*, Cambridge University Press, Cambridge, UK.

Fiske, M. and Chiriboga, D.A. (1985). The interweave of societal and personal change in adulthood. In J. Munichs, P. Mussen, E. Olbrich and P.G. Coleman, (eds.). *Life-span and Change in a Gerontological Perspective*, Academic Press, New York.

Folkman, S., Lazarus, R.S., Pimley, S. and Novacek, J. (1987). Age differences in stress and coping processes. *Psychology and Aging*, **2** (2), 171—84.

George, L.K. (1980). *Role Transitions in Later Life: A Social Stress Perspective*, Brooks/Cole, Monterey, CA.

Holmes, R.S. and Holmes, T.H. (1970). Short-term intrusions into the life style routine. *Journal of Psychosomatic Research*, **11**, 213—18.

Holmes, T.H. and Rahe, R.H. (1967). The social readjustment scale. *Journal of Psychosomatic Research*.

Horoitz, M.J. and Wilner, N. (1980). Life events, stress and coping. In L. Poon (ed.) *Aging in the 1980s; Psychological Issues*, American Psychological Association, Washington D.C.

Kahana, E., Fairchild, T. and Kahana, B. (1982) Adaptation. In D.J. Mangen and W.A. Peterson (eds.) *Research Instruments in Social Gerontology. Volume 1: Clinical and Social Psychology*, University of Minnesota Press, Minneapolis.

Kahana, E.F., Kahana, B., and Young, R. (1987). Influences of diverse stress on health and well-being of community aged. In A.M. Fowler (ed.) *Post Traumatic Stress: The Healing Journey*, Veterans Administration, Washington, DC.

Kanner, A.D., Coyne, J.C., Schaefer, C. and Lazarus, R.S. (1981). Comparison of two modes of stress measurement: Daily hassles and uplifts versus major life events. *Journal of Behavioral Medicine*, **4**, 1—39.

Kiyak, A., Liang, J. and Kahana, E. (1976). A methodological inquiry into the Schedule of Recent Life Events. Paper presented to the Meetings of the American Psychological Association, Washington, DC, August.

Kobasa, S.C., Maddi, S.R. and Courington, S. (1981). Personality and constitution as mediators in the stress-illness relationship. *Journal of Health and Social Behavior*, **22**, 368–78.

Krause, N. (1986a). Stress and coping: Reconceptualizing the role of Locus of Control beliefs. *Journal of Gerontology*, **41**, 617–22.

Krause, N. (1986b). Life stress as a correlate of depression among older adults. *Psychiatry—Research*, **18** (3), 227–37.

Krause, N. (1986c). Stress and sex differences in depressive symptoms among older adults. *Journal of Gerontology*, **41** (6), 727–31.

Lawton, M.P. (1977). Morale: What are we measuring? In C.N. Nydegger (ed.) *Measuring Morale: A Guide to Effective Assessment*, Gerontology Society, Washington, DC.

Lazarus, R.S. and Folkman, S. (1984). *Stress, Appraisal and Coping*, Springer, New York.

Lazarus, R.S. and Launier, R. (1978). Stress-related transactions between person and environment. In L.A. Pearlin and M. Lewis (eds.) *Perspectives in Interaction Psychology*, Plenum, New York.

Lewinsohn, P.M. and MacPhillamy, D.J. (1974). The relationship between age and engagement in pleasant activities. *Journal of Gerontology*, **29** (3), 290–4.

Lewinsohn, P.M., Mermelstein, R.M., Alexander, C. and MacPhillamy, D.J. (1983). The unpleasant events schedule: A scale for the measurement of aversive events. Unpublished research document, University of Oregon.

Lewinsohn, P.M., Mermelstein, R.M., Alexander, C. and MacPhillamy, D.J. (1985). The unpleasant events schedule: A scale for the measurement of aversive events. *Journal of Clinical Psychology*, **41** (4), 483–98.

Lewinsohn, P.M. and Talkington, J. (1979). Studies on the measurement of unpleasant events and relations with depression. *Applied Psychological Measurement*, **3** (1), 83–101.

Lin, N., Ensel, W.M. and Dean, A. (1986). The age structure and the stress process. In N. Lin, A. Dean, and W.M. Ensel (eds.) *Social Support. Life Events and Depression*, Academic Press, Orlando, FL.

Lowenthal, M.F., Berkman, P.L. and Associates. (1967). *Aging and Mental Disorder in San Francisco: A Social Psychiatric Study*, Jossey-Bass, San Francisco.

Lowenthal, M.F., Thurnher, M. and Chiriboga, D.A. (1975) *Four Stages of Life: A Comparative Study of Women and Men Facing Transitions*. Jossey-Bass, San Francisco.

Lynch, J.J. (1977). *The Broken Heart; the Medical Consequences of Loneliness*, Basic Books, New York, NY.

MacPhillamy, D.J. and Lewinsohn, P.M. (1982). The pleasant events schedule: Studies on reliability, validity, and scale intercorrelation. *Journal of Consulting and Clinical Psychology*, **50** (3), 363–80.

MacPhillamy, D.J. and Lewinsohn, P.M. (1976). *Manual for the Pleasant Events Schedule*, Unpublished research document, University of Oregon.

Masuda, M. and Holmes, T.H. (1978). Life events: Perceptions and frequencies. *Psychosomatic Medicine*, **40**, 236–61.

Mensh, I.N. (1983). A study of a stress questionnaire: The later years. *International Journal of Aging and Human Development*, **16** (3), 201–7.

Miller, F.T. (1980). Measurement and monitoring of stress in communities. In L.W. Poon (ed.) *Aging in the 1980s: Psychological Issues*, APA, Washington, DC.

Murrell, S.A., Norris, F.H. and Grote, C. (1988). Life events in older adults. In L.H. Cohen (ed.) *Life Events and Psychological Functioning: Theories and Methodological Issues*, Sage Publications, Newbury Park.

Murrel, S.A., Norris, F.H. and Hutchins, G.L. (1984). Distribution and desirability of life events in older adults: Population and policy implications. *Journal of Community Psychology*, **12**, 301–11.

Neugarten, B.L. (1977). Personality and aging. In J.E. Birren and K.W. Schaie (eds.) *Handbook of the Psychology of Aging*, Van Nostrand Rheinhold, New York.

Norris, F.H. and Murrell, S.A. (1984). Protective functions of resources related to life events, global stress, and depression in older adults. *Journal of Health and Social Behavior*, **25**, 424–37.

Norris, F.H. and Murrell, S.A. (1987). Transitory impact of life-event stress on psychological symptoms in older adults. *Journal of Health and Social Behavior*, **28**, 197–211.

Pearlin, L.T. (1980). Life strains and psychological distress among adults. In N.J. Smelser and E.H. Erikson (eds.) *Themes of Love and Work*, Harvard University Press, Cambridge, MA.

Pearlin, L.T., Menaghan, E.G., Lieberman, M.A., and Mullins, J.T. (1981). The stress process. *Journal of Health and Social Behavior*, **22**, 337–56.

Pilisuk, M., Boylan, R. and Acredulo, C. (1987). Social support, life stress, and subsequent medical care utilization. *Health Psychology*, **6** (4), 273–88.

Pollack, H.M. (1925). What happens to patients during the first year of hospital life? State Hospital Commission, Albany, New York.

Preston, D.B. and Mansfield, P.K. (1984). An exploration of stressful life events, illness and coping among the rural elderly. *The Gerontologist*, **24** (5), 490–4.

Proshansky, H.M., Ittelson, W.H. and Rivlin, L.G. (eds.) (1970). *Environmental Psychology: Man and His Physical Setting*, Holt, Rinehart and Winston, New York.

Pruchno, R.A. and Resch, N.L. (1988). Intrainstitutional relocation: Mortality effects. *The Gerontologist*, **28** (3), 311–17.

Rabkin, J. and Streuning, E. (1976). Life events, stress and illness. *Science*, **174**, 1013–20.

Radloff, L. (1977). The CES-D scale: A self-report depression scale for research in the general population. *Applied Psychological Measurement*, **1**, 385–401.

Rahe, R.H. (1978). Life change measurement clarification. *Psychosomatic Medicine*, **40**, 95–8.

Rahe, R.H. and Arthur, R.J. (1978). Life change and illness studies: Past history and future directions. *Journal of Human Stress*, **4**, 3–15.

Rahe, R.H., Meyer, M, Smith, M., Kjaer, G., and Holmes, T.H. (1964). Social stress and illness onset. *Journal of Psychosomatic Research*, **15**, 19–24.

Sarason, I.G., Johnson, J.H., and Siegel, J.M. (1978). Assessing the impact of life changes: Development of the life experiences survey. *Journal of Consulting and Clinical Psychology*, **48**, 932–46.

Sarason, I.G., Sarason, B.R., Potter, E.H. and Antoni, M.H. (1985). Life events, social support, and illness. *Psychosomatic Medicine*, **47** (2), 156–63.

Selye, H. (1956) *The Stress of Life*, New York: McGraw-Hill.

Spielberger, C.D., Gorsuch, R.L., Lushene, R.E. and Vagg, P.R. (1977) *The State-Trait Anxiety Inventory: Form Y*, Tampa: University of South Florida.

Suzman, R. (1977). Effects of employment and occupation on ego-level. Paper presented at the 30th annual scientific meeting of the Gerontological Society of America, San Francisco, CA, November, 17–22.

Tausig, M. (1986). Measuring life events. In N. Lin, A. Dean and W.M. Ensel (eds.) *Social Support, Life Events, and Depression*, Orlando, FL: Academic Press.

Teri, L. and Lewinsohn, P. (1982) Modification of the pleasant and unpleasant events schedules for use with the elderly. *Journal of Consulting and Clinical Psychology*, **50** (3), 444−5.

Thoits, P.A. (1983) Dimensions of life stress that influence psychological distress: An evaluation and synthesis of the literature. In H.B. Kaplan (ed.) *Psychosocial Stress: Trends in Theory and Research*, New York: Academic Press.

Tobin, S.S. and Lieberman, M.A. (1978) *Last Home for the Aged*, San Francisco: Jossey-Bass.

VanderPlate, C., Aral, S.O. and Magder, L. (1988). The relationship among genital herpes simplex virus, stress and social support, *Health Psychology*, **7**(2), 159−68.

Wallerstein, J.S. (1986). Women after divorce: Preliminary findings from a ten year follow-up, *American Journal of Orthopsychiatry*, **56**, 65−77.

Weinberger, M., Hiner, S.L., and Tierney, W.M. (1987). In support of hassles as a measure of stress in predicting health outcomes, *Journal of Behavioral Medicine*, **10**(1), 19−31.

Whitbourne, S.K. (1985). The psychological construction of the life span. In J.E. Birren and K.W. Schaie (eds.) *Handbook of the Psychology of Aging*, New York: Van Nostrand Rheinhold.

Zautra, A.J., Guarnaccia, C.A., Reich, J.W. and Dohrenwend, B.P. (1988). The contribution of small events to stress and distress. In L.H. Cohen (ed.) *Life Events and Psychological Functioning: Theories and Methodological Issues*, Newbury Park: SAGE Publications.

Chapter 3

Issues of Measurement and Analysis in Studies of Social Support, Aging and Health

Neal Krause

Although gerontologists have shown continuing interest in the relationship between stress, social support, and health, research findings have failed to provide consistent evidence that supportive social relations play an important role in reducing the deleterious effects of stress. Some studies indicate that older adults with strong social support systems are less likely to be affected by life stressors than elderly persons with inadequate social relations (e.g. Krause, 1986; Curtona, Russell and Rose 1986; Cohen, Teresi and Holmes, 1985), while other studies fail to detect significant effects (e.g. Simons and West, 1985; Linn, 1986; Fuller and Larson, 1980). These equivocal findings have prompted some researchers to argue that social support may be a less effective coping resource than the individual psychological attributes (e.g. Henderson, 1983).

However, these assertions may be premature because social support research is plagued by serious problems in conceptualization, measurement, and statistical analysis. If we hope to determine whether social support is an important coping resource and if we are to understand the role played by supportive social relations in the stress process, then these methodological and data analytic problems must be confronted and resolved.

Three specific questions will be examined in this chapter that reflect these methodological problems: (1) What is the correct functional form (i.e. model) of the relationship between stress, social support and health? (2) Which approach to the measurement of social support will allow us to estimate the stress-buffering properties of social support with the greatest amount of precision? (3) What data analytic problems must be addressed if these stress-buffering effects are to be estimated properly? The overall goal of this chapter is to argue that theory and methodology are intimately related. Further advances in the field depend upon our ability to specify our theories in a clear and explicit manner and to select measures of social support that best reflect these theoretical specifications. However, advances in theory and measurement will be in vain if inadequate statistical procedures are used to estimate stress-reducing effects.

Aging, Stress and Health Edited by K.S. Markides and C.L. Cooper
© 1989 John Wiley & Sons Ltd

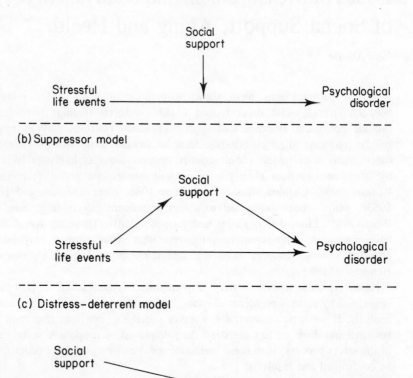

Figure 1 Models of the stress-buffering process

MODELS OF THE STRESS-BUFFERING PROCESS

In his cogent discussion of stress-buffering models, Wheaton (1985) identifies a series of conceptual schemas that are designed to explain how social support and stress affect health and well-being (see Lin., 1986, and Dohrenwend and Dohrenwend, 1981, for the specification of additional models of this process). Three of the models identified by Wheaton (1985) will be reviewed below: the moderator model, the suppressor model, and the distress-deterrent model.

Moderator model

The moderator model is depicted in the top panel of Figure 1. This model predicts that a statistical interaction effect exists between stress and social support on well-being. The moderator is typically evaluated within a multiple regression framework by creating a multiplicative term (stress × support) and then adding this term to the regression equation in a hierarchical fashion. It is assumed in this model that the correlation between stress and support is low: if stress and social support were correlated highly, the interaction effect between stress and support could become confounded with the effect of stress on support (see Thoits, 1982, for a more detailed discussion of this problem). Because the stress-buffering effects are nonadditive, it is further assumed that social support is progressively more effective in reducing the effects of stress, and that maximum buffering effects occur at high levels of stress. As Wheaton (1985) points out, this is perhaps the most frequently examined stress-buffering model.

Suppressor model

The suppressor model is shown in the middle panel of Figure 1. Here it is assumed that the relationships between stress, social support and well-being are additive. The key characteristic of the additive suppressor model is that the level of support is dependent upon the amount of stress that is present. This model assumes a resource mobilization approach that specifies that as stress increases, individuals act to increase (or mobilize) support from significant others (see Alloway and Bebbington, 1987, for a recent review of this crisis support perspective).

Another major characteristic of the suppressor model becomes evident when the direct, indirect, and total effects of stress on well-being are examined. The suppressor model predicts that although stress reduces feelings of well-being, the total effects of stress are diminished by the indirect effects that operate through social support. In this model, stress increases support, and support, in turn, tends to bolster well-being, thereby suppressing or limiting the total effects of life stress.

Distress-deterrent model

The distress-deterrent model is presented in the bottom panel of Figure 1. This scheme has also been referred to as the 'counter-balancing' model by Cohen and Wills (1985). As shown in Figure 1, stress and social support both exert an additive effect on well-being, but there is no relationship whatsoever between stress and support. Proponents of this view have devised a number of hypotheses in an attempt to explain the direct and independent impact of support on well-being, but perhaps the most convincing explanation has been offered by Rook (1987). In this recent work, Rook (1987) makes a distinction between companionship and social support. She defines companionship as shared leisure or other activities that are undertaken primarily for the intrinsic goal of enjoyment whereas social support refers to interaction that is problem-focused and that involves the exchange of aid or assistance. Companionship affects well-being by creating the opportunity for self-disclosure, the discussion of aspirations and fantasies, and the expression of affection. Rook (1987) provides empirical evidence indicating that social support buffers the impact of stress on well-being in the manner prescribed by the moderator model while companionship exerts only a direct effect.

As Wheaton (1985) points out, the distress-deterrent model is not a stress-buffering model because support does not intervene in the relationship between stress and well-being in any fashion. Therefore, despite the widespread testing of this model, it will not be discussed further in this chapter because it does not provide any information on how support might reduce the deleterious effects of stress.

MEASURING SOCIAL SUPPORT

A major challenge in the life stress field is to determine whether the moderator or suppressor model best describes the stress-buffering functions of social support. Although these models need not be mutually exclusive, it is imperative that researchers select an index of social support that reflects the processes that are thought to be embodied in these conceptual schemas. Presently four broad categories of social support measures have been devised: measures of social embeddedness, indices of the perceived availability of support, scales of satisfaction with social support, and measures of enacted support. Each of these measures will be examined in greater detail below. After briefly describing each measure, the advantages and disadvantages of each type of scale will be discussed. Throughout, an emphasis will be placed on identifying the type of index that is best suited for evaluating the suppressor and moderator models.

Social embeddedness

The first category of social support measures are what Barrera (1986) refers to as indices of 'social embeddedness'. Other investigators have used the term 'social integration' to label this class of indicators (see, for example, Liang and

Bollen, 1981). This type of index attempts to count or describe the connections that individuals maintain with significant others. Social embeddedness is frequently measured by enumerating the number of social relationships available to a respondent or the number of social contacts made by a study participant during a specified time period.

There are at least three different ways in which social embeddedness has been operationalized: some investigators rely soley on the basic demographic indicators, others count the number of confiding social relationships maintained by respondents, while other researchers conduct social network analysis. Each of these approaches will be discussed briefly below.

At the crudest level, social embeddedness is measured with basic demographic indicators, such as marital status or house hold composition. Researchers who use this approach assume that the presence of social ties ensures that social support is being provided. Although these measures are useful for specifying the conditions under which support *might* be provided, there is no way of determining whether support was *actually* provided. Merely knowing whether someone has a relationship with others overlooks the possibility that such interaction could have negative or undesirable consequences (Rook, 1984; Wortman, 1984).

Perhaps in response to these criticisms, other investigators attempted to assess the number of confiding relationships that study participants maintain (see, for example, Lowenthal and Haven 1968). Although this appears to make an improvement over the mere enumeration of social ties, there is still some slippage between what this type of indicator measures and what is needed to test the suppressor and moderator models. As a recent study by Brown *et al.* (1986) suggests, having a confiding relationship does not necessarily guarantee that support will be forthcoming in times of stress. In fact, 40% of the married women in this longitudinal study who reported that they confided in their husbands at the baseline interview failed subsequently to receive support from them when a crisis emerged during the follow-up period.

Social network analysis represents a more sophisticated way of measuring social embeddedness. Here an attempt is made to describe an individual's social network along a number of dimensions including density (i.e. determining the number of direct ties among network members) and homogeneity (i.e. determining the extent to which network members have similar personal attributes, such as gender) (see Hall and Wellman, 1985, for a detailed discussion of social network analysis). As discussed earlier, describing social network characteristics tells us that support may be exchanged within these relationships, but this measurement strategy may also inadvertently include social relations that are in fact a source of distress. Social network analysis is also time-consuming and costly to conduct (House and Kahn, 1985). This is an important consideration for a researcher who wishes to assess a number of constructs in the same study, such as stress, health, and psychological well-being.

In my opinion, social embeddedness measures are not well-suited for testing either the suppressor or moderator models. Both of these conceptualizations require data on specific supportive behaviors that were made in response to stressful situations. We have no way of knowing whether members of an individual's social network were even aware that a stressor had occurred, much less whether they actually did anything in response to that event.

The perceived availability of support

Indices of the perceived availability of support attempt to gauge an individual's estimation of the amount of support that would be made available to them should the need arise. In fact, some researchers argue that the expectation or belief that support would be forthcoming in time of need is a more potent stress-reduction factor than the amount of support that has actually been provided (Wethington and Kessler, 1986). These researchers maintain that the mere knowledge that support is available allows individuals to, '... take more risks, to pursue the practical resolution of their problems more single-mindedly than they would have otherwise' (Wethington and Kessler, 1986, p. 85) (see also Lieberman, 1982).

Two problems with measures of the perceived availability of support will be discussed below. The first concerns the lack of documentation on the sources of these perceptions while the second arises from the fact that individuals may incorrectly assume that support that will be provided and that such misperceptions can actually heighten the effects of stress.

It is not entirely clear how perceptions of available support arise. One would expect that perceptions of the availability of support are based upon the actual receipt of support from significant others in the past. To the extent that this is true, we would expect to observe fairly high correlations between measures of perceived support and support that has actually been provided. However, Wethington and Kessler (1986) only found correlations ranging from 0.02 to 0.20 between these types of indicators. This means that at best, there is only 4% common variance that is shared by these scales. This finding suggests that, to a large extent, perceptions of support are determined by something other than support that has actually been provided.

A potential source of perceived support is identified by Gore (1981). She argues that such measures are confounded with psychological distress and that individuals who are suffering from psychological distress tend to report less available support than persons who enjoy better mental health. Unfortunately, gerontologists have not attempted to determine the direction of causality between these measures in an empirically rigorous manner.

Measures of the perceived availability of support suffer from a second, potentially more serious problem. Respondents may misjudge or misperceive the amount of support that others are actually willing to provide when a crisis occurs. We have all experienced the disappointment of discovering that we cannot count on someone we thought would support us. This may lead to a feeling of being let down by significant others. Instead of being a stress-reducing mechanism, feeling let down by others in time of a personal crisis may actually heighten the negative effects of stress (see Brown *et al.*, 1986, for empirical evidence of this effect).

It is evident that measures of the perceived availability of support cannot be used to test the suppressor model because this conceptual framework predicts that stress mobilizes social support systems. That is, stress increases the amount of support provided by significant others. Perceived availability of support is largely an intrapsychic construct: perceived support lies in the eye of the beholder. If we attempt to use this type of measure in a suppressor model framework, we are forced to predict that stress somehow leads to the perception that additional support is available above and beyond what was believed to exist previously. If we exclude support that has actually been provided from this process, it is not at all clear how or why this perceived increase occurs.

Perhaps measures of the perceived availability of support are more appropriate for tests of the moderator model because changes in perceived support do not have to be linked with changes in stress. Instead, it can be assumed that perceptions of available support are fairly stable and independent of life events. However, I would still be hesitant to use this type of measure to test the moderator model because of the problems created by the misperception of available support as well as those that may be attributed to the prior influence of psychological distress.

Satisfaction with social support

As the social support literature evolved, it became evident that the qualitative or evaluative aspects of supportive social relations should be examined. Researchers began to realize that individuals confronted with the same stressful experience did not use the same amounts or types of social support (Ward, 1985). The social measures discussed to this point cannot assess these individual variations in need directly. As a result, researchers began to ask study participants whether they were satisfied with the amount of support they had received as a way of assessing variations in the need for social support (see, for example, Henderson *et al.*, 1986).

Earlier, measures of social embeddedness were criticized for not reflecting the negative side of social interaction. Of all the indices examined in this chapter, measures of satisfaction with social support are probably most capable of capturing these effects because study participants are required to judge the adequacy of the support that has been provided to them. Clearly those respondents who have experienced a good deal of negative support will not tend to report that they find such relations to be satisfying.

A number of researchers have argued that there are problems involved in attempting to measure the qualitative or evaluative aspects of social relations because such assessments may be influenced by the psychological state of the respondent (e.g. Dohrenwend, Dohrenwend, Dodson and Shrout 1984; Arling, 1987). More specifically, they argue that individuals who are initially suffering from significant emotional disorder may subsequently be less satisfied with their social relations than persons who enjoy better mental health.

However, I have recently completed a study that challenges this conclusion (Krause, Liang and Yatomi, forthcoming). Working with data from a panel study of older adults, we found evidence that qualitative evaluations of support are not contaminated by psychological distress and that changes in satisfaction with support actually precede changes in depressive symptoms through time.

Despite their intuitive appeal, measures of satisfaction with social support may not be appropriate for evaluating the suppressor or moderator models because a number of complex factors may enter into the overall evaluation of the adequacy of social support. For example, the norm of reciprocity dictates that older adults not become overly dependent upon others, which may lead them to evaluate low levels of support in a satisfactory manner because others are not expected to provide extensive assistance to them.

Enacted support

Measures of enacted support assess the amount of social support that has actually been provided to a respondent by his or her significant others during a specified time period (typically one month to one year). Indices of enacted support are usually administered in the following fashion: first, respondents are asked to report all of the stressful events that they have experienced in the last year (or perhaps the last six months); then the study participants are asked to report the amount of social support that was actually provided to them during the same time period.

A major advantage of enacted support measures is that specific types of social relations can be assessed, such as instrumental or emotional support. As I have argued elsewhere (Krause, 1986), aggregate indices of support that attempt to assess the benefits of diverse types of supportive behaviors create interpretational problems because it is impossible to determine whether all forms of social support buffer the effects of life stress or whether the benefits of support are restricted to a few specific types of helping behaviors. Examining the dimensions of support may be especially important because some researchers suspect that specific types of support are beneficial in reducing the impact of specific types of life stress, and that no single kind of supportive behavior is beneficial in all stressful situations (Gottlieb, 1983).

It is for this reason that a panel at the National Academy of Sciences concluded that scales assessing social support should include indicators of emotional, tangible, and informational support (these dimensions of support are defined in Krause, 1986). In addition to these specific kinds of supportive behavior, I have found that another kind of social support has been especially helpful in my work with the stress process. I initially called this type of support 'integration', but it is probably best thought of as 'support provided to others'. In developing a measure of support provided to others, I attempted to determine the amount of informational, tangible, and emotional support that a respondent has provided to others in his or her social network. It is important to include a measure of assistance provided to others because research indicates that individuals who provide support to others frequently profit themselves from the help-giving role (Reisman, 1965). In fact, a number of self-help groups, such as Alcoholics Anonymous, have been based on this principle. Presumably, providing help to others bolsters the self-esteem of the help provider because they feel as though they are doing something worthwhile for someone in need. Moreover, by helping others, the attention of the help provider may be diverted from his or her own problems or general self-concerns. Finally, it is particularly important to assess the provision, as well as the receipt, of support in studies of the elderly because research indicates that the maintenance of reciprocity in social relations is especially important to elderly people (see Antonucci, 1985, for a review of this research).

Researchers have recently proposed two ways in which measures of enacted support may be further refined: (1) Specific supportive acts should be linked directly with particularly stressful experiences; and (2) measures should be devised to identify the source of supportive behaviors. As discussed earlier, scales of enacted support are administered by asking respondents to report the life events and the amount of support they received during a given time period. It is assumed in this approach that the support that was provided during this specified time period was in fact given in response to the events that also occurred during that time. However, there is no way of testing this assumption directly with this kind of data. Support that is provided may be unrelated to the crises at hand. Assume that we are interested in assessing stress and support in the six-month period to the time the data are gathered. A respondent reports that he/she suffered from a major financial problem during that time and that he/she also received a good deal of tangible support at some point in the same time period. Given this type of data, a researcher would proceed with the analyses under the assumption that the tangible support was in fact given in response to the financial crisis. However, we cannot rule out the possibility that the tangible support was provided for some totally unrelated reason and that it might even have been provided before the financial crisis occurred.

Perhaps in response to this kind of problem, Brown and his colleagues devised a more focused way of obtaining data on stress and enacted social support (Brown *et al.*, 1986). First, respondents are asked to identify any major life crisis that they have experienced in the six months prior to the interview. The study participants are then asked to provide information about the types of support that were provided in response to each stressful event. For example, if a respondent indicated that he or she had experienced the death of a loved one, they are subsequently asked to indicate the types of support they received in response to that loss. In this manner distinct types of support are linked directly with individual stressful experiences.

Despite the apparent intuitive appeal of this technique, there are two reasons why I suggest that researchers do not use the procedure devised by Brown *et al.* (1986). First, it is impossible to test either the suppressor or moderator models by gathering information on enacted support from only those persons who experienced stress. As discussed earlier, the suppressor model predicts that stress leads to the mobilization of support. This hypothesis specifies that there is an increase in support among those persons who are exposed to a stressor while there is no change in the amount of support provided to those individuals who have not experienced a stressful event. This can only be tested if data on social support is also gathered from those who did not experience a stressor. Unfortunately, this type of information is not obtained with Brown's technique.

Similar problems are encountered when attempts are made to test the moderator model. The moderator model predicts that the effects of social support are diminished (technically they are nonexistent) in the absence of stress, but this cannot be evaluated if information on enacted support is not gathered from those persons who did not experience a stressor.

The second reason for rejecting the procedure devised by Brown *et al.* (1986) arises from the fact that this technique does not rule out an important competing hypothesis. When analyzing data gathered with this procedure, stress is treated as a constant because information is obtained only from those persons who report that a life event had occurred. As a result, the analyses merely involve estimating the direct effect of support on well-being within this group. Such analyses make it impossible, however, to rule out the possibility that social support may also have exactly the same effect among those persons who did not experience a stressful event. In fact, this is precisely what has been predicted by the distress-deterrent model, and as noted earlier, this model does not assess stress-buffering effects.

Brown and his colleagues propose another way of refining measures of enacted support that appears to be more promising (Brown *et al.*, 1986). They propose that the source of support should be taken into consideration when information on enacted support is gathered. In conducting their research, Brown *et al.* (1986) make a distinction between core support and resource support. Core support is support provided by individuals who are especially close to the focal person, such as a spouse. In contrast, resource support is provided by others with whom the respondent feels less close. Brown and his colleagues report that while core support reduces the deleterious effects of stress, resource support appears to be a less effective stress-buffering resource.

The reasons for these findings, however, are not clear. Brown *et al.* (1986) suggest that core support sources involve relationships that are relatively long-standing and that are characterized by a high degree of reciprocity. Presumably such relations foster a sense of acceptance and individuals will not feel weak or ashamed if they seek support from this type of relationship. On the other hand, resource support is provided in relationships that do not involve the same amount of closeness or acceptance as core resources. As a result, individuals may experience a loss of self-esteem if they seek support from this type of relationship.

It is impossible to tell at this point whether identifying the source of enacted support will increase our understanding of the stress-buffering process among older adults because the existing empirical work has been conducted solely with younger persons. However, because the norm of reciprocity may play an important role in the social relations of older adults (see Lee, 1985, for a review of this research), they may be more willing to seek and receive support from core relationships than from relationships characterized by unequal exchange (i.e. resource relations). I encourage further work in this area and I recommend that researchers interested in the measurement of social support follow the development of these indices carefully.

In general, measures of enacted support are not without their shortcomings. Two of these problems will be discussed below. The first deals with contamination of self-reported social support with psychological distress while the second pertains to problems with the retrospective recall of support that has been provided.

If we are interested in obtaining information about support that has been provided or that was made available when an event occurred, then this type of data can only be gathered retrospectively. That is, we must wait for a stressor to occur and then subsequently assess the amount of support that was provided in response to that event. However, the stressor may also increase psychological distress which may, in turn, influence retrospective reports of support provided. The extent to which this type of contamination actually takes place, however, has not been examined in a rigorous manner in the literature. Until such findings are forthcoming, researchers should be aware of the potential bias that may be created by this problem.

Depending upon the time interval that is selected, researchers may encounter problems with the retrospective recall of enacted social support. This may be an especially difficult problem when elderly respondents are involved. However, two pieces of evidence suggest that this problem may not be as great as it appears to be. First, investigators have attempted to determine whether respondents have difficulty recalling stressful life events (see, for example, Funch and Marshall, 1984). This research suggests that while some events are forgotten quickly, individuals have little difficulty recalling stressors that are important or salient. If social support in fact reduces the deleterious effects of stress, then it is likely that it will be perceived as being important or salient by the respondent. If this is true, then like salient stressors, support that is perceived as important may also be less likely to be forgotten.

It should be emphasized that the research involving the recall of life stressors has not been conducted with samples of older adults, making it difficult to determine whether elderly people are especially likely to encounter this type of problem. However, the general issue of memory problems in survey research with the elderly has been examined carefully by Rodgers and Hertzog (1987). These researchers report that recall problems are no more serious for older adults than for persons in other age groups.

Taken together, these studies suggest that older adults may not experience problems in recalling enacted social support, although this issue has not been studied directly. Clearly this is an area in need of further study and until this issue is resolved, researchers should be sensitive to the fact that recall problems may exist.

In spite of these limitations, indices of enacted support appear to be the measure of choice for evaluating either the suppressor or the moderator models. In essence, both stress-buffering models imply that life stress creates adjustment challenges and that successful adaptation is facilitated by the support that others make available to the stressed individual. Measures of enacted support are best suited for testing this process because they come closest to measuring what is taking place and what is actually being provided in a supportive relationship. In comparison, measures of social embeddedness can only tell us what might have been provided, while satisfaction with support measures and indices of the availability of support rely too heavily on intrapsychic judgements or perceptions. As such, they are not measuring social support per se. Instead, they are at best assessing the concomitants of support. In my opinion, personality attributes are likely to strongly influence perceptions of available support (Henderson, Byrne and Duncan-Jones, 1981). To the extent that this is true, then it is incumbent upon researchers to identify and measure these attributes in order that the impact of the perceived availability of support on well-being may be assessed net of these intrapsychic or psychological factors. By following this approach, it will be possible to demonstrate that the causal mechanism is in fact social support, and not merely the manifestation of some intrapsychic phenomena.

DATA ANALYTIC PROBLEMS

Two major problems will be discussed in this section that arise when researchers attempt to estimate stress-buffering effects statistically. The first problem involves the effects of measurement error in the estimation of the moderator model while the second problem area is related to estimation of stress-buffering effects within a longitudinal framework. When such panel analyses are designed, the causal lag between the occurrence of a stressor and the subsequent development of psychological distress or physical problems must be specified correctly.

Measurement error and the moderator model

Most variables in the social and behavioral sciences are measured imperfectly. Although measurement error can lead to biased estimates of effect parameters, this problem has been largely ignored by gerontologists. As the reliability estimates for scales of enacted support and stressful events reveal, these measures contain a sizable amount of measurement error. For example, the internal consistency estimates for four scales of enacted support that I developed ranged from approximately 0.65 to 0.85 (Krause, 1986), while Tennant, Bebbington and Hurry (1981) suggest that the reliability of stress measures (i.e. test–retest reliability) typically falls between 0.50 and 0.75.

As Bollen demonstrates, when only one of several independent variables is measured imperfectly, the resulting parameter estimates linking that construct with an outcome measure will underestimate the true relationship between these indicators. In addition, if the fallible measure is correlated with the remaining independent variables, then error in the imperfectly measured indicator will affect the relationships between the remaining perfectly measured independent variables and the outcome measure.

The impact of multiple fallible measures is even more serious because the resulting parameter estimates become highly unstable, with coefficients becoming greater, equal, or less than their true values. As the literature reviewed above indicates, researchers seeking to estimate the stress-buffering effects of social support are working with multiple fallible measures.

Fortunately, advances in structural equation modeling make it possible to take the effects of measurement error into account when the relationships between stress, social support, and well-being are examined. The structural equation modeling program devised by Joreskog and Sorbom (1986) (i.e. LISREL) is especially useful for this purpose. However, it is easier to use this structural equation modeling program to estimate the suppressor model than it is to assess the moderator model.

As discussed earlier, the suppressor model predicts that the relationships between stress, social support, and well-being are all additive. That is, the direct effect of stress on well-being is not contingent upon the level of support that is present. In this case, estimating the relationships between stress, support, and well-being with LISREL is a relatively straightforward task.

However, difficulties are encountered in estimating the moderator model because tests must be performed for statistical interaction effects: the direct impact of stress on well-being varies according to the amount of social support that is provided. Tests of the moderator model are usually performed by estimating the following ordinary least squares multiple regression equation:

$$D = b_0 + b_1SE + b_2SS + b_3(SE \times SS) + \Sigma c_i Z_i + e \qquad (1)$$

where D denotes psychological distress, SE stands for stressful life events, social support is depicted by SS, the expression (SE $\times$ SS) represents a multiplicative term created by multiplying stress by support, the Z_i stand for control variables in the equation (e.g. age sex, education), and e is a disturbance term. Finally, the b_i and the c_i represent unstandardized regression coefficients.

The multiplicative term (SE $\times$ SS) captures the nonadditive or interaction effect that is specified by the moderator model, but its presence in the equation creates additional problems with measurements error that make it difficult to derive estimates with LISREL. The problem arises from the fact that measurement error in SE and SS is correlated with the measurement error in the multiplicative term (SE × SS). This occurs because the multiplicative term is nothing more than the product of SE and SS and as a result it contains the error associated with these indicators. This correlated measurement error can result in estimates of the b_i that are biased and inconsistent. Moreover, this bias can severely affect the relative magnitudes and even the signs of these estimates (see Busemeyer and Jones, 1983, for a detailed discussion of this problem).

Researchers have attempted to incorporate multiplicative terms into structural equation models (see for example, Lin, 1986), but as Busemeyer and Jones (1983) point out, the statistical properties of the estimates produced by this approach are unknown. More specifically, it is not known whether the resulting estimates are consistent.

An alternative to estimating the moderator model within a structural equation framework is to use ordinary least squares multiple regression analysis (OLS). Unfortunately, even greater problems are encountered when OLS is used for these purposes. First, as discussed above, error in SE and SS is correlated with the error in (SE × SS). In addition, unlike LISREL, OLS assumes that SE, SS, and (SE × SS) have all been measured perfectly. As the literature reviewed earlier suggests, this is an unrealistic assumption. However, problems with unreliability arising from measurement error are especially troublesome in OLS analyses when multiplicative terms are involved. As Bohrnstedt and Marwell (1978) demonstrate, the reliability of the multiplicative term (SE × SS) is lower than the reliability of either of the component parts (SE or SS), indicating that the effects of measurement error become compounded when cross-product terms are created.

An example may help to further clarify the nature of this problem. Working with data described elsewhere (Krause, 1987), I used the complex formulas provided by Bohnrstedt and Marwell (1978) to compute the reliability of a cross-product term that was created by multiplying a measure of tangible social support (a = 0.669) by a global measure of undesirable stressful life events. An estimate of the reliability of the stress measure could not be computed directly from these data because the appropriate test–retest information was not available (see Cleary, 1981, for a discussion of why it is not appropriate to compute internal consistency estimates with this type of scale). However, as discussed earlier, literature reviewed by Tennant *et al.* (1981) suggests that the test–retest reliability of life stress indices generally ranges from 0.50 to about 0.75. Based on this information, I assumed that the reliability of my stress measure was 0.67. Substituting that figure into the formulas provided by Bohrnstedt and Marwell (1978) revealed that the reliability of the resulting cross-product term was only 0.581, which is clearly lower than the reliability of either of the component parts. Perhaps more important, a reliability of 0.581 indicates that this multiplicative term contains a sizable amount of measurement error and that estimates of the relationships involving this variable are likely to be biased substantially.

It should be clear from this discussion that it is inappropriate to use OLS procedures to estimate the moderator model because of the serious problems that are created by measurement error when estimates are derived with this technique. In view of the difficulties with both OLS and standard applications of structural equation techniques, what alternatives are available to researchers interested in estimating the moderator model? I would like to examine two options below. The first deals with recent efforts to adapt structural equation techniques to the special estimation problems created by multiplicative terms while the second option makes use of the subgroup approach to study statistical interaction effects.

Recently, a statistical software program has been devised (COSAN) that some researchers believe can handle the complex correlated error problem that arises when multiplicative terms are used within a structural equation framework (Fraser, 1980). However, this program is not available in many universities. In addition, the statistical properties of the estimates derived with this program are unknown, leading Busemeyer and Jones (1983, p. 558) to warn that use of this approach is 'risky at best' (see Kenny and Judd, 1984 for a detailed discussion of this technique).

Given the problems associated with the use of the COSAN program, the only other option available to researchers for estimating statistical interaction effects is the use of the subgroup approach with the structural equation program devised by Joreskog and Sorbom (1986) (i.e. LISREL). The subgroup approach involves partitioning the sample into two or more groups. In the two group case the sample is typically divided with the mean or median support score, creating a group with a high level of social support and a second group consisting of those individuals with low levels of social support. Identical structural equation models are then created for each group and the models are estimated simultaneously. In the process, the relationship between stress and well-being can be assessed systematically by conducting these simultaneous analyses twice. In the first estimation, the parameter representing the effects of stress on well-being is constrained to be equal in the high and low support groups; in the second estimation, the parameter representing the impact of stress on well-being is allowed to vary freely across groups. The resulting chi-square values for the fit of these models to the data can be compared and the difference between the two (with one degree of freedom) can be used to determine whether the relationship between stress and well-being differs significantly across groups. If these estimates are significantly different and the impact of stress is greater in the low social support group than in the high support group, then we can conclude that social support is buffering or reducing the impact of stress on well-being for those respondents who enjoy high levels of social support.

The advantage of the subgroup approach is that random error is handled easily within the LISREL framework. Perhaps more important, problems arising from the use of multiplicative terms are avoided because it is no longer necessary to include such cross-product terms in the model.

However, researchers may encounter two problems when they attempt to use subgroup analysis: The first is associated with the selection of the cutpoint score that is used to partition the sample while the second problem arises from the loss of statistical power that is created by dividing the sample into subgroups.

A thorough examination of the social support literature reveals that researchers have yet to establish norms for social support indices that would enable us to identify a cutpoint score that successfully differentiates subjects with high levels of social support from respondents with low levels of support. Instead, researchers must arbitrarily select a cutpoint for this purpose. However, as both Blalock (1982) and Zedick (1971) point out, aggregation bias may arise from the improper assignment of cases to high and low support groups. Merely deciding to create two instead of three subgroups (e.g. high, medium, and low support) may also lead to aggregation bias. As a result of these arbitrary decisions, the findings may vary depending upon where the cutpoints are made and how many subgroups are created.

The only advice that I can offer at this point is to select a number of cutpoints and observe how much the findings change when the analyses are repeated using each cutpoint. Similarly, researchers may wish to examine the stability of their findings by estimating models consisting of two and perhaps three subgroups. I wish to emphasize that this solution is not entirely satisfactory. Clearly trade-offs are involved. Nevertheless, I would rather risk the problems created by subgroup analyses than encounter the more serious problems created by measurement error and the use of multiplicative terms.

Further problems may arise from partitioning the sample into two or more groups because the reduced number of cases in each subgroup may fail to provide the statistical power necessary for hypothesis testing. Fortunately, the solution to this problem is straightforward: a researcher must keep this important data analytic issue in mind when a study is being designed and insure that a sample is interviewed that is sufficiently large to accommodate subgroup analyses (see Cohen, 1977, for a detailed discussion of the procedures involved in sample size estimation).

Unfortunately, this solution is of no value for researchers performing secondary data analyses. The only solution that I can offer under these circumstances is to make liberal use of equality constraints when the identical models are analyzed simultaneously across subgroups. Within a LISREL framework, this would involve constraining all of the parameters in the measurement model for the low support group to equal the corresponding parameters in the measurement model for the high social support group. However, it should be emphasized that this is really a stopgap measure and that under more ideal circumstances an adequate number of cases should be available to determine in a more systematic manner whether it is appropriate to constrain the elements in the measurement model to be invariant across groups.

Selecting the appropriate causal lag

As the literature on the stress-buffering functions of social support evolves, it should be evident that longitudinal data are essential if further progress is to be made in the field. Data of this type are needed because it is very difficult to use cross-sectional data to determine whether stress creates psychological disorder or whether psychological disorder subsequently leads to greater exposure to life stress. Similar problems arise when researchers attempt to assess the direction of causality between social support and well-being with data that have been gathered at only one point in time.

Selecting an appropriate between-round interval represents an extremely important issue in the design of such longitudinal studies. To resolve this problem, a research must determine how much time should elapse between the baseline and follow-up interviews. Ideally, the between-round interval should correspond to the time it takes for stressful events and social support to exert a maximum effect on psychological distress or health. It is imperative that this causal lag be specified correctly because, as Kessler and Greenberg (1981) argue, the resulting parameter estimates will be biased if data are gathered using inappropriate between-round intervals.

If the knowledge base was more well-developed, a researcher could determine the correct causal lag by merely consulting the literature to find out how much time elapses between the occurrence of a stressful event and the subsequent development of psychological distress or physical health problems. Unfortunately, very little is known about the time required for symptoms to develop following exposure to life stress, and even less is known about the time required for these symptoms to abate (see Thoits, 1983, and Sandler and Guenther, 1985, for a more detailed discussion of this issue). Perhaps more important, most of what is known about the appropriate causal lag comes from studies of younger adults (see, for example, Brown and Harris, 1978).

As Kessler and Greenberg (1981) point out, when little is known about the proper causal lag, a researcher is likely to err in one of two ways: the follow-up data may be gathered too soon or too long after a stressor occurs. A partial solution to this dilemma may be found by examining the relative disadvantages that arise in each of these situations.

If the true causal lag lies beyond the time interval of the study (i.e. the follow-up data were gathered too soon), then Kessler and Greenberg (1981) argue that the situation is hopeless and the resulting parameter estimates will fail to capture the full effects of stress. If, however, the true lag lies within the interval between observations (i.e. a researcher waited too long to gather follow-up data), then the problem is difficult, but it can be solved.

Kessler and Greenberg (1981) provide a complex data analytic technique that can be used to estimate the appropriate causal lag, but it can only be used when the true lag lies within the interval between observations. This technique is quite involved and the interested reader is referred to Kessler and Greenberg (1981) for a more detailed presentation of their procedure. Given the availability of this technique, Kessler and Greenberg (1981) feel that it is better to wait too long to gather follow-up data than to use a between-round interval that is too short.

Although the technique devised by Kessler and Greenberg (1981) appears to be useful, I have been unable to find an empirical study where it has been applied. As a result, it is not entirely clear how well the procedure performs in actual study settings.

I believe that researchers have a second option available to them to determine the appropriate causal lag. I would propose that a study be designed so that data could be gathered a number of times (at least three and perhaps four) over fairly short periods of time (every three months). By the time the final wave of data is collected, a researcher could determine the causal lag systematically by first examining the effects involving data from wave one and wave two, then wave one and wave three, and finally data from wave one and wave four.

The recommendation that researchers use a three-month between-round interval and conduct at least two follow-up interviews was based on existing studies in the literature. Research conducted with members of the general population suggests that the three-month interval may be appropriate. Work by Brown and his colleagues, for example, indicates that psychological disorder is precipitated by stressors occurring between three weeks and six months prior to the onset of symptoms (Brown and Harris, 1978). However, researchers may wish to select a longer between-round interval if they are attempting to examine changes in physical health status (see Creed, 1985, for a discussion of the causal lag between stress and changes in health).

Kessler and Greenberg (1981) demonstrate that it is essential to gather at least three waves of data because there are likely to be reciprocal (i.e. contemporaneous) as well as cross-lagged effects between stress and well-being. This means, for example, that a respondent's mental health status at the follow-up interview is likely to be influenced by prior stressful experiences (i.e. stressors as assessed at the baseline interview) as well as current life events (i.e. events measured at the follow-up interview). Normally it would be difficult to estimate reciprocal and cross-lagged effects simultaneously with two waves of data because the model would not be identified. In order to resolve this problem, a researcher would have to be constrained to equal a selected value, which is a highly restrictive assumption. As Kessler and Greenberg (1981) argue, it is much more desirable to collect at least three waves of data so that both lagged and contemporaneous effects can be estimated without having to make such restrictive assumptions.

Although there are sound reasons for determining the causal lag by gathering multiple waves of data over relatively short time periods, there are some drawbacks with this approach. First, if short between-round intervals are selected, sufficient change may not have occurred in the independent variable (life stress) or the dependent variable (psychological distress). In addition, the causal lag may vary from stressor to stressor, creating problems for studies that are designed to assess the effects of multiple stressful events. Each of these problems will be examined in detail below.

Research suggests that older adults experience fewer life stressors than younger persons (see, for example, Chiriboga, 1984). If this is true, then relying on brief three-month intervals may not provide a sufficient amount of time for older adults to experience an adequate number of stressors for data analytic purposes. Stated simply, there may not be sufficient variance in the independent variable.

Unfortunately, this issue is quite complex. In the first place, it has not been demonstrated conclusively that the elderly do in fact experience fewer stressors than members of younger generations. Some researchers have pointed out that data reflecting such age differences may be biased because these studies rely on life event indices that include many items that are inappropriate for older adults (e.g. employment-related stressors and questions about recent pregnancies), thereby insuring that elderly study participants will receive lower life event scores (Lazarus and DeLongis, 1983).

Even if it is true that older adults experience fewer stressful life events that younger persons, research suggests that the elderly may actually experience greater exposure to other kinds of stressors. In their classic study of life stress, Pearlin, Meneghan, Lieberman and Mullan (1981) make a distinction between stressful life events and chronic life strains. Essentially, the two are separated by a temporal distinction, in which stressful life events are viewed as discrete experiences limited by time, whereas chronic life strains are thought to be continuous and ongoing. The identification of different types of stressors may be particularly important for studies of older adults because research indicates that chronic life strains exert a greater impact on psychological well-being than stressful life events (Pearlin *et al.*, 1981) and the elderly experience more chronic strains than younger adults (Pearlin, 1980).

Taken together, the research findings reviewed above suggest that brief between-round intervals may not create problems with restricted variance in life stress measures if careful attention is paid to stress measurement. More specifically, problems may be avoided and more meaningful results may be obtained if researchers gather information on chronic life strains as well as stressful life events (see Krause, 1987, for empirical evidence on the impact of chronic strains on older adults).

Even though problems with restricted variance in the life stress measure may be avoided by careful attention to the measurement of stress, sufficient change may not have taken place in the dependent variable during brief between-round intervals. Based on research reviewed by Creed (1985), I suspect that this may be more of a problem with physical health measures than with measures of psychological distress. However, I will limit my comments here to psychological well-being because data on this type of outcome measure has been gathered in a more systematic fashion.

Research by the late Duncan-Jones (1987) indicates that the stability of neurosis over a four-month period among members of the general population is 0.73. Although I have been unable to find comparable data with older adults for a four-month between-round interval, evidence for a slightly longer interval is provided by Norris and Murrell (1984). These researchers report a stability coefficient of only 0.37 for a measure of depressive symptoms over a six-month interval in an elderly sample. This figure indicates that a sizable amount of change takes place in six months.

Taken as a whole, evidence on the stability of psychological distress in the elderly indicates that significant change can occur in fairly brief periods of time. This suggests that researchers probably will not encounter problems created by restricted variance in this type of measure if they elect to conduct re-interviews within three months of the baseline data collection. However, further research on this issue is clearly needed.

By far, the majority of studies on life stress and social support in the elderly have relied on event checklists as the primary tool for gathering information on stressful experiences. These checklists typically elicit information on a wide range of events ranging from a traffic ticket to the death of a spouse. Researchers usually compute life stress scores by simply summing the number of stressors reported by a respondent. However, the use of such aggregate measures rests on the assumption that the causal lag for each stressful experience is the same. As the literature reveals, however, this may not be a valid assumption.

Research reviewed by Minkler (1985) suggests that rates of serious illness following retirement (one type of stressful event) generally peak three to six years after termination of employment whereas illness following bereavement (another type of stressful event) appears within the first six months after the death of a significant other. When viewed from the perspective of selecting an appropriate causal lag, the aggregation of these diverse stressors into a single composite score can create serious problems in longitudinal studies.

A cursory review of the life stress literature reveals that researchers frequently gather data on stressful events that occur during a one-year period. What kind of effect can we expect to observe if the maximum impact of one life event occurs in six months while the peak effects of another event in the same index does not occur until three years later? The one-year lag used in this example will be too long for the first stressor and too short for the other.

Obviously, the resolution of this dilemma involves avoiding the use of aggregate indices of stressful life events. Instead, only events with a similar causal lag should be combined in the same stress measure. Elsewhere, I have appealed for the disaggregation of global life events indices on more substantive grounds (Krause, 1986). The present discussion merely bolsters this argument by suggesting that there are methodological reasons for doing so as well.

CONCLUSIONS

Designing a study on the stress-buffering effects of social support is a difficult task involving a number of critically important decisions. Among the more important choices confronting an investigator is selection of a measure of social support. All too often, however, these decisions are made without careful consideration of the issues that are involved.

In this chapter I have tried to provide a more systematic framework for approaching and overcoming these problems. First, studies of stress-buffering effects must begin with specific ideas or models of how this process takes place. The suppressor and moderator models were introduced to provide two elementary examples of the types of conceptual schemas that are needed. The nature of the relationship between stress, support, and well-being was examined carefully in each model.

Having decided on the model (or models) to be tested a researcher must then select a measure of support. Four types of social support measures were reviewed. I attempted to show that the selection of a measure should be guided by the model being tested. Measures must be used that come closest to capturing the precise mechanisms responsible for the stress-buffering effect so that we are able to test what we are in fact hypothesizing. Within this context, I made a case for selecting measures of enacted support to test either the suppressor or moderator models.

However, selecting a model and an appropriate measure of social support will not insure that a study will be successful. Many (if not most) researchers have failed to pay attention to a number of key data analytic issues. Perhaps the most important of these are the problems created by measurement error. In addition, for those investigators conducting longitudinal studies, issues in the selection of an appropriate causal lag were examined.

Clearly there are a host of other methodological issues that were not examined in this chapter. For example, problems arising from the confounding of measures of social support with measures of stress were not discussed. Similarly, issues involving the use of confirmatory factor analysis to verify the independence of dimensions of enacted support were not reviewed. The issues that were examined here were selected because I felt that they had received relatively little attention elsewhere in the gerontological literature.

Rather than providing an exhaustive review, I hope to convey a sense that progress can be made if the interface between conceptualization, measurement, and data analysis is made explicit. By carefully studying the interrelatedness among these domains, I believe that researchers will not only be able to design better studies, but they will also be in a better position to understand why the literature on the stress-buffering effects of social support is in such chaos. Instead of indicating that support is not an important coping resource, I believe that this disarray expresses our inability to recognize or resolve key problems in the measurement and analysis of social support.

REFERENCES

Alloway, R. and Bebbington, P. (1987). The buffer theory of social support. *Psychological Medicine*, **17**, 91–108.

Antonucci, T. (1985). Personal characteristics, social support, and social behavior. In R.H. Binstock and E. Shanas (eds) *Handbook of Aging and the Social Sciences*, Van Nostrand Reinhold, New York pp. 94–128.

Arling, G. (1987). Strain, social support, and distress in old age. *Journal of Gerontology*, **42**, 107–13.

Barrera, M. (1986). Distinctions between social support concepts, measures, and models. *American Journal of Community Psychology*, **14**, 413–45.

Blalock, H. (1982). *Conceptualization and Measurement in the Social Sciences*, Sage, Beverly Hills, CA.

Bohrnstedt, G. and Marwell, G. (1978). The reliability of products of two random variables, In D. Schuessler (ed.) *Sociological Methodology*, Jossey-Bass, San Francisco, pp. 254–73.

Brown, G. and Harris, T. (1978). *Social Origins of Depression: A Study of Psychiatric Disorder in Women*, Free Press, New York.

Brown, G., Andrews, B., Harris, T., Adler, Z. and Bridge, A. (1986). Social support, self-esteem, and depression. *Psychological Medicine*, **16**, 813–31.

Busemeyer, J. and Jones L. (1983). Analysis of multiplicative combination rules when the causal variables are measured with error. *Psychological Bulletin*, **93**, 549–62.

Chiriboga, D. (1984). Social stressors as antecedents of change. *Journal of Gerontology*, **39**, 468–77.

Cleary, P. (1981). Problems of internal consistency and scaling in life event schedules. *Journal of Psychosomatic Research*, **25**, 309–20.

Cohen, C., Teresi, J. and Holmes, D. (1985). Social networks and adaptation. *The Gerontologist*, **25**, 297–304.

Cohen, J. (1977). *Statistical Power Analysis for the Behavioral Sciences*, Academic Press, New York.

Cohen, S. and Wills, T. (1985). Stress, social support, and the buffering hypothesis. *Psychological Bulletin*, **98**, 310-57.

Creed, F. (1985). Life events and physical illness. *Journal of Psychosomatic Research*, **29**, 113–23.

Curtona, C., Russell, D. and Rose, J. (1986). Social support and adaptation to stress. *Journal of Psychology and Aging*, **1**, 47–54.

Dohrenwend, B.S. and Dohrenwend, B.P. (1981). Life stress and illness: formulation of the issues. In B.S. Dohrenwend and B.P. Dohrenwend (eds.) *Contexts*, Prodist, New York, pp. 1–27.

Dohrenwend, B.S., Dohrenwend, B.P., Dodson, M. and Shrout, P. (1984). Symptoms, hassles, social support, and life events: problem of confounding measures *Journal of Abnormal Psychology*, **93**, 222–30.

Duncan-Jones, P. (1987). Modeling the aetiology of neurosis: long-term and short-term factors. In B. Cooper (ed.). *The Epidemiology of Psychiatric Disorders*, Johns Hopkins University Press, Baltimore, pp. 178–91.

Fraser, C. (1980). *COSAN User's Guide*, The Ontario Institute for Studies in Education, Ontario.

Fuller, A. and Larson, S. (1980). Life events, emotional support, and health of older people. *Research in Nursing and Health*, **3**, 81−90.

Funch, D. and Marshall, J. (1984). Measuring life stress: factors affecting fall-off in the reporting of life events. *Journal of Health and Social Behavior*, **25**, 453−64.

Gore, S. (1981). Stress-buffering functions of social supports: an appraisal and clarification of research methods. In B.S. Dohrenwend and B.P. Dohrenwend (eds.) *Stressful Life Events and Their Contexts*, Prodist, New York, pp. 202−22.

Gottlieb, B. (1983). *Social Support Strategies: Guidelines for Mental Health Practice*. Sage, Beverly Hills, CA.

Hall, A. and Wellman, B. (1985). Social networks and social support. In S. Cohen and S. Syme (eds.) *Social Support and Health*, Academic Press, New York, pp. 23−41.

Henderson, A. (1983). Vulnerability to depression: the lack of social support does not cause depression. In. J. Angst (ed.) *Current Concepts and Approaches*, Springer-Verlag, New York, pp. 107−19.

Henderson, A., Byrne, D. and Duncan-Jones, P. (1981). *Neurosis and the Social Environment*, Academic Press, New York.

Henderson, A., Grayson, D., Scott, R., Wilson, J., Rickwood, D. and Kay, D. (1986). Social support, dementia, and depression among the elderly living in the Hobart Community. *Psychological Medicine*, **16**, 379−90.

House, J. and Kahn, R. (1985). Measures and concepts of social support. In S. Cohen and S. Syme (eds.) *Social Support and Health*, Academic Press, New York, pp. 83−108.

Joreskog, K. and Sorbom, D. (1986). *LISREL VI: Analysis of Linear Structural Relationships by Maximum Likelihood, Instrumental Variables, and Least Squares Methods*, Scientific Software, Mooresville, IN.

Kenny, D. and Judd, C. (1984). Estimating nonlinear and interactive effects of latent variables. *Psychological Bulletin*, **96**, 201−10.

Kessler, R. and Greenberg, D. (1981). *Linear Panel Analysis: Models of Quantitative Change*, Academic Press, New York.

Krause, N. (1986). Social support, stress, and well-being among older adults. *Journal of Gerontology*, **41**, 512−19.

Krause, N. (1987). Chronic strain, locus of control, and distress in older adults. *Psychology and Aging*, **2**, pp. 375−82

Krause, N., Liang, J. and Yatomi, N. (forthcoming). Satisfaction with social support and depressive symptoms: a panel analysis. *Psychology and Aging*.

Lazarus, R. and DeLongis, A. (1983). Psychological stress and coping in aging. *American Psychologist*, **38**, 245−54.

Lee, G. (1985). Kinship and social support of the elderly: the case of the United States. *Aging and Society*, **5**, 19− 38.

Liang, J. and Bollen, K. (1981). Dimensions of social integration. Paper presented at the 34th Annual Meeting of the Gerontology Society of America, Toronto.

Lieberman, M. (1982). The effects of social supports on responses to stress. In L. Goldberger and S. Breznitz (eds.) *Handbook of Stress*, Free Press, New York, pp. 143−56.

Lin, N. (1986). Modeling the effects of social support. In N. Lin, A. Dean and W. Ensel (eds.) *Social Support, Life Events, and Depression*, Academic Press, New York, pp. 173−209.

Linn, M. (1986). Elderly women's health and psychological adjustment: life stressors and social support. In S. Hobfoll (ed.) *Stress, Social Support, and Women*, McGraw-Hill, New York, pp. 223−35.

Lowenthal, M. and Haven, C. (1986). Interaction and adaptation: intimacy as a critical variable. In B. Neugarten (ed.) *Middle Age and Aging*, University of Chicago Press, Chicago, pp. 390– 400.

Minkler, M. (1985). Social support and health of the elderly. In S. Cohen and S. Syme (eds.) *Social Support and Health*, Academic Press, New York, pp. 199–216.

Norris, F. and Murrell, S. (1984). Protective function of resources related to life events, global stress, and depression in older adults. *Journal of Health and Social Behavior*, **25**, 424–37.

Pearlin, L. (1980). Life strains and psychological distress among adults. In N. Smelser and E. Erikson (eds.) *Themes of Work and Love in Adulthood*, Harvard University Press, Cambridge, MA, pp. 174–92.

Pearlin, L., Meneghan, E., Lieberman, M. and Mullan, J. (1981). The stress process. *Journal of Health and Social Behavior*, **22**, 337–56.

Reisman, F. (1965). The helper principle. *Social Work*, **10**, 27–32.

Rodgers, W. and Hertzog, A. (1987). Interviewing older adults: the accuracy of factual information. *Journal of Gerontology*, **42**, 387–94.

Rook, K. (1984). The negative side of social interaction: impact on psychological well-being. *Journal of Personality and Social Psychology*, **46**, 1097–108.

Rook, K. (1987). Social support versus companionship: effects on life stress, loneliness, and evaluations by others. *Journal of Personality and Social Psychology*, **52**, 1132–47.

Sandler, I., and Guenther, R. (1985). Assessment of life stress events. In P. Karoly (ed.) *Measurement Strategies in Health Psychology*, Wiley, New York, pp. 555–600.

Simons, R. and West, G. (1985). Life changes coping resources, and health among the elderly. *International Journal of Aging and Human Development*, **20**, 173–89.

Tennant, C., Bebbington, P. and Hurry, J. (1981). The role of life events in depressive illness: is there a substantial causal relation? *Psychological Medicine*, **11**, 379–89.

Thoits, P. (1982). Conceptual, methodological, and theoretical problems in studying social support as a buffer against life stress. *Journal of Health and Social Behavior*, **23**, 145–59.

Thoits, P. (1983). Dimensions of life event that influence psychological distress: An evaluation and synthesis of the literature. In H. Kaplan (ed.) Academic Press, New York, pp. 33–103.

Ward, R. (1985). Informal networks and well-being in later life: a research agenda. *The Gerontologist*, **25**, pp. 55–61.

Wethington, E. and Kessler, R. (1986). Perceived support, received support, and adustment to stressful life events. *Journal of Health and Social Behavior*, **27**, pp. 78– 89.

Wheaton, B. (1985). Models of the stress-buffering functions of coping resources. *Journal of Health and Social Behavior*, **26**, 352–64.

Wortman, C. (1984). Social support and the cancer patient: conceptual and methodological issues. *Cancer*, **53**, 2339–60.

Zedick, S. (1971). Problems with the use of moderator variables. *Psychological Bulletin*, **76**, 295–310.

Major Events or Transitions

Chapter 4

Widowhood and Health

Kenneth F. Ferraro

With the widespread understanding that stress is related to health outcomes, considerable research has focused on how life events, either desirable or undesirable, influence health over the life course. Even before Holmes and Rahe (1967) documented that widowhood is perceived as the most significant life-changing event, researchers from a variety of disciplines wrote about the health consequences of losing a spouse to death. In the last two decades this research has continued by examining the contingencies under which widowhood has deleterious effects upon individuals throughout the life course. The effect of widowhood on the health of older adults is now known not to be as simple as an inevitable decline in health status. The purpose of this chapter is to systematically review the literature on widowhood and health in order to gain a better understanding of the situations in which widowhood is likely to precipitate health problems. As we shall see, both the designs of studies conducted as well as the measures of health used are important considerations in drawing conclusions about this subject.

WIDOWHOOD AS A LIFE TRANSITION

When considering the widowed as a social category in the United States, it is important to realize that there are approximately 13.5 million widows, and almost 10 million of these are 65 years of age or older (US Bureau of the Census, 1986). The majority of widowed Americans are women (84%) and, with present demographic trends, it appears that the widowed population will increasingly be characterized as female. The average age at which people experience loss of spouse is 56 years (Lopata, 1973). Considering that most women marry men older than themselves, the probability of widowhood is very high for women; and most widowed women will spend approximately 20 years of their life in that status.

Whereas marriage is regarded as beneficial to human development, the dissolution of such a relationship generally challenges individual functioning and autonomy. Unlike divorce and separation, the experience of widowhood does not imply conflict in the conjugal relationship. Thus, the loss is much more likely to be seen as both painful and overpowering, particularly for people married for long periods of time. Other forms of marital dissolution offer opportunities—however

Aging, Stress and Health Edited by K.S. Markides and C.L. Cooper
© 1989 John Wiley & Sons Ltd

limited—to modify or alter the course of the relationship. The sense of both the finality and fatality of widowhood spur what many term a life crisis, commonly accompanied by adverse effects (Vachon, 1976).

Lopata (1973) notes in her research on widows that some women reported 'compensations' or benefits derived from the death of one's spouse. This may especially be the case when (a) conjugal conflict is extensive or (b) if a long-term illness of the person dying has affected the health of the spouse caring for their mate—what we now often euphemistically term 'caregiver strain'. With regard to conjugal conflict, however, Lopata noted that women frequently engaged in husband sanctification; they remembered and focused upon the positive qualities of the man after his death, perhaps because the grieving process is structured to elicit positive verbalizations about the deceased. The effect of widowhood may bring compensations, but initially, at least, the profound sense of loss seems to implode on the self. When one considers older adults facing widowhood—after many years of marriage—the individual is also faced with massive changes in lifestyle and daily activities. Some scholars have asserted that familiarity with one's surroundings is more important to older than younger people. Thus, widowhood is a time of tremendous transitions which challenge ontological security and lifestyle. These transitions have been propitiously regarded within the framework of a stress process.

Stress is defined in various ways which means that common definitions are typically in very general terms. Stress may be regarded for this review as the nonspecific response of the body when an individual confronts a situation where the usual modes of acting are insufficient (Eisdorfer and Wilkie, 1977; House, 1974). A situation which may precipitate the *stress process* is usually one where demands exceed current abilities or where barriers appear to preclude fulfilling the demands. This process has generated so much interest among investigators of the life course because the response to stressful situations (sometimes called stressors) is closely related to the wear and tear of the body—and, concomitantly, disease processes. As posited by Eisdorfer and Wilkie (1977, p. 258):

> With increasing age, there is presumed to be a loss of physiologic adaptability and the older person is reported to be less able to cope with a stress or environmental change.

Older adults may not be able to handle the effects of stress reactions as well because of decreased physical ability. However, older adults may enjoy advantages when facing life events such as widowhood. For instance, while they may not be as physiologically adept, they may be more psychologically prepared: caring for an elderly dying spouse challenges one to consider widowhood on a more regular basis than would be the case among younger persons.

The framework employed here to consider widowhood and health is based on the work of House (1974). Central to understanding this model is the recognition that the individual *perceives* whether or not a situation is stressful; there are no conditions which automatically initiate the stress process. Granted, some conditions are likely to produce adverse outcomes, but the individual judges the presence or absence as well as the severity of the stress. Moreover, a number of conditioning variables influence the individual's judgment about the situation and the person's response to the situation. One such conditioning variable—social support—has been shown to influence the process and the outcomes of the stress process. After reviewing the empirical research on widowhood and health, the role of these conditioning variables is discussed.

CHARACTERISTICS OF THE LITERATURE

Previous research on widowhood has provided the scientific community with many useful findings, but it also contains some contradictions and inconsistencies within the major findings. A review of the literature indicates that the divergence of findings is largely due to variations in the methodological procedures used (Ferraro, 1984). In order to be able to effectively evaluate previous research on widowhood and health, it may be helpful to consider important methodological characteristics of the research. This review focuses on three methodological characteristics—study design, sampling, and measures used—though it is readily recognized that other features of the research, such as the time frame and the statistical procedures used, may also affect the findings.

Study design

Previous researchers have used different study designs to assess the impact of widowhood on health. Studying this life event implies that the primary interest lies in the change that occurs as a result of the loss of spouse. There have been basically three different approaches for examining changes due to widowhood. First, the vast majority of the previous research on widowhood and health has focused on assessing differences between married and widowed people through the use of *cross-sectional designs* (e.g. Clayton, 1974; Gerber *et al.*, 1975). These studies attempt to infer changes from the observed differences between the two categories. While cross-sectional designs are appropriate for some types of research, the use of such designs is accompanied by certain problems in studying life events or aging in general. It is generally not recognized as an appropriate way to assess intra-individual change.

A second approach to assess changes due to widowhood is through the use of *retrospective questions*, generally employed in cross-sectional studies. For instance, Maddison and Viola (1968) examine health deterioration by *reports of change*, not by measuring the degree of change at two times. Retrospective questions have been shown to be somewhat unreliable (Nachmias and Nachmias, 1976), and the use of such questions may be particularly problematic in the study of stressful life events such as widowhood, where the individual may have difficulty in accurately recalling what life was like before confronting bereavement. This is especially the case when Lopata (1973) notes that many women exaggerate certain characteristics of their husbands and/or their marriages.

The third approach that has been used to assess changes due to widowhood is the *longitudinal design*. It has been heralded as the superior design to examine changes due to widowhood or life events in general (Dean and Lin, 1977). Having actual measures of health before and after widowhood enables one to better assess changes that result from it. Longitudinal studies of widowhood and health are still relatively few in number but have recently been appearing with greater frequency (Fenwick and Barresi, 1981; Ferraro *et al.*, 1984). Longitudinal designs are generally more appropriate for this type of research but it should be noted that they are not without their problems— especially selective drop-out and testing effects (Baltes, 1968).

Sampling

There are two basic types of study samples that have been used, the first of which studies both widows and married persons. Cross-sectional designs measure *between-group differences* to infer changes about the transition from the married to the widowed status. Longitudinal studies of both married and widowed persons generally compare the *rates of change* in health for the two groups (e.g. Ferraro, Mutran and Barresi, 1984; Wan, 1984). These studies are most often based on sample surveys of populations.

The second type of study sample is comprised of widows only (e.g. Dimond, Lund and Caserta, 1987; Gerber *et al.*, 1975; Solie and Fielder, 1987). In this type of research *within-group differences* are emphasized in cross-sectional designs and *personal change* in longitudinal designs. As such, the emphasis is not upon the change in health that the widowed experience as a group, but rather on what types of widows are more likely to experience health decline. Many of these studies are based on either clinical data or samples of spouses listed as survivors in obituary notices. Thus, empirical generalizations from these studies may be more limited.

In attempting to evaluate an inventory of research findings on the subject of widowhood and health, it is readily apparent that other features of sample composition may affect the process of developing empirical generalizations. For example, some studies examine only women. Many of the samples utilized in previous research are constrained by regional variations; only a few have used national studies. Regional variations in sample composition may be particularly important given the consequences of age density in community settings. If we expect social support to influence the individual's reaction to this life crisis, then region may spuriously affect findings of some research.

Finally, the age of the respondents in various samples should also be considered when interpreting the findings. While studies of older widows are emphasized in this review, several studies use unique age parameters in their

Table 1 Research designs used in assessing widowhood and health

Type of design	Widows only	Widowed/comparison group*
	Sample composition	
	A	B
Cross-sectional	Within-group differences	Between-group differences
	C	D
Longitudinal	Within-group change (personal change)	Between-group change (comparison of change rates)

* Comparison groups may be married only or may include other marital statuses or other bereaved groups.

sample, and some purposely avoid older adults (e.g. Parkes, 1975). Table 1 portrays the cross-classification of the major elements of these two characteristics: study design and sampling. The table is not intended to exhaust the possible types of research strategies for this subject but rather to note the differences in the commonly used strategies. Comparison groups for cells B and D are most often married people, but some investigators use similarly aged people in other marital statuses. A growing number of studies compare bereaved adults with nonbereaved adults (e.g. Bass, Noelker, Townsend and Deimling, 1986). Unfortunately, some of these studies, such as the work of Norris and Murrell (1987), do not consider each type of bereavement separately but lump together those who were bereaved of a spouse, child, or parent. For the present study, such investigations do not aid our purpose—assessing the effect of widowhood on health.

Measurement

Health status has been conceptualized and measured in a variety of ways. Three types of indicators predominate in this literature: mortality, morbidity, and service use, with the first two receiving considerably more attention. The present review is structured around these three indicators although others are noted where appropriate.

While there are no complete and infallible measures of health, all three of these dimensions provide some insight into how adults adjust to widowhood in terms of their health status. The first two enjoy a rich tradition in epidemiological studies (Klerman and Clayton, 1984), while service use studies have mushroomed in the last two decades, some of which include widowhood as a variable. The focus of this chapter is on physical health; but, as will be evident, psychological health is intricately intertwined with many health measures and understanding this relationship should aid the prevention or treatment of various physical maladies. Because the measures used are so critical to empirical generalizations, the specific indicators used in the majority of studies reviewed are presented in the Appendix at the end of the chapter and discussed in the next section.

REVIEW OF LITERATURE

Several other reviews on this and related subjects are available (Berardo, 1970; Bowling, 1987; Klerman and Clayton, 1984; Kosten, Jacobs and Kasl, 1985; Rando, 1986; Walker, MacBride and Vachon, 1977). The focus of the present review, however, is on published empirical research on widowhood and health. The Appendix lists many of these empirical studies and briefly describes the sample, measures used, and salient findings. Excluded from the Appendix and detailed discussion are the clusters of reports that examine widowhood and suicide, morale, social life, or depression. The only exception to this exclusion rule is if measures of health were also considered in those studies; but if no mention of health—at least psychophysical health—was offered, the study was not identified here. This review is not construed to be exhaustive but representative of the core of studies on widowhood and health. Over 30 studies are listed in the Appendix; a variety of journals is represented as well as a few books.

Mortality

Can the stress of losing a spouse be so severe that it can kill the survivor? Different answers are offered to this question from studies conducted over the last 25 years. Clayton's work (1974, 1975) on older widows suggests the answer is no. However, studies of a broader age range of subjects hint at higher mortality for the widowed, although the magnitude of the effect varies. Studies of only widowed persons (cells A or C in Table 1) point to a substantial effect (Cox and Ford, 1964; Ward, 1976), while one comparative study (cells B or D in Table 1) indicates the mortality risk is only modest (Helsing and Szklo, 1981). Moreover, sex differences appear to be important.

Helsing and Szklo (1981), Helsing, Szklo and Comstock (1981), Rees and Lutkins (1967), and Ward (1976) all indicate that the mortality risk of widowhood is greater for men. A number of other writers have echoed the special problems of widowers (Berardo, 1970; Bock and Webber, 1972; Durkheim, 1951; Hyman, 1983). Many medical sociologists and social gerontologists note that older men, and especially older widowers, are less socially integrated than their female counterparts, and are thus more susceptible to a host of problems from loneliness to suicide. By contrast, a longitudinal study of mortality in England and Wales reports that higher mortality due to widowhood is likely for women—not men—especially during the first year of bereavement (Jones, 1987; Jones and Goldblatt, 1986). The sex difference is not simply a British and an American difference, for Rees and Lutkins' (1967) report of higher male mortality risk from widowhood is also based on data from England, albeit rural England. It seems likely that social context, and more specifically, social support, influences the ability to confront the stress of widowhood; and the literature tends to point to men's having a more difficult time avoiding the mortality risk of widowhood. It is possible that the average age at which widowhood occurs, and its indication of social involvement, is at least partly responsible for the sex difference in mortality risk.

Morbidity

If widowhood can in some cases precipitate death for the bereaved, then it should come as no surprise that heightened morbidity accompanies the grieving process of widowed people. The major recent questions in the study of widowhood and threats to health are when, how severe, and upon whom are these effects most likely to occur. Therefore, it may come as somewhat of a surprise that one of the first longitudinal studies of widowhood showed no significant decline in health status (Heyman and Gianturco, 1973). Closer examination of this study shows that it assesses within-group change in health as measured by a physician during a medical exam (cell C in Table 1). It is possible that either the small sample ($N = 41$) in this type of design, the health measure used, or perhaps some combination of the two, is responsible for this null finding. Physician ratings, or what are sometimes referred to as the more objective health measures may be less sensitive to change, particularly psychophysiological symptoms. On the other hand, it could be argued that the self-reports of health upon which so many of these studies are based inflate the degree of *physical* health decline because they also carry considerable information on psychological health (see Ferraro, 1980, 1987, for fuller discussions of measuring health among older people).

The vast majority of empirical studies of widowhood do, in fact, show some sort of health decline (Bass *et al.*, 1986; Clayton, 1974, 1975; Fenwick and Barresi, 1981; Ferraro, 1985; Ferraro *et al.*, 1984; Hyman, 1983; Maddison and Viola, 1968; Owen, Fulton and Markusen 1982; Parkes, 1970, 1975; Parkes and Brown, 1972; Vachon *et al.*, 1982; Wan, 1982, 1984). As noted earlier, most of these studies use some type of self-reported data, ranging from self-ratings of health (e.g. Fenwick and Barresi, 1981; Hyman, 1983) to illness symptoms (e.g. Clayton, 1974) or a physical disability index (e.g. Ferraro, 1985). Most of the studies which examined the duration of any effect conclude that the health decline is most likely shortly after the loss of spouse (Fenwick and Barresi, 1981; Ferraro *et al.*, 1984; Parkes, 1970; Vachon *et al.*, 1982; Wan, 1984). The long-term effects tend to be modest or nonexistent unless there were complicating conditions.

Some of the complicating conditions were those observed on the mortality measures as well. For instance, the more isolated adults were more likely to show enduring signs of health decline (e.g. Dimond *et al.*, 1987; Vachon *et al.*, 1982). This is certainly what one would expect from the social stress literature. Yet, it is important to note that resources such as social support can act as both a cause of better health and a product of it as well (Ferraro *et al.*, 1984). Advantage can accumulate. Similarly, social class operates to enhance both social involvement and health and, therefore, the change in these over time. Finally, a few studies indicate that widowed men manifest higher overall levels of morbidity than widowed women (e.g. Parkes and Brown, 1972; Wan, 1984).

One other factor that notably affects the health outcomes of bereavement is the degree of anticipation associated with the death of spouse. Both Lundin (1984) and Parkes (1975) show that health decline is more likely when the loss of spouse occurred with a shorter preparation time—the 'shock' of widowhood takes its toll. Gerber *et al.* (1975) found no differences in morbidity outcomes when comparing survivors of spouses who died because of acute or chronic illness. However, among those widowed because of chronic fatal illnesses, a lengthy time of preparation—and caregiving—was associated with greater morbidity. Although the verdict is tentative, it appears that there is a curvilinear relationship between length of time anticipating the death and morbidity. Sudden and unexpected loss of a spouse creates special problems, but so may attempting to provide care for a spouse over several years. Death stings in most cases, but the former resembles a sharp pain demanding reorganization while the latter is a dull, chronic pain that delays life reorganization. It is in this latter type that the 'compensations' Lopata (1973) refers to may emerge: relief for and from the suffering process of a loved one's death.

Service use

Whether or not actual changes in health have transpired following widowhood may be discerned from changes in medical service use. Although service use does not imply physical morbidity, it may indicate the development of such problems or at least psychophysical distress. Two studies reveal that the widowed may have a higher risk of hospitalizaiton or institutionalization. Parkes and Brown (1972) found that widowed adults in the Harvard Bereavement Project spent more days sick in a hospital than did married controls. Fenwick and Barresi (1981) found a similar effect but only among adults who were widowed for at least 15 months. Elderly people who were recently widowed (14 months or less) did not show higher rates of hospitalization/institutionalization. Works by Clayton (1974, 1975) and Homan *et al.* (1986) found no differences in the frequency of contacting a physician, especially when controlling for other factors. Gerber *et al.* (1975) found that physician visits were higher for widows bereaved of a spouse who suffered a lengthy chronic illness.

The amount of quality research on widowhood and medical service use is small. This is certainly an area that merits more detailed examination. From what can be discerned from the few studies conducted, it appears that service use does not immediately increase after widowhood but that it may increase somewhat over the long run. It is possible that the lack of a partner to provide care when symptoms of illness arise increases the likelihood of seeking professional help—and perhaps total care (Fenwick and Barresi, 1981). Others have previously noted that larger families with more extensive interaction are more likely to provide informal help and thus delay contact with the formal medical care system (Salloway and Dillon, 1973). Thus, one might anticipate that the loss of a spouse may spur more contacts with the medical service system. Yet, because we are considering health behaviors in advanced adulthood, it may be that lifelong patterns of helpseeking will prevail. More research is needed to answer this question definitively. The issue is critical for the proper assessment and treatment of illness symptoms following the death of spouse.

ATTENUATING THE STRESS OF WIDOWHOOD

The empirical research reviewed here has permitted some sincere conclusions to be drawn as well as suggested a few avenues for further research. Mortality risk following widowhood is greatest for men during the first six months of bereavement. It appears that women do not generally have a higher mortality risk from widowhood, but if they do, it is more likely to occur a couple years after death of spouse. Widowhood does precipitate a decline in health, especially psychophysical health status. This decline is rapid for a year or two and then levels off. Medical service use appears to remain fairly similar to when a person is married but may increase a year or two after widowhood. With all these empirical generalizations there are exceptions or countervailing forces. Better understanding of these countervailing forces should enable the initiation or potentiation of interventions to reduce the adverse effects of conjugal bereavement.

Social support

The major avenue for attenuating the adverse effects of widowhood is through social relations that offer some form of support. Several researchers have noted that close interpersonal relationships buffer the adverse effects of life events or normative crises (Berardo, 1970; Parkes and Brown, 1972; Vachon *et al.*, 1982). In short, the buffering hypothesis, described in chapters 3 and 11, asserts that people who are involved in supportive relationships provide each other with assistance to lessen the negative effects of the stress process (Stroebe and Stroebe, 1983). There are numerous problems in the research purporting to test the buffering hypothesis which are well summarized by Thoits (1982). Even with appropriate caution, however, there are no studies reviewed here which indicate that social support *adversely* affects the longevity or health status of adults confronting bereavement. Some studies may show no effect of social network variables on health status (e.g. Heyman and Gianturco, 1973), but a number of others show positive effects of such social variables on health while confronting bereavement (Dimond *et al.*, 1987;

Ferraro *et al.*, 1984; Parkes and Brown, 1972; Vachon *et al.*, 1982). It is possible that, as stated earlier, family members, including spouses, may delay contact with the formal medical service system; this *may* in turn heighten morbidity or mortality risk, but there is still no evidence to strengthen such an assertion. Rather, numerous studies show that social support greatly benefits those who can claim it as their own. The question therefore is not so much, can social support help people facing crises, but which dimensions of this global concept termed social support really make a difference in the lives of individuals confronting a stress process.

Social support has been an omnibus concept, taking on a variety of meanings. It seems from where the research has gone thus far that there are two general dimensions of support that are of crucial interest in assessing the buffering hypothesis; structure of social networks and commodities exchanged. The two are no doubt related but each may play an important role in assessing the buffering hypothesis.

Structure of social networks

Social networks can be described in a number of ways. Walker *et al.* (1977) define five characteristics that are relevant for studying stressful life events. (1) *Size* refers to the number of people with whom some social contact is made. (2) *Strength of ties* refers to the amount of time spent together, emotional intensity, and intimacy. The strength of a tie is probably the best predictor of the commodities exchanged therein. (3) *Density* refers to the proportion of people in a person's network who know and contact one another. (4) *Homogeneity of membership* is the extent to which network members share attributes. (5) *Dispersion of membership* is the difficulty encountered for network members to make face-to-face contact.

For people confronting widowhood, I would assert that certain structural properties are more important for providing support. Size is probably not very important in itself, but strength of ties is critical. Lopata's (1973) study of widows indicates that homogeneity of network members is often the case and this appears to strengthen ties. Various intervention groups such as the Widow-to-Widow program are similarly premised on homogeneity of contacts. These groupings are generally quite helpful, but properly structured heterogeneous groups may be as well. It could also be anticipated that strong ties are critical in the early stages of bereavement but not nearly so after two years of living in the widowed status.

Another important consideration with regard to the structure of social networks is that they are often dynamic. Widowhood itself may fracture some relationships that were rooted in either the couple orientation or the bereaved spouse. Yet, most studies show networks to be fairly stable for at least a year after widowhood (Ferraro *et al.*, 1984; Heyman and Gianturco, 1973). Both Ferraro *et al.* (1984) and Wan (1982) report that some *increases* in network characteristics are possible following widowhood, especially after the first year.

Again, compensations are possible; and, while some relationships may shrink, others may grow.

Commodities exchanged

By commodities exchanged, I refer to any items given or received which possess value to those who participate in the relationship. These items may be very practical such as warm meals or housework, or relatively intangible such as spending time together or listening. The latter are sometimes referred to as informal, caregiving tasks and have been noted to play an extremely potent role (Walker *et al.*, 1977). The type of commodities valued will vary according to the individuals receiving them. Practical commodities are frequently exchanged just after the death of a spouse but may also be highly valued thereafter depending upon the physical condition of the bereaved. Gender differences in value assigned to commodities as well as the expectation to provide commodities also exist.

Status characteristics

Another major difference in how people cope with widowhood is based upon the status characteristics of the individuals involved. While many of these cannot be altered, it is helpful to consider the social position of the bereaved in understanding special needs and the likelihood of success for interventions designed to help widowed people. Among the status characteristics considered, none has received as much attention as gender. The evidence is equivocal, but men probably suffer more (Stroebe and Stroebe, 1983). Recall that the event of widowhood is normative among women but not among men. Women will likely know more individuals of the same sex who have experienced the event to turn to for consolation and help in facing bereavement; this means they may be better off than widowed men in terms of social support. The structure of widowers' networks is not going to be as homogeneous in membership as their female counterparts. Thus, what appears as a gender difference may, in fact, be a social support difference.

Without confronting genetic or physiological explanations in this chapter, it is also possible that social expectations for expressivity also favour women when facing a life crisis. If men are not socialized to express their loneliness or depression, then they may not make as great a use of support networks and may permit the accumulation of stress-related outcomes. Both of these may explain the higher mortality risk of men, especially for suicide (Bock and Webber, 1972). In short, expressivity as a cultural norm may predispose women to do more active grief-work and thereby avoid some of widowhood's deleterious effects. One study examining sex roles and adjustments to widowhood found that androgynous widows fared better (Solie and Fielder, 1987); this topic deserves further consideration.

Without exception, studies which considered the social status of widowed people found that those with more education and income fared better. Being higher up on the socioeconomic ladder has repeatedly been found to offer advantages: better health, larger social networks, and more coping resources. Interventions, therefore, should be geared to address those less fortunate on the socioeconomic scale.

Finally, the age at which widowhood occurs is also an important consideration when assessing health outcomes. As mentioned at the beginning of this chapter, some gerontologists have suggested that stress may be harder on older adults because of a presumed reduction in physiologic ability (Eisdorfer and Wilkie, 1977). While this is certainly a tenable thesis, again, there must be countervailing forces. Studies of the relatively younger adults confronting bereavement show an intensity of psychophysical distress not generally reported among older adults (Maddison and Viola, 1968; Parkes, 1970, 1975). This is not meant to trivialize the trauma of the event for older adults. There is plenty of grief associated with the event. Rather, it should amplify our concern for the younger adults facing this event. Remarriage rates are another indicator of how different ages face bereavement. Although younger adults have more opportunities for remarriage, they also desire it much more strongly—as Durkheim (1951) asserted—to reorganize a disorganized life. Older adults are not nearly as interested in remarriage, for they have anticipated the disorganization (Lopata, 1973).

The other implication of the findings on various ages of widowhood is that older adults may be more resilient than is popularly portrayed. Widowhood is an intense struggle for most, but older adults seem no less able to wage the fight, especially if they are able to draw upon the resources known to help in the process (Gallagher, Thompson and Peterson, 1982).

ACKNOWLEDGEMENTS

I would thank Linda Ferraro for helpful comments on an earlier version of this paper, Kimberly Robinson and Lisa Stone for library research assistance, and Gloria Halsey for processing the manuscript.

REFERENCES

Baltes, P.B. (1968). Longitudinal and cross-sectional sequences in the study of age and generation effects. *Human Development*, **11**, 145−71.

Bass, D.M., Noelker, L.S., Townsend, A.L. and Deimling, G.T. (1986). The loss of an aged relative: perceptual differences between spouses and adult children, *Omega*.

Berardo, F.M. (1970). Survivorship and social isolation: the case of the aged widower. *The Family Coordinator*, **19**, 11− 25.

Bock, E.W. and Webber, I.L. (1972). Suicide among the elderly: isolating widowhood and mitigating alternatives. *Journal of Marriage and the Family*, **34**, 24−31.

Bowling, A. (1987). Mortality after bereavement: a review of the literature on survival periods and factors affecting survival. *Social Science and Medicine*, **24**, 117−24.

Clayton, P.J. (1974). Mortality and morbidity in the first year of widowhood. *Archives of General Psychiatry*, **30**, 747–750.
Clayton, P.J. (1975). The effect of living alone on bereavement symptoms. *American Journal of Psychiatry*, **132**, 133– 7.
Clayton, P.J., Halikas, J.A., Maurice, W.L. and Robins, E. (1973). Anticipatory grief and widowhood. *British Journal of Psychiatry*, **122**, 47–51.
Cox, P.R. and Ford, J.R. (1964). The mortality of widows shortly after widowhood. *Lancet*, **1**, 163–4.
Dean, A. and Lin, N. (1977). The stress-buffering role of social support. *Journal of Nervous and Mental Disease*, **165**, 403–17.
Dimond, M., Lund, D.A. and Caserta, M.S. (1987). The role of social support in the first two years of bereavement in an elderly sample. *The Gerontologist*, **27**, 599–604.
Durkheim, E. (1951). *Suicide: A Study in Sociology*, Free Press, Glencoe, IL.
Eisdorfer, C. and Wilkie, F. (1977). Stress, disease, aging and behavior. In J.E. Birren and K.W. Schaie (eds.) *Handbook of the Psychology of Aging*, Van Nostrand Reinhold, New York, pp. 251–75.
Fenwick, R. and Barressi, C.M. (1981). Health consequences of marital-status change among the elderly: a comparison of cross-sectional and longitudinal analyses. *Journal of Health and Social Behavior*, **22**, 106–16.
Ferraro, K.F. (1980). Self-ratings of health among the old and the old-old. *Journal of Health and Social Behavior*, **20**, 377–83.
Ferraro, K.F. (1984). Widowhood and social participation in later life: isolation or compensation?. *Research on Aging*, **6**, 451–68.
Ferraro, K.F. (1985). The effect of widowhood on the health status of older persons. *International Journal of Aging and Human Development*, **21**, 9–25.
Ferraro, K.F. (1987). Double jeopardy to health for black older adults?. *Journal of Gerontology*, **42**, 528–33.
Ferraro, K.F., Mutran, E. and Barresi, C.M. (1984). Widowhood, health, and friendship support in later life. *Journal of Health and Social Behavior*, **25**, 245–59.
Gallagher, D.E., Thompson, L.W. and Peterson, J.A. (1982). Psychosocial factors affecting adaptation to bereavement in the elderly. *International Journal of Aging and Human Development*, **14**, 79–95.
Gerber, I., Rusalem, R., Hannon, N., Battin, D. and Arkin, A. (1975). Anticipatory grief and aged widows and widowers. *Journal of Gerontology*, **30**, 225–9.
Helsing, K.J. and Szklo, M. (1981). Mortality after bereavement. *American Journal of Epidemiology*, **114**, 41–52.
Helsing, K.J., Szklo, M. and Comstock, G.W. (1981). Factors associated with mortality after widowhood. *American Journal of Public Health*, **71**, 802–9.
Heyman, D.K. and Gianturco, D.T. (1973). Long term adaptation by the elderly to bereavement. *Journal of Gerontology*, **28**, 359–62.
Holmes, T.H. and Rahe, R.H. (1967). The social readjustment rating scale. *Journal of Psychosomatic Research*, **11**, 213–18.
Homan, S.M., Haddock, C.C., Winner, C.A., Coe, R.M. and Wolinsky, F.D. (1986). Widowhood, sex, labor force participation, and the use of physician services by elderly adults. *Journal of Gerontology*, **41**, 793–6.
House, J.S. (1974). Occupational stress and coronary heart disease: a review and theoretical integration. *Journal of Health and Social Behavior*, **15**, 12–27.
Hyman, H.H. (1983). *Of Time and Widowhood*, Duke University, Durham, NC.
Jones, D.R. (1987). Heart disease mortality following widowhood: some results from the OPCS longitudinal study. *Journal of Psychosomatic Research*, **31**, 325–33.

Jones, D.R. and Goldblatt, P.O. (1986). Cancer mortality following widow(er)hood: some further results from the office of population censuses surveys longitudinal study. *Stress Medicine*, **2**, 129–40.

Klerman, G.L. and Clayton, P.J. (1984). Epidemiological perspectives on the health consequences of bereavement. In M. Osterweis, F. Solomon, and M. Green (eds.) *Bereavement: Reactions, Consequences, and Care*, National Academy, Washington, DC, pp. 15–44.

Kosten, T.R., Jacobs, S.C. and Kasl, S. (1985). Terminal illness, bereavement, and the family. In D.C. Turk and R.D. Kerns (eds.) *Health, Illness, and Families: A Life-Span Perspective*, Wiley, New York, pp. 311–37.

Lawton, M., Moss, M. and Kleban, M.H. (1984). Marital status, living arrangements, and the well-being of older people. *Research on Aging*, **6**, 323–45.

Lopata, H.Z. (1973). *Widowhood in an American City*, Schenkman, Cambridge, MA.

Lundin, T. (1984). Morbidity following sudden and unexpected bereavement. *British Journal of Psychiatry*, **144**, 84–8.

Maddison, D. and Viola, A. (1968). The health of widows in the year following bereavement. *Journal of Psychosomatic Research*, **12**, 297–306.

Nachmias, D. and Nachmias, C. (1976). *Research Methods in the Social Sciences*, St Martin's, New York.

Norris, F.H. and Murrell, S.A. (1987). Older adult family stress and adaptation before and after bereavement. *Journal of Gerontology*, **42**, 606–12.

Owen, G., Fulton, R. and Markusen, E. (1982). Death at a distance: a study of family survivors. *Omega*, **13**, 191–225.

Parkes, C.M. (1970). The first year of bereavement. *Psychiatry*, **33**, 444–67.

Parkes, C.M. (1975). Determinants of outcome following bereavement. *Omega*, **6**, 303–23.

Parkes, C.M., Benjamin, B. and Fitzgerald, R.G. (1969). Broken heart: a statistical study of increased mortality among widowers. *British Medical Journal*, **1**, 740–3.

Parkes, C.M. and Brown, R.J. (1972). Health after bereavement. *Psychosomatic Medicine*, **34**, 449–61.

Parkes, C.M. and Weiss, R.S. (1983). *Recovery from Bereavement*, Basic, New York.

Rando, T.A. (ed.) (1986). *Loss and Anticipatory Grief*, Lexington, Lexington, MA.

Rees, W.D. and Lutkins, S.G. (1967). Mortality of bereavement. *British Medical Journal*, **4**, 13–16.

Salloway, J.C. and Dillon, P.B. (1973). A comparison of family networks and friend networks in health care utilization. *Journal of Comparative Family Studies*, **4**, 131–42.

Solie, L.J. and Fielder, L.J. (1987). The relationship between sex role identity and a widow's adjustment to the loss of a spouse. *Omega*, **18**, 33–40.

Stroebe, M.S. and Stroebe, W. (1983). Who suffers more? Sex differences in health risks of the widowed. *Psychological Bulletin*, **93**, 279–301.

Thoits, P.A. (1982). Conceptual, methodological, and theoretical problems in studying social support as a buffer against life stress. *Journal of Health and Social Behavior*, **23**, 145–59.

US Bureau of the Census. (1986). *Statistical Abstracts of the United States: 1987*, Washington, DC.

Vachon, M.L.S. (1976). Grief and bereavement following the death of a spouse. *Canadian Psychiatric Journal*, **21**, 35– 44.

Vachon, M.L.S., Sheldon, A.R., Lancee, W.J., Lyall, W.A., Rogers, J. and Freeman, S.J.J. (1982). Correlates of enduring distress patterns following bereavement: social network, life situation, and personality. *Psychological Medicine*, **12**, 783–8.

Walker, K.N., MacBride, A. and Vachon, M.L.S. (1977). Social support networks and the crisis of bereavement. *Social Science and Medicine*, **11**, 35–41.

Wan, T.T.H. (1982). *Stressful Life Events, Social-Support Networks, and Gerontological Health*, Lexington, Lexington, MA.

Wan, T.T.H. (1984). The health consequences of major role losses in later life: a panel study. *Research on Aging*, **6**, 469–89.

Ward, A.W.M. (1976). Mortality of bereavement. *British Medical Journal*, **1**, 700–2.

Young, M., Benjamin, B. and Wallis, C. (1963). The mortality of widowers. *Lancet* **2**, 454–6.

APPENDIX

Empirical studies of widowhood and health

Study (Sample)	Measurement	Salient results
Bass *et al.* (1986) (19 bereaved spouses and 47 bereaved adult children, Cleveland, OH)	1. Six-item index of negative health change 2. Four-item index of depression	1. Loss of spouse associated with health decline and increased depression among those bereaved <30 months
Clayton (1974) (109 bereaved adults, mean age of 61, matched with married controls, St Louis)	1. 15 illness symptoms 2. 26 symptoms of psycho-logical distress 3. Medical treatment 4. Mortality	1. Bereaved experienced significantly more psychological and illness symptoms 2. No differences observed in medical treatment or mortality
Clayton (1975) (same as above)	(similar to above)	1. Results noted above are not due to living alone 2. Health problems are more substantial for younger widows than older widows
Clayton, Halikas, Maurice and Robins (1973) (same as above)	1. 20 symptoms of depression	1. Duration of spouse's terminal illness was not related to depression 2. Anticipatory grief is related to heightened depression immediately after death of spouse
Cox and Ford (1964) (60 000 women under age 70 who were awarded widows pension, England)	1. Mortality	1. Mortality risk is greatest two years after widowhood
Dimond *et al.* (1987) (192 widowed older adults from Utah; several data collection points *after* widowed)	1. Self-rating depression scale (Zung) 2. Self-reports of physical health and stress	1. Depression was greatest among widows with smaller social networks 2. High quality of networks—in terms of interaction—were associated with better health and less depression

Study	Measures	Findings
Fenwick and Barresi (1981) (National sample of low- and middle-income elderly; longitudinal data on all marital statuses)	1. Perceived health 2. Reported illness days (in bed) 3. Reported hospitalized days	1. Recently widowed report health decline but spend fewer days in bed than married respondents
Ferraro (1985) (National sample of low- and middle-income elderly; longitudinal data on married and widowed only)	1. Perceived health 2. Nine-item disability index 3. Frequency of chronic conditions	1. Widowhood results in an immediate health decline but the long-term effects are minimal 2. Widowed elderly with poorer perceived health showed increased disability
Ferraro et al. (1984) (same as above)	1. Perceived health	1. Recently widowed report greater declines in health than either long-term widowed or married persons 2. Widowed elderly in better health increased friendship involvement over time
Gerber et al. (1975) (Cross-sectional data on 81 bereaved spouses from New York City: 16 whose spouses died of acute illness/remainder chronic illness)	1. Number of physician office visits 2. Number of times when ill without contacting a physician 3. Number of psychotropic medications used	1. No significant differences between reports from chronic illness and acute illness groups 2. No significant differences between widows and widowers of acute illness deaths 3. More health problems for those who were bereaved because of a lengthy chronic fatal illness than those whose spouses died of a short-term chronic illness
Helsing and Szklo (1981) 4032 adults widowed between 1963 and 1974 matched with married persons from Maryland)	1. Mortality	1. Widowhood increased mortality for men but not for women 2. Little evidence for higher mortality in the first year after death of spouse
Helsing, Szklo and Comstock (1981) (same as above)	1. Mortality	1. Mortality rates for widowed men who remarried were lower than those who did not 2. Remarriage did not affect mortality among widowed women

Appendix (continued)

Study (Sample)	Measurement	Salient results
Heyman and Gianturco (1973) 41 bereaved older adults, Piedmont, NC; longitudinal study before and after widowhood)	1. Activities and attitudes (Havighurst): 20 activity items and 56 attitude items 2. Cavan Adjustment Rating Scale (social workers' evaluation) 3. Psychiatric evaluation 4. Physical Function Rating, MD medical exam	1. No significant difference in health before and after widowhood 2. Respondents manifested (a) emotional stability; (b) stable social network; (c) few life changes; (d) only time related health deterioration
Homan et al. (1986) (18 441 adults 55 and over from 1978 Health Interview Survey)	1. Use of ambulatory physician services	1. Widowhood is not associated with higher physician use once living arrangements and sex are controlled
Hyman (1983) (NORC surveys; pooled, cross-sections)	1. Two health ratings	1. Widowhood is associated with poorer health, especially among men
Jones (1987) (OPCS Longitudinal Study of England and Wales)	1. Mortality (by cause)	1. Widowhood increases mortality during the first year of bereavement, especially for women 2. The higher mortality associated with bereavement is not due to ischaemic heart disease
Jones and Goldblatt (1986) (same as above)	1. Mortality (by cause)	1. Same as 1 above 2. No peak in postbereavement mortality from cancer by sex
Lawton, Moss and Kleban (1984) (Two national samples and one from Philadelphia)	1. Functional health (different measure(s) for each survey)	1. Living arrangements affect health more than widowhood: healthier can live alone

Study	Measures	Findings
Lundin (1984) (87 bereaved relatives in Sweden, 32 of whom suffered sudden and unexpected bereavement)	1. Frequency of sick days per year	1. Increased morbidity among those bereaved suddenly and unexpectedly
Maddison and Viola (1968) (132 middle aged widows, Boston; 243 middle aged widows, Australia; cross-section of women whose husbands died before reaching 60 years—married controls)	1. 57-item questionnaire for symptoms and complaints (physical and mental)	1. Psychological symptoms differentiate most consistently between the bereaved and controls. One widow in eight had consulted physician for treatment of depression 2. Boston—21.2% of widows sustained health deterioration compared with 7.2% for the controls; Australia—32.1% and 2.0% respectively
Owen, Fulton and Markusen (558 bereaved persons including 434 bereaved spouses, Minnesota)	1. Perceived emotional and behavioral reactions to bereavement 18-item questionnaire	1. Nature of the relationship severed shapes the grief response. Surviving parents and spouses displayed more illness than bereaved adult children
Parkes (1970) (22 widows *under* age 65, London; longitudinal study with several data points)	1. Guttman scale of anger, guilt, and social withdrawal 2. Perceived and observed psychiatric reactions to bereavement	1. Anger and guilt closely related in the first month, lessened over time 2. Insomnia, sleep disturbances, anorexia and weight loss common in the first three months 3. A year after spouse's death, the widow may often experience depression, but this gradually diminishes
Parkes (1975) (68 widows and widowers with mean age of 36 years, Boston, MA; 'longitudinal' data over one year)	1. 168-item health questionnaire asked only at final interview 2. Additional variables used to assess overall adjustment—psychological and physical	1. Socioeconomic status is related to health outcomes 2. Patients with shorter preparation for bereavement were more likely to suffer a 'depressive symptom complex'

Appendix (continued)

Study (Sample)	Measurement	Salient results
Parkes and Brown (1972) (49 widows and 19 widowers *under* age 45; matched with married controls, Boston, MA; see also Parkes and Weiss (1983) for details)	1. External anxiety (14 questions) 2. Depression (10 questions) 3. Compulsive self reliance (10 questions) 4. Autonomic reactions (12 questions) 5. Stimulus seeking (7 questions) 6. Interpersonal fear (11 questions) 7. Additional items: medical care use, psychological symptoms, personality	1. Widowers reported more acute physical symptoms than widows and neither sex reported more chronic symptoms than controls 2. Bereaved spent more days sick in bed and had more hospital admissions than controls 3. Two to four years later there was little difference in health between bereaved and control groups but evidence of persistent 'disengagement' among bereaved who differed from controls in feeling more apart or remote even among friends
Parkes, Benjamin and Fitzgerald (1969) (4486 widowed men 55 years or older, England; follow-up of Young *et al.*, 1963)	1. Mortality	1. Mortality risk is greatest six months after widowhood 2. Thereafter mortality risk is roughly equal to married men
Rees and Lutkins (1967) (903 bereaved close relatives matched with control groups from a small town in Great Britain; longitudinal groups)	1. Mortality rates over six years following death of close relative	1. Mortality rate for widowed people was higher than controls during first two years of bereavement, especially first six months 2. Mortality of widowers is higher than that of widowed women during first year of bereavement
Solie and Fielder (1987) (45 women, 21 to 70 years of age, widowed at least one year; MN)	1. Adult form, Adjustment Inventory: health, social, emotional 2. Adjustment/Depression Scale for Widows	1. Androgynous widows showed the best adjustment, especially in terms of health and social functioning

Study (Sample)	Measure	Results
Vachon et al. (1982) (99 women bereaved of their husband; 27 to 69 years old)	1. Goldberg Questionnaire to assess nonpsychotic psychiatric illness	1. Approximately one-third of respondents reported high distress for two years 2. Deficits in social support, health, and finances were correlated with enduring high distress
Wan (1982) (Longitudinal Retirement History Study (LRHS), 1969–1975; about 5000 adults)	1. Perceived health 2. Disability	1. Widowhood is associated with a decline in perceived health and an increase in disability
Wan (1984) (Similar to above: LRHS; 2476 adults)	1. Latent variable of poor health based on three indicators	1. Recently widowed men showed poorer health; among women, widowhood did not affect health status
Ward (1976) (87 men and 279 women who lost their spouse, England and Wales)	1. Mortality	1. Mortality risk is significant for men only during the first six months of widowhood
Young et al. (1963) (4486 widowed men, 55 years or older, England)	1. Mortality	1. Mortality risk is greatest six months after widowhood 2. Suggested slightly higher mortality risk after one year of widowhood

Chapter 5

Stress, Early Retirement and Health

Ann E. McGoldrick

Retirement from employment has been viewed as a major transition in the individual's life—perhaps the most major transition of all. Its impact in terms of physical and mental health is much disputed in the literature. Likewise, a 'folklore' of retirement has arisen relating to the feasibility and means of avoiding adverse effects, which is often quoted to researchers at interviews. It too comes to diametrically opposed views—retirement necessarily brings deleterious consequences, even death, or retirement induces health improvement. At retirement, however, the individual is moving out of the work environment, where he spent his adult life. Work, it has been argued, provides far more than mere financial security for the majority. While individual cultures may differ in the extent to which they emphasize the values of the outcomes of work, in most cultures work has much greater significance than merely obtaining an income (e.g. Triandis, 1973). Perhaps one of the most frequently quoted commentators on the losses ensuing has been Miller (1965), who saw retirement as a 'socially debilitating loss', a 'degrading withdrawal of all legitimate identity'.

The individual on retiring leaves the work environment, where he has developed well-defined roles and interpersonal relationships. His occupational status, it is proposed, is his major source of identity, both within the work setting and in the non-work domain. From this comes self-image, self-respect, a feeling of making a useful contribution and a place in the social system, determining the nature of his relations with others. To withdraw the central life role is therefore seen as critical for the majority, since it cannot be replaced in leisure because it lacks social value. He moves to a 'roleless role' (Burgess, 1960), lacking in cultural value and any real role specifications. If this is the case, would it be surprising therefore if the consequences of retirement were severe physical and psychological problems? Will retiring early or having the choice of retirement timing have an ameliorating effect on this? In this chapter, retirement will be considered as an important life event or transition. The evidence regarding subsequent expectancy and health will be assessed. The focus of our investigation will be on new trends towards early retirement, seen in the United States from the late 1960s and 1970s, then following in other industrialized countries. Can this be only the result of reduction in labour needs or does it demonstrate changing attitudes towards retirement itself? Are there positive benefits for the individual? On the

Aging, Stress and Health Edited by K.S. Markides and C.L. Cooper
© 1989 John Wiley & Sons Ltd

other hand, what do we know about the potential stressors which may arise with earlier retirement? In conclusion, we will examine the buffering influences which may reduce the impact of this transition, considering particularly the role of social support, practical and attitudinal preparation.

THE RETIREMENT TRANSITION

The beginnings of 'retirement' as we know it are comparatively recent. It was the end of the eighteenth century in the United States and the beginning of the nineteenth century in the United Kingdom before the transition known as 'retirement' started to be standardized at a set age. Previously leaving the workforce was an independent decision, based on a wide range of personal and family circumstances. For the majority, it was to be delayed as long as possible on financial grounds. Ill-health was consequently the major cause of retirement, which was generally associated with an inability to work. The change was facilitated by the introduction and growth of superannuation or 'pension schemes', firstly in public then in larger private organizations. While ostensibly these were of direct benefit to older employees, they also permitted a rationalization of the workforce, removing those whom it was believed were less fit for regular and efficient employment. With the blessing of trade unions and philanthropic organizations State pension schemes followed for the elderly. These changes brought some financial relief for the sick and those unfit to work, although it has been suggested that the result could be dependency or poverty for some of those who could have effectively worked on (Walker, 1980).

Early retirement trends

Since this time it has been argued that public and official attitudes towards retirement have been closely related to changes in demand for labour. In both the United States and the United Kingdom incentives to continue in employment have been introduced in times of labour need, as in the years of the Second World War. Retirement policy has likewise been used in an attempt to relieve unemployment, with discouragement of continuing working and the fostering of more positive views of retired life, as in the 1920s slump and during the depression years in the United States (e.g. Phillipson, 1978; Graebner, 1980). From this perspective, the early retirement options arising from the later 1960s in the United States and following elsewhere through the 1970s can be viewed merely as the latest in this series of manipulations of the older employee. The changing mood suggested that retirement and leisure was a reward for those who had already contributed sufficiently. The move was based on developments in State and private pension scheme provision in both the United States and other industrialized societies. These included a widening of schemes generally to permit earlier retirement, reduction of actuarial infringements, and in some special schemes, supplemental benefits and 'golden handshakes'. While at first company schemes were mainly compulsory, more recently, with union influence, they have tended to be operated on a voluntary basis (McGoldrick and Cooper, 1978).

While political expediency is obvious, what of the uses for the company? Early retirement has, in fact, been found to be an effective 'management tool', which compensates for the expense of increased pension scheme support and lump-sum payments. Its uses include numbers' reduction, re-establishing promotion prospects, dealing with workforce 'bulges' and response to changing technology. A slightly younger and potentially healthier workforce can be established with benefits to morale generally by providing long-service rewards and increasing the security of younger employees (McGoldrick and Cooper, 1978). Government statistics in both the United States and the United Kingdom reveal dramatic declines in the labour participation of older employees, particularly men (e.g. United States Department of Labor, 1978; Department of Employment, 1978). A significant proportion of the figures, of course, still relate to the disabled and long-term sick, who we will not generally be dealing with here. Likewise, attention cannot be focused on those unfortunate victims of the unemployment situation who are made redundant in later life, with little prospect of re-employment.

Here we will concentrate on these new early retirement initiatives. Since political and organizational requirements suggest that it is here to stay, we must ask whether it is desirable and beneficial for the employee himself. Will it bring improvements to lifestyle and avoidance of health problems, or alternatively does an earlier retirement add to the stresses of this particular life event? Does it bring forward the implied status change of retiring, increasing psychological pressures as well as the practical implications of an earlier move from employment, thus increasing the likelihood of deleterious health outcomes?

Retirement as a psychosocial crisis

A major distinction in conceptual approaches to retirement and the aging process generally occurs between the type of framework employed by social gerontologists and the psychological approach. Sociological approaches have stressed role loss, changing role expectations and their impact on the individual. An early and influential approach was that of 'disengagement' (Cumming and Henry, 1961), stressing the universal and inevitable process of mutual withdrawal between society and the aging individual, with retirement as the symbol of the socially specified time. Many criticisms have been levelled and the theory has largely given way to the 'activity' framework. This is almost a converse of disengagement, concentrating on replacement of roles and readjustment of social self (e.g. Atchley, 1976). Both share a lack of emphasis on personality factors and the psychological dynamics of response.

Psychological literature relating to life events and the potential stresses induced has developed rapidly through the last two decades. The fundamental proposition is that all individuals experience a variety of such life changes and major adaptation may be required, with consequent social adjustment. While the impact may be mollified by social buffers and personality variables, to some degree all individuals necessarily suffer stresses from these occurrences. It is proposed that individual functioning may be seriously affected in reaction to such changes, on account of psychological and physical coping demands. Aetiological significance will be dependent on the amount of adjustment required (Holmes and Rahe, 1967; Masada and Holmes, 1967; Dohrewend and Dohrenwend, 1974; Rahe, 1974). The Social Readjustment Rating Scale, and others developed from it, have been used widely in empirical studies to relate life stress to a variety of dynamic and minor illnesses, psychiatric disorders, anxiety and depression. Critical reviews have, however, pointed to weaknesses in the scales and methodologies employed (e.g. Birley and Connolly, 1976; Rabkin and Struening, 1976; Kasl, 1980, 1983).

Retirement is a major life change. Can the concept be useful therefore to the study of retirement? One reviewer, in fact, referred to it as 'simplistic and impoverished' (Kasl, 1980), advising workers in the field of retirement not to look to the stressful life events literature to augment the viewpoint that retirement may bring adverse health consequences. As far as the Social Readjustment Rating Scale is concerned, retirement is only one item, which will not even apply to large numbers of subjects who have completed it. Such a measure is consequently irrelevant. Likewise the concept requires careful consideration.

Firstly, retirement will necessarily have different meanings for individuals, ranging from complete rejection to a positive welcoming of the life change implied. The response will be determined by a wide range of attitudes, beliefs and personal circumstances. The 'meaning' of retirement will vary in terms of both relevance and desirability on an individual basis. Secondly, retirement does not occur in isolation. As part of the aging process, it is accompanied by other changes for the individual. Some employees now volunteer to retire before the norm. Will retirement likewise be a stressful event for them, bringing adverse health consequences? In considering retirement, we need to place it firmly within a wider perspective, assessing the significance of interacting elements of the individual's life. This will include attitudes towards work and leisure, employment pressures and changes, the relevance of the non-work domain, family and social relationships, health and physical aging, personality variables and other life events occurring at the same time, including the possibility of bereavement.

A wider view does exist, which considers life-course development. This conceptual orientation assumes that aging must be viewed as the outcome of a life-long process, with multidimensional effects producing change (e.g. Neugarten and Hagestad, 1976; Lowenthal, 1977; Neugarten, 1977). From this perspective, the complex nature of the aging process is acknowledged, with the interaction of many biological, social and personal changes. The essence is to examine retirement as one of a series of life 'transitions', which the individual deals with in terms of his own varied circumstances. His pattern of response will be determined by his own coping style, which is developed over time and used to adapt to new situations and problems encountered. These are evolving patterns, although nonetheless rooted in the past. It is claimed, in fact that there is no sharp discontinuity of personality with increasing age, rather 'increasing consistency' (Neugarten *et al.*, 1968).

The meaning of 'retirement'

Before going on to examine empirical evidence in relation to approaches outlined, it is necessary to examine one conceptual issue which is a potential cause of confusion between findings. A major problem in assessing retirement studies is how 'retirement' is actually defined. The wide range of meanings the term has in ordinary usage can be ascertained from any dictionary. In empirical studies various definitions have been adopted in terms of the subjects of the particular research investigation. Definitions which have been used relating to observable characteristics of the respondents include: receipt of a pension, taking a specific retirement option, reaching a set age, not working or working under a certain number of hours, relying totally on pension income or being substantially reliant on such. Other studies have relied on self-report measures, leaving respondents to decide for themselves if they are retired or not. The diversity increases in the study of early retirement, resulting in virtually a complete continuum (Parnes and Nestle, 1975). At one end is complete labour force withdrawal, with a second career or further full-time employment at the other extreme. While it can be argued that it is legitimate to use different definitions for differing purposes, bitter exchanges have occurred between researchers. In studying early retirement, one definition has been withdrawal from the main job on eligibility under pension scheme terms (e.g. Messer, 1969; Schmitt, Coyle, Rauschenberger and White, 1979; Schmitt and McCune, 1981); others have focused on special schemes (e.g. Barfield and Morgan, 1969; Orbach, 1969; Katona, Morgan and Barfield 1969; Pollman, 1971a,b; Burkhauser and Tolley, 1978). Post-retirement employment activity, with consequent financial gain and other gains from work involvement, here does not affect eligibility. Other definitions have been based on registering for employment benefits (e.g. Reno, 1971). Boskin (1977), on the other hand, argued that the common perception of retirement was a reduction in work and income rather than cessation of work, using 'quarter time' work as the basis of his definition. Parker (1980) defined retirement as those not working or seeking employment, pension income not being considered essential. Older redundant employees could therefore qualify. Subjectively defined retirement was used, for example, in the Retirement History Study (Quinn, 1977). Other studies have included a wider range of early retirement options, although requiring pension arrangements (e.g. McGoldrick and Cooper, 1989). The basic problem is therefore comparability and the interpretation of findings. A good demonstration was provided by the National Longitudinal Survey (Parnes and Nestle, 1975, 1981), where subjective assessment by respondents and substantial curtailment of labour force participation were both utilized. While results were sometimes similar, at times findings could be significant by one definition but not the other. Definitions employed are likely to account for some differences between studies and the actual effects cannot easily be determined.

LIFE EXPECTANCY AND HEALTH AFTER RETIRING

An examination of the empirical literature relating to health after retirement is instructive in assessing the appropriateness of the life event approach. On the one hand, strong adverse effects have been deduced or assumed to be directly related to the retirement act, because of the importance of the life event occurring (e.g. Carp, 1977; Kutash and Schlesinger, 1980). Opposed to this is literature, mainly of a social gerontological nature, which suggests such outcomes are rare, even suggesting improvements in health and psychological outlook (e.g. Streib and Schneider, 1971; Friedmann and Orbach, 1974; Atchley, 1976). We need to consider two sets of studies: those connecting retirement with increases in mortality and physical health change, as well as those dealing with mental adjustment. While there are major methodological problems and some of the literature is somewhat dated, the overall conclusion, it seems, must fall on the side of the more positive interpretation.

Retirement and longevity

Early views particularly tended to assert that the impact of retirement may result in premature death. Often quoted, for instance, is the early study by Myers (1954), which claimed to demonstrate increases in mortality in the first two years after retiring, after which trends returned to anticipated levels. Could this be the 'shock' of the life crisis? The study's validity must be questioned, however, on the grounds that it is impossible to isolate 'retirement impact' from other variables (e.g. health, social class, economic status), which are likely to affect the outcome. Such factors will, of course, also variously affect the control group upon which expected mortality rates were constructed. The insensitive nature of this type of approach soon determined that it would become less fashionable.

Other studies at the time had found a lack of such impact. A study of 3971 rubber tyre workers in the United States compared correlates of survival after early and normal retirement (Haynes, McMichael and Tyroler, 1977, 1978). No significant mortality excesses were observed. Comparison of deaths in a five year control period after retirement with a control sample of survivors showed the only significant predictor to be pre-retirement health status. Higher mortality rates for the early retired in the year following retirement can again be related to their health reasons for retiring, rather than any subsequent impact. Risk of dying was better assessed from medical history, sickness absence and lower social status. A further study of employees from a Canadian communications company (Tyhurst, Salk and Kennedy, 1957) came to similar conclusions. No evidence appeared that mortality rates of groups retiring at different ages differed, nor that age at retirement affected life expectancy. Finally, McMahan and Ford (1955) assessed survival rates of a population of United States army and airforce officers. The population studied necessarily causes problems, since re-entry to the labour market would be an obvious option. Also, retirement would occur at differing ages and with wide variation in health status. Mortality rate was, in fact, somewhat higher for younger age groups, presumably as a result of ill-health retirements. Overall, no direct evidence was found to support the proposition that 'entry into retirement is an especially deadly transition'.

Analysing British census data, Parker (1982) quotes evidence that in the case of both men and women under State pension age those who are retired have death rates nearly two times those of groups still in employment. A less marked difference exists for those over pension age, which he explains as a consequence of retirement after pension age being much less often linked to ill-health. Again this cannot be directly linked to the impact of retirement, since there will be other important social correlates intervening, especially prior health status on retiring. A comparison of poor health and mortality among the retired and the working is not sufficient to establish the 'reasons' for any differences which might be found. A related issue raised by Parker is that of suicide rates. Data from the United States demonstrates a high rate of attempted suicide in the over 65 age band. Since suicide is frequently linked to life crises, can this be evidence for this interpretation of retirement? Again it is necessary to consider the full complexity of the aging process. Other factors, such as health problems, bereavement and financial strain, cannot be ignored. Furthermore, similar analysis of British census data did not indicate a higher suicide rate for the retired than for the employed, whether they retired early or over State pension age.

The impact of retiring on physical health

Available evidence therefore suggests that retirement cannot be assumed to be directly related to early mortality. Ill-health is, of course, a major determinant of early retirement, which would seem to be more likely to be associated with higher mortality rates than the act of retirement itself. What of the evidence, however, relating retirement to physical health problems and decline? Again there are major methodological problems in the studies. Many, for instance, are cross-sectional designs rather than longitudinal analyses, with health status and changes to health being a matter of self-report. Other indications include the reporting of minor ailments, changes to eating and sleeping patterns, tiredness, visits to doctors, with only a limited amount of attention to physician ratings or before and after retirement designs. Despite such weaknesses their conclusions are generally similar and positive, overall suggesting that retirement cannot be associated directly with health decline. There is, in fact, some evidence that there may be improvements to health status.

The Canadian study previously referred to (Tyhurst *et al.*, 1957), for example, used company absence records and post-retirement interviews to assess changes in health status before and after retiring. No changes were found, with no differences here occurring as a result of pre-retirement attitudes or between volunteers and the compulsorily retired. Both objective and subjective data was used to assess the health after retirement of 500 older men and women in the United States, aged 60–70 years (Ryser and Sheldon, 1969). The outcome was positive: no difference to health was reported by over two-thirds, while twice as many respondents reported improvement in comparison to decline. In the Cornell longitudinal study (Streib and Schneider, 1971), no change in health was found on the basis of early retirement. By self-assessment, the early retired were, in fact, more likely to report improved health, while those in employment over the same period tended to suggest a slight decline. Since the retired initially had poorer health, the authors suggest that it could demonstrate the beneficial effect of retirement, which occurred similarly for both sexes and different occupational groups. Physician examination of a sub-sample again revealed improvement for the retired (Streib and Thompson, 1957). While the health of the retired declined slightly after 65, this was not directly attributed to retirement, since workers showed similar decline.

Similar findings come from British studies. One investigation (Emerson, 1959), for example, used the Cornell Medical Index on a small sample of retired and employed men, finding no differences, despite the fact that early leavers would have included subjects already in poorer health. Interview reports were used to compare a sample of 604 retired and working men, aged 55 and over (Martin and Doran, 1966). No differences were found in respect of serious health problems, with lower incidence of serious illness in the two years following retirement and a slower rate of increase thereafter, especially it seems for blue-collar workers. Crawford (1972) interviewed a small sample of 53 married couples before and after retirement, also finding self-assessed health to be the same. Suggestion of decreased appetite and increased weight here could be related to lack of early adjustment to the more relaxed pace of retirement for the mainly blue-collar sample, since the study only extended one year into retirement.

Little of the literature relating specifically to early retirement assists here, since few researchers have examined the outcome. Barfield and Morgan (1969) found that early retired automobile workers were more likely to report health improvement, while those planning to retire rather than work on were more likely to suggest health decline. Owen and Belzung (1967) found that a small sample of voluntarily early retired men from a Texas oil refining company reported health status to be better or equivalent to that when working, with few reporting decline. In a study in the United Kingdom (McGoldrick and Cooper, 1989), over half of the 1208 early retired men reported improved health to be a benefit after their retirement, with a quarter seeing it as a major benefit. Health problems tended to be associated with older respondents and lower social groups. Perceived improvement in terms of a 'healthier lifestyle' were also significantly associated with volunteering to retire, while perceived reduction in general well-being related to compulsory retirement.

Mental health and adjustment

In assessing the effect of retirement on mental health, problems occur as a result of lack of comparability between studies. Sample composition varies in terms of type of retirement, age, time in retirement, social class, industry and prior health. Likewise, differing approaches are adopted and different measures of adjustment are utilized. Kasl (1980) suggests four approaches: 'medical-psychiatric', emphasizing specific diagnosis or rating of symptoms; 'sociological', distinguishing ability to perform normal roles and activities; 'psychological', with a variety of indictors of well-being and satisfaction; and the 'positive mental health' approach, emphasizing competence and mastery. Findings will obviously be affected. Likewise measures include rating scales, indices of mental health and of life-satisfaction, with many studies only employing some form of global assessment by respondents.

Whatever approach is taken or measure used, however, results appear remarkably similar, suggesting that individual study weaknesses cannot account for the outcome. Overall, evidence suggests that retirement does not lead directly to mental health problems for the majority, although differences in respect of sub-group characteristics will be investigated further. Commentators have suggested that between two-thirds and three-quarters are generally satisfied with the retirement experience, adapting well to their new circumstances and suffering no adverse psychological effects as a result of it (e.g. Atchley, 1975; Kasl, 1980; McGoldrick and Cooper, 1985). Both cross-sectional analyses (e.g. Shanas *et al.*, 1968; Bell, 1974, 1975; Atchley, 1975) and longitudinal studies in the United States (e.g. Thompson, Streib and Kosa, 1960; Streib and Schneider, 1971) of normal retirement have produced similar results. Their conclusions have been supported by studies examining the life quality of different age groups (e.g. Campbell, Converse and Rodgers, 1976) as well as comparisons between the retired and employed respondents (e.g. Streib, 1956; Simpson and McKinney, 1966). One such study (Thompson, 1973), in fact, examined 1589 older men, concluding that the retired did have lower morale than workers. When the combined effects of health, age and income were partialled out, however, the relationship almost disappeared.

Here the complexity of the retirement transition is demonstrated, with difficulty in isolating components of the retirees' situation. Any indication of lower morale for the retired could therefore be primarily explained in terms of lower incomes, poor health and more advanced aged, rather than simply by retirement itself. Turning to the studies of early retirement, a generally high level of satisfaction is again found, although early retirement as a result of poor health must be separately considered (e.g. Parker, 1980). For the majority, negative mental effects do not occur, with similar proportions adjusting well as at normal retirement age. An early investigation by Messer (1969), for example, of 3299 employees who had been eligible for early retirement under pension scheme terms found that the vast majority would have elected to retire early again. Pollman (1971b) compared 258 automobile workers with 442 early retirees under a liberalized benefits programme, using a shortened version of Life Satisfaction Index-Z (Wood, Wylie and Sheafor, 1966). The retired group demonstrated a significantly higher degree of life satisfaction. The author distinguished between the 'rocking chair' concept of retired life still suggested by many and newer approaches, with a 'myriad of leisure activities', or even further employment.

The Michigan studies undertaken by Barfield and Morgan (1969) produce further evidence of satisfaction with early retirement. Part of the work focused on a relatively homogeneous group of older blue-collar automobile workers, who qualified for a liberalized pension plan. Of the 477 who were retired at interview, 75% reported satisfaction. In a re-survey two years later (Barfield, 1970), 67% were still satisfied, while an overwhelming majority (89%) indicated that their decision to retire when they did had been right. The author concluded that 'autoworker retirees are overwhelmingly happy with their lot'. By 1976, however, when the retired sample were contacted a third time (Barfield and Morgan, 1978a, 1978b; Morgan, 1979), an increased sense of dissatisfaction was found amongst the retired from what seemed to be a stable high level of satisfaction when observed eight to 10 years previously. The authors associated this with declining health and the effects of high levels of inflation in the intervening years on retirement finances. A United Kingdom study of 1208 men retiring early under a variety of circumstances, other than disability retirement, showed again that almost 80% were satisfied with their experience and the lifestyles they adopted. When asked to compare their current life and life preceding retirement, approximately 60% reported improvement, while a further 30% indicated that they were the same. Three-quarters of the men also declared a preference to retire early again (McGoldrick, 1983; McGoldrick and Cooper, 1989). This and other studies mentioned here frequently relate, of course, to voluntary retirement, sometimes with special early retirement financial arrangements, although in this case it also included compulsory retirements. Ill-health retirement must necessarily have a depressing effect on general well-being after retirement. In a survey of men and women in the United Kingdom up to age 72, Parker (1980) reported health to be the most common reason still for early retirement, with approximately 50% of men aged 45 to 64 and women aged 45 to 59 years on retiring giving it as their principal reason. While 76% of the men also reported an illness or handicap which interfered with their activities, however, just over half were enjoying retirement. Only one in five expressed dissatisfaction, the remainder having mixed feelings. The level of satisfaction is perhaps surprisingly high considering the nature of most of these retirements, together with their reported post-retirement health and financial problems.

EARLY RETIREMENT AS A STRATEGIC RESPONSE

If retirement itself has not been shown directly to cause adverse health affects, is it possible that it may not be a 'life crisis' for many older employees, but instead may provide a positive response to their situation? Evidence does suggest that early retirement on a financially viable basis may, in fact, represent a 'double-edged strategy' for many older workers, providing both a basis for coping and an opportunity for personal development outside the work role (McGoldrick, 1983). If financial arrangements are appropriate, it may release them from the confines of working on when health problems exist which are not sufficient to warrant disability retirement. For others, improved health or health preservation may be the goal, with the acknowledgement of growing problems with their job or the work environment. Many employees have indeed been found to hold preferences for lower ages of retirement and a small body of evidence exists to suggest that, with reasonable financial security, early retired lifestyles may be a positive attraction.

A methodological note

In studies of the retirement decision comparability is limited by differences in approach. Studies employ either a retrospective or a projective framework, each having advantages and posing problems. In the retrospective studies (e.g. Barfield and Morgan, 1969; Streib and Schneider, 1971; Parnes and Nestle, 1975; Schmitt *et al.*, 1979; McGoldrick and Cooper, 1989) it is possible to include an accurate measure of retirement timing, although retrospective discussion may be affected by post-retirement experience. It is suggested, for example, that health may be emphasized as a reason for retiring on account of social acceptability, while financial motives may be taken for granted or suppressed if subsequent problems have arisen. Likewise the surprisingly low significance of work problems in some studies may indicate lack of current relevance, or a preference to retain positive memories of employed life. On the other hand, in projective studies, even for older subjects, later circumstances and events will influence attitudes and ultimate behaviour. It is even difficult to compare studies with others of the same type, since age ranges of respondents vary considerably. Furthermore, the actual preference examined differs. Examples include 'preferred age of retirement' (Rose and Mogay, 1972; Ekertd, Rose, Bosse and Costa, 1976), 'willingness to retire' (Jacobson and Eran, 1980), 'expected retirement age' (Hall and Johnson, 1980; Usher, 1981), 'preference for retirement' (Jacobson and Eran, 1980) and 'if they want to retire before 65' (Barfield and Morgan, 1969; Parnes and Nestle, 1975).

A further drawback has been the limited range of factors covered in the analyses, with early studies examining only a handful of global concepts, such as 'health', 'job', 'finances', 'leisure' (e.g. Messer, 1969; Orbach, 1969). Longitudinal or panel studies are few in number. They deal mainly with ill-health retirement and factors are likewise limited, since the retirement decision is not the only focus (e.g. Parnes and Nestle, 1975; Boskin, 1977). Many samples are small (e.g. Owen and Belzung, 1967; Peretti and Wilson, 1975; Schmitt and McCunne, 1981), a limitation which even applies to national surveys once discussion moves to those who have actually retired (Parnes and Nestle, 1975; Parker, 1980). The different industries and schemes selected for study cannot easily be compared, nor assumed to be representative of the general situation. It is notable, for example, that the United States car industry, with its history of industrial conflict, is the basis of a number of the enquiries. Some studies are limited to either blue-collar (e.g. Barfield and Morgan, 1969; Orbach, 1969) or white-collar samples (e.g. Eden and Jacobson, 1976; Jacobson and Eran, 1980), while the majority relate only to men. Having specified so many comparability issues, it is surprising that their findings are generally so consistent.

Health and finances as reasons for early retirement

Early studies of the retirement decision naturally placed great emphasis on the part played by poor health, since financially viable early retirement was rarely available (e.g. Corson and McConnell, 1956; Steiner and Dorfman, 1957; Shanas *et al.*, 1968). Later studies have demonstrated the association between early retirement and financial considerations, in response to the newly introduced options. Evidence from national surveys in the United States have shown pension eligibility at both State and company levels to be a dominant influence (e.g. Barfield and Morgan, 1969; Reno, 1971; Parnes, Fleischer, Miljus and Spitz, 1975; Parnes and Nestle, 1975, 1981; Boskin, 1977; Quinn, 1977, 1981; Morgan, 1980). Plans to retire tend to rise as expected post-retirement income increases. Similar results were found in the study in the United Kingdom, covering a range of types of early retirement (McGoldrick and Cooper, 1980, 1989).

Likewise studies of specific groups and individual occupations reach similar conclusions (e.g. Katona *et al.*, 1969; Orbach, 1969; Pollman, 1971 a,b; Pollman and Johnson, 1974; Patton, 1977; Schmitt *et al.*, 1979; Schmitt and McCune, 1981; Prothero and Beach, 1984). In one study, early acceptance was, in fact, shown to be increased when an actuarial penalty was imposed for delay (Burkhauser and Tolley, 1978; Burkhauser, 1979). Other financial factors which have been found to be influential include having fewer financial dependents, economic assets, mortgage security, private pensions, savings, partner's earnings, receipt of lump-sum payments and a positive financial outlook (Barfield and Morgan, 1969; McGoldrick and Cooper, 1989).

On account of these changes, there has been a tendency recently to minimize the relevance of health in retirement decisions (e.g. Boskin, 1977). Poor health must still be seen as a major determinant of labour force status in the United States and Britain (e.g. Quinn, 1977; Parker, 1980). Health issues also remain important decision criteria, even under voluntary options. They are frequently found in second rank in studies which examine primary reasons for retiring. While suitable finances are the vehicle enabling early retirement, declining health, the feeling that health is being affected by work or inability to cope well with work can also be relevant (e.g. Barfield and Morgan, 1969; Messer, 1969; Barfield, 1970; Pollman, 1971; Burkhauser, 1979; Morgan, 1980). Only a small number of studies have found health to be unrelated (e.g. Schmitt *et al.*, 1979; Schmitt and McCune, 1981). British studies have similarly shown the relevance of self-appraised health, as well as the significance of beliefs that retirement is beneficial to health status (e.g. Jacobson, 1972 a,b; Eden and Jacobson, 1976; Eran and Jacobson, 1976; McGoldrick and Cooper, 1989). The latter study also demonstrated the importance of tiredness in later working years, recognition of the effects of aging and the relevance of the partner's health status, as well as a desire to preserve better health by freeing oneself from the stresses of the work environment.

Later years at work

This leads us on to consider in more detail the stresses which individuals may encounter as they grow older in their working situation. Some attention has been given to occupational status in respect of preferring to retire early (e.g. Draper , Lundgren and Strother, 1967; Barfield and Morgan, 1969; Jacobson, 1972 a, 1972 b), which indicates that more positive views are associated with blue-collar work, low skill levels and jobs with higher rates of physical strain. Higher education and employment status, on the other hand, and more desirable occupations have been associated with preference for later ages (e.g. Barfield, 1970; Streib and Schneider, 1971; Boskin, 1977; Parnes and Nestle, 1981). It has been suggested that the older worker in general has to cope with declining physical and mental abilities, which affect job performance. Reviews have demonstrated that such changes are not inevitable and occur slowly, while older employees show high levels of moti- vation, job attitudes and involvement (e.g. Fleischer and Kaplan, 1981; Doering, Rhodes and Schuster, 1983). What they do have to cope with, however, are the stereotypes which still exist in many industries and increasing insecurity in the work environment (e.g. Rosen and Jerdee, 1979; Brousseau, 1981).

There is also some evidence that job elements may be influential in the decision to retire, in respect of both job attitudes and actual features of later working years. Both lower job satisfaction and placing less emphasis on the value of work have shown some association with preference for earlier retirement (e.g. Johnson and Strother, 1962; Messer, 1969; Barfield and Morgan, 1969; Streib and Schneider, 1971; Parnes and Nestle, 1975; McGoldrick and Cooper, 1989). A problem is that measures used are often global self-report, although where the relevance of autonomy, intrinsic satisfaction and challenge were investigated using more sophisticated measures (Schmitt *et al.*, 1979; Schmitt and McCune, 1981), an association was found. Lack of autonomy has been fairly consistently related to a preference for earlier retirement (e.g. Barfield and Morgan, 1969; Jacobson, 1972a; Quinn, 1977), as have changes in the nature of work, including the effects of automation and new technology (e.g. Barfield and Morgan, 1969; McGoldrick and Cooper, 1989). Other more detailed problems suggested include overwork, the need for reduced hours, boredom and travel to and at work. At the same time, little attention has been given to the effect of colleagues and peers. There seems to be some evidence that influential factors may be management attitudes and changing company structures, younger workers' attitudes, supervisory responsibilities and dislike of union practices and policies (McGoldrick and Cooper, 1989).

Another area which has so far not received a great deal of attention is that of job stresses experienced in later years. Older employees often feel less able to cope well with their jobs in the changing industrial environment. This does not only apply to the physical requirements of manual work but also to the pressures in managerial and professional employment. At the manual level, preference to retire early has been shown to increase with job strain, measured in terms of such factors as noise, fumes, repetitiveness and atmospheric conditions (Jacobson, 1972a, 1972b), while job related tension, including conflict, overload and ambiguity, was associated with lower effectiveness and favourable attitudes towards retiring in a study of male executives (Eden and Jacobson, 1976). Likewise a combination of greater stress, less job satisfaction and a lower competence evaluation were combined in association with preference for retirement in respect of a sample of physicians (Jacobson and Eran, 1980). This lowered ability to cope at work and greater efforts required can result in tiredness and stress symptoms, as well as affecting enjoyment of leisure. Likewise it can be carried over into the non-work domain, exerting stress on marital and family relationships (McGoldrick and Cooper, 1989).

Changing attitudes to work and retirement

A growing body of evidence suggests that attitudes towards work are, in fact, changing, indicating that many workers do not obtain their primary personal outcomes from their work role. For them, financial security is indeed the overriding purpose for working. Identity, status, self-fulfilment and the 'meaning' of their lives can be obtained elsewhere (e.g. Gechman, 1974; Kahn, 1974). While a strong positive orientation towards work has been found to remain for some retired people, this is not necessarily accompanied by either a dislike of retirement or withdrawal from other activity (Atchley, 1971). People can be buffered from the impact of retirement by other roles in family and community (Cottrell, 1970), which may indeed be more significant for many (e.g. Cantril and Roll, 1971; Campbell *et al.*, 1976). This was shown in the Quality of Employment Survey in the United States, for example, where work was strongly related to economic needs. Almost a third of workers indicated they would miss nothing about work, while a further third would miss only colleagues and workmates (Quinn and Sheppard, 1974).

Lower skilled workers particularly have been shown to gain little fulfilment from their jobs, high involvement being reserved for stimulating and more autonomous occupations (e.g. Strauss, 1974; Rabinowitz, Hall and Goodale, 1977). Acceptance of leisure roles, on the other hand, has been found to be high amongst middle-aged people (e.g. Pfeiffer and Davis, 1971). Furthermore, as the concept of retirement becomes incorporated into a culture, the tendency to look on work as a temporary part of life increases, causing people to put emphasis elsewhere.

Another area of debate has been the relationship between attitudes towards work and retirement. Are these diametrically opposed or can they be linked, representing personality factors and a more general approach to life? Even Friedmann and Havighurst (1954), in their early study of the 'meaning' of work and retirement, admitted that there were exceptions to their general finding that it was those less involved in work who were most willing to retire. Studies reporting an inverse relationship have perhaps dominated (e.g. Tuckman and Lorge, 1953; Saleh and Otis, 1963; Stokes and Maddox, 1967). Inconsistencies have been detected, however, and the most satisfactory formulation seems to be a wider, more complex response. One study, for example, suggested four types of relationship: a positive attitude to both, giving on easy transition; dissatisfaction with the job and looking forward to leaving it; a negative view of retirement, with resentment at the change implied; and dissatisfaction at work, combined with negative anticipation of the non-work role (Goudy, Powers and Keith, 1975).

Evidence of changing attitudes towards retirement also exists. While earlier studies suggested that the majority of workers approached retirement with negative feelings (e.g. Donahue, Orbach and Pollack, 1960; Katona, 1965), more recent projective studies amongst the working population have shown preferred retirement age to be lower than expected age (e.g. Draper *et al.*, 1967; Barfield and Morgan, 1969; Rose and Mogey, 1972; McGoldrick and Cooper, 1985). There is some evidence that younger respondents are more positive, with a decline as actual retirement age approaches (e.g. Crook and Heinstein, 1958; Rose and Mogey, 1972; Eden and Jacobson, 1976; Riffault, 1978). The problems of cross-sectional analysis may confound issues here, demonstrating cohort effects, with younger workers now preferring earlier retirement ages. A large-scale longitudinal study (Ekerdt *et al.*, 1976), however, drew similar conclusions. Preferred age overall was nonetheless typically younger than expected age. Contradictory evidence also exists. In the National Longitudinal Study in the United States (Parnes and Nestle, 1975), early retirement intentions were found to increase with age rather than decline between two waves of the survey, as did actual retirements. A Canadian longitudinal study (Crawford and Matlow, 1972) showed increase in positive retirement attitudes as men moved into their 50s, with increasing numbers of respondents specifying preference for early retirement. Positive attitudes were likewise detected in a British study (Stafford and Mould, 1982), with the majority desiring an earlier retirement, even if on a reduced pension.

Information regarding positive perceptions of early retirement lifestyles is practically non-existent in studies. The desire for more free time and to leave while it is still possible to enjoy life has been noted (e.g. Barfield and Morgan, 1969; Messer, 1969; Orbach, 1969; Pollman, 1971a; Manion, 1972; Kimmel, Price and Walker, 1978; Price, Walker and Kimmel, 1979). Results suggested that the retirement decision could represent a positive attempt for some to pursue more interesting, challenging activities. The 'development strategy' which may be involved, with opportunities for a new and positive lifestyle, has still received little attention. In the United Kingdom, the patterns desired have been found to categorize broadly into traditional retired roles, family involvement, more active pursuit of hobbies and activities, voluntary work and further education (McGoldrick, 1983). Likewise, desire for further employment is comparatively unstudied, although significant numbers of the early retired have been found to make this a part of their decision (e.g. Messer, 1969; Orbach, 1969; Manion, 1972; Patton, 1977). It can, however, give the potential of self-employment, a second career, an easier job or part-time employment (McGoldrick, 1983).

POTENTIAL STRESSORS AFTER RETIRING EARLY

It must be borne in mind that a significant minority of retirees do experience problems, which can be severe. It has, in fact, been estimated that amongst the third of retirees with adjustment problems, finances and health are the chief causes of dissatisfaction for almost three-quarters (Atchley, 1976). Again this appears to be the case after early retirement, even though many of those studied would have retired with special early retirement financial packages. Not all those who retire early are able to adjust mentally to their new situation, with evidence of the development in some cases of psychological problems associated with loneliness, boredom and decline in self-image. It might also be anticipated that a major source of stress would relate to involuntary early retirement, since such individuals might be less prepared practically and attitudinally for this transition.

Financial status and health

As one would expect, the early retired generally consider themselves as well or better prepared financially than those retiring at normal age, often having better assets and savings (e.g. Messer, 1969; Greene, Pyron, Manion and Winklevoss, 1969). Those retiring on disability grounds, of course, must be excluded (e.g. Parnes and Nestle, 1975; Parker, 1980). Small numbers can be better off, due to a new full-time job or part-time work boosting pension income. For the majority, however, retirement means some reduction in income, although this might have been anticipated and accepted as a cost of earlier freedom (McGoldrick and Cooper, 1989). Dissatisfaction has been found to be significantly associated with financial problems: mortgage constraints, dependents, low pension income, decreased savings, poor assets (Barfield and Morgan, 1969; McGoldrick and Cooper, 1989). Bitter resentment can ensue when drastic economies are necessary. Major stresses and worries about finances can affect mental and physical health, preventing retirees from achieving leisure goals. A significant cause of distress could be the need to work again because of financial constraints, possibly in unsuitable or poorly paid employment. High levels of inflation have been shown as a concern in many studies, while in a re-survey, Barfield and Morgan (1978b) were able to show a significant decline in satisfaction as a result of it. In the study in the United Kingdom, finances were of major concern to a fifth of the sample, while even more respondents had some problems. Lower status men, older retirees and the compulsorily retired were most at risk. The early retired obviously have a greater number of years in which financial assets can decline.

Declining health and reduction of physical abilities have been shown to represent a second potential stress source, with consequent lifestyle restrictions. Obviously severe illness is likely to result in a negative outlook on retirement potential, although the limitations imposed by more minor conditions can have an effect. In the Barfield and Morgan (1978b) follow-up study, the percentage of respondents alleging significant health problems increased from 10 to 33%. This was strongly associated with growth in dissatisfaction. In the United Kingdom, Parker (1980) found that the majority of early retired men reported illness or handicap which interfered with their activities. A fifth of an early retired sample (McGoldrick and Cooper, 1989) had major concerns about health, although disability retirements had been excluded. Lower social groups and those older on retiring and at the time of survey were most at risk. The health of a partner was likewise a considerable source of stress for a similar number, while smaller sub-sets of the men reported sleeping less well, worrying more and being less mentally active. While these were sometimes attributed by respondents themselves to the effects of aging rather than retirement itself, they had negative effects on satisfaction.

Serious mental adjustment problems also exist. Retirees more active in leisure pursuits, hobbies, charitable work and those with more social contacts, have been found to be more satisfied than their less active counterparts (e.g. Barfield and Morgan, 1969; McGoldrick, 1983). In the United Kingdom survey boredom, loneliness and depression were ranked as serious problems by approximately 5%, although representing a minor problem for rather more men. Problems suggested included being at home too much, strains on the marital situation, bereavement, reduced social contact and social activity. Again older and lower status respondents were more likely to exhibit such concerns, reinforcing the linkage betweeen successful aging and financial security. Some of these problems, of course, can be directly related to loss of work. For some retirees the significance of work, in terms of role loss and identity problems, remains and such losses are irreplaceable in the retired situation. Estimates suggest that up to a third of the retired would have preferred to work on or would like to work again, particularly younger retirees and those in good health (e.g. Shanas *et al.*, 1968; Campbell *et al.*, 1976). In the United Kingdom sample over a third had intended to work again and a similar number had done so. Finances were, of course, a major motivation and some would have preferred not to. Compulsory retirees were more likely to do so, as were lower income groups and those with more financial dependents. Inability to find employment or the need to accept an unsuitable job were strongly associated with dissatisfaction and emotional disturbance (McGoldrick and Cooper, 1989). More generally the retired missed the companionship of colleagues and work mates, with smaller numbers missing satisfaction, status and responsibility, which they had been unable to attain through leisure.

Voluntary and involuntary retirement

Only a small number of studies permit comparison on the basis of type of retirement, and some studies compare the early retired with mandatory retirement or workers, with consequent influences from age and health criteria. The importance as a policy issue, however, merits examination. Tuckman (1956), for example, compared compulsory retirees at mandatory age with those free to choose retirement timing. Reactions were similar, although the compulsory group actually had more active retirement plans and felt more able to have continued working. Their younger age and health effects were obviously intervening variables here. The Cornell study also distinguished administrative retirees from those with choice, as well as isolating the 'willing' and 'reluctant' amongst each group (Thompson, 1958; Thompson *et al.*, 1960). Volunteers, in fact, were more satisfied and 'willing' retirees were significantly so. The 'reluctant' to retire, whether voluntary or administrative, suffered greater reductions in life satisfaction and more symptoms of dejection. When health status and poor economic position were controlled for, this difference was reduced but did not disappear.

Peretti and Wilson (1975) found volunteers to be more positive, with higher emotional satisfaction. For compulsory retirees, retirement had been more of an abrupt and unplanned change, carrying negative stigma. They had more emotional problems, suffered from more conflict and depression, having less social involvement. Volunteers demonstrated a greater sense of usefulness and self-confidence, in comparison to the negative self-images of many of the compulsory retired. Unfortunately, the sample was small and confined to skilled and semi-skilled men. A larger questionnaire survey of 1436 subjects biased towards higher social groups (Kimmell *et al.*, 1978; Price *et al.*, 1979) found little difference between normal aged retirees and early retirees in terms of retirement impact, positive views being paramount for both. In contrast, marked differences existed by type of retirement. Compulsory retirees were significantly less positive in terms of satisfaction and attitudes, more negative about health, had planned less for retirement, had more worries about not working and were more likely to want to work again. In the United Kingdom (McGoldrick and Cooper, 1989), a third of a sample of 1208 early retired men had been compulsorily retired. The volunteers had significantly more positive views on lifestyles and leisure, were more satisfied financially and had prepared more for their retirement. While not all compulsory retirees suffered hardship and many did adapt well, it seems clear that it is the least positive way to retire and promotes vulnerability.

COPING MECHANISMS AND SOCIAL SUPPORT

It is relevant to consider information we have to suggest which individuals may be at risk on retiring, as well as the support mechanisms and buffers which may assist adaptation and reduce ill effects. Categories of coping resources may come from within the individual himself or from his environment. A growing theme in recent literature has focused on the personality and cognitive processes as mediators of stress and coping. A second area of enquiry has concentrated on social support systems. We will consider the former, before moving on to examine the relevance of home and family as support networks and assistance which can be provided by organizations. Here evidence from the United Kingdom early retirement study will provide illustration of points explored.

The individual's response

There is little emphasis in retirement studies to date on the role played by personality factors in respect of adjustment. We know that tolerance of stress and life changes differs between individuals. It may be assumed that response to any potentially stressful situation or life change will depend significantly on the individual's health and general morale. Those retiring in good health and with a positive outlook would be expected to succeed more frequently in their response to retirement or early retirement, which has been demonstrated in studies quoted earlier. Likewise, it seems relevant to consider belief systems and attitudinal response to the change in respect of the likely emotional outcome. People interpret life events in different ways. What is desirable for one is undesirable or even threatening to another. Coping is a process based on individual cognitive appraisal, which involves judgement of the importance of the event and its relevance for future well-being (e.g. Vinokur and Selzer, 1975; Mueller, Edwards and Yarvis, 1977; Sarason, Johnson and Siegel, 1978). With choice of retirement timing, individuals can assess their circumstances and form a balanced view of the appropriateness of the transition at that point.

Positive response would also be expected to be associated with higher levels of self-efficacy (Bandura, 1977) and internal locus of control (Rotter, 1966), a belief in personal ability to face change and master the new situation, attaining primary personal goals from it. Lack of control and a disbelief in self-efficacy, on the other hand, have been strongly linked with feelings of helplessness, passivity and depression. Prior expectations of retirement have been found to exert a significant influence on adaptation. Expectations of positive retirement experiences, in terms of finances, friends and social activity, are more likely to induce a positive attitude (e.g. Glamser, 1976; Kelley, 1982). Adjustment has also been found to be significantly improved if individuals make adequate re-appraisals of life prior to retiring, re-assessing goals and value orientations (e.g. Ludwig and Eichhorn, 1967; Thurner, 1974). In the United Kingdom study those retirees who had previously expected to retire early rather than at the norm tended to show significantly better adaptation patterns. They were better prepared in practical terms, as well as emotionally for this transition. This brings us to consider the information available regarding the change. Time is required to make this mental adjustment, which is not always provided in such situations. This applies particularly in the case of the compulsorily retired, for whom announcement of the impending transition can be a severe shock. As will be noted below, the company can assist here by providing adequate information and assisting with pre-retirement preparation.

Another major area of coping resource, which is of obvious relevance, is that of financial provision for retirement. The preceding discussion would strongly suggest that it is unwise to underestimate the buffering effect adequate and secure pension arrangements can bring, determining the retirees' ability to cope with life effectively. Finances are a major source of concern for many of those currently retired in the United Kingdom (e.g. Parker, 1982), severely limiting the potential of retirement and bringing a range of stresses. Those retiring early face a longer and potentially more active retirement. Many are amongst the more fortunate retired, having been long-service members of good occupational pension schemes, sometimes also receiving lump-sum payments. Those at risk include people compulsorily retired with inadequate benefits or personal financial security. Likewise some employees are not fully aware of entitlement rules; in particular some lower status employees may expect benefits which are not available to them. In the United Kingdom study considering oneself to be personally well prepared, in financial and attitudinal terms, was found to be of immense importance in respect of subsequent well-being.

The role of social support

The importance of social support systems in facilitating morale and good health is an area of growing interest to social scientists and epidemiologists (e.g. Cobb, 1976; Kaplan, Cassel and Sore, 1977). At times of crisis and life change, close personal relationships have been found to be beneficial in buffering people against stresses experienced (e.g. House, 1981). It is likely therefore that at retirement the support of a partner and close family members will be an effective coping resource. This reinforces a view frequently expressed, that the widowed and single may experience more problems after retirement due to social isolation. Increasing geographical mobility separates the old from their children and close relatives. Retirees are often warned about the dangers of house moves, although after early retirement some men in the United Kingdom study effectively used such a move. They exchanged a house in a suburban environment, with distant relationships with neighbours, for example, for the closer contact and inter-dependency of a village community or a retired residential area. New developments in housing initiatives for the elderly are now following trends witnessed much earlier in the United States. It is, of course, the individual's own circumstances which must determine suitable coping styles. It should be noted that lack of family support can in itself be a major source of conflict and stress. Some United Kingdom early retirees found that wives and children resented the implied status change to a 'retired' household, or the re-entry of the husband into the domestic domain caused disruption of established lifestyles.

The role of the organization in support terms is of interest. In the first place, it has control of the voluntary or compulsory nature of the early retirement option. In a voluntary situation, employees may have the opportunity to elect a time of retirement to suit their own needs and circumstances. The individual will consequently have control over his own situation, which is obviously more likely to produce a satisfactory outcome. As discussed earlier, compulsory retirees have been found to be more likely to be ill-prepared financially and attitudinally for the retirement transition, associating negative stigma with their new situation. Voluntary situations can set up their own pressures, however, either direct or of a more subtle form. In the United Kingdom study volunteers described a range of pressures from management, unions, fellow workers and the influence of 'social' conscience', beliefs that older employees should make way for the young. The closer men came to the retirement norm, the stronger this became as an influence which eventually compelled them to leave at least a few years early. On account of pressures experienced, in fact, when asked to define their type of retirement, some volunteers redefined it in compulsory terms. The advantages of personal control will be lost in such circumstances, leading to a potentially inappropriate decision and placing them at a similar level of risk as a compulsory scheme.

The company must also bear some responsibility towards preparing the individual for early retirement, as it has trained him throughout his working life for role change. This is particularly relevant when the decision is sudden or retirement is enforced, since personal preparedness is likely to be lower. The vast majority of United Kingdom early retirees believed that a company ought to do so, although only a quarter even had the option of attending a pre-retirement course, which frequently was immediately before retiring and of a general nature. There is evidence of a new emphasis on life-long education and training, with a move away from earlier reluctance to participate in such (e.g. Gilmore, 1980). Not many companies are using courses designed for the special needs of the early retired, while in the United Kingdom major re-thinking is necessary towards increasing initiatives earlier in the career rather than immediately prior to retiring. Few companies as yet provide adequate counselling services and detailed information before the decision is made to retire, while later support services and assistance in finding alternative employment are also relevant. Again the United Kingdom study demonstrated that retirees appreciate continued company contact after their retirement. Long-service workers, particularly, do not dissociate from their former organizations, wanting to remain to some degree 'attached'. Needs varied according to age and health, while even those who required no immediate contact often felt the company should remain one of their suppport mechanisms in time of future need.

A RESEARCH NOTE

In general, assessment of existing evidence would suggest that we cannot directly associate retirement with either physical or mental health decline. We cannot therefore assume that retirement is a stressful life event for all individuals. Response to voluntary early retirement schemes in particular suggests that it can hold attractions for those employees who feel that their circumstances are adequate for retiring and who hold positive perceptions of post-retirement opportunities. It can, in fact, itself represent a strategic response to stresses experienced in later working years and increasing difficulties in coping with the modern industrial environment.

Nonetheless, not all individuals view retirement positively and for the minority adaptation problems may be severe, especially in respect of financial problems and health decline. The experience of early retirement has so far received little research attention, with most studies focusing instead on factors in the decision to retire, presumably as a result of its importance at governmental and organizational levels. If it is to remain a viable manpower planning tool, however, we need to examine subsequent satisfaction, lifestyles and problems more extensively. Schemes will ultimately be discredited if those opting for them become disillusioned. In relation to the retirement decision, an area where evidence is weak is reaction to job stresses and work problems. In the study of retirement generally, attention to personality factors and coping mechanisms has been neglected. Little is known of the support of partner and family, since the majority of studies focus only on the retiree. We should also be looking at the feasibility of other alternative approaches to retirement, which would more effectively enable individuals to cope with the transition. These include gradual or phased retirement, re-training, skills up-grading and job re-design to suit older workers' needs. In addition, literature in respect of women and retirement is still slow growing. Nor have studies tended to take a 'family' perspective on the subject, which is surprising, since retirement can mean a re-establishment of the couple's joint activities and the partner may be an important support resource or may, in fact, increase the pressures experienced.

REFERENCES

Atchley, R.A. (1971). Retirement and leisure participation: continuity or crisis. *The Gerontologist*, **11**, 13–17.

Atchley, R.C. (1975). Adjustment to loss of job at retirement. *International Journal of Aging and Human Development*, **6**, 17–27.

Atchley, R.C. (1976). *The Sociology of Retirement*, Halstead Press, Wiley, New York.

Bandura, A. (1977). Self-efficacy: towards a unifying theory of behavioural change. *Psychological Review*, **84**, 191–215.

Barfield, R.E. (1970). *The Automobile Worker and Retirement: A Second Look*, Survey Research Centre, Institute of Social Research, University of Michigan, Ann Arbor.

Barfield, R.E. and Morgan, J.N. (1969). *Early Retirement: The Decision and the Experience*, Institute of Social Research, University of Michigan, Ann Arbor.

Barfield, R.E. and Morgan, J.N. (1978a). Trends in planned early retirement. *The Gerontologist*, **18**, 12–18.

Barfield, R.E. and Morgan, J.N. (1978b). Trends in satisfaction with retirement. *The Gerontologist*, **18**, 19–23.

Bell, B.D. (1974). Cognitive dissonance and life satisfaction of older adults. *Journal of Gerontology*, **24**, 564–71.

Bell, B.D. (1975). The limitations of crisis theory, as an explanatory mechanism in social gerontology. *International Journal of Aging and Human Development*, **6** (2), 153–68.

Birley, J.L. and Connolly, J. (1976). Life events and physical illness. In O. Hill (ed.) *Modern Trends in Psychosomatic Medicine*, **3**, Butterworths, London.

Boskin, M.J. (1977). Social Security and retirement decisions. *Economic Inquiry*, **15**, 1–25.

Brousseau, K.R. (1981). After age forty: Employment patterns and practices in the United States. In C.L. Cooper and D.P. Torrington (eds.) *After Forty*, John Wiley & Sons, Chichester.

Burgess, E.W. (1960). Aging in Western culture. In E.W. Burgess (ed.) *Aging in Western Society: A Comparative Study*, University of Chicago Press, Chicago.

Burkhauser, R.V. (1979). The pension acceptance decision of older men. *Journal of Human Resources*, **14** (1), 63–75.

Burkhauser, R.V. and Tolley, G.S. (1978). Older Americans and market work. *The Gerontologist*, **18**, 449–53.

Campbell, A., Converse, P.E. and Rodgers, W.L. (1976). *The Quality of American Life*, Russel Sage Foundation, New York.

Cantril, A.H. and Roll, C.W. (1971). *Hopes and Fears of American People*, Universe Books, New York.

Carp, F.M. (1977). Retirement and physical health. In S.F. Kasl and F. Reichsman (eds.) *Advances in Psychosomatic Medicine, Vol. 9: Epidemiologic Studies in Psychosomatic Medicine*, S. Karger, Basil.

Cobb, S. (1976). Social support as moderators of life stress. *Psychosomatic Medicine*, **38**, 300–14.

Corson, J.J. and McConnel, J.W. (1956). *Economic Needs of Older People*, Twentieth Century Fund, New York.

Cottrell, F. (1970). *Technical Change and Labor in the Railroad Industry*, D.C. Heath, Lexington, Mass.

Crawford, L. and Matlow, J. (1972). Some attitudes towards retirement among middle-aged employees. *Industrial Relations Industielles*, **27**, 616–31.

Crawford, M.P. (1972). Retirement as a psychosocial crisis. *Journal of Psychosomatic Research*, **16**, 375–80.

Crook, G.H. and Heinstein, M. (1958). *The Older Worker in Industry*, Institute of Industrial Relations, University of California.

Cumming, E. and Henry, W.E. (1961). *Growing Old: The Process of Disengagement*, Basic Books, New York.

Department of Employment, (1978). Measures to alleviate unemployment in the medium term: early retirement. *Department of Employment Gazette*, March, 283−5.

Doering, M., Rhodes, S.R. and Schuster, M. (1983). *The Aging Worker, Research and Recommendations*, Sage, Beverley Hills.

Dohrenwend, B.S. and Dohrenwend, B.P. (eds.) *Stressful Life Events: Their Nature and Effects*, John Wiley & Sons, New York.

Donahue, W., Orbach, H.L. and Pollack, O. (1960). Retirement: The Emerging Social Pattern. In C. Tibbits (ed.) *Handbook of Social Gerontology*, Chicago University Press, Chicago.

Draper, J.E., Lundgren, E.F. and Strother, G.B. (1967). *Work Attitudes and Retirement Adjustment*, University of Wisconsin, Bureau of Business Research and Service, Madison.

Eden, D. and Jacobson, D. (1976). Propensity to retire among older executives. *Journal of Vocational Behaviour*, **8**, 145−54.

Ekerdt, D.J., Rose, C.L., Bosse, R. and Costa, P.T. (1976). Longitudinal change in preferred age of retirement. *Journal of Occupational Psychology*, **49**, 161−9.

Emerson, A.R. (1959). The first year of retirement. *Occupational Psychology*, **49**, 167−208.

Eran, M. and Jacobson, D. (1976). Expectancy theory prediction of the prevalence to remain employed or to retire. *Journal of Gerontology*, **31**, 605−610.

Fleischer, D. and Kaplan, B.H. (1981). Characteristics of older workers: Implications for restructuring work. In P.K. Ragan (ed.) *Work and Retirement: Policy Issues*, Andrus Gerontology centre, Los Angeles.

Friedmann, E.A. and Havighurst, R.J. (eds.) (1954). *The Meaning of Work and Retirement*, University of Chicago Press, Chicago.

Friedmann, E.A. and Orbach, H.L. (1974). Adjustment to retirement. In S. Arieti (ed.) *American Handbook of Psychiatry*, Vol. 1, Basic Books, New York.

Gechman, A.S. (1974). 'Without work life goes...' *Journal of Occupational Medicine*, **16**, 749−51.

Gilmore, F. (1980). Education for retirement. *European Journal of Education*, **15**, 191−9.

Glamser, F.D. (1976). Determinants of a positive attitude toward retirement. *Journal of Gerontology*, **31** (1), 104−7.

Goudy, W.J., Powers, E.A. and Keith, P. (1975). Work and retirement: a test of attitudinal relationships. *Journal of Gerontology*, **30**, 193−8.

Graebner, W. (1980). *A History of Retirement: The Meaning and Function of an American Institution, 1885−1978*, Yale University Press, New Haven.

Greene, M.R., Pyron, H.C., Manion, U.V. and Winklevoss, H. (1969). *Pre-retirement Counseling, Retirement Adjustment and the Older Employee*, Graduate School of Management and Business, University of Oregon.

Hall, A. and Johnson, T.R. (1980). The determinants of planned retirement age. *Industrial and Labour Relations Review*, **33**, 241−54.

Haynes, S.G., McMichael, A.J. and Tyroler, H.A. (1977). The relationship of normal, involuntary retirement to early mortality among US rubber workers. *Social Science and Medicine*, **11**, 105−14.

Haynes, S.G. McMichael, A.J. and Tyroler, H.A. (1978). Survival after early and normal retirement. *Journal of Gerontology* **33**, 269−78.

Holmes, T.H. and Rahe, R.H. (1967). The social readjustment rating scale. *Journal of Psychosomatic Research*, **11**, 213−18.

House, J.S. (1981). *Work Stress and Social Support*, Addison-Wesley, Reading, Mass.

Jacobson, D. (1972a). Willingness to retire in relation to job strain and type of work. *Industrial Gerontology*, **13**, 65−74.

Jacobson, D. (1972b). Fatigue-producing factors in industrial work and pre-retirement attitudes. *Occupational Psychology*, **46**, 193−200.

Jacobson, D. and Eran, M. (1980). Expectancy theory components and non-expectancy moderators as predictors of physicians' preference for retirement. *Journal of Occupational Psychology*, **53**, 11−26.

Johnson, J. and Strother, G.B. (1962). Job expectations and retirement planning. *Journal of Gerontology*, **17**, 418−23.

Kahn, R.L. (1974). On the meaning of work. *Journal of Occupational Medicine*, **16**, 716−19.

Kaplan, B.H., Cassel, J.C. and Gore, S. (1977). Social support and health. *Medicine Care*, **15**, 47−58.

Kasl, S.V. (1978). Epidemiological contributions to the study of work stress. In C.L. Cooper and R. Payne (eds.) *Stress at Work*, John Wiley & Sons, Chichester.

Kasl, V. (1980). The impact of retirement. In C.L. Cooper and R. Payne (eds.) *Current Concerns in Occupational Stress*, John Wiley & Sons, London.

Katona, G. (1965). *Private Pensions and Individual Saving*. Survey Research Centre, University of Michigan, monograph No. 40, Anabor, Michigan.

Katona, G., Morgan, J.N. and Barfield, R.E. (1969). Retirement in prospect and retrospect. *Trends in Early Retirement*, Occasional Papers in Gerontology No. 4, University of Michigan.

Kelley, G. (1982). Orientations towards retirement: a predictable transition. *Personnel Review*, **11**, 33−7.

Kimmel, D.C., Price, K.F. and Walker, J.W. (1978). Retirement choice and retirement satisfaction. *Journal of Gerontology*, **33**, 575−85.

Kutash, I.L., Schlesinger, L.B. and Associates (1980). *Handbook on Stress and Anxiety*, Jossey-Bass, San Francisco.

Lowenthal, M.F. (1977). Some potentials of a life-cycle approach to the study of retirement. In F.M. Carp (ed.) *Retirement*, Behavioural Publications, New York.

Ludwig, E.G. and Eichhorn, R.L. (1967). Age and disillusionment: a study of value changes associated with aging. *Journal of Gerontology*, **22**, 59−65.

Manion, U.V. (1972). Why employees retire early. *Personnel Journal*, **51** (3), 183−7.

Martin, J. and Doran, A. (1966). Evidence concerning the relationship between health and retirement. *Sociological Review*, **14**, 329−43.

Masada, M. and Holmes, T.H. (1967). Magnitude estimations of social readjustment. *Journal of Psychosomatic Research*, **11**, 219−25.

McGoldrick, A.E. (1983). Company early retirement schemes and private pension scheme options: scope for leisure and new lifestyles. *Leisure Studies*, **2**, 187−202.

McGoldrick, A.E. and Cooper, C.L. (1978). Early retirement for managers in the U.S. and the U.K. *Management International Review*, **3**, 35−42.

McGoldrick, A.E. and Cooper, C.L. (1980). Voluntary early retirement—taking the decision. *Employment Gazette*, August, 859−64.

McGoldrick, A.E. and Cooper, C.L. (1985). Stress at the Decline of one's Career. The Act of Retirement? In T.A. Beehr and R.S. Bhagat, *Human Stress and Cognition in Organizations: An Integrated Perspective* John Wiley & Sons, New York.

McGoldrick, A.E. and Cooper, C.L. (1989). *Early Retirement*, Gower Press, Aldershot.

McMahan, C.A. and Ford, T.R. (1955). Surviving the first five years of retirement. *Journal of Gerontology*, **2**, 212−15.

116   *Aging, Stress and Health*

Messer, E.A. (1969). Thirty-Eight Years is A Plenty. In H.I. Orbach *et al.*, (Eds.) *Trends in Early Retirement*, Occasional Papers in Gerontology No. 4, University of Michigan.
Miller, D.R. (1965). The study of social relationships: situations, identity and social interaction. In S. Koch (ed.) *Psychology: A Study of Science*, Vol. 5, McGraw-Hill, New York.
Morgan, J. (1979). What with inflation and unemployment, who can afford to retire? In M.W. Riley (ed.) *Aging from Birth to Death. Interdisciplinary Perspectives*, Westview Press, Boulder, Colorado.
Morgan, J.N. (1980). Retirement in prospect and retrospect. In G. Duncan and J. Morgan (eds.) *Five Thousand American Families—Patterns of Economic Progress*, Vol. 8, Michigan: Institute for Social Research, Ann Arbor.
Mueller, D.P., Edwards, D.W. and Yarvis, R.M. (1977). Stressful life events and psychiatric symptomatology: change or undesirability? *Journal of Health and Social Behaviour*, **18**, 307–17.
Myers, R.J. (1954). Factors in interpreting mortality after retirement. *Journal of the American Statistical Association*, **49**, 499–509.
Neugarten, B.L. (1977). Personality and aging. In J.E. Birren and K.W. Schaie (eds.) *Handbook of the Psychology of Aging*, Van Nostrand Reinhold, New York.
Neugarten, B.L. and Hagestad, G.O. (1976). Age and the life course. In R.H. Binstock and E. Shanas (eds.) *Handbook of Aging and the Social Services*, Van Nostrand Reinhold, New York.
Neugarten, B.L., Havighurst, R.J. and Tobin, S.S. (1968). Personality and patterns of aging. In B.L. Neugarten (ed.) *Middle Age and Aging*, University of Chicago Press, Chicago.
Owen, J.P. and Belzung, D. (1967). Consequences of voluntary early retirement: a study of a new labour force phenomenon. *British Journal of Industrial Relations*, **5**, 162–89.
Parker, S. (1980). *Older Workers and Retirement*, HMSO, London.
Parker, S. (1982). *Work and Retirement*, Allen and Unwin, London.
Parnes, H.S., Fleischer, B.M., Miljus, R.C. and Spitz, R.S. (1975). *The Pre-Retirement Years: Five Years in the Work Lives of Middle-Aged Men*, United States Department of Labour Manpower Administration.
Parnes, H.S. and Nestle, G. (1975). Early retirement. In H.S. Parnes (ed.) *The Pre-Retirement Years: Five Years in the Work Lives of Middle-Aged Men*, United States Department of Labor Administration, Washington.
Parnes, H.S. and Nestle, G. (1981). The retirement experience. In H.S. Parnes *et al.*, (ed.) *Work and Retirement: A Longitudinal Study of Men*, MIT Press, Cambridge, MA.
Patton, C.V. (1977). Early retirement in academia, making the decision. *The Gerontologist*, **17** (4), 347–54.
Peretti, P.O. and Wilson, C. (1975). Voluntary and involuntary retirement of aged males and their effect on emotional satisfaction, usefulness, self-image, emotional stability and interpersonal relationships. *International Journal of Aging and Human Development*, **6**, 131–8.
Pfeiffer, E. and Davis, G.C. (1971). The use of leisure time in middle life. *The Gerontologist*, **11**, 187–95.
Phillipson, C. (1978). *The Emergence of Retirement*, Working Papers in Sociology, No. 14, Durham University Press, Durham.
Pollman, A.W. (1971a). Early retirement: a comparison of poor health to other retirement factors. *Journal of Gerontology*, **26**, 41–5.
Pollman, A.W. (1971b). Early retirement: relationship to variation in life satisfaction. *The Gerontologist*, **11**, 43–7.

Pollman, A.W. and Johnson, A.E. (1974). Resistance to change, early retirement and managerial decisions. *Industrial Gerontology*, **1**, 33−41.

Price, K.F., Walker, J.W. and Kimmel, D.C. (1979). Retirement timing and retirement satisfaction. *Aging and Work*, **2**, 235−45.

Prothero, J. and Beach, L.R. (1984). Retirement decisions: expectation, intention and action. *Journal of Applied Social Psychology*, **14**, 162−74.

Quinn, J.F. (1977). 'Microeconomic determinants of early retirement: a cross-sectional view of white married men. *Journal of Human Resources*, **12**, 329−46.

Quinn, J.F. (1981). The extent and correlates of partial retirement. *The Gerontologist*, **21**, 634−42.

Quinn, R.P. and Shepard, L.J. (1974). *The 1972−73 Quality of Employment Survey*, University of Michigan, Survey Research Centre, Ann Arbor.

Rabinowitz, S., Hall, D.T. and Goodale, J.G. (1977). Job scope and individual differences as predictors of job involvement: independent or interactive? *Academy of Management Journal*, **20**, 273−81.

Rabkin, J.G. and Struening, E.L. (1976). Life events, stress and illness. *Science*, **184**, 1013−20.

Rahe, R.H. (1974). The pathway between subjects' recent life change and their near-future illness reports. In B.S. Dohrenwend and B.P. Dohrewend (eds.) *Stressful Life Events: Their Nature and Effects*, John Wiley & Sons, New York.

Reno, V. (1971). Why Men Stop Working Before Age 65. In V. Reno, *et al.*, (eds.) *Reaching Retirement Age. Findings from a Survey of Newly Entitled Workers, 1968−70*, US Department of Health, Education and Welfare. Social Security Administration, Office of Research and Statistics, Research Report No. 47.

Riffault, H. (1978). *The Attitude of the Working Population to Retirement*, the Directorate-General for Employment and Social Affairs of the Commission of the European Communities, Brussels.

Rose, C.L. and Mogey, J.M. (1972). Aging and preference for later retirement. *Aging and Human Development*, **8**, 152−6.

Rosen, B. and Jerdee, T.H. (1979). Influence of employee age and job status on managerial recommendations for retirement. *Academy of Management Journal*, **22**, 169−73.

Rotter, J.B. (1966). Generalized expectancies for internal versus external control of reinforcement. *Psychological Monographs*, **80**, Whole No. 609.

Ryser, C. and Sheldon, A. (1969). Retirement and health. *Journal of the American Geriatrics Society*, **17**, 180−90.

Saleh, S.D. and Otis, J.L. (1963). Sources of job satisfaction and their effects on attitudes towards retirement. *Journal of Industrial Psychology*, **1**, 101−6.

Sarason, I.G., Johnson, J.H. and Siegal, J.M. (1978). Assessing the impact of life changes: development of the life experiences survey. *Journal of Consulting and Clinical Psychology*, **46**, 932−46.

Schmitt, N., Coyle, B.W., Rauschenberger, J. and White, J.K. (1979). Comparison of early retirees and non-retirees. *Personal Psychology*, **32**, 327−40.

Schmitt, N. and McCune, J.T. (1981). The relationship between job attitudes and the decision to retire. *Academy of Management Journal*, **24**, 795−802.

Shanas, E., Townsend, P., Wedderburn, D., Friis, H., Milhoj, P. and Stenhouner, J. (1968). *Old People in Three Industrial Societies* Routledge & Kegan Paul, London.

Simpson, I.D. and McKinney, J.C. (eds.) (1966). *Social Aspects of Aging*, Duke University Press, Durham, North Carolina.

Stafford, M. and Mould, R. (1982). *Retirement and the Older Worker*, Work and Society Report, London.

Steiner, P.O. and Dorfman, R. (1957). *The Economic Status of the Aged*, University of California Press, Berkeley.

Stokes, R.G. and Maddox, G.L. (1967). Some social factors on retirement adaptation. *Journal of Gerontology*, **22**, 329−33.

Strauss, G. (1974). Is there a Blue Collar Revolt Against Work? In J. O'Toole (ed.) *Work and the Quality of Life*, MIT Press, Cambridge.

Streib, G.F. (1956). Morale of the retired. *Social Problems*, **3**, 270−6.

Streib, G.F. and Schneider, C.J. (1971). *Retirement in American Society: Impact and Process*, Cornell University Press, Ithaca, New York.

Streib, G.F. and Thompson, W.E. (1957). Personal and social adjustment in retirement. In W. Donahue and C. Tibbits (eds.) *The New Frontiers of Aging*, University of Michigan Press, Ann Arbor.

Thompson, G.B. (1973). Work versus leisure roles: an investigation of morale among employed and retired men. *Journal of Gerontology*, **29**, 339−44.

Thompson, W.E. (1958). Pre-retirement anticipation and adjustment in retirement. *Journal of Social Issues*, **14**, 35−45.

Thompson, W.E., Streib, G.F. and Kosa, J. (1960). The effect of retirement on personal adjustment: a panel analysis. *Journal of Gerontology*, **15**, 165−9.

Thurner, M. (1974). Goals, values and life evaluations at the pre-retirement stage. *Journal of Gerontology*, **29**, 85−96.

Triandis, H.C. (1973). Work and nonwork: interculture perspectives. In M.D. Dunnette (ed.) *Work and Nonwork in the Year 2001*, Brooks/Coke Publishing Co., Monterey, California.

Tuckman, J. (1956). Retirement attitudes of compulsory and noncompulsory retired workers. *Geriatrics*, December, 569−72.

Tuckman, J. and Lorge, I. (1953). *Retirement and the Industrial Worker: Prospects and Reality*, Columbia University, New York.

Tyhurst, J.S., Salk, L. and Kennedy, M. (1957). Mortality, morbidity and retirement. *American Journal of Public Health*, **47**, 1434−44.

United States Department of Labor, (1978). *Employment and Training Report to the President*, US Government Printing Office, Washington DC.

Usher, C.E. (1981). Alternative work options for older workers: Part 1—Employees' Interest. *Aging and Work*, **4**, 74−81.

Vinokur, A. and Selzer, M.L. (1975). Desirable versus undesirable life events: their relationship to stress and mental distress. *Journal of Personality and Social Psychology*, **32**, 329−37.

Walker, A. (1980). The social creation of poverty and dependency in old age. *Journal of Social Policy*, **9**, 45−49.

Wood, V., Wylie, M. and Sheafor, B. (1966). *An Analysis of a Short Self-Report Measure of Life Satisfaction: Correlation with Rater Judgements*, Paper presented at the Annual Meeting of the Gerontological Society, New York.

Chapter 6

Residential Relocation and Health of the Elderly

A.J. Baglioni, Jr

While the propensity of Americans in general to change residence has often been noted by historians (Kopf, 1977) and social commentators (Packard, 1972), until recently little attention has been given specifically to the issue of residential relocation among the elderly (Lawton, 1980). Most research that has been performed on relocation issues relevant to the aged has focused only on the demographic predictors of mobility (Biggar, 1980; Litwak and Longino, 1987).

Relocation has long been hypothesized as being a potentially stressful life event (Holmes and Rahe, 1967). As such, it is expected to have some negative effects on the well-being of the individuals involved. In the case of the elderly, who may be more vulnerable to the effects of stress than other age groups, the period of adjustment to relocation may be more extended and more intensive. However, considerable research on the consequences of relocation among the elderly suggests that, although such relocation can have negative effects, it can also have no effects, or even positive effects—depending on the specific population and parameters of the study.

Research on the effect of relocation of the elderly to institutions has a history dating at least to 1945 (Camargo and Preston, 1945) but despite this research within the relatively controlled conditions of an institution, the identification and impact of factors affecting adaptation to relocation are still the subject of serious debate (see Borup, Gallego, and Heffernan, 1980; and Bourestom and Pastalan, 1981). The limited scope of residential relocation research restricts knowledge in that area even more than with institutions. An overview of research indicates that residential relocation among the elderly appears to be determined by a complex interaction of personal, social, and environmental variables. Income, previous residential history, race, marital status, health, social integration, economic status, and whether a person owns or rents his/her home have all been associated with the desire and the decision to relocate (Lawton, 1980). Further information is needed, however, about voluntary residential relocation among the elderly concerning not only who moves, but also the consequences of relocation, what factors contribute to successful adjustment to the new environment, and perhaps most importantly, the processes involved in the adjustment.

Aging, Stress and Health Edited by K.S. Markides and C.L. Cooper
© 1989 John Wiley & Sons Ltd

This chapter presumes that both unique and common issues influence adjustment to relocation among the institutionalized elderly and those who change their personal residence. The common features would include the type of preparation made for the relocation, individual health and personality characteristics, length of time in the new environment, as well as factors unique to the new environment such as whether it is segregated by age, the extent of age-specific facilities available, and the presence of support personnel.

Identification of the specific variables involved is only a prelude to the development of theories of the processes involved in relocation adjustment. Most of the studies to be examined are focused on issue identification. Several possible explanations exist for this lack of a process orientation in the relocation literature. As noted, early studies are needed for the identification of the variables relevant to process models. The puzzle parts need to be gathered before they can be connected. Concomitant with variable identification is the issue of obtaining valid and accurate measurement of the variables. The interpretation of an 'objective' variable such as health is confused by whether the measure is self-reported health or physiological indices or limitations on daily living activities. In the area of social support, much effort is still focused on the question of measurement (see Chapter 3). Similarly, the identification of environmental factors which may influence adjustment to relocation has been hindered by questions of how to measure such concepts as environmental stressors. Finally, a process research orientation requires facility with complex statistical techniques, such as path analysis or structural equation modeling. Until recently these techniques were difficult to employ and not readily available to most researchers.

Research findings on both institutional and residential relocation will be presented. A meta-analysis of the extant research from a process orientation is beyond the goals of this chapter. Nevertheless, some of the isolated findings may be integrated via a process theory approach. As the literature describing the adjustment of the aged to institutional relocation is the more extensive, these studies will be discussed first, followed by a summary of the limited information more specifically concerning residential relocation.

OUTCOMES OF INSTITUTIONAL RELOCATION

The basic research designs that have been used in studies of institutional relocation are as follows: if the move was planned (e.g. Liebowitz, 1974), baseline characteristics of the about-to-be-relocated group were gathered; if the move was abrupt and unexpected (e.g. Aleksandrowicz, 1961), patient records were reviewed in an attempt to construct the relevant baselines. Following the move, various dependent measures were gathered. These measures generally included the following: some indication of psychological well-being, such as satisfaction with life or morale; measurement of the social behaviour of the relocated elderly; and a measure of their physical characteristics, generally via self-reported health and/or staff monitoring of functional health. In addition to the psychological, social, and medical measures, the death rate, or 'mortality experience' (Markson and Cumming, 1974), of the relocated group was almost universally provided as a primary indicator of the impact of relocation. Pre- and post-move death rates were compared and reported along with one or more of the previously cited dependent measures.

Most of the research on the effects of institutional relocation has focused on relocation from home to institution or from one institution to another (Ferraro, 1982). Since 1945, at least 200 studies reported in the literature concern the impact of institutional relocation on the elderly (Bourestom and Pastalan, 1981). For example, Camargo and Preston (1945) report a three-year survey of first admissions of patients over 65 years of age to the Maryland state mental hospitals. A total of 683 cases were examined. In the first year following admission, 47% of the patients died, approximately 16% during the first month. During the second year, another 11% died. Whittier and Williams (1956) conducted a similar investigation and report a 20% mortality rate within 30 days from the date of admission. After one year, half of the study population had died.

Replications of the basic designs (and mortality findings) described in these early studies are legion. Aldrich and Mendkoff (1963) followed a group of 182 elderly patients who were transferred to alternate facilities when a chronic-disease home was closed. Expected mortality rates, corrected for age, were computed using the records of the home for the previous 10 years. Within the first year following transfer, 32% of the elderly patients had died. By comparison, the death rate in the same institution had averaged 19% during the previous 10 years.

A similar increase in the average number of deaths is reported by Killian (1970), who examined the impact of relocation on several groups of geriatric patients who were forced to move because of the closing of a California state hospital. One group of patients was transferred to another state hospital; a second group went to a nursing home or another community-based facility. In addition, since part of the hospital was to remain open, a control group of non-movers was available for comparison. The groups were matched for age, race, sex, physical condition, and approximate length of hospitalization. At a four-month follow-up, compared with the control group, five times as many persons transferred to another state hospital had died, and nine times as many persons transferred to a nursing home had died. Many other studies in the literature report similar findings of increases in the death rates, decreases in functional health, and decreased psychological well-being following institutional relocation (e.g. Bourestom and Tars, 1974; Goldfarb, Shahinian, and Burr, 1972; Kral, Grad, and Berenson, 1968; Lieberman, 1974; Miller and Lieberman, 1965; Ogren and Linn, 1971; Pino, Rosica, and Carter, 1978; Smith and Brand, 1975).

As might be expected, however, not all of the findings are clear cut or in total agreement. Borup, Gallego, and Heffernan (1980) reviewed some of the literature examining the impact of relocation on health, functioning, and mortality and note that most relocation studies used mortality as the primary dependent variable—ignoring the different effects that health and functioning may have on the mortality of relocated patients. They cite research suggesting alternative explanations for the apparent negative effects of relocation. Storandt and Wittels (1975) report that relocation did not affect self-evaluated health. Markson and Cumming (1974) examined the results of a mass transfer of 2174 patients and conclude that relocating primarily middle-aged and elderly, chronic patients does not seem to place them at an excessively high risk of dying. The authors suggest that death is more related to age than to other factors and that the extensive mortality noted in many studies might not even be a function of age, but rather of patient characteristics such as poor health and mental confusion. Thus relocation may hasten an already impending death but not necessarily speed mortality among the relatively well. Markson and Cumming (1974) found no significant difference in mortality among transferred patients when compared with two other groups—one in the community and one in another state hospital that were not relocated during a similar time period.

Zweig and Csank (1975) investigated the voluntary transfer of about 350 male war veterans who were over 64. From the year before transfer to one year after, there was about a 7% decrease in mortality. Jasnau (1967) compared a group who were mass-moved with another group in which each person was given extensive individual attention. The mass-moved group had a 35% increase in mortality over the previous year's rate. The group given individual attention had, as one might anticipate, lower than expected mortality.

A review of the literature concerning the effects of relocation (e.g. Borup, Gallego, and Heffernan, 1979, 1980; Bourestom and Pastalan, 1981; Brand and Smith, 1974; Coffman, 1981, 1983; Gopelrud, 1979; Kasl, 1972; Lieberman, 1974; Markus, Blenkner, Bloom, and Downs, 1970, 1971; Schulz and Brenner, 1977; Smith and Brand, 1975; and Turner, Tobin, and Lieberman, 1972), reveals widely discrepant findings about the adjustment of elderly patients to institutional relocation. Clearly other factors are involved beyond the simple act of relocating persons into an institution, between institutions, or even within the same institution. The amount of pre-relocation orientation or preparation, the pre-move status of the individuals (i.e. their age, sex, diagnosis and prognosis, length of hospitalization) as well as environmental variables relating to the original and receiving settings have been shown to have an influence on the post-relocation adjustment and 'mortality experience' of persons moved.

A study by Novick (1967) examined the impact of one of these factors, preparatory counseling, on adjustment to relocation. Staff members prepared residents far in advance of an impending move by taking them on frequent trips to the new site and by constructing a full-size model of the future bedroom, including furniture. Additionally, residents decided what type of bedroom, fixtures, windows, and doors they desired. Novick (1967) concludes that the increased space at the new facility, the increased privacy, and the subsequent separation of medical and psychiatric residents were all important factors that resulted in fewer patient deaths than expected after relocation to a new hospital. However, the lack of a control group, requires that all of the conclusions be evaluated with caution. The degree of autonomy granted the patients in this study should also be considered a major factor contributing to the lower than expected mortality rate (Langer and Rodin, 1976; Schulz, 1976).

The previously cited studies by Jasnau (1967) and Zweig and Csank (1975) represent research designs using a voluntary population sample. In addition, both studies involved carefully designed pre-relocation preparation programs. In the study by Jasnau, all patients were prepared for the move, and no patient was moved against his or her will. The individually relocated group was also given extensive psychological and emotional preparation. Similarly, the Zweig and Csank (1975) study involved voluntary transfers of patients who received a preparation program designed to alleviate many of the fears and anxieties concerning their post-relocation future. Persons in these studies who received the orientation and had control over the decision to relocate did not suffer from the move.

Other variables have been found to influence the impact of institutional relocation. Lieberman (1974) examined factors associated with the post-transfer outcome of 427 state mental patients who were abruptly relocated to other institutions. He found that the most powerful predictors of post-transfer trauma were physical health and cognitive capacity. In the Aldrich and Mendkoff (1963) study cited earlier, those patients who showed neurotic or psychotic symptoms prior to relocation and whose reaction to the news of the transfer was classified as regressive, depressive, or denying had higher than average mortality. Those persons whose reactions were satisfactory or angry/demanding and whose responses were philosophical or angry showed low death rates. In a re-analysis of the Aldrich and Mendkoff (1963) data, Adlrich (1964) found that 80% of the patients diagnosed as psychotic at the time of the move had died by follow-up while three times as many patients considered satisfactory, angry, or demanding had survived transfer as had died.

Kral, Grad, and Berenson (1968) report evidence which suggests that transfer may have a more prolonged and severe impact on high-risk patients than on normal patients. Psychotic patients (all but one with organic disorders) reacted to relocation more than nonpsychotic patients. After relocation, significantly more psychotic patients than normal patients showed signs of physical deterioration. After a 23-month follow-up period, psychotics had a higher mortality rate. Kral *et al.*, (1968) also found that elderly males, psychotic and normal, reacted to transfer with significant increases in indicators of physiological stress; nonpsychotic women showed no corresponding increases. Also, significantly more normal men than women died within the first six months after relocation.

Lieberman (1974) examined the role of the institutional environment in adjusting to relocation. As noted earlier, post-transfer mortality was best predicted by physical health and cognitive capacity. The environment did not seem to affect the outcome among those who died. However, for those who

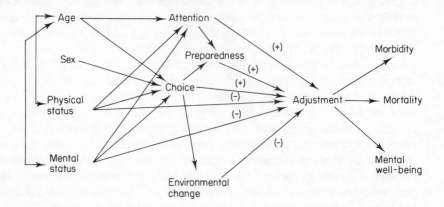

Figure 1   Structural model of the factors affecting adjustment
to institutional relocation

survived but either deteriorated or improved following relocation, environmental factors seemed to play a critical role. Environments where patients improved were characterized by relatively high degrees of autonomy that fostered personalization of patients and community interactions; patients in these environments were treated as adults, given responsibility, and allowed privacy. Also, the boundaries between the institution and the community were more permeable than in other environments. Facilitative environments had high expectations for residents' behavior, were more tolerant of deviancy, and tended to be low on care-giving. Lieberman suggests that 'tender loving care,' when it appears to infantilize the person, seems to be not only nonfacilitative, but potentially destructive. This evidence may support Blenkner's (1967) finding that those persons receiving maximal care following relocation had higher mortality rates than those receiving less care.

   In summary, eight factors have been identified with institutional relocation and mortality effects: age, sex, physical status, mental status, degree of choice, pre-paredness, environmental change, and individualized attention (Coffman, 1983). The influence of these factors on morbidity, mortality and psychological adjust-ment has not been fully determined and is still strongly debated in the literature (e.g. Coffman, 1983; Horowitz and Schulz, 1983). Perhaps much of the debate could be resolved, however, if the individual variables were viewed as parts of a larger process. For example, Figure 1 presents a structural model suggested by the above variables. A person−environment (P−E) fit theory of stress would adequately describe the process inferred by the model. Individual characteristics (age, sex, physical status, and mental status) have a direct effect on the degree of choice a person is able to maintain, the need for individual attention, and on adjustment. Choice, in turn, may directly influence the amount of environmental change to which the person may expose him/herself. In addition, choice may have a positive direct effect on the amount of preparation for the move undertaken by the individual. Finally, the amount of attention (which is a source of social support as well as increased predictability for the person) received and the degree of preparedness should have a positive effect on outcome while greater environmental change may lead to greater difficulty in adjustment.

All the data needed to test the above model have not been presented in a single study of institutional relocation, although Lieberman and Tobin (1983) present a more complex model and test it thoroughly. In the Lieberman and Tobin research, two of the predictors of outcomes were person–environment congruence and environmental discontinuity which would be consistent with the proposed model. Environmental quality was identified as a third predictor variable by Lieberman and Tobin. This may be also viewed as an alternate measure of change with the direction of the change taken into account.

Beyond the Lieberman and Tobin study, in the context of institutional relocation, most information relevant to the model exists only in fragments. As the next section shows, with respect to noninstitutional relocation, the research and analysis of the fragments is even less advanced.

OUTCOMES OF RESIDENTIAL RELOCATION

The studies on residential relocation among the aged are scarce, and much of the knowledge is derived from studies of nonvoluntary moves caused by urban renewal or highway construction during the period 1945–1970 (Lawton, 1980). More recently, the conversion of apartments to condominiums and the rediscovery of the advantages of central-city living by the young and middle-aged has resulted in many aged persons being priced out of their living quarters. Condemning of buildings, continually rising rents and property taxes, and simple evictions of the elderly insure that nonvoluntary residential relocation by the elderly will continue. Furthermore, voluntary residential relocation among the more affluent elderly is expected to continue to increase. Thus there is a continuing and growing need for increased knowledge about those factors that contribute to successful adjustment to residential relocation.

Nonvoluntary residential relocation

Lawton (1980) notes that few studies of nonvoluntary residential relocation are available in the literature, and most of these studies were performed after the fact, that is, after the change of residence had occurred. Kasteler, Gray, and Carruth (1968) present the results of a study performed to determine the effect of involuntary relocation on a sample of elderly residents forced to move because of highway construction. They hypothesized that the stress experienced by the (48) older persons because of relocation would result in poorer personal and social adjustment relative to (268) comparable persons who had not been so relocated. The data supported the hypothesis and the general conclusion that 'involuntary relocation was an especially stressful experience for older persons whose ties are generally more firmly established and who, by the process of aging, may be more resistant to change than younger persons' (Kasteler *et al.*, 1968, p. 279). Again referring to Figure 1, the disruption of the support network of the relocated elderly may be a key variable to understanding the experienced stress. This deprives the elderly of a formerly reliable resource for coping in a stressful situation exacerbated by the lack of choice and preparedness as well as the high degree of environmental change.

Lawton (1980) describes a study by Kasl that may be the only longitudinal study of involuntary relocation using an adequate control group. The experimental subjects had to move for various reasons, and all moved into public housing designed for the elderly. Movers were matched with nonmovers from the same neighborhoods. Even though they had to move, 63% of the persons *perceived* that they had made the choice to move voluntarily. There were few significant differences between the relocated and nonrelocated groups in the amount of change in social behavior, activities, or mental stress. The relocated group experienced a marked increase in environmental satisfaction, but there was a gradual decline in their health. No difference in the mortality rates of the two groups was reported. It is important to note that a majority of the relocated persons maintained the perception that they had a choice in the matter of relocation. Clearly, the perceived volition of the movers may be suggested as somehow attenuating any stress-induced negative health outcomes. Thus, Figure 1 should be revised to reflect not only actual degree of choice but also the perception of choice. The environment into which these elderly persons moved was housing designed specifically for elderly people and was more physically comforting and psychologically supportive of the new residents than their originating environments. Both the positive environmental change and the degree of preparedness would also help explain the lack of significant differences between the groups.

Eckert (1983) used a quasi-experimental design to assess the consequences of forced relocation on the mental and physical health, social networks and supports, and psychosocial adjustments of relocated older persons. Data were gathered on 137 persons living in single-room occupancy (SRO) hotels. The experimental group ($N = 62$) and control group ($N = 75$) did not differ significantly on demographic, health, and social network variables used at Time 1. The experimental group was forced to relocate by urban renewal and development. At Time 2, only 38 persons (60%) in the experimental group and 32 persons (43%) in the control group could be re-interviewed. The results of the Time 1 and Time 2 comparisons between the two groups were surprising. There were few negative outcomes experienced by the relocated persons; persons forced to move were more satisfied with their new environment. They exhibited no major declines in health or in their well-being and few changes in their social networks. While the study may be confounded by a number of flaws, such as the loss of subjects at Time 2, it does suggest that many older persons maintain adaptive strengths that can offset the expected negative consequences of enforced relocation. In trying to interpret the results, Eckert suggests that, since the social networks of the older persons were dispersed, the disruption of one sector, in this case their hotel residence, did not mean the person was left completely without sources of support. An intact social support network and the increased satisfaction with the environment would contribute to the positive adjustment of the relocated individuals.

Eckert and Haug (1984) provide further support for the P−E fit model of adjustment for persons forced to relocate. They report few pre−post differences within a group of 38 SRO dwellers forced to relocate. For this group, only emotional health changed significantly; unexpectedly, the change indicated that emotional health improved. Relative to a comparison group of nonmovers, the movers showed increased emotional health; however, they also had a decline in functional health status. A follow-up hierarchical multiple regression suggests that control variables—unspecified demographic and attitude variables— explained more variance in the outcome measures that did whether or not an individual was forced to relocate. Eckert and Haug hypothesize that the high congruity between the originating and receiving environments, the lack of transfer trauma, and per-sonal characteristics of the individuals made relocating an unstressful event, thus accounting for the lack of negative outcomes.

Voluntary residential relocation

A second type of residential change among the elderly is voluntary relocation. It may be to senior housing projects, which are characterized as age-homogeneous settings; it may include return migration to the community of one's youth; or migration to one of the Sunbelt states; or it may include relocation within the same community. The studies reported in general support the P−E fit hypothesis of Figure 1.

A major study evaluating the impact on the social and psychological well-being of elderly tenants was performed by Carp (1966), who compared movers ($N =$ 204) into Victoria Plaza, one of the first housing projects for the elderly, with a group of persons ($N = 148$) who had applied for but were not accepted into the new housing. The research design included an extensive series of pre- and post-move measures to assess change over time. At one-year follow-up, the rehoused group showed many favorable effects of the improved housing and living environment. They were more satisfied with their housing, their neighborhood, and their ability to obtain services than previously. In addition, they displayed improved morale and functional health and an increase in social interactions. The study reported on the first year of tenancy, which might represent a 'honeymoon' period, but a validation across time using data gathered over an eight-year period supported the early conclusions and demonstrated the persistence of the improved housing's positive impact (Carp, 1975).

Lawton and Cohen (1974) assessed the social and psychological characteristics of tenants in five urban housing environments immediately before they moved and about one year after the move. After a year the rehoused were poorer in functional health and higher in morale, perceived more changes for the better, were more satisfied with their housing, and were more involved in external activities than a group of persons who remained in the community. Of particular interest is the decline in functional health contrasted to indications of a positive adjustment to relocation in other areas. Lawton and Cohen (1974) suggest that persons moving into the planned housing had already begun a gradual decline in health, which explained the appeal of the planned housing. The new, improved environment may have buffered the effects of failing health. It is also possible, however, that the stress of moving may have initiated the decline in health, and the 'honeymoon' period may have masked negative adjustment in other areas.

In an earlier study, Lawton and Yaffe (1970) compared three groups of moved and nonmoved persons matched for sex, age, and health at the beginning of the study: (1) a congregate-housing relocation group composed of new residents in an apartment building for the elderly; (2) a congregate-housing nonrelocated group composed of persons residing at least 18 months in a second apartment building; and (3) a community nonrelocated group drawn from a pool of community residents. At 12-month follow-up, there were no statistical differences in mortality among the three groups, but the relocated subjects were more likely than the nonrelocated to have had changes in health, i.e. more had improved and more had declined. Lawton and Yaffe (1970) speculate that the stimulation or satisfaction associated with moving into a new environment may be causally related to the improved health of some relocated persons, while the stress of relocation may result in a decline for others. They suggest that the voluntary nature of the move may have moderated the impact of the stress, thus attenuating the potential increase in mortality among the relocated persons.

Finally, Beaver (1979) attempted to identify some of the correlates of successful adjustment of voluntary entrants to a new retirement apartment complex in Los Angeles. The 108 elderly residents had lived in the apartment for an average of about 24 months at the time of the study. The sample was divided into 56 persons identified as successful adjusters and 52 as unsuccessful adjusters. Only two factors differed significantly between the successful and unsuccessful adjusters. First, the majority of successful adjusters (52%), but only 29% of the unsuccessful group, had felt it important to consider the activities available at the setting prior to relocating. The second factor concerned the number of choices of residence available to persons prior to the decision on where to move. Thirty-four percent of the successful adjusters and only 10% of the unsuccessful adjusters considered two other choices, 23% of the unsuccessful adjusters compared with 9% of the successful adjusters considered three or more choices. Beaver (1979) concludes from this finding that successful decision making occurs when neither too little nor too much information is available; i.e. having too many choices becomes confusing, while having too few choices may exclude the truly desirable option. The only other major finding of this study was that good physical health was the most powerful predictor of success in relocation.

A study by Bell (1976) examined the impact of housing relocation on the patterns of interaction and life satisfaction of a sample of older, married adults. Comparisons were made between matched samples of 115 persons living in congregate housing and 105 individuals living in independent residential units. The primary focus of the study was the role that social interactions play in life satisfaction of relocated elderly. It was hypothesized that persons in congregate housing would engage in more social interactions and report greater satisfaction. Length of time in the new environment was also hypothesized to be positively related to social interaction. None of the hypotheses were confirmed. No differences were found in the number or type of social interactions for persons in congregate or independent housing. Furthermore, a weak (nonsignificant) inverse relationship was observed between duration of residence and number of social interactions as well as between duration of residence and life satisfaction for persons in congregate housing. Finally, a significant difference in life satisfaction was noted; however, the higher levels of life satisfaction were reported by persons in independent dwellings.

These studies concur on only one of their primary findings: low-cost housing for the elderly can be beneficial for those persons who *choose* to live in it and who possess some minimal level of social and functional competence. However, in each of these studies there are a number of unmeasured variables which may potentially influence the outcome measures, thus, confounding the results.

For older persons with the personal and financial resources to make a big move, long-range relocation, or migration, is becoming an increasingly popular alternative to either not moving or moving locally. Senior migrants to Sunbelt states, primarily Arizona, California, and Florida, are largely motivated by a desire to spend retirement years in a warm, tranquil environment (Kahana and Kahana, 1983). Little empirical knowledge is available, however, concerning factors leading the elderly to successful adaptation and satisfaction with these new environments (Lawton, 1980). Beyond some recent demographic descriptions (e.g. Litwak and Longino, 1987), only a handful of studies have been reported.

Bultena and Wood (1969) report a study that investigated differences in the personal adjustment of older persons who had moved to age-integrated and age-segregated communities in Arizona. Their goal was to test the general hypothesis that planned communities (i.e. age-homogeous settings) facilitate adaptation of older migrants to the retirement role. Within the framework of P−E fit, this hypothesis summarizes a series of research questions concerning the role of social support, preparedness, environmental change, and the degree of choice in the move. An additional variable, predictability, would also enter the model as a direct influence on adjustment, i.e. greater predictability leads to fewer problems of adjustment. Comparisons were made among persons living in retirement communities ($N = 322$) and persons in age-integrated communities ($N = 199$). A third comparison group was composed of 284 persons who had retired in their hometowns in Wisconsin. A larger portion of migrants to retirement communities perceived their health as being very good or good than did those persons in the regular communities (75% and 59%). Similarly, persons in the retirement communities obtained a score indicating high morale over twice as often as migrants to heterogeneous communities in Arizona (57% and 27%). The relationship between type of community and morale was retained when statistically controlling for age, occupational status, income, educational attainment, and perceived health. Bultena and Wood (1969) suggest that the environment of the planned retirement community is more conducive for facilitating social interaction and the formation of new friendships. The retirement communities provide a 'supportive reference group' which is important to increased morale.

Results supporting the P−E fit approach to adjustment are also presented by Hendrick, Wells, and Faletti (1982) who compared the adjustment of 175 retired persons who had relocated to south Florida to the adjustment of 139 retired persons who had resided in the south Florida area prior to retirement. The type of residence (regular versus retirement community) was also included in the design. The respondents had been retired at least 1.5 years but not more than 15 years. The Srole Anomie Scale (Srole, 1956) was the major dependent measure. This scale assesses the degree of alienation and isolation perceived, in this case by the retirees. Health, general satisfaction with life, and the occurence of major life problems were also measured. On the health measure, over 70% of the respondents assessed their health to be either good or excellent; less than 5% of both groups rated themselves to be in poor health. While 10% reported a decline in health since retirement, approximately 66% perceived an improvement in health. Retirement preparation emerged as an important factor in adjustment to retirement and relocation, and those persons with less control over retirement decisions and fewer resources were less likely to have had preparation for retirement, leading to higher alienation. Persons at the highest risk for alienation were those in nonnormative situations, i.e. migrant elderly persons who moved into the general community and nonmigrants who moved into a retirement community. Respondents with poor perceived health ratings were more likely to feel alienated than persons with good perceived health. Alienated persons had a slightly greater difference in income from pre-retirement to post-retirement than the nonalienated. Alienated respondents were more likely to have experienced increases in transportation assistance and less likely to have obtained assistance with household chores—implying greater likelihood for social isolation. Persons classified as alienated had poorer health ratings in a discriminant analysis; however, there is no way to determine from the reported results whether a reversed causal path from alienation to poor health is also possible.

Overall, no more than 15% of the total sample could be classified as alienated on the Srole scale, which suggests that, at least within the first decade of retirement, most people adjusted quite well. The data also indicate that relocation per se had very few negative consequences, but that congruence between type of housing and social needs of the aged may enhance life satisfaction following retirement. Thus, for persons who remain in the same area after retirement, a traditional community situation may be best; for persons relocating to a new environment, a planned retirement community may be optimal. These conclusions define the P−E fit model. Unfortunately, the authors are not more explicit in making this definition. Nor do they test the full model even though they possess the data to do so.

Kahana and her colleagues (Kahana and Kahana, 1983) described an ongoing longitudinal study of adaptation to voluntary, long-distance moves. The study examined predictors of positive post-relocation outcomes for 259 older Americans who relocated to Florida retirement communities. Using improved health, high morale, and satisfaction with life in Florida as outcome variables, the authors found that stepwise multiple regression resulted in different predictors being identified as significant. Those in better health, females, and married persons exhibited high post-move morale; improvement in health was related to age, the sex of the respondent (female), the perception of the move as not permanent, and positive views of Florida. Satisfaction with life in Florida was correlated with length of residence in Florida, enthusiasm for moving there, and the perception that few adjustments were required. The authors suggest that the voluntary nature of the move to Florida resulted in high levels of satisfaction for most aged in spite of the major adaptation required. This interpretation concurs with previous research on local moves (e.g. Beaver, 1979; Ferraro, 1981), which suggests that the desire to move was an important factor in post-relocation adjustment.

The work by Kahana and her colleagues suggests that perceptions may play a greater role in establishing 'fit' than is generally thought. One theory in recent psychological research on subjective well-being (see Diener, 1984) suggests that happiness is experienced when particular goals are obtained or needs fulfilled. If people vary greatly in their goals and needs, it is not surprising that individuals will have varying perceptions of when goals and needs are satisfied—when fit between environmental demands and personal resources to meet those demands has been attained. Thus, in the above study the perception that the move need not be permanent may satisfy the need to be in control of where a person resides. This, in turn, may lead to the perception of fewer required adjustments since, as dissonance theory would predict, if the transition were very difficult, the person would simply leave.

Ferraro (1982), in a study of moves within the community at large, concludes that relocation is associated with a decline in health status among older people, and that the adverse affects of moving on the health of older people appears to be unaffected by the degree to which the move is considered voluntary. Ferraro also considered the possibility that declining health was a factor in the relocation decision and was unable to reject the hypothesis that relocation of older people is dependent on prior health status; such a relationship would, of course, suggest that the moves might not be entirely voluntary. Ferraro added change in housing setting and change in satisfaction with housing in the new setting in order to determine if there were environmental features that affected health status but neither of these variables was significant. Ferraro may have overgeneralized from these two proxy measures of environmental features, however, in concluding that 'the decline in health is not due to environmental change, (Ferraro, 1982, p. 94).

The contradictory conclusions obtained from isolated studies on voluntary residential relocation mirror those obtained from research on institutional relocation and underscore the need for more complex theoretical approaches to the question of adjustment. The issue of individual control over the decision to relocate has potential as a major explanatory variable, but the few studies that have incorporated sense of control into their research designs have produced conflicting results. Beaver (1979) and Ferraro (1981) conclude that greater volition led to more successful personal adjustment, while Ferraro (1982) provides evidence that the degree of voluntarism is not associated with post-relocation health.

Health status prior to the move is also strongly related to post-relocation health in these studies, but the more statistically rigorous techniques for examining this relationship have not been used. The causal role of health as a factor in the choice to relocate versus its role as a result of relocation has not been clearly explored for residential relocation. Studies among the elderly have tended to use health as a variable predicting life satisfaction (e.g. Baglioni, 1986; Edwards and Klemmack, 1973; Spreitzer and Snyder, 1974). Studies among relocated elderly are needed to explore evidence that the reverse may, in fact, represent the causal path. Moreover, unlike studies concerning institutional relocation, which regularly report pre- and post-relocation morbidity and mortality, studies of voluntary residential relocation with health as a primary outcome variable are rare (e.g. Hendrick, Wells, and Faletti, 1982; Lawton and Yaffe, 1970).

Both the originating and the receiving environments have been implicated as significant in the successful adjustment to relocation. When the originating environment is low-quality, inner-city type housing, relocation to an environment designed for the aged has led to improvements in reported health. The previously cited study by Hendrick, *et al.* (1982) suggested the receiving environment may contribute to successful adjustment. On the other hand, Ferraro (1982) suggests that type of housing in the receiving environment is not significantly associated with change in health status, even though his sample was composed of low- and middle-income older people.

SUMMARY AND IMPLICATIONS FOR FURTHER RESEARCH

The literature cited here makes apparent that many of the factors identified as influential in determining adjustment to institutional relocation are also functional when residential relocation occurs. While research has begun to isolate specific variables, however, no comprehensive model has emerged that can provide coherency to the *process* of adjustment.

Schulz and Brenner (1977) suggest that adjustment to relocation is, at least in part, determined by perceived predictability and controllability in the environment and by the degree of similarity between the originating and receiving environments. Their suggestion may be interpreted as a detailed statement of the more general person−environment (P−E) fit hypothesis of stress, which proposes that discrepancies between characteristics of the individual and the environment produce stress. If the imbalance is prolonged, the strain of continually trying to achieve a more homeostatic relationship eventually leads to negative psychological and physiological consequences. The reaction to relocation is to try to re-establish control within one's environment. To the extent that the relocation is unpredictable and involuntary and there is a lack of familiarity with the new environment, these factors may combine to decrease the amount of P−E fit and thus increase strain. Individual characteristics such as age, health, psychological well-being, preparedness, and social and emotional supports may work to reduce the initial discrepancy. Conversely these same factors may help to restore the balance. Environmental characteristics can function in similar roles.

The ongoing debate about the health consequences of relocation has centered on specific variables without acknowledging the processes involved. Future research will need to achieve a greater process orientation with efforts made to use more sophisticated statistical techniques in order to understand the complex questions being addressed. Some studies of life satisfaction among the elderly (Baglioni, 1986; Markides and Martin, 1979; and Medley, 1976) have begun to develop process models using path analytic and structural equation approaches that are direct extensions of more simple regression models (e.g. Edwards and Klemmack, 1973; Spreitzer and Snyder, 1974). Path and structural models of health-related reactions to relocation are also needed. Research designs in which multiple dependent health variables are measured both physiologically and via self-reports of physical well-being and more general functional health will be required. Multiple indicators of the independent variables also need development in order to increase the validity of the constructs being measured.

There are several advantages to adopting a process orientation in studying the phenomena related to relocation among the elderly. The first, and most obvious, is that such an approach will allow the assimilation of much more information than

134 *Aging, Stress and Health*

before. The growing number of researchers examining the impact of relocation insures that isolated bits of knowledge will continue to be amassed. Without an overriding paradigm of adjustment, it will become virtually impossible for most researchers to maintain control of the new information. The second advantage is that such a paradigm will guide further research and analysis of the adjustment-to-relocation issues. Recent research has seemingly applied a shotgun approach to studying isolated factors. This tactic has contributed to the inconsistent findings because there has been little agreement on definitions and parameters for analysis. Finally, deficiencies in a paradigm lead to further research. Attempts to replicate the unexpected findings may find faults with the original research and/or lead to corrections in the paradigm. Either result advances the knowledge base and may suggest applications that may assist the adjustment process.

As the field must come to recognize, true experimental designs with random assignment of respondents are rarely possible. To control for the many potentially confounding factors, advanced statistical techniques as well as detailed research designs must be invoked. These methodologies must be theory driven, however, or the question of the process by which elderly persons achieve a healthy adjustment to relocation will continue to be debated long past the lifetimes of most of the advocates of any particular factor.

REFERENCES

Aldrich, C. (1964). Personality factors and mortality in the relocation of the aged. *Gerontologist*, **4**, 92–3.
Aldrich, C. and Mendkoff, E. (1963). Relocation of the aged and disabled: a morbidity study. *Journal of the American Geriatric Society*, **11**, 185–94.
Aleksandrowicz, D.R. (1961). Fire and its aftermath on a geriatric ward. *Bulletin of the Meninger Clinic*, **25**, 23–32.
Baglioni, A.J., Jr (1986). A Structural Equation Approach to Life Satisfaction Among Elderly Migrant Women. Unpublished doctoral dissertation, University of Virginia.
Beaver, M.L. (1979). The decision-making process and its relationship to relocation adjustment in old people. *Gerontolgist*, **19**, 567–74.
Bell, B.D. (1976). The impact of housing relocation on the elderly: an alternative methodological approach. *International Journal of Aging and Human Development*, **7**, 27–38.
Biggar, J.C. (1980). Who moved among the elderly, 1965 to 1970: a comparison of types of elderly moves. *Research on Aging*, **2**, 73–91.
Blenkner, M. (1967). Environmental change and the aging individual. *Gerontologist*, **7**, 101–5.
Borup, J.H., Gallego, D. and Hefferman, P. (1979). Relocation and its effect on mortality. *Gerontologist*, **19**, 135–40.
Borup, J.H., Gallego, D. and Heffernan, P. (1980). Relocation: Its effect on health, functioning, and mortality. *Gerontologist*, **20**, 468–79.
Bourestom, N. and Pastalan, L. (1981). The effects of relocation on the elderly: a reply to Borup, J.H., Gallego, D.T., and Heffernan, P.G. *Gerontologist*, **21**, 4–7.
Bourestom, N. and Tars, S. (1974). Alterations in life patterns following relocations. *Gerontologist*, **14**, 506–10.

Brand, F.N. and Smith, R.T. (1974). Life adjustment and relocation of the elderly. *Journal of Gerontology*, **29**, 336–40.

Bultena, G.L. and Wood, V. (1969). The American retirement community: bane or blessing. *Journal of Gerontology*, **22**, 209–17.

Camargo, O. and Preston, G.H. (1945). What happens to patients who are hospitalized for the first time when over 65 years of age. *American Journal of Psychiatry*, **102**, 168.

Carp, F.M. (1966). *A Future for the Aged*, University of Texas Press, Austin.

Carp, F.M. (1975). Long-range satisfaction with housing. *Gerontologist*, **15**, 68–72.

Coffman, T.L. (1981). Relocation and survival of institutionalized aged: a re-examination of the evidence. *Gerontologist*, **21**, 583–600.

Coffman, T.L. (1983). Toward an understanding of geriatric relocation. *Gerontologist*, **23**, 453–9.

Diener, E. (1984). Subjective well-being. *Psychological Bulletin*, **95**, 542–75.

Eckert, J.K. (1983). Dislocation and relocation of the urban elderly: social networks as mediators of relocation stress. *Human Organization*, **42**, 39–45.

Eckert, J.K. and Haug, M. (1984). The impact of forced residential relocation on the health of the elderly hotel dweller. *Journal of Gerontology*, **39**, 753–5.

Edwards, J.N. and Klemmack, D.L. (1973). Correlates of life satisfaction: a re-examination. *Journal of Gerontology*, **28**, 497–502.

Ferraro, K.F. (1981). Relocation desires and outcomes among the elderly: a longitudinal analysis. *Research on Aging*, **3**, 166–81.

Ferraro, K.F. (1982). The health consequences of relocation among the aged in the community. *Journal of Gerontology*, **37**, 90–6.

Goldfarb, A.I., Shahinian, S.P. and Burr, H.T. (1972). Death rates of relocated residents. In D.P. Kent, R. Kastenbaum and S. Sherwood (eds.) *Research Planning and Action for the Elderly*, Behavioral Publications, New York.

Gopelrud, E.N. (1979). Unexpected consequences of deinstitutionalization of the mentally disabled elderly. *American Journal of Community Psychology*, **7**, 315–28.

Hendrick, C., Wells, K.S. and Faletti, M.V. (1982). Social and emotional effects of geographical relocation on elderly retirees. *Journal of Personality and Social Psychology*, **42**, 951–62.

Holmes, T.H. and Rahe, R.H. (1967). The social readjustment rating scale. *Journal of Psychosomatic Medicine*, **11**, 213–18.

Horowitz, M.J. and Schulz, R. (1983). The relocation controversy: criticism and commentary on five recent studies. *Gerontologist*, **23**, 229–35.

Jasnau, K.F. (1967). Individualized versus mass transfer of non-psychotic geriatric patients from mental hospitals to nursing homes with special reference to death rates. *Journal of the American Geriatric Society*, **15**, 280–4.

Kahana, E. and Kahana, B. (1983). Environmental continuity, futurity, and adaptation of the aged. In G.D. Rowles and R.J. Ohta (eds.) *Aging and Milieu: Environmental Perspectives on Growing Old*, Academic Press, New York.

Kasl, S. (1972). Physical and mental health effects of involuntary relocation and institutionalization: a review. *American Journal of Public Health*, **62**, 379–84.

Kasteler, J.M., Gray, R.M. and Carruth, M.L. (1968). Involuntary relocation of the aged. *Gerontologist*, **8**, 276–9.

Killian, E.C. (1970). Effect of geriatric transfers on mortality rates. *Social Work*, **15**, 19–26.

Kopf, E. (1977). Untarnishing the dream: mobility, opportunity, and order in modern America. *Journal of Social History*, **11**, 206–27.

Kral, V.A., Grad, B. and Berenson, J. (1968). Stress reactions resulting from relocation of an aged population. *Canadian Psychiatric Association Journal*, **13**, 201–9.

Langer, E. and Rodin, J. (1976). The effects of choice and enhanced personal responsibility for the aged. *Journal of Personality and Social Psychology*, 34, 191−8.

Lawton, M.P. (1980). *Environment and Aging*, Brooks/Cole, Monterey, CA.

Lawton, M.P. and Cohen, J. (1974). The generality of housing impact on the well-being of older people. *Journal of Gerontology*, **29**, 194−204.

Lawton, M.P. and Yaffe, S. (1970). Mortality, morbidity, and voluntary change of residence by older people. *Journal of the American Geriatric Society*, **18**, 823−31.

Lieberman, M.A. (1974). Relocation research and social policy. *Gerontologist*, **14**, 494−501.

Lieberman, M.A. and Tobin, S.S. (1983). *The Experience of Old Age*, Basic Books, New York.

Liebowitz, B. (1974). Impact of intra-institutional relocation. *Gerontologist*, **14**, 293−5.

Litwak, E. and Longino, C.F., Jr. (1987). Migration patterns among the elderly: a developmental perspective. *Gerontologist*, **27**, 266−72.

Longino, C.F., Jr (1982). American retirement communities and residential relocation. In A. Warnes (ed.) *Geographical Perspectives on the Elderly*, Wiley, New York.

Markides, K.S. and Martin, H.W. (1979). A causal model of life satisfaction of the elderly. *Journal of Gerontology*, **34**, 86−93.

Markson, E.W. and Cumming, J.H. (1974). A strategy of necessary mass transfer and its impact on patient mortality. *Journal of Gerontology*, **29**, 315−21.

Markus, E., Blenkner, M., Bloom, M. and Downs, T. (1970). Relocation stress and the aged. *Interdisciplinary Topics in Gerontology*, **7**, 60−71.

Markus, E., Blenkner, M., Bloom, M. and Downs, T. (1971). Some factors and their association with post relocation mortality among aged persons. *Journal of Gerontology*, **26**, 537−41.

Medley, M.L. (1976). Satisfaction with life among persons sixty-five and older: a causal model. *Journal of Gerontology*, **31**, 448−55.

Miller, D. and Lieberman, M.A. (1965). The relationship of affect state and adaptive capacity to react to stress. *Journal of Gerontology*, **20**, 492−7.

Novick, L.J. (1967). Easing the stress of moving day. *Hospitals*, **41**, 469−74.

Ogren, E.H. and Linn, M.W. (1971). Male nursing home patients: relocation and mortality. *Journal of the American Geriatric Society*, **19**, 229−39.

Packard, V. (1972). *A Nation of Strangers*, McKay, New York.

Pino, C.J., Rosica, L.M. and Carter, T.J. (1978). The differential effects of relocation on nursing home patients. *Gerontologist*, **10**, 167−72.

Schulz, R. (1976). Effects of control and predictability on the physical and psychological well-being of the institutionalized aged. *Journal of Personality and Social Psychology*, **33**, 563−73.

Schulz, R. and Brenner, D. (1977). Relocation of the aged: a review and theoretical analysis. *Journal of Gerontology*, **32**, 323−33.

Smith, R.T. and Brand, F.N. (1975). Effects of enforced relocation on life adjustment in a nursing home. *International Journal of Aging and Human Development*, **6**, 249−60.

Spreitzer, E. and Snyder, E.E. (1974). Correlates of life satisfaction among the aged. *Journal of Gerontology*, **29**, 454−8.

Srole, L. (1956). Social integration and certain corollaries. *American Sociological Review*, **21**, 709−16.

Storandt, W. and Wittels, I. (1975). Maintenance of function in relocation of community-dwelling older adults. *Journal of Gerontology*, **30**, 608−12.

Turner, B.F., Tobin, S.S. and Lieberman, M.A. (1972). Personality traits as predictors of institutional adaptation in the aged. *Journal of Gerontology*, **27**, 61−8.

Whittier, J. and Williams, D. (1956). The coincidence of constancy of mortality figures for the aged psychotic patients admitted to state hospital. *Journal of Nervous and Mental Disease*, **124**, 618–20.

Zweig, J.P. and Csank, J.Z. (1975). Effects of relocation on chronically ill patients on a medical unit: mortality rates. *Journal of Gerontology*, **23**, 132–6.

Chapter 7

The Effects of Institutionalization

Sheldon S. Tobin

INTRODUCTION

Institutionalization is a specific kind of relocation that refers, for the elderly, to relocating from a noninstitutional to a long-term care setting. The process of becoming institutionalized when old begins before the actual relocation when, for example, the resident-to-be anticipates admission and is aware of the impending event. Psychological effects during this anticipatory period are a result of feelings of abandonment and, also, of a redefinition of self as a person who can only survive if provided with institutional care. Then, after admission, there is a first month syndrome. Most newly admitted residents become disoriented but also some become extremely depressed, others manifest quite bizarre behaviors and still others deteriorate rather rapidly. The syndrome is not only a result of the more conscious psychological appraisals of the stressfulness of living in a total institution, as well as the less conscious inner experience of being more physically vulnerable and closer to death, but also of the social dislocation following the move to a foreign environment. After the first month syndrome, some residents recover to reestablish their pre-admission status whereas others continue to deteriorate including having their death hastened. These phases will be discussed more fully, borrowing heavily from the Tobin and Lieberman (1976) longitudinal study of becoming institutionalized when old in nursing homes reported in *Last Home for the Aged*.

Following the discussion of effects throughout the process of becoming institutionalized when old, the focus will shift to causes for differential effects, i.e. for differential vulnerability to the stress of institutionalization. Personal characteristics that sensitize elderly persons to the stresses inherent in institutional adaptation will be considered. Vulnerability to institutionalization is increased, for example, when passivity is in evidence preceding the move. Replicated also in three additional longitudinal studies of relocation, reported in the Lieberman and Tobin (1983) book *The Experience of Old Age*, is how the inability to magically master the situation is associated with adverse outcomes. Conversely those who can transform involuntary relocation into a voluntary choice and who can transform an unwelcomed relocation environment into a rather ideal setting are likely to evade adverse outcomes. Simply put, those who are aggressive and

Aging, Stress and Health Edited by K.S. Markides and C.L. Cooper
© 1989 John Wiley & Sons Ltd

who use magical mastery are more likely to survive intact in all relocation situations. In addition to personal characteristics, qualities of environments also predict outcomes. The study of institutionalization, however, encompassed three location environments that were too similar to assess how environmental quality affects outcome. Thus, there shall be a reliance on two of the four Lieberman—Tobin studies in which relocation was to a range of long-term care facilities. Moreover, in examining psychosocial quality of environments, there will also be discussion of person—environment fit and environmental discrepancy hypotheses. Whereas person-environment fit refers to the congruence between personal characteristics and adaptive demands of the relocation setting, environmental discrepancy refers to discrepant demands between pre- and post-relocation environments. It has been assumed that the better the fit of personal characteristics with environmental adaptive demands and the less the environmental discrepancy, as well as the better the psychosocial quality, the less the adverse effects from institutionalization.

The assumption underlying our studies was that relocation is a stressful event because of new adaptive demands on individuals. Indeed, in all our relocation studies, adverse outcomes were found. About one-half of those relocated manifested adverse outcomes, mostly excess morbidity but sometimes excess mortality. The kinds of adverse outcomes varied by relocation situation. Excess mortality was most in evidence only when very debilitated aged persons were involuntarily located *en masse* from a state mental hospital to long-term care facilities. In this our fourth study, within one year of relocation 18% of the 427 had died as compared to only 5% among a carefully matched control group of 100 who were not relocated. In the other three studies, adverse outcomes were reflected primarily in excess morbidity. Thus, the lingering controversy regarding the presence of 'relocation trauma' or 'transplantation shock' as occurring only when there is evidence for excess mortality must be put to rest. Borup (1983) attempted to do so when he responded to Horowitz and Schulz (1983) who focused on mortality rates in reviewing relocation studies. Many still falsely believe that only excess mortality reveals the presence of relocation effects (see, for example, Coffman, 1983).

After discussing both the process of becoming institutionalized when old and the predictors of differential vulnerability, issues will be covered related to caring, and to reducing excess morbidity and mortality.

Finally, in the last section, a research agenda will be discussed; first, explicitly for the study of institutionalization and, then, for studies beyond institutionalization, for understanding adaptation to stress in aging and for normative aging, as well as for all persons independent of age.

BECOMING INSTITUTIONALIZED WHEN OLD

Before our longitudinal study of the effects throughout the process of becoming institutionalized, it was common to identify effects by comparing an institutionalized to a community sample. Beyond the obvious problems in developing matched samples, a cross-sectional design masks effects from two different sources. That is, even if the two samples were perfectly matched, it would be impossible to differentiate effects during the anticipatory period after admission has been sought from the effects after entering and living in the institutional setting. Also purposeful in our design was the selection of the best of long-term care facilities because of an interest in identifying the irreducible effects of institutionalization.

Effects before admission

What happens to the elderly frail person when told 'It's time?' That is, 'It's time to go to a nursing home.' One octogenarian, Mrs V., who expected to return to her home after hospitalization, became extremely depressed when told she could not live alone and needed home care. The alert geriatric nurse observed the increasing depression and asked for a psychiatric consultation. The psychiatrist prescribed psychotropic medication and both he and the nurse were heartened to see the depression lift. They falsely, however, attributed the lifting of the depression to the medication. Rather the patient, a feisty person all her life, had regained her determination. She ceased to be compliant and decided for herself that the county nursing home would permit her to carry on. She badgered the hospital discharge planner to arrange admission to the nursing home of her choice and when the social worker successfully gained admission for her, celebrated her victory by refusing her anti-depressant medication. Still, she was not happy to know that she soon would be relocating to a nursing home where her survival could be assured.

Mrs V., akin to those in our institutionalization study, had to cope with a redefinition of herself as a person who could only survive in an institutional setting. In all, 85 elderly individuals (mean age = 79) were followed, on the average, from four months before admission while on the waiting lists to three sectarian homes through two months after admission and, then, one year after admission. At each time, if interviewable, respondents were interviewed for 12 to 16 hours in four to six sessions. Two control groups were developed: 37 persons who had been residents of the facilities for one to three years and 40 persons living independently in the community who would apply to those excellent homes if institutional care was sought. To assess the fears of becoming institutionalized, Kuypers (1969) developed an interview guide that permitted the assessment of latent, as well as manifest, attitudes toward the home. The subsample of 14 from the community control sample had a rather positive appraisal of the sectarian institution to which they would apply if institutionalization was warranted. For example, they felt that old-age homes were necessary, that the staff met the needs of the residents, that a resident could maintain self-respect, and that the home provided companionship. The people who went into the homes were clearly different because they were no longer independent. More latent attitudes were then revealed in the focused interview that followed the questionnaire. For 12 of the 14 respondents, entering the home would be a calamity. One respondent said 'it would be giving up everything' and that she would go 'only if helpless,' another compared it to 'a jail' and a third, to 'a place to die.' Although it may be giving up everything, a jail, and a death house, they would enter these excellent homes, as have others before them, to assure survival.

Given the attitude of elderly before admission is contemplated, it is not at all surprising that if admission is later sought, the resident-to-be becomes depressed and withdrawn before actually entering and living in the home. Also not surprising was that the deteriorating psychological portrait, a portrait usually attributed to living in a total institution, was accompanied by feelings of being abandoned by their family, as revealed, for example, by their reconstruction of earliest memories (Tobin, 1972; Tobin and Etigson, 1968).

Feelings of abandonment can best be understood if institutionalization is considered a family process. Indeed, families go to extremes to avoid institutionalizing a member. Although a disproportionate percentage of those who reside in long-term care facilities may be without nuclear family members, most do have families. Among those elderly who do have family members involved in the decision-making process to seek institutional care, the situation evokes problems in family relationships that are persistent, but often veiled, and the family manifests, according to Brody (1977), 'internalized guilt-inducting injunctions against placing an elderly spouse or parent regardless of the most reality-based determinants of that placement' (p. 115). More recently Brody (1985) attributed the myth of how previous generations cared better for their elderly members to these kinds of feelings. Cath (1972) labeled the institutionalization of a parent, 'a nadir of life' because one of the most unhappy times in life may be when a child must make a decision to institutionalize a parent. Mrs V.'s daughter, whose life situation precluded caring for her at home, had these kinds of feelings and Mrs V., had feelings of being abandoned.

Given the redefinition of self as a person who can only survive in a nursing home and who feels abandoned, it is understandable why the psychological portrait approximates those who have lived in these homes rather than those who live independently in the community. A contrast of the waiting list sample with the two control samples revealed (Lieberman, Prock and Tobin, 1968) that waiting list respondents were more like institutionalized elderly persons in being depressed, apathetic, and cognitively constricted and so forth. Because adverse physical and social changes that provoked application to the homes where not more in evidence among waiting list respondents than among community respondents who did not apply for admission, it is most sensible to conclude that psychological status was a result not of precipitants that evoked applying for admission but, rather, was a result of the redefinition of self as a person who has been abandoned with no place to go but to a setting that has always been dreaded. Three cases of persons from the community sample who later applied for admission and were interviewed while on the waiting list were used to poignantly illustrate the transition to becoming a waiting list person (see Tobin and Lieberman, 1976). They, like Mrs V., focused on the gains in personal care, people and activities in their future home as a way of coping with the underlying painful feelings (see Pincus, 1968).

Effects from the initial stress of institutionalization

The timing of the interview after entering and living in facilities, six weeks to two months post-admission, was purposefully chosen to follow the impact of the initial stress, i.e. six weeks to two months post-admission. Jerome Grunes, my clinical mentor and psychiatric consultant at Drexel Home for the Aged in Chicago for over a quarter of a century, labeled it the first month syndrome. It is when the newly admitted resident does not show a first month syndrome that there is cause for concern. The presumptions must be either that the resident is insufficiently lucid to comprehend the situation or has fled into fantasy to deal with it.

Stein, Linn and Stein (1985) investigated the sources of anticipatory stress among 223 residents newly admitted to 10 nursing homes. Direct queries of residents revealed five factors, or dimensions. The first was relocation orientation expressed by questions such as 'Where do I sleep?' and 'When do I eat?' A second source of stress, labeled severance anxiety, was associated with separation from family. Another dimension encompassed medical concerns including worries about illness, pain, medication and doctor visits. A fourth, tender loving care, referred to being treated with concern and respect. The fifth, and final dimension, was personal space encompassing needs for privacy, personal possessions and flexibility in schedules.

To live, according to Goffman (1961), in a total institution is to reside in a setting that restricts contact with the outside world, that attempts to handle human needs the bureaucratic management of blocks of people and that encompasses a basic split between resident and staff. Bennett and Nehemow (1965) observed that the extent of institutional totality among geriatric facilities affects both residents and staff. Gubrium (1975) similarly noted how institutional totality provides for differences between staff and residents in the perceived environment. Using Lemke and Moos' (1987) data, as well as additional interview data, Smith and Nierke (1987), in turn, found increasing perceived discrepancies between staff and residents as institutional totality increased; i.e. the greatest amount of discrepancies were found in skilled nursing home facilities, with lesser amounts in intermediate care facilities and the least in residential age-segregated apartments. It is apparent that nursing homes are not only total institutions but more total than other long-term care facilities.

All total institutions not only reduce autonomy but also force an identification with peers that is distinct from staff. The shared identification of residents in nursing homes includes self-perceptions of frailty and dependency. The realization of how autonomy is reduced, as reflected in the specific stresses reported to Stein *et al.*, (1985), and the forced identification as only one among other impaired residents are indeed stressors that must be overcome. Concurrently, an alien setting must become familiar. A social dislocation at any age can be disorienting. To the elderly person who may have been accustomed to the same familiar home environment for half a century or more, negotiating the new environment may be devastating. Invariably, for example, persons of advanced age sleep in spurts and arise at night to urinate. This behavioral pattern may be counter to practices of facilities where residents are expected to remain in bed at night and where toileting is associated with possible hip fractures. For the fastidious resident who attempts to toilet at night without fracturing a bone, finding the bathroom may be a challenge in an unfamiliar environment. Not quick enough in locating the toilet, a slight accident may occur. The wetting of undergarments may be negligible but it can be frightening to the resident who fears incontinence and confusion, both of which are observed as common among other residents. These fears become added to, and escalate the many other fears and anxieties of the newly admitted resident. Only after familiarity with surroundings and an acceptance of the reality of survival in the institution, can there be a return to a former level of adaptation.

Even under the best of circumstances, living in a foreign environment is likely to cause adverse effects. Witness the culture shock among Peace Corps recruits who eagerly volunteer to work and live in a different culture. The discrepancy between their home environment in the United States and the foreign one in a strange land is an extreme social dislocation. Lazarus (1966) refers to the source of stress as social rather than psychological because the situation may not be appraised as threatening and interpreted as harmful or dangerous. Disorientation, as well as other symptoms of culture shock, are evoked by the disparity in environments.

Effects following the initial stress

By two months or so, residents in excellent facilities have been able to reestablish a resemblance of self. Indeed data gathered before and after admission suggest more stability than changes two months post-admission. Constrictions in cognition and affective responsiveness persisted and also there was a continuation, and thus a stability, of moderate levels of well-being, anxiety and depression. Changes found were limited to an increase in hopelessness, an increase in bodily preoccupation, a perception of less capacity for self-care and a lessening of affiliation in interaction with others. The self-system, however, remained remarkably intact and stable in contrast to the deselfing process which Goffman (1961) has described as occurring when entering a state mental hospital. Rosner (1968) found, for example, on the interpersonal self-sort task (a pool of 48 self-descriptive items) that respondents who entered the homes were similar to respondents in the community and institutional contrast groups in selecting four of five items the second time that had been selected the first time. Even when those items selected by 70% or more of respondents were eliminated, the percentage of items chosen after admission that had been chosen before was very high, specifically three of four self-descriptive items. On this index of the more idiosyncratic items, there was also no apparent effect on the consistency of the self-view as a result of entering and living in the homes. The only shift that did occur was on the dimension of affiliative – hostile, which suggests a perception of less friendliness and more hostility toward others.

Does this diminution in affiliation toward others suggest a decline in interaction with others? Responses to one instrument, the Personal Resources Questionnaire, an 11 item scale that required respondents to mention the names of one or more specific other who can, for example, be turned to when lonely, for help, or when happy, suggested that residents interact with a range of peers and staff, and also with family. Regarding family, there is an amelioration of feelings of abandonment reflected in diverse parts of our data (see also Smith and Bengtson, 1979), and a tendency toward mythicizing of living children, reflected specifically in reminiscent data which apparently, is an exaggerated expression of an age-associated process of mythicizing significant figures from the past. Although a child may still be alive and a frequent visitor, the increased psychological distance created by institutionalization and the need to preserve the self in the face of institutional demands and distance may cause an exaggeration in the adaptative process of mythicizing the child. The exaggerated response is probably reinforced by the institutional environment where the coin of the realm is famous offspring who are attentive and caring and where family attention provides leverages for personal and also for more attentive staff caring.

Entering and living in institutional environments were, therefore, not associated with changes that would support a belief in the destructiveness of institutions. Apparently the institution forces the adoption of the patient role, including increasing the preoccupation with bodily concerns and personal vulnerability, which, in turn, reduces the elderly resident's expectations for future experiences that can give purpose to life. Yet, the shift at the more latent level was not as modest as the manifest changes in psychological status.

The earliest memories revealed a significant shift toward the introduction of themes of mutilation and death. This shift in recollection sometimes occurred when the same incident was reported at both times. For example, before admission one elderly woman offered the following earliest memory: 'I remember my mother. She had hair like braids, open and falling upon her shoulder. She was sitting up in her bed and near her on her table was a bottle of honey and I remember asking her for honey. That's all I remember—nothing before and nothing behind. I still can see her sitting in bed. I must have been two years, two or three. Closer to two, I guess. But that's a picture I have.' After admission she recalled: ' I remember my mother's death. I remember at least one moment of it. She had honey on her bed and I wanted some of that honey. I didn't really understand that she was dying. I was almost three years old. That's all I remember. I can see her face clearly even now. She had two braids hanging down. This picture is all I remember of her.' The contrast between the two memories suggests that a breakthrough of repression had occurred in which previously withheld, archaic material was now being expressed. It would appear that in the first report the pain of mother's death is defended against, but breaks through in the second telling of the same incident. In the reconstruction of the same incident at both times, there is a central theme of oral deprivation (e.g. wanting, but not getting, the honey), as well as the personally meaningful symbolism of mother's braids.

More often, however, the increase in loss when becoming institutionalized was associated with a shift in the incident, as in the following example of the repeat earliest memory. When on the waiting list: 'I liked to go swimming and mother wouldn't let me. Once I stood on the pier and fell in. I remember how they took me out and took me to my mother. That's all I remember. I wasn't sick.' And after admission: 'Didn't have coffins in the old country like they do here. My father died. I remember my sister was still a breast baby... It was a cold day. My mother said don't go, but he was a stubborn man and so he got pneumonia and died.'

Contrasts with thematic changes in the control groups suggest that one-third would not have shifted to these themes of more narcissistic loss had they not entered the home. The shift is apparently specifically related to entering and living in the homes, and to living in a total institutional environment with sick elderly in a home that is to be the last one. With such a significant shift, from abandonment to increased vulnerability, it was indeed surprising that so little change was observed in psychological status. Most likely the ability to successfully contain, to defend against, the latent meaning is a function of entering the best of contemporary long-term care facilities. Yet even these facilities exact their toll, as reflected in the latent meaning of institutional life itself, in the adoption of the patient role, a lessening of futurity, and portraying oneself as less affiliative in relation to others.

By the end of one year post-admission, about one-half of the sample had either died (13 of the 85, or 15%) or had deteriorated extremely (28 or 33%). Those able to be interviewed again showed only a lessening of affiliation in relation to others and a lessening of body preoccupation. All other measures did not show a change. This pattern of stability with only focal changes in affiliation and body preoccupation among the intact survivors masks the previously noted global outcomes; 41 of the 85 had died or had become extremely deteriorated. To what extent these 41 would have shown these outcomes had they not entered and lived in the houses is impossible to know. Although similar outcomes were found for 18% of the community sample, such outcomes were found for 47% of the institutional control sample. The latter statistic suggests no excess morbidity and mortality for those who entered the homes. This issue will be incorporated into the discussion of differences between the deteriorated or dead and the intact survivors, i.e. into the discussion of predictors of vulnerability to the stress of institutionalization.

PREDICTING OUTCOMES TO INSTITUTIONALIZATION

There are two classes of predictors: personal and environmental characteristics (see Carp, 1987). Personal characteristics refer to attributes that vary among individuals that either reduce or increase the capacity to cope with the stressful situation whereas environmental characteristics refer to aspects of the ecology that diminish or heighten the stressfulness of the situation.

Personal characteristics as predictors

Intact and nonintact respondents did not differ on age, for example, but they did differ in living arrangements prior to admission. Of the 85 respondents, 17 had lived in nursing homes prior to admission, the other 65 were living with others or alone in noninstitutional settings. Of the 17 admitted from nursing homes, 13 (77%) were in the nonintact group as opposed to only four (23%) in the intact group. Relocation from a nursing home to a home for the aged is obviously associated with more negative outcome than relocation into the home from independent community living. Yet, those admitted from nursing homes were similar to those admitted from the community on most of our measures. Neither, for example, did they differ on functional adequacy nor with the severity or number of events leading to the decision to seek institutional care. It is also possible that their deterioration partially resulted from the earlier relocation. They had to adapt to the stress of two relocations in a rather brief time interval. This double relocation may explain the few differences that were found between those elderly who lived transitionally in a nursing home and those who did not. The elderly admitted from the nursing homes tended to be more passive, to use denial more, and to have a lowered sense of futurity, characteristics that in many ways reflect an institutional profile. Their lower anxiety and greater comfort in relating to the interviewers may have related to their assurance of care while in the nursing home and to their being further along in their resolution of the issues of loss and abandonment than the respondents who were admitted directly from the community.

As implied, we determined the psychological predictors of morbidity and mortality, by using baseline measures, assessments made while on the waiting list. Measures were sorted out into nine dimensions that have either been explicitly discussed as, or inferred to be, predictions of outcome to stress: functional capacities, affects, hope, the self-system, personality traits, reminiscence, coping with the impending event, interpersonal relations, and accumulated stress. We then contrasted the two outcome groups (the intact survivors and the nonintact on these measures) and, simultaneously, we contrasted the corresponding two outcome groups for the two control samples. Thus any measure that differentiated, or predicted, for the sample that underwent the stress of institutionalization and also predicted for the sample not undergoing this stress could not be a predictor of vulnerability to the stress of institutionalization but, rather, would be a characteristic that is associated with survival. Stated another way, only if a measure predicted for the sample undergoing stress could the attribute being measured be considered a sensitizer to the stress of institutionalization and not associated with intact survival per se. Measures in several dimensions were associated with intact survival; function capacities, affect, hope, self-system, coping, and interpersonal relations. Only one dimension, and then only one type of measure within the dimension, was a sensitizer to the stress of institutionalization; passivity among the personality traits. Passivity, that is, was associated with morbidity and mortality among those entering the homes but not with morbidity and mortality for those in stable environments.

A dimension that was not relevant for control samples was coping with the impending event of institutionalization. When residents on the waiting list were assessed, however, for how they were mastering the impending event of institutionalization, if was found that those who transformed the situation so as to make the move totally voluntary and also to perceive their relocation environment as ideal were those most likely to survive intact through one year following admission. This kind of magical mastery, as well as aggressiveness and hopefulness (but not the absence of clinical depression), were found to enhance adaptation in the three additional relocation situations.

Environmental predictors

The most obvious environmental dimension is the quality of the relocation environmental. Building on Moos' (1974) seminal work on assessing environments, ten psychosocial scales were developed; an eleventh scale was added that measured the capacity of the environment to provide for the physical care of elderly residents. Dimensions were assessed by a skilled judge who spent half a day in each facility and made, in all, 216 ratings. The dimensions were:

1. Achievement fostering: the extent to which the environment provides opportunities for and encourages residents to achieve meaningful tasks or engage in goal-directed activities, and rewards them for doing so.
2. Individuation: the extent to which residents of the environment are perceived and treated as individuals in being allowed and encouraged to express individuality.
3. Dependency fostering: the extent to which residents are provided for, 'coddled,' and protected in ways that discourage or prevent the development of self-sufficiency and autonomy.
4. Warmth: the warmth and humanity of the staff in its attitudes toward or relation with residents. Also, the extent to which these same qualities are expressed in the residents' attitudes toward and relations with each other.
5. Affiliation fostering: the extent to which social interaction occurs in, and is encouraged by, the environment.
6. Recognition: the extent to which the environment recognizes, responds to, and rewards both the activities and the accomplishments of residents.
7. Stimulation: the extent to which the environment provides a variety of sights, sounds, and activity, and other stimuli to perceive and interact with.

8. Physical attractiveness: the attractiveness or aesthetic appeal of the physical plant, including interior, exterior, and immediate surroundings.
9. Cue richness: the extent to which the environment functions to differentiate or provide cues for perceptual orientation, such as signs, distinctive colors, odors, textures, sounds, varied furnishings, clutter, and so on.
10. Tolerance for deviancy: the extent to which the staff tolerate 'deviant' behaviors on the part of residents, such as aggression, drinking, wandering, complaining, and incontinence.
11. Health care adequacy: the extent to which the environment is equipped and staffed to provide health care, in the form of physical examinations, physical therapy, nursing, doctor's care, and drugs, and handle medical emergencies.

More recently Moos and his colleagues (see, for example, Lemke and Moos, 1986) have generated eight dimensions to assess residential settings for elderly adults that are comparable to our 11 dimensions. Moos and Lemke found that nonprofit facilities tended to score higher on the eight dimensions affirming findings by others (see, for example, Greene and Monahan, 1981 and Kosberg and Tobin, 1972).

Psychosocial quality, as noted earlier, is not the only environmental variable that can be explored as a predictor of outcomes to institutionalization. Also considered were person−environment fit and environmental discrepancy. Person−environment fit refers to the congruence between characteristic of individuals and adaptive demands of situations. The greater the fit between coping styles and environmental adaptive demands, the less stressful the situation. Similarly, the greater the similarity in pre- and post-relocation environments, the less the environmental discrepancy and, therefore, also the less stressful the situation. The assumption is that independent of psychosocial quality, and even when the relocation is welcomed and perceived as non-threatening, the extent of social dislocation will cause a kind of culture shock that was discussed earlier when focusing on the first month syndrome.

The studies of environmental predictors (the third study, the relocation of the institutionalized elite and particularly the fourth study, the *en masse* relocation, reported in *The Experience of Old Age*) revealed that those most physically impaired are likely to have their death hastened independent of psychosocial quality. Even when environments are of better quality, the initial impact of institutionalization and relocation in general, as well as all stressors, may cause a downward irreversible course leading to a hastened death. When investigated further, support was not found for Lawton's (1977) docility hypothesis in which it is posited that more impaired persons are more affected by their environments than the less impaired.

It was found that environmental factors were stronger predictors of adverse outcomes than personal characteristics. Linn, Surel and Linn (1977) also found that differential outcomes were associated with nursing care quality. Simply stated negative environmental conditions could not be compensated for by aggressiveness and magical coping. Additionally, person−environment fit was found to have a direct role in causing adverse effects (Turner, Tobin and Lieberman, 1972). Among others (Carp, 1966; Gubrium, 1975; Kiyak, 1978; and Nierke *et al.*, 1981), Kahana and her associates (Kahana, Liang and Felton, 1980) have provided further evidence for this association. Yet in our work, as well as in Kahana's, it appears that the critical personal characteristics are aggressiveness and magical coping. Apparently, facilities that permit aggressiveness and magical coping are particularly helpful for institutional adaptation. Can the same be said for environmental discrepancy? Apparently not. All factors, in addition to the degree that aggressiveness and magical coping are permitted, were important dimensions of discrepancy that predicted adaptation.

ISSUES IN INSTITUTIONAL CARE

A first issue relates to how to assure a high level of psychosocial quality of the institutional environment. Our dimensions tapped the personalizing of the environment and individualizing of care. Yet to do so can be costly and, also, conflict with organizational efficiency. Most monies are spent and are reimbursed for the hotel and hospital functions and not for the home functions of institutional care. Here, however, the focus is not on the many organizational issues but, rather, on psychosocial issues. Yet, it is obvious that when resources are committed to enhancing resident care, and thereby psychosocial quality, positive adaptation can be increased. For many residents there can be increased morale (Morris, 1975; Kahana, Kahana and Young, 1987; and Spassof *et al.*, 1978). As noted by Kahana (1987): 'Improved nutrition and medical care, availability of activities and opportunities to be exposed to social interaction as well as cognitive stimulation have been cited as enhancing lives of institutionalized aged' (p. 356).

Facilitating institutional adjustment: restoration of the self

Whose responsibility is it to mobilize aggressiveness, enhance magical coping, and instill hopefulness before admission? When admission occurs quickly, as when the resident arrives directly from the hospital, it may not be possible for staff of the facility to work directly with the resident before admission. If, in turn, there is any waiting period before admission, staff must prepare residents-to-be for the move. This issue is inseparable from how elderly patients are discharged from hospitals, particularly now when they are being discharged 'quicker and sicker'.

After admission, the first month syndrome of disorientation, depression or other symptoms of extreme distress can be expected. Thus it is essential that the functional status of the new resident be considered temporary with the assumption that the initial gross psychopathology will diminish as residents returns to pre-admission levels of intactness. Only, however, if this assumption is made will new residents be

helped to recover from the initial shock of the social dislocation. Indeed the quality of an institution can be determined by the level of acknowledgement and awareness of the initial first month syndrome. Facilities in which staff say 'everybody does fine when they first come in' are likely to be precisely those facilities associated with greater deterioration following the relocation. Fortunately, there are ways to assist the transition. A service plan can be developed at admission in which the attempt is to anticipate the course of adjustment and to minimize distress as much as possible. Over the years, we became rather creative at Drexel Home for the Aged. One example was providing the newly admitted paranoid resident with a room-mate who was a 'paranee', someone whose sense of self was dependent upon criticisms of others. This approach, of course, incorporates the principle of environmental discrepancies in institutional adaptation.

As discussed previously, even in the best of facilities, there are irreducible effects in becoming a resident in a total institution. Whereas at a latent level the inner experience will be that of being more physically vulnerable and closer to death, these feelings can be contained. Most residents of facilities of high psychosocial quality are able to preserve their identity, their sense of self-sameness, albeit with less hopefulness, with less of an expectation that they can make a fulfilling future for themselves, and also with a greater preoccupation with bodily concerns. Unavoidable, even with only a modicum of cognitive intactness, is the awareness that to live in a long-term care facility is to live with other old impaired persons with whom you are grouped together in daily routines. Only through individualizing care can these propensities be counteracted. And it is through the hands-on staff that individualizing of care can occur.

Enhancing life in the institution: preservation of the self

An institutional orientation to enhancing residents' functioning and their preservation of self must penetrate interactions between residents and staff at all levels. Such penetrations occur through staff's understanding of residents' behavior, but there are many barriers that must be overcome if there is to be accurate appraisals of behaviors, particularly of demented residents. Now as many as three-fourths of the residents may have mental impairments (Larsen, Llo and Williams, 1986). Particularly among these residents, staff find it difficult to understand how seemingly pathological processes are actually functional. Aggressiveness, even nastiness and paranoid behaviors, are facilitatory for adaptation to stress. Staff must learn to understand, tolerate and even nurture verbally abusive aggressive and paranoid behaviors directed at them by residents. Obviously this is a difficult task, a task too difficult for some staff. It is also a task that is not assumed by staff in many facilities where even the most minor of deviations from ideal compliance and gratefulness are not tolerated.

Yet lower level staff cannot begin to understand the meanings of these seemingly pathological behaviors unless professionals do. Professionals, however,

can too easily interpret facilitatory mechanisms as psychopathological if they use models developed for younger persons. Mental health professionals are taught that good coping necessitates realistic appraisal of personal capacities and that abusive behavior toward others reflects bad object relations. Although such generalizations may generally be correct, they may be completely wrong when applied to the very old, particularly when under duress. Professionals must teach staff that bizarre behaviors often have meanings related to the striving for preservation of self. Once this principle is understood it becomes increasingly possible to see continuity between bizarre behavior and premorbid personality traits. In turn, as the bizarre behaviors become intelligible, staff can tolerate, or even encourage, seemingly aberrant behaviors that help the patient be him/herself.

It is not easy for staff to be objective. They have good reasons for feeling angry, helpless and demoralized, frustrated and even betrayed (Dobrof, 1983). Feelings of anger toward residents are reflected in comments such as 'How can he say these things to me? After all I have done for him?' Anger toward the family may be justified in a comment such as 'Don't they even care about that old man? He probably just sits there like that because they never visit him.' Thoughts about the other staff members and supervisors include 'They leave all the dirty work for me. Nobody ever shows any appreciation around here.' Feelings of helplessness and demoralization are reflected in 'It doesn't seem to matter what we do, they never get any better.' Should not the aide feel frustrated when saying to herself 'I must have explained that to her six times already.' The terrible feeling of betrayal is captured by the comment 'After everything I have done for her, she doesn't even know who I am.' There is obviously no easy way to reduce these painful feelings. It is necessary, however, to provide to the hands-on staff a sense of efficacy and potency.

Burnside (1981), a nurse with experience in long-term settings, in reviewing techniques for managing patients with cognitive impairments, divided them into three categories: techniques for the helper, for memory development, and for manipulation of the environment. Her 'bedside' helper techniques include: reinforce reality, use touch, support denial if it is therapeutic, approach slowly, do not argue, do not take client's behavior personally, do not alter long-standing personality patterns, use both short and frequent contacts, reduce client's need to employ functions which have been lost, identify feelings and help clients to express them, assess physical and psychological liabilities early, preserve functions, gain knowledge of premorbid personality characteristics, talk with the patient and not about him or her, gain the attention of the patient, use affection and praise, enhance self-expression, do not push and give orders, become aware of your tone of voice and approach and how the client will respond and react, do not take problems home, and eliminate or reduce unexpected situations that cause duress.

Reducing duress is particularly important. Situations that provoke agitation, including most new situations, must be recognized. Obviously when the resident cannot communicate the source of the agitation, disorganized and aberrant

behavior is likely to escalate. Staff education in communication is indeed very helpful. Can staff in turn, become more comfortable, more competent and feel more efficacious in working with demented patients? Certainly our observations at Drexel Home were that it is possible to enhance staff's functioning and feelings but only by support and reassurance of the more prestigious professional staff. The more staff are expected to put out, the more nourishment staff must be provided with.

Regarding Burnside's concept for memory development, she has provided a list that is appropriate for reality orientation groups, as well as recommendations for interaction outside of groups. For example, she suggests providing sufficient cues to aid memory and orientation (e.g. props to indicate change of seasons), consistent cues that encourage recognition instead of recall, and multiple cues; avoiding pressure to perform; being sure to communicate what is expected to be remembered; and being sure that familiar objects that reaffirm the continuity are rather obvious such as using a night light; bright colors and decoration, color coded doors, keeping the same staff working with individuals, providing a safe environment, that is not too boring but not over-stimulating, a nonthreatening environment, providing clocks and calendars, and making special efforts to provide a milieu that reduces sundowners syndrome.

In vogue now are behavioral interventions. What is meant by behavioral approaches to intervention? Simply stated, interaction between the resident and the environment is first analyzed for factors that encourage dysfunctional behavior; then, new kinds of interactions are substituted that encourage restoration of activities of daily living (ADL) (see, for example, Pinkston *et al.*, 1982). Different terminology, however, is used by behaviorists: environmental contingencies that reinforce dysfunctional behavior are analyzed; new contingencies introduced; and targeted behavior charted for extinction of dysfunctional aspects and for increased frequence of functional aspects. Regardless of language, successful restoration of functioning has been demonstrated for a diversity of deficits including an inability to use eating utensils by use of one-to-one skill training at every meal; daytime urinary incontinence for wheelchair-bound residents by use of a bell and then toileting at a fixed two hour or so interval; and incoherent speech by constant positive reinforcement of intelligible speech and negative reinforcement (ignoring) unintelligible speech.

If the successes are so impressive, why have behavorial approaches not been embraced with enthusiasm? Too often a graduate student in psychology applies the intervention devoting a great deal of time to an individual resident while providing relief for overburdened staff who invariably are delighted to have the added, and optimistic, assistance. Unfortunately, when the student leaves, the intervention ceases. Also, the most successful interventions have occurred in facilities of the poorest quality where, indeed, anything works to restore function behavior. Witness Langer and Rodin's (1976) work on enhancing feelings of control. Feelings of more control may have persisted (Rodin and Langer, 1977) because of the paucity of the psychosocial environment; giving residents even simple choices can indeed be a potent force.

It may not, however, be appropriate to discuss the work on control within the context of behavioral interventions. Whenever stress is overwhelming, as it is likely to be in institutionalization, feelings of helplessness and lack of control are generated which inhibit appropriate mobilization, such as the mobilization reflected in aggressiveness and magical mastery. Helplessness is clearly a potent force leading to adverse consequences (Seligman, 1975). The effort to reduce helplessness through enhancing control is certainly one way to mobilize institutionalized elderly persons. Thus, Langer and Rodin's work on perceived control is important, as well as the work of Schulz (1976) and Schulz and Hanusa (1978). Yet even under the best of circumstances as, for example, in facilities of high quality and with excellent training of staff in interventions, improvements rarely extend beyond the period of intervention. That is, and again in the appropriate terminology, unless prosthetic environments are developed to reinforce desired behaviors, reestablished functioning will decay and previously extinguished behaviors return (see, for example, Lindsley, 1964).

Albeit the exaggerated optimism regarding behaviorial approaches, some important lessons have been learned. The presence of eager graduate students is indeed immensely valuable for improving morale and performance of residents. This was certainly so on the unit where the doctoral student applied a behavioral approach to helping residents to empty their bladders on a fixed schedule. During the period he was on the unit, morale was noticeably better. Staff like the affable student who was always courteous and respectful and, also, was most willing to lend a hand when called upon to help lift a resident or to carry a tray. In turn, only through their assistance to him, was he able to show that a bell that rang on a fixed schedule followed by the staff assisting the resident to urinate successfully kept residents dry. When he left, however, the staff felt an emptiness and soon reverted to letting residents become incontinent during the day. Only by assigning a staff member to empty residents' bladders when the bell rang would it have been possible to maintain this program.

A most important lesson from behaviorial interventions is that unless appropriate levels of reinforcement are maintained, both outside of the minutes or even hours in a formal program, and beyond a fixed period of weeks and even months, improvements do not stay. But probably the most important lesson is that unless staff members are taught why what they are doing is particularly helpful to the resident, there is no generalization. When teaching staff the reason for interventions, they are being provided not only with the prerequisite knowledge for their actions but they are also receiving support, the necessary nourishment, for the arduous tasks of caring. Unless nourished, burnout quickly occurs. One kind of knowledge that too frequently is not the focus of behaviorists' analysis is that the identification of dysfunctional behavior that necessitates change must be based on the purpose of the behavior for the individual. To reiterate, a behavior that appears grossly dysfunctional, and therefore a most appropriate behavior to change, may indeed be a behavior that is most needed by the resident because it is most critical for the preservation of self.

Put another way, behaviorist interventions must not be targeted on behaviors that preserve the self but, rather, on behaviors that diminish the self. For reinforcement to be effective, procedures must be incorporated into the service plan and be part of every day routine. Implementation must be by staff who, whether as members of nursing, occupational therapy or social service departments, assure the creation of a prosthetic environment for each resident. Using these principles, a behaviorally oriented psychogeriatric program was developed by Mallya and Fitz (1987), Project Adapt, that employed therapeutic assistants who provided hands-on behaviorial interventions. The therapeutic assistants implemented an individualized treatment plan developed by an interdisciplinary team most of whom had extensive experience working with mentally ill elderly persons. In common with behaviorial approaches, group interventions must also be augmented by a continuous prosthetic environment. Groups can be particularly helpful. Lesser *et al.* (1981) reported that a reminiscence group for psychotic impatients of a mental hospital facilitated structured thinking. Other groups, particularly reality orientation groups, have been reported to be helpful. Yet none of these group programs for elderly residents with cognitive impairments have been demonstrated to be helpful beyond their duration. Unless programs are continuous and, also, unless restored residual functioning is reinforced outside of group programs improvements are not maintained.

Beyond these kinds of programs, as well as periodic staffing of residents that includes modifying service plans that encompass implementation by aides, additional innovations can be initiated (Hegeman and Tobin, 1987). A Wander-Proof Lounge, for example, was developed at the Long Beach Memorial Home in Long Island, New York, for wanderers who spent two hours per day in the lounge participating in structured programs and where they could roam freely and, also, provide a needed respite for floor staff. The lounge becomes a stable environment in which the wanderers can freely explore many artifacts of interest. Purposeful behavior is encouraged, and even aggressive purposeful behavior and, additionally, participants are urged to reminisce and form coherent images and expressions of the past, mechanisms discussed earlier as adaptive components of the unique psychology of the very old. When participants return to their floor, the staff reports less random wandering and better sleeping at night.

Changes, however, will be resisted, especially the kinds of reorganization necessary to meet the needs of mentally impaired elderly residents (Edelson and Lyons, 1985). The obvious challenge to professionals is to facilitate change. The paradox is that facilities must be assisted in changing so that they become settings where identities are not changed. Fortunately, mental health professionals are precisely those professionals who know only too well how hard it is to reduce resistance to change but, also, at the same time, know how to reduce the resistance.

Family members must become allies in the attempt to modify institutional life so that the self is preserved. A project was developed at the Jewish Home and Hospital for the Aged in New York to enhance communication between families and residents, particularly for family members of confused residents. Initially for families it has been expanded to staff. Project CONNECT (Communication Need Not Ever Stop) included a series of lectures and small discussion groups (Marchico-Greenfield, 1986). In addition to Burnside's suggestions, participants were encouraged to be natural; share ideas, thoughts, and problems; encourage verbalizing as much and as often as possible; speak more slowly, more loudly, more vividly, more concretely, more descriptively and more clearly; choose topics that are more interesting, familiar, important, and are preferred; stick to a topic for a while and avoid shifting too much; keep talking whenever appropriate; accept any form of communication; use gestures and accept them; give hints to facilitate the message; allow extra time for responding; accept answers which are close approximation; elicit and prompt answers without forcing them; do not begin visits with crucial messages but rather allow for warmup; allow for turn-taking during the conversations if possible; do not over-correct; acknowledge breakdowns in communication; when all else fails, provide things to talk about; be sensitive to changes in attitude and energy; if misunderstood, revise what you said and repeat what you said; if unsure, revise what you have heard and seek clarification; summarize your conversations frequently; if one approach is not working be creative and try another; do not, if possible, speak for the resident; include the resident in all discussion; give the resident choices and facilitate all decisions; be a good listener; and allow for reminiscing. These techniques, prepared for families, are precisely those that must be encouraged among staff.

What about the feelings of family members? By the time a decision is made to institutionalize an elderly member, the family often feels relieved but not without feeling of guilt and inadequacy and, moreover with great rage, i.e. rage at oneself for being inadequate and rage toward the elderly person for inducing feelings of inadequacy. Too often workers focus on the family's feelings of guilt, rather than on the accompanying feelings of inadequacy and rage, as well as sense of relief, after institutionalization. Given this mixture of painful feelings, it is expected the reassurances of competent care by staff would be welcomed by families; and also welcomed would be subtle, and not so subtle, messages that it is not necessary to visit so much. It is indeed painful to visit a mother who is quickly deteriorating and may not recognize you. Visits by family members, however, are particularly important because of the effects of becoming institutionalized when old.

When an elderly person is institutionalized in a long-term setting, the potentially deselfing process can be attenuated, in part, by interaction with family members. One common example is the importance of family visits to the seemingly intractably confused elderly resident of an institution. The elderly person may seem to be totally unaware of the family visitor at the time of the visit. Shortly after the visit, however, the elderly resident may become quite agitated, reflecting an awareness at some level of the visit; often organized reminiscence replaces psychotic like ramblings. Despite the importance to the resident, the visit can be quite upsetting to the family visitor and serve only to heighten the previously discussed feeling of guilt, impotence and rage. Unless someone explains to the family the specific meaningfulness of the visit, the family may reduce their visiting which can be quite harmful to the elderly resident. We developed guidelines for a successful visit.

For those without family, or families who are unable or unwilling to visit, a deselfing process can accelerate. Not only are these residents without the benefit of significant others who can reinforce the self but, also, staff are less likely to see the resident as a real person. For these family-less residents we, at Drexel Home for the Aged, used volunteers who committed themselves to continual visits to the same resident. Most often through careful preparation and pairing, visiting persisted over a long time period.

Constant and persistent efforts must be made to educate family and staff. Some efforts must be continual, occurring in both formal regular staff meetings or in informal supervision of staff. Other efforts will be sporadic as in family group meetings which usually are held when the resident is newly admitted. Occasionally there will be special programs, as when family groups are convened to learn how to communicate with their impaired resident. At Drexel Home a social experiment was developed where it was determined that aides could be helped in relating to families. Particularly helpful to aides was knowing how and to whom specific complaints could be referred rather than accepting the blame of family members and becoming resentful, bitter, and angry toward the family and the resident.

We, too, at Drexel Home discovered that family meetings were not sufficient to increase, and sometimes to even maintain, visiting. Thus a more ambitious structural change was implemented that consisted of assigning a one half-time BA-level worker to each unit of 40 or so residents. Of critical importance, however, was the reorientation of staff to the families of residents: BA-level workers were selected and trained to be perceived by family members as all-loving and all-giving caregivers to the elderly resident and, in turn, administrative staff were encouraged to let themselves be targets for hostile expressions by family members regarding the dereliction of the home in caring for their relatives.

Drexel Home, in common with the best of homes, had always encouraged family visiting. As with many homes, however, as the residential population deteriorated, becoming more impaired mentally, it became apparent that although family members visited the home, there was a tendency for lessened visiting of family members. Attempts to maintain visiting patterns through family groups, such as family members of new residents or Friends of Drexel Home (which was formed to raise money for special projects), did keep families involved in the home. Yet, as Safford (1980) found, members of more confused residents participated in these groups but did not necessarily visit either the floor of their resident family members or the resident her/himself. In withdrawing from interaction with deteriorating residents, some family members simply deny that their visiting has lessened while others become terribly upset with themselves and their inability to tolerate the deterioration, and still others vociferously blame the home for causing the deterioration. Ubiquitous, as always, among all families was the anger toward themselves and toward the resident that is displaced onto the home.

The extreme pain in passively watching the deterioration of a loved one is quite evident. As noted earlier, families would have welcomed relief from their psychological pain through being encouraged not to visit. Occasionally, of course, family members were not encouraged to visit if it was too upsetting to them or to the resident. Certainly, however, a general discouragement of family visiting would have provided great relief to families but would have been dysfunctional for residents in reducing the maintenance of their identities and diminishing the perception of their uniqueness by staff. Thus our task was to develop an approach to families that would encourage their presence on residents' floors and, also, encourage face-to-face contact with even the most intractably confused family member.

Another kind of observation was important to our developing a structural approach. That is, those family members who continued to visit a slowly deteriorating resident until the time of death were less likely to have a protracted mourning process following the death of the resident. These family members, however, were not without feelings of inadequacy and rage during stages of deterioration. Thus, our approach would have to allow for displaced rage that we know was more beneficial to family members than rage turned inward causing heightened depression and, certainly better than rage expressed toward the resident.

Fortunately, the home had a long history of acceptance of anger expressed by both residents and family members. Aggressiveness by residents, expressed by staff in such terms as 'complaining' and 'griping', and sometimes as 'bitchiness', was perceived as facilitating adaptation and, when absent, this was cause for alarm. Unless complaining was tolerated, or even encouraged, staff would become complacent and administrative needs would outweigh residents' needs.

From another perspective, we were aware that an institutional relationship, or transference, is developed by families that includes both positive and negative projections. The home, that is, becomes both the life-sustaining all-giving other and, also, the life-impeding other that is the cause of the present, as well as further, deterioration in their family member. To direct this institutional transference (for discussion of institutional transference, see Gendel and Reiser, 1981; Safirstein, 1967; Van Eck, 1972; and Wilmer, 1962) into usefulness for the resident, the structured approach to the institutional psychosocial environment was developed in which, as noted earlier, a split transference occurred wherein a BA-level unit social worker became the all-giving, all-loving other, and administrative personnel the life-impeding others (for further details, see Tobin, 1987).

A RESEARCH AGENDA

A research agenda that follows from the previous discussion should include development of programs and their systematic evaluation in institutions and, also, knowledge-building that permits generalizing beyond institutionalization, specifically related to factors that facilitate adaptation to stress and in normative aging.

Programs in institution

Practice wisdom too often goes unheeded by researchers. Indeed, the usefulness of aggression for institutional adaptation was first taught to me by Grunes before collaborative studies with Lieberman. Also, before our finding (Revere and Tobin, 1980–81) that the very old make their reconstructions vivid in comparison to those in their middle years, Grunes had developed an orientation to psychotherapy with the elderly based on recapturing the past (see, for example, Grunes, 1982). In turn, Goldfarb (1959), a long time psychiatric consultant to a home for the aged, had discussed the use of 'over inflated' beliefs in mastery as essential to his psychotherapy with the elderly before we discovered the benefit of magical coping for intact survivorship following institutionalization. Similarly, the use of the split transference, the wanderers' lounge, ethics rounds and many other programs have emerged from practice wisdom rather than from the findings of studies. The task now is to refine, replicate, and evaluate these innovations. To do so, however, it is necessary that facilities adopt an experimenting approach to care for their elderly residents and, additionally, that researchers sufficiently appreciate the problems in applied research so as not to interfere with, or be dysfunctional for, the necessary administrative tasks inherent to managing a complex human service organization. Our approach at Drexel Home for the Aged was to use research as program. Every research initiative, whether basic or applied, had to enhance the home's service to its residents.

Generalizing beyond institutionalization

Are the personal characteristics found to be facilitatory for adaptation to institutionalization among the elderly, facilitatory under other stressful conditions? Observations, largely anecdotal in nature, exist regarding how passivity and the lack of magical coping is detrimental to older persons in, for example, hospitals or in encounters with physicians. Still needed are systematic studies to determine the usefulness of aggressiveness and magical coping for elderly persons when they are in a diversity of stressful situations.

Recall that we found that personal characteristics which reduced vulnerability to the stress of institutionalization were not necessarily functional for elderly persons who were not in stressful situations. Aggressiveness before admission, for example, reduced vulnerability to institutionalization as evidenced by intact survivorship. Yet, aggressiveness was not associated with greater intact survivorship in the community control sample. Thus, attributes that facilitate adaptation to stress among elderly persons may not be the same attributes that facilitate adaptation when not under stress. When not under stress, there is less need to mobilize inner resources and aggressiveness. Indeed aggressiveness, especially when expressed in abusive ways towards others, may only cause an alienation of those providing social supports.

Some attributes, in turn, may be helpful to adaptation in both circumstances, when under stress and when not under stress. Sherman (1987) found, for example, that group reminiscing by noninstitutionalized elderly persons enhanced their support of one another and, moreover, that focusing on feelings when reminiscing enlivened reminiscence and their integration. Although we did not find that our reminiscence variables were associated with outcomes, it is sensible to believe that had we enhanced the use of reminiscence by using Sherman's approach, institutional adaptation would have been facilitated.

The awareness of the use of reminiscence by elderly people has, apparently, not gone unnoticed by those interested in psychological processes used by younger persons. Although the mutuality of reminiscence, and particularly regarding how the reconstruction of the past changes to serve adaptational needs, is not new (see, for example, James, 1890). The renewed attention to the personal narrative is inseparable from an awareness, and the communication of the awareness, that the remembered past serves some critical functions in aging. What is needed, therefore, is a research agenda in which there is an interaction between practice wisdom and systematic studies. Practice wisdom can provide hypotheses to guide studies and their interpretation, and studies can provide hunches for practitioners. In turn, practice wisdom about, and findings from studies of, effects throughout the process of becoming institutionalized when old and the predictors of differential outcomes, can lead to hypotheses regarding adaptation to stress in general by elderly persons and adaptation also when not under stress. Lastly, these kinds of knowledge can lead to an understanding of adaptational processes among persons of all ages.

REFERENCES

Bennett, R. and Nahemow, L. (1965). Institutional totality and criteria of social adjustment in residences for the aged. *Journal of Social Issues*, **21**, 44–78.

Borup, J.H. (1983). Relocation mortality research: assessment, reply, and the need to refocus on the issues. *The Gerontologist*, **23**, 235–42.

Brody, E.M. (1977). *Long Term Care of Older People*, Human Science Press, New York.

Brody, E.M. (1985). Parent care as a normative stress. *The Gerontologist*, **25**, 19–29.

Burnside, I.M. (1981). *Nursing and the Aged*, McGraw-Hill, New York.

Carp, F.M. (1966). *A Future for the Aged: The Residents of Victoria Plaza*. University of Texas Press, Austin, Texas.

Carp, F.M. (1987). Environment and aging. In D. Stokols and I. Altman (eds.) *Handbook of Environmental Psychology*, Wiley & Sons, New York, pp. 329–360.

Cath, S.H. (1972). The institutionalization of a parent: A nadir of life. *Journal of Geriatric Psychiatry*, **5**, 25–46.

Coffman, T.L. (1983). Toward an understanding of geriatric relocation. *The Gerontologist*, **23**, 453–9.

Dobrof, R. (1983). *Training Workshops on Caring for the Mentally Impaired Elderly*, the Brookdale Center on Aging of Hunter College, New York.

Edelson, J.S. and Lyons, W. (1985). *Institutional Care of the Mentally Impaired Elderly*, Van Nostrand Reinhold, New York.

Gendel, M.H. and Reiser, D.E. (1981). Institutional countertransference. *American Journal of Psychiatry*, **138**, 508–11.

Goffman, E. (1961). *Assylums*, Aldine Publishing company, Chicago.

Goldfarb, A.I. (1959). Minor Maladjustment in the Aged. In S. Arieti (ed.) *American Handbook of Psychiatry*, Basic Books, New York.

Greene, V.L., and Monahan, D.J. (1981). Structural and operational factors affecting quality of patient care in nursing homes. *Public Policy*, **29**, 399–415.

Grunes, J.M. (1982). Reminiscence, regression and empathy—A psychotherapeutic approach to the impaired elderly. In S.I. Greenspan and G.H. Pollock (eds.) *The Course of Life* NIMH, Washington, D.C.

Gubrium, J.F. (1975). *Living and Dying at Murray Manor*, St. Martin's Press, New York.

Hegeman, C. and Tobin, S.S. (1988). Enhancing the autonomy of mentally impaired nursing home residents. *The Gerontologist*, Supplementary Issue, **28**, 71–5.

Horowitz, M.J. and Schulz, R. (1983). The relocation controversy. *The Gerontologist*, **23**, 229–34.

James, W. (1890). *)Principles of Psychology*, Henry Holt, New York.

Kahana, E. (1987). Institutionalization. In G.L. Maddox (ed.) *Encyclopedia of Aging*, Springer, New York.

Kahana, E.F., Kahana, B. and Young, R. (1987). Strategies of coping and postinstitutional outcomes. *Research on Aging*, **9**, 182–99.

Kahana, E., Liang, J. and Felton, B.J. (1980). Alternative Models of Person–Environment Fit: Prediction of Morale in Three Homes for the Aged. *Journal of Gerontology*, **35**, 584–95.

Kiyak, H.A. (1978). A multidimensional perspective on privacy preference of institutionalized elderly. In W.E. Rogers and W.H. Ibels (eds.) *New Directions in Environmental Design Research*. Proceedings of the Environmental Design Research Association, University of Arizona, Tuscon, Arizona.

Kosberg, J.I. and Tobin, S.S. (1972). Variability among nursing homes. *The Gerontologist*, **12**, 214–19.

Kuypers, J. (1969). Elderly persons en route to institution: a study of Changing Perceptions of Self and Interpersonal Relations. Unpublished doctoral dissertation, University of Chicago.

Langer, E. and Rodin, J. (1976). The effects of choice and enhanced personal responsibility for the aged: A field experiment in an institutional setting. *Journal of Personality and Social Psychology*, **34**, 191–8.

Larsen, E.B., Lo. B. and Williams, N.E. (1986). Evolution and care of elderly patients with dementia. *Journal of General Internal Medicine*, **1**, 116–26.

Lawton, M.P. (1977). The impact of the environment on aging and behavior. In J.E. Birren and W.K. Schaie (eds.) *Handbook of the Psychology of Aging*. Van Nostrand Reinhold, New York.

162   *Aging, Stress and Health*

Lazarus, R.S. (1966). *Psychological Stress and the Coping Process*, McGraw-Hill, New York.

Lemke, S. and Moos, R.H. (1986). Quality of residential settings for elderly adults. *Journal of Gerontology*, **41**, 268–76.

Lemke, S. and Moos, R. (1987). Measuring the social climate congregate residence for older people: Sheltered Care Environment Scale. *Psychology and Aging*, **2**, 20–9.

Lesser, Jary, M.D., Lazarus, L.W., Frankel, R. and Hauasy, S. (1981). Reminiscence group therapy with psychotic geriatric inpatients. *The Gerontologist*, **21** (3), 291–6.

Lieberman, M.A., Prock, V. and Tobin, S.S. (1968). Psychological effects of institutionalization. *Journal of Gerontology*, **23**, 343–53.

Lieberman, M.A. and Tobin, S.S. (1983). *The Experience of Old Age: Stress, Coping, and Survival*, Basic Books, New York.

Lindsley, O.R. (1964). Geriatric behavioral prosthetics. In R. Kastenbaum (ed.) *New Thoughts on Old Age*, Springer, New York.

Linn, M.W., Gurel, L. and Linn, B.S. (1977). Patient outcome as a measure of quality of nursing home care. *American Journal of Public Health*, **67**, 337–44.

Mallya, A. and Fitz, D. (1987). A Psychogeriatric Rehabilitation Program in Long Term Care Facilities.

Marchico-Greenfield (1986). C-O-N-N-E-C-T (Communication Need Not Ever Cease Totally): A Communication Enrichment Project for Families at the Jewish Home and Hospital for Aged. Unpublished paper.

Moos, R. (1974). *Evaluating Treatment Environments*, John Wiley & Sons, New York.

Morris, J.N. (1975). Changes in morale experienced by elderly institutional applicants along the institutional path. *The Gerontologist*, **15**, 345–9.

Nierke, M.F., Hulicka, I.M., Whitbourne, S.K., Morgaut, J.B., Cohen, S.H., Turner, R.R., and Cataldo, J. (1981, November). Environmental perception differences between staff and elderly domiciliary residents. Paper presented at the 34th Annual Scientific Meeting of the Gerontological Society of America, Toronto, Canada.

Pincus, M.A. (1968). Toward a Conceptual Framework for Studying Institutional Environments in Homes for the Aged. Unpublished doctoral dissertation, University of Wisconsin.

Pinkston, E.M., Levitt, J.L., Green, G.R., Linsk, N.L. and Rzepnicki, T.L. (1982). *Effective Social Work Practice*, Jossey-Bass, San Francisco.

Revere, V. and Tobin, S.S. (1980–81). Myth and reality: The older person's relationship to his past. *International Journal of Aging and Human Development*, **12**, 15–26.

Rodin, J. and Langer, E.J. (1977). Long-term effects of a control-relevant intervention within the institutionalized aged. *Journal of Personality and Social Psychology*, **35**, 897–902.

Rosner, A. (1968). Stress and the Maintenance of Self-Concept in the Aged. Unpublished doctoral dissertation, The University of Chicago.

Safford, I. (1980). A program for families of the mentally impaired elderly. *The Gerontologist*, **20**, 656–60.

Safirstein, S. (1967). Institutional transference. *Psychiatric Quarterly*, **41**, 557–66.

Schulz, R. (1976). The effects of control and predictability on the psychological well-being of the institutionalized aged. *Journal of Personal and Social Psychology*, **33**, 563–73.

Schulz, R. and Hanusa, B.H. (1978). Long-term effects of control and predictability on enhancing interventions: findings and ethical issues. *Journal of Personality and Social Psychology*, **36**, 194–201.

Seligman, M.E.P. (1975). *Helplessness: On Depression, Development and Death*, Freeman, San Francisco.

Spassof, R.A., Krauss, A.S., Beattie, E.J., Holden, D.E.W., Lawson, J.S., Rodenburg, M. and Woodcock, G.M. (1978). Longitudinal study of elderly residents of long-study institutions. *The Gerontologist*, **18**, 281−92.

Sherman (1987). Reminiscence groups for community elderly. *The Gerontologist*, **20**, 3−11.

Smith, K.F. and Bengtson, V.L. (1979). Positive consequences of institutionalization: solidarity between elderly parents and their middle-aged children. *The Gerontologist*, **19**, 438−47.

Smith, G.C. and Nehrke, M.F. (1987 November). Staff-resident perceptual differences in long-term care settings. Paper presented at the 40th Annual Scientific Meeting of the Gerontological Society of America, Washington, DC.

Stein, S., Linn, M.W., and Stein, E.M. (1985). Patients' anticipation of stress in nursing home care. *The Gerontologist*, **25** 88−94.

Tobin, S.S. (1972). The earliest memory as data for research. In D. Kent, R.Kastenbaum and S. Sherwood (eds.) *Research, Planning and Action for the Elderly: Power and Potential of Social Science*, Behavioral Publications, New York.

Tobin, S.S. (1987). A structural approach to families. In T.H. Brubaker (ed.) *Aging, Health and Family*, Sage Publications, Newbury Park, CA, pp. 42−55.

Tobin, S.S. and Etigson, E.C. (1968). Effects of stress on the earliest memory. *Archives of General Psychiatry*, **19**, 435−44.

Tobin, S.S. and Lieberman, M.A. (1976). *Last Home for the Aged: Critical Implications of Institutionalization*, Jossey-Bass, San Francisco.

Turner, B.F., Tobin, S.S. and Lieberman, M.A. (1972). Personality traits as predictors of institutional adaptation among the aged. *Journal of Gerontology*, **27**, 61−8.

Van Eck, L.A. (1972). Transference to the hospital. *Psychotherapy and Psychosomatics*, **20**, 135−8.

Wilmer, H.A. (1962). Transference to a medical center. *California Medicine*, **96**, 173−80.

Chapter 8

Social Support, Prognosis and Adjustment to Breast Cancer

Sally W. Vernon
and Gilchrist L. Jackson

INTRODUCTION

This review focuses on the role of social support in the prognosis of and adjustment to breast cancer. Fox (1983) has suggested that if psychosocial factors exert any effect at all in the etiology or prognosis of cancer, there is a sounder theoretical basis for expecting a prognostic rather than an etiologic role. Several researchers (Bloom 1986; Levy, 1986; Weisman and Worden, 1975) have noted that repeated clinical observations suggest that some cancer patients survive longer than others despite similarity in type and location of lesion, dissemination, and treatment. Levy (1986, p. 290) succinctly states the questions as follows: 'Why do two patients with the same stage of disease at diagnosis of apparently identical tumor systems, similar treatment history, and essentially identical cellular histology have different disease outcomes?, and 'How much of this differential outcome can be accounted for by emotional and behavioral factors?' Although there is an increasing literature on the subject of psychologic, behavioral, and social factors and cancer prognosis and adjustment, the studies which have included social support are relatively few.

The term prognosis is used here to mean length of survival or time to recurrence of disease. The term adjustment encompasses a range of outcomes including physical, marital, sexual, and social functioning, psychologic adjustment and psychiatric morbidity, and self-concept, each of which has been defined and measured in a number of ways (Bloom, 1982a, 1986; Satariano and Eckert, 1983; Wright, 1960). In addition, social support has been conceptualized and measured in many ways (Bloom, 1982a and 1986; Wortman, 1984).

There are several conceptual and methodologic issues related to the study of social support that deserve mention at the onset, but they will not be discussed in detail because they have been considered elsewhere (Bloom, 1982b; Cobb and Erbe, 1978; Lindsey, Norbeck, Carrien and Perry, 1981; Thoits, 1982; Wortman, 1984; Wortman and Dunkel-Schetter, 1979, 1987), including other chapters in this book. Two general conceptual models have been proposed for considering the effects of social support on illness or disease outcomes. These models have

Aging, Stress and Health Edited by K.S. Markides and C.L. Cooper
© 1989 John Wiley & Sons Ltd

been termed the direct effects and the buffering models (Thoits, 1982). Early research studies hypothesized that social support would act as a mediating or buffering factor in the association between life stress and disease while more recent studies also have examined its direct effects. Only a few studies of social support and breast cancer have explicitly tested either model (Bloom, 1982b; Bloom and Spiegel, 1984; Funch and Marshall, 1983; Funch and Mettlin, 1982; Woods and Earp, 1978).

Another important issue in comparing the evidence from studies of social support and breast cancer is the diversity of conceptual definitions and operational measures of social support. Several articles have addressed this subject in the context of research on social support and cancer (Bloom, 1982a, 1986; Lindsey *et al.*, 1981; Satariano and Eckert, 1983; Wortman, 1984). At this point, the consensual view is that the concept is multidimensional, that at the minimum, researchers should make explicit their conceptual definitions and operational measures, and that existing measures need to be modified when used in studies of cancer patients. We reviewed all studies in which one or more components of social support, including marital status, were included or could be inferred from the variables measured.

A more fundamental issue that was not addressed in the studies reviewed here is the nature of the underlying biologic mechanisms through which social support, as well as other social and behavioral factors, brings about its effects. Several recent articles (Baltrusch and Waltz, 1985; Greer and Watson, 1985; Henry, 1982; McQueen and Siegrist, 1982; Peteet, 1986; Pettingale, 1985) have discussed what these psychobiologic pathways may be. As emphasized by Pettingale, there are many possible mechanisms which may play different roles at different stages of tumor development. We will return to the importance of considering these hypothesized mediating pathways in the discussion section of this chapter.

The first section of this chapter reviews studies which examined the relationship between social support and survival from or reccurence of breast cancer while the second section reviews studies of social support and adjustment. Those studies which included measures of stress are discussed in some detail. Most studies of the relationships between social support and prognosis and adjustment do not look at specific age groups, and many do not include women over 70 years of age. Where possible this review focuses on the evidence for these relationships by age and highlights the findings for older women.

SURVIVAL

Very few studies examined the relationship between social support and survival from breast cancer (Cassileth *et al.*, 1985a; Funch and Marshall, 1983; Goodwin, Hunt, Key and Smet, 1987; Greer, Morris and Pettingale 1979; Hislop *et al.*, 1987; Marshall and Funch, 1983; Neale, Tilley and Vernon, 1986; Pettingale,

Table 1 Characteristics of studies of social support and survival from breast cancer

Study	Study population	Age range	Time frame of the study (length of follow-up)	Sample size (response rates)	Outcome
Cassileth et al. (1985a)	Patients hospitalized at the University of Pennsylvania Cancer Center with stage 2 breast cancer or malignant melanoma	—	—	93 breast 62 melanoma (99%)	Time to recurrence categorized as ≤6 months, 7–12 months, 13–24 months, ≥25 months
Funch and Marshall (1983) Marshall and Funch (1983)	White women diagnosed with stages 1 and 2 primary breast cancer at Roswell Park Memorial Institute, NY	15–90	1958–60 (1958–79)	283 (80%)*	Length of survival between diagnosis and death followed through 1979
Goodwin et al. (1987)	Newly diagnosed epithelial cancers (all stages) in Hispanic and non-Hispanic white residents of New Mexico identified through the state tumor registry	>20	1969–82 (same)	25,706	(1) Survival (2) Stage at diagnosis (3) Type of treatment
Greer et al. (1979) Pettingale et al. (1985)	Women admitted to King's College Hospital, London, England, with breast cancer ($T_{0,1}N_{0,1}M_0$) treated by simple mastectomy	<70	— (5 years/10 years)	69	(1) Survival (2) Disease-free survival
Hislop et al. (1987)	Women referred to the A. Maxwell Evans Clinic in Vancouver, British Columbia, with a confirmed diagnosis of primary ductal breast cancer (all stages)	<55	6/80–5/81 (4 years)	133 (79%)	(1) Survival (2) Disease-free survival
Neale et al. (1986)	White married or widowed women with a histologically confirmed diagnosis of breast cancer (all stages) referred to U of TX Cancer Center, M.D. Anderson Hospital	—	1949–68 (same)	910 married 351 widowed	10-year survival

* Only verified deaths were included.

Table 2 Operational measures of social support in studies of survival from breast cancer

Study	Measures
Cassileth *et al.* (1985a)	(1) Marital status (married, never married, or separated, divorced, widowed) (2) 'Eight items were included in the social ties subscale of the questionnaire...two items requested information about marital status; the remainder, taken from Berkman and Syme's (1979) scale, were designed to obtain patients' views on the number and adequacy of their social relationships' (Cassileth *et al.*, 1985a, p. 1552)
Funch and Marshall (1983) Marshall and Funch (1983)	(1) Marital status: married or not currently married, i.e. never married, divorced, widowed, separated (2) Number of friends and relatives (3) Organizational involvement (number of religious and nonreligious meetings usually attended)
Goodwin *et al.* (1987)	Marital status: currently married versus unmarried (i.e. never married, divorced, separated, widowed)
Greer *et al.* (1979) Pettingale *et al.* (1985)	(1) Marital status: married versus unmarried (2) Rating scales measuring social adjustment with respect to marital, sexual, interpersonal relationships, and work record
Hislop *et al.* (1987)	(1) Expressive activities at home including social activities within the home such as entertaining, hobbies, and playing indoor games (2) Expressive activities away from home including social activities such as club meetings, church, outside entertainment, active sports, and visiting friends
Neale *et al.* (1986)	Marital status: married versus widowed. Divorced, separated and never married women were excluded due to small numbers.

Morris, Greer and Haybittle, 1985). Characteristics of the study populations and methodology are summarized in Table 1. The reports by Funch and Marshall (1983) and Marshall and Funch (1983) came from the same data source as did the reports by Greer *et al.* (1979) and Pettingale *et al.* (1985).

As shown in Table 1, the sample sizes in these studies ranged from 69 to 25 706 patients, and in two studies (Cassileth *et al.*, 1985a; Goodwin *et al.*, 1987) breast cancer patients were grouped with patients who had other cancer diagnoses. In three studies (Cassileth *et al.*, 1985a; Funch and Marshall, 1983; Greer *et al.*, 1979), women with advanced breast cancer were excluded from the sample. The age range of the patients in these studies varied considerably, and only one considered patterns by age in the analysis (Funch and Marshall, 1983 and Marshall and Funch, 1983). In the reports by Funch and Marshall and Marshall and Funch, three age groups were chosen to approximate the pre-, peri-, and post-menopausal stages which may reflect the importance of hormonal factors in the etiology and prognosis of breast cancer. For similar reasons, Neale *et al.* (1986) used the three age groups of <45, $45-54$, and >54, and Hislop *et al.* (1987) excluded women over 54 years.

The time interval when cases were diagnosed also varied across studies. In the reports by Funch and Marshall (1983) and Marshall and Funch (1983) cases were diagnosed between 1958 and 1960, those studied by Goodwin *et al.* (1987) between 1969 and 1982, those in the study by Hislop *et al.* (1987) between 1980 and 1981, and those in the Neale *et al.* (1986) report between 1949 and 1968. Two reports (Cassileth *et al.*, 1985a; Greer *et al.*, 1979) do not give the time frame of studies.

All studies were prospective from the time of diagnosis with length of follow-up ranging from four to 21 years (Table 1). In general, the outcomes measured were length of survival and/or disease-free survival or time to recurrence, although one study (Goodwin *et al.*, 1987) also included stage of diagnosis and type of treatment. A wide array of social and psychologic factors was measured in addition to social support. Psychosocial data were obtained either by interview (Funch and Marshall, 1983; Greer *et al.*, 1979) or by self-report (Cassileth *et al.*, 1985a; Hislop *et al.*, 1987), in most instances using standardized instruments. Goodwin *et al.* and Neale *et al.* obtained information on marital status from tumor registries or medical records. Clinical and outcome data generally were ascertained through medical record review or tumor registries.

As shown in Table 2 the most commonly used indicator of social support was marital status. Most contrasts were between the married and the unmarried, i.e. never married, separated, widowed, and divorced. The other indicator of social support frequently used in these studies was social ties or contacts, although the operational definitions differed (Table 2). Only one study measured quality of relationships (Greer *et al.*, 1979).

It is difficult to summarize succinctly the findings of these studies in part because different variables, both dependent and independent, were analyzed, and even when the same variables were considered, different operational definitions and analytic procedures were often used. Moreover, the age range differed across studies, and so failure to replicate findings could be due to actual differences in the patterns of association by age or to other differences in the composition of the samples, the time frame of the studies, or study methodology.

Four studies (Cassileth *et al.*, 1985a; Goodwin *et al.*, 1987; Greer *et al.*, 1979; Neale *et al.*, 1986) examined the association between marital status and survival or time to recurrence. Greer *et al.* reported a tendency for patients who were unmarried or who reported poor marital relationships at the time of diagnosis to have a less favorable outcome (those who were alive with no recurrence were compared to those who had died or who were alive but had a recurrence). Their primary finding, however, was a significant difference in five-year outcome depending on the patient's initial psychologic response to a diagnosis of cancer: those who were categorized as having a fighting spirit or denial were more likely to survive than those characterized by stoic acceptance or a helpless/hopeless response. None of the other social or psychologic factors examined was significantly associated with five-year outcome in bivariate analysis. In a subsequent report, Pettingale *et al.* (1985) reexamined these associations for the 10-year follow-up data. Using multivariate analysis which included age, menopausal status, clinical stage of disease, type of operation, treatment with radiotherapy, tumor size, histologic grade, and psychologic response, they found that psychologic response was still the most important factor for three outcomes: death from any cause, death from breast cancer, and first recurrence of disease. They did not report on marital status.

In a recent study by Goodwin *et al.* (1987), the effect of marital status (married versus unmarried) on stage at diagnosis, type of treatment, and survival was examined in a large group of cancer patients. Although most of the analysis grouped cancers from all sites, the authors briefly summarized the findings for a number of specific sites including breast cancer. The odds of being diagnosed at a nonlocal stage of breast cancer were elevated for unmarried as compared with married women (relative risk = 1.24, 95% confidence interval = 1.09 to 1.42) as were the odds of not receiving definitive therapy (relative risk = 1.34, 95% confidence interval = 1.02 to 1.76). The relative risk of death, however, was not elevated (relative risk = 1.03, 95% confidence interval = 0.92 to 1.16). In contrast, Neale *et al.* (1986) found an effect of marital status on 10-year survival (married survived longer than widowed) even after adjusting for the effects of age, socioeconomic status, delay, and stage of disease.

Cassileth *et al.* (1985a) found no association in bivariate analysis between any psychologic or social variables, including marital status, items on social contacts, and perceived support (see Table 2) and time to recurrence in their sample of breast cancer and melanoma patients. In subsequent analyses reported in a letter to the editor (Cassileth *et al.*, 1985b), they controlled for age, sex, occupation, and education without changing their results. None of their analyses was not done separately for breast cancer cases, however.

In another recent study, Hislop *et al.* (1987) examined the effects of a number of psychosocial and clinical factors in relation to survival and disease-free survival over a four-year period. Although they did not use the term social support, information was obtained about types of usual activities (Table 2), some of which have been used elsewhere as indicators of social support. After adjusting for clinical and other psychosocial factors, expressive activities at home (Table 2) was a statistically significant prognostic factor for both measures of survival (i.e. survival and disease-free survival) while expressive activities away from home was statistically associated only with disease-free survival. The only other psychosocial factors that were significant predictors after adjusting for both clinical and psychosocial variables were extroversion and a low level of anger for survival, and a low level of cognitive disturbance for disease-free survival. The authors suggest in their discussion that implicit in the measure of extroversion is the psychologic dimension of willingness and ability to reach out to others and that this may be associated with a network of social and emotional relationships. Hislop (personal communication, 1987) said additional analyses showed that women who were single or employed or who had a large network of friends had better survival. As mentioned, this study was limited to women under 55 years of age at diagnosis.

Marshall and Funch (1983) and Funch and Marshall (1983) examined the effects of measures of life stress, social involvement, prior history of cancer, and stage of disease on length of survival for three age groups among women known to have died during a 19- to 21-year follow-up period. In particular, they examined whether or not social support mediated the relationship between life stress and survival.

Despite the fact that both reports came from the same data source, there were differences in the construction of the measures of social support (Table 2) and life stress and in the analytic procedures used, and these differences made if difficult to compare the findings from the two studies. In one study (Marshall and Funch, 1983), only 'objective' measures of life stress were used including number of deaths, serious illnesses, divorces, and periods of unemployment. Composite measures of life stress and of social support were constructed because a preliminary analysis of each of the measures was consistent with the hypothesis that life stress decreased survival and social support increased survival (Marshall and Funch, 1983).

In the other article (Funch and Marshall, 1983), subjective measures of life stress were included in addition to the objective measure of life events: number of months in which a woman felt tired, felt upset, or perceived the family income as inadequate. In this article, the authors reported that 'Concerning social support, neither marital status nor the number of friends and relatives were [sic] significantly related to survival although organizational involvement was related' (p. 78). (This statement seems inconsistent with those made in their other paper unless the associations were in the predicted direction but were not statistically significant.)

Somewhat different patterns of association were found among the variables for the three age groups. In multivariate analysis, the most important predictors were stage of disease, cancer history, and age; the social environmental variables did not increase predictive ability in the older two age groups (Marshall and Funch, 1983). In the younger age group (less than 46 years), some of the variance was explained by stress and social support, but including these variables did not increase predictive ability (Marshall and Funch, 1983).

In the other report (Funch and Marshall, 1983), the interaction between life stress and social support was considered in relation to survival, and no interaction effect was found; thus, social support did not mediate the effects of life stress. In multivariate analysis, the model which best fitted the data was one which included stage alone. When the analysis was done excluding women age 46 to 60, the model which best fitted the data included life stress and social support (i.e. organizational involvement) as well as stage of disease. This finding is somewhat inconsistent with the other report which found no effect of social support and life stress for the older two age groups, nor is it consistent with the authors' report of the results. In one report (Marshall and Funch, 1983, p. 1550), the investigators concluded that 'Objective social conditions and support appear to have their most significant role among younger patients.' Yet the data in the other report (Funch and Marshall, 1983, p. 80) show that objective life stressors are most important in the oldest age group.

Summary

The findings for marital status are inconsistent. Greer *et al.* (1979) found that married cases had better survival than unmarried cases as did Neale *et al.* (1986). Goodwin *et al.* (1987) found that the married did better than the unmarried on two of three outcomes measured. Goodwin *et al.* (1987), Cassileth, *et al.* (1985a) and Funch and Marshall (1983) found no association between marital status and survival or time to recurrence. In contrast, Hislop *et al.* (1987) reported that single women had better survival.

Four of these studies examined other indicators of social support. Greer *et al.* (1979) reported that women who had poor marital relationships at the time of diagnosis had a less favorable outcome. Cassileth *et al.* (1985a, 1985b) found no association with any social or pyschologic variables, but their sample was not limited to breast cancer cases. Hislop *et al.* (1987) found that expressive activities at home independently predicted both survival and disease-free survival and that expressive activities away from home predicted disease-free survival. Funch and Marshall (1983) and Marshall and Funch (1983) found that social support and life stress predicted survival differentially by age.

ADJUSTMENT

As mentioned, the term adjustment was used by the various investigators to denote a range of outcomes including short- and long-term physical, social, marital, and sexual functioning, psychologic adjustment and psychiatric morbidity, self-concept, and fear of death or recurrence. Moreover, even when the same concept was used by more than one researcher, for example psychologic adjustment, the same operational definition rarely was (Table 3). In general, studies of adjustment were more systematic in the conceptualization and measurement of social support than studies of survival (Table 4). Most studies used cross-sectional designs with concurrent or retrospective ascertainment of adjustment measures. In most studies the sample size was small, and the target population was not always

Table 3 Citations for the dependent variables used in studies of social support and adjustment to breast cancer

	Citations for dependent variables		
Study	Psychologic/psychiatric	Self-concept	Functioning
Bloom (1982)	McNair *et al.*, 1971*	Janis, 1958§; Wallston *et al.* 1976§	
Bloom and Spiegel (1984)	Heimler, 1965§		Heimler, 1965§
Dean (1987)	Wing *et al.*, 1974; Spitzer *et al.*, 1978; Feighner *et al.*, 1972		
Dunkel-Schetter (1984)	Derogatis, 1975	Rosenberg, 1965	Gilson *et al.*, 1975§; Stewart *et al.*, 1978§
Funch and Mettlin (1982)	Bradburn, 1969		(χ)
Funch and Mettlin (1984)	Bradburn, 1969		
Hughes *et al.* (1986)	APA, 1980 Zigmond and Snaith, 1983		
Jamison *et al.* (1978)	(χ)		(χ)
Metzger *et al.* (1983)	Radloff, 1977		
Morris *et al.* (1977)	Hamilton, 1967		(χ)
Penman *et al.* (1987)		Rosenberg, 1965; Berscheid *et al.*, 1972; Polivy, 1977; Schain, 1977§	Donald and Ware, 1982§; Gilson *et al.*, 1975§; Holmes and Rahe, 1967; Spitzer *et al.*, 1978§
Smith *et al.* (1985)	(χ)		
Spiegel *et al.* (1983)	McNair *et al.*, 1971		
Woods and Earp (1978)	(χ)		(χ)

* References are given if the investigators used existing instruments. A § indicates that the investigators stated they modified the instrument. An (χ) indicates the investigators developed their own instruments.

Table 4 Operational measures of social support in studies of adjustment to breast cancer

Study	Measures
Bloom (1982)	(1) Marital status; four measures constructed from a number of social support items; (2) the woman's perception of the cohesiveness of her family (4 items from the Moos' Family Environment Scale, (Moos, 1974)); (3) social affiliations: (a) perception of social contact (1 item); (b) perception of amount of leisure activity (1 item); (4) presence or absence of a confidant.
Bloom and Spiegel (1984)	(1) Marital status; (2) emotional support: the sum of 3 subscales (cohesiveness, conflict, and expressiveness from the Moos' Family Environment Scale (Moos, 1974); (3) social activity: the extent to which the woman was able to carry out six activities including dressing and caring for her personal appearance, planning and cooking, housework, entertaining, doing errands and shopping, and attending social functions.
Dean (1987)	(1) Marital status; (2) presence of a confidant; (3) quality of the marital relationship.
Dunkel-Schetter (1984)	Three measures constructed for the study: (1) quantity of support, e.g. number of relationships, frquency of interaction (8 items); (2) satisfaction with support from spouse or closest significant other (one item each on love, understanding, approval, advice, and assistance); (3) interviewer rating of overall strength of support on a 5-point scale.
Funch and Mettlin (1982)	Three measures constructed for the study: (1) perceived support based on the extent to which the subject perceived she could rely on and talk to network members; (2) professional support based on general satisfaction with care, satisfaction with preparation for surgery, ability to talk with physician, and degree of information received on follow-up care; (3) financial support: (a) reported annual family income; (b) a scale based on insurance coverage of surgery and prosthesis and perceived financial impact of breast cancer.
Funch and Marshall (1984)	Three measures constructed for the study: (1) availability measured by an index based on number of people potentially available to the patient as represented by marital status, number of children, number of years in the neighborhood, and proximity of friends and relatives; (2) involvement measured by the woman's degree of participation in religious and non-religious organizations and the extent to which individuals were visited by or went to the homes of friends and relatives; (3) perceived support as measured by Funch and Mettlin (1982).
Hughes *et al.* (1986)	Did not measure social support.
Jamison *et al.* (1978)	The authors stated that the questionnaire inquired about 'perceptions of effects of the mastectomy on relationships with spouses (both sexually and generally), and attitudes toward surgeons and the nursing staff in the hospital' (p. 432).
Metzger *et al.* (1983)	Marital status: married, never married, widowed, and divorced or separated.

Table 4 (continued)

Study	Measures
Morris *et al.* (1977)	Not clearly defined: '...interpersonal adjustment ratings assessed the frequency of contact with friends and family, and evidence of disturbance in both these and more remote relationships, on a four point scale' (p. 2382).
Penman *et al.* (1987)	(1) Marital status; (2) social contacts; (3) group participation scales from the Social Health Index (Donald and Ware, 1982); (4) the Perceived Social Support Scale by Flamer (1977) which is a list of 15 emotional and social supports from persons close to the respondent.
Smith *et al.* (1985)	(1) Martial status; questions on: (2) the type of networks used and the degree of benefit derived from specific network members (adapted from Berkman and Syme, 1979), (3) the tasks others performed during the patient's illness that the patient viewed as helpful or unhelpful; (4) a list of support activities based on previous research on cancer patients including (a) listening or talking about the illness, (b) helping with housework, (c) taking care of the children, (d) preparing meals, etc.
Spiegel *et al.* (1983)	Family Environment Scale (Moos, 1974), the 40-item version with 10 subscales.
Woods and Earp (1978)	Two measures developed for the study: (1) social support—help: measured the amount of help the woman could expect from spouse, other family members, relatives, friends and neighbors, people at work, minister, doctors and nurses; (2) social support—listen: measured the extent to which these persons were willing to listen to her problems when she was not feeling well.

clearly defined (Table 5). In order to facilitate comparison of the findings across studies, this discussion is organized around three broad categories of outcomes: psychologic/psychiatric, self-concept, and functioning. Findings are considered in the context of the strengths and limitations of the studies. Again, where possible, findings related to age are emphasized.

Psychologic adjustment and psychiatric disorders

The preponderance of studies of adjustment included some indicator of psychologic adjustment or distress. Most of these were measures of symptoms of depression or general mood state (Table 3). Studies of this outcome generally used a cross-sectional design in which women were interviewed at varying time intervals post-surgery and in which the outcomes were ascertained at that time

Table 5 Characteristics of studies of social support and adjustment to breast cancer*

Study	Source	Age range and mean	Time interval between surgery and study	Study design	Sample size (response rates)
Bloom (1982b)	Breast cancer cases (nonmetastatic) who were members of an HMO in northern CA identified consecutively from medical records	$\bar{x}=51.3$	1 week to 2½ years	Cross-sectional	133 (—)
Bloom and Spiegel (1984)	Breast cancer cases with metastatic disease referred by 11 oncologists	$\underline{35-79}$ $\bar{x}=54$	$\bar{x}=28$ months since Dx $\bar{x}=12$ months since Dx of metastases	Cross-sectional	86 (78.9%)
Dean (1987)	Consecutive breast cancer cases ($T_{1,2}N_{0,1}$) who had mastectomies at Longmore Hospital in Edinburgh; comparison group from a community-based study	$\underline{20-60}$ $\bar{x}=48.7$	1 week before surgery and at 3 and 12 months post-surgery	Prospective	122 (97.6% baseline) (92.6% 3 months) (83.6% 12 months)
Dunkel-Schetter (1984)	Breast and colorectal cancer cases (all stages identified from tumor registry at Northwestern University) who had their cancers diagnosed within a 12-month period	$\underline{30-70}$ $\bar{x}=56$	7 to 20 months	Cross-sectional	60 breast 19 colon (67% breast) (45% colon)
Funch and Marshall (1984)	Breast cancer cases (nonmetastatic) identified from the NY tumor registry who had mastectomies in 1979	$\underline{29-92}$ $\bar{x}=59.5$	3–12 months	Cross-sectional	151 (72.6%)§
Funch and Mettlin (1982)	Same as Funch and Marshall, 1984	$\underline{29-92}$ $\bar{x}=59.5$	3–12 months	Cross-sectional	151 (72.6%)
Hughes et al. (1986)	Women with clinical signs of breast disease referred to a breast clinic for biopsy over a 9-month period. Some were found to have BrCa (all stages) and some BBD	$\underline{35-64}$ $\bar{x}=52$ BrCa $\bar{x}=47$ BBD	Prior to biopsy	Prospective	33 BrCa 107 BBD (90.9% overall) (79.0% BrCa)
Jamison et al. (1978)	Breast cancer cases from Women for Women self-help recovery group in LA and from the ACS	$\underline{32-70}$ $\bar{x}=52.7$	$\bar{x}=22$ months Median=10 months	Cross-sectional	41 (—)

Study	Sample description	Age	Assessment timing	Design	N (response)
Metzger et al. (1983)	Breast cancer cases (nonmetastatic) diagnosed between 5/78–1/79 identified from the NY tumour registry	18–65 $\bar{x}$=52	~1 year	Cross-sectional	652 (59.8%)§
Morris et al. (1977)	Women consecutively admitted to King's College Hospital, London for breast tumour biopsy and diagnosed with BrCa ($T_{0,1,2}N_{0,1}M_0$) or BBD	<70 $\bar{x}$=58 BrCa $\bar{x}$=48 BBD	Prior to biopsy and at 3, 12 and 24 months post-surgery	Prospective	69 BrCa 91 BBD

Morris et al. (1977) — response rates:

	BrCa	BBD
(3 months	91.3%	87.9%
(12 months	76.8%	82.4%
(24 months	65.2%	71.4%

Study	Sample description	Age	Assessment timing	Design	N (response)
Penman et al. (1987)	Women meeting specific criteria recruited between 1/78 and 7/79 from 61 hospitals in 11 states. Four groups: (1) women who had a mastectomy for stage 1 or 2 breast cancer; (2) women who had a biopsy for BBD; (3) women who had a cholecystectomy; (4) women with no known health problems	30–69 stratified by age	1–3 months and at 6, 12, and 15 months	Cross-sectional and prospective	1715 overall 412 in the longitudinal study (88% of 412)
Smith et al. (1985)	Women with breast, ovarian or endometrial cancer (all stages) identified from the Iowa SEER cancer registry who were part of a national study on the use of steroid hormones and female reproductive cancer	20–54 $\bar{x}$=45.6	Within 6 months of Dx; $\bar{x}$=10 weeks	Cross-sectional	272 BrCa 46 ovarian 43 endometrial (98.1%)
Spiegel et al. (1983)	Subset of women studied by Bloom and Spiegel (1984)	35–79 $\bar{x}$=54.5	$\bar{x}$=25 months since Dx of metastases	Cross-sectional	58 (67.4%)
Woods and Earp (1978)	Breast cancer cases (stages 1–3) who had a mastectomy in 1972 at 6 of 24 hospitals in the NC tumor registry	25–71 $\bar{x}$=51.8	~4 years after surgery	Cross-sectional	49 (48.5%)§

* ACS = American Cancer Society; BBD = benign breast disease; BrCa = breast cancer; Dx = diagnosis; HMO = health maintenance organization.
§ 72.6% of women whose physicians gave permission, 41.9% overall; 58.9% of women whose physicians gave permission, 52% overall; 48.5% of women alive and eligible at the time of the study.

and/or retrospectively (Bloom, 1982b; Bloom and Spiegel, 1984; Dunkel-Schetter, 1984; Funch and Marshall, 1984; Funch and Mettlin, 1982; Jamison, Wellisch and Pasnau, 1978; Metzger, Roger and Bauman, 1983; Smith, Redman, Burns and Sagart, 1985; Spiegel, Bloom and Sottheil, 1983; Woods and Earp, 1978). Only three studies interviewed women prior to surgery for breast symptoms (Dean, 1987; Hughes, Royle, Buchanan and Taylor, 1986; Morris, Greer and White, 1977), and unfortunately, these contained limited measures of social support.

Cross-sectional studies

Bloom (1982b) interviewed 133 women with nonmetastatic breast cancer whose surgery had occurred from one week to two and one-half years earlier (Table 5). Five measures of social support were examined (Table 4) in relation to psychologic distress (Table 3). Two support measures—family cohesiveness and perception of social contact—were indirectly associated with distress through their effect on coping response, and controlling for time since surgery did not alter these associations.

Bloom and Spiegel (1984) also analyzed the effects of three measures of social support (Table 4) on outlook using a sample of 86 women with metastatic breast cancer. In multivariate analysis, two measures of support—family support and social activity—had direct effects on the patient's outlook. They did not control for time since surgery or recurrence.

Spiegel *et al.* (1983) studied a subset of the women reported on by Bloom and Spiegel. Fifty-eight of the 86 women with metastatic breast cancer completed interviews at four-month intervals over the course of one year. Although baseline mood disturbance was the strongest predictor of a change in mood over the year ('to the extent that it was less at baseline, mood became worse during the year, and vice versa' (p. 40)), three subscales from the Family Environment Scale (Moos, 1974) also were independently associated with mood disturbance. Patients who rated their families as more expressive, i.e. openly discussed problems and feelings, in the baseline measurements and as showing less conflict experienced less mood disturbance. An unexpected finding was that a deemphasis on moral—religious orientation was associated with less mood disturbance over the year.

Funch and Mettlin (1982) studied 151 women who had had a mastectomy for nonmetastatic breast cancer within three to 12 months prior to interview to examine the effects of three indicators of social support (Table 4) on psychologic adjustment (Table 3). After controlling for other variables, perceived emotional support and professional support were associated with adjustment, but financial support was not. Life stress following, but unrelated to, surgery was not associated with psychologic adjustment. Funch and Marshall (1984) used the same data source to examine whether or not an ad hoc measure of self-reliance mediated the relationship between social support and psychologic adjustment. Self-reliance was not associated with psychologic adjustment, physical outcome, or any of the independent variables including social support indicators, but there was a different pattern of association between social support indicators and psychologic adjustment for self-reliant compared with other-reliant women. For other-reliant women, perceived support was associated with less negative affect while for self-reliant women, it was associated with more negative affect. Greater availability of support also was associated with more negative affect for the self-reliant women, and there was a tendency for stress to have more impact on adjustment for the self-reliant.

Woods and Earp (1978) interviewed 49 women four years after mastectomy and examined whether two measures of perceived support (Table 4) mediated the association between persistent physical symptoms related to breast surgery and depression. Their data showed that social support buffered a person from experiencing symptoms of depression only at low levels of physical symptoms; among those with few physical symptoms and high social support, only about 10% were categorized as depressed whereas 30% were depressed among those having few physical symptoms and low support. Among those with many physical symptoms, the proportion of persons categorized as depressed was approximately 60% regardless of the level (or measure) of social support.

Jamison *et al.* (1978) examined emotional adjustment to mastectomy and symptoms of depression among 41 breast cancer patients whose surgery occurred an average of 22 months before the study. They did not do any multivariate analysis, including controlling for time since diagnosis, and their measure of social support was not clearly defined (Table 4). Women who reported better emotional adjustment also perceived significantly more understanding and emotional support from their spouses, children, physicians, surgeons, and the nursing staff in the hospital. Younger women (<45 years) rated their post-mastectomy adjustment as poorer and were more likely to seek professional help for psychologic problems secondary to mastectomy. The association between social support and symptoms of depression was not reported.

Metzger *et al.* (1983) looked at the effects of age (<50, 50 to 59, and >59 years) and marital status on psychologic distress. Marital status was associated with depression scores, but the findings were inconsistent with respect to a protective effect of being married, and they were mediated by age. Under age 50 years, there were no differences in depression by marital status. For women over 50 years, however, never married women were less depressed than women who were married, divorced or separated, or widowed, but married women were less depressed than their widowed, divorced, or separated counterparts. When marital, parental, socioeconomic, and employment status were controlled, age was significantly associated with depression scores: younger women were more likely than older women to be depressed. Although younger women were more likely than older women to be troubled by the disfiguring surgery, older women who expressed this concern were more likely to be depressed than were younger women with this concern.

Two studies (Dunkel-Schetter, 1984; Smith *et al.*, 1985) which examined the effects of social support on psychologic adjustment did not limit their samples to breast cancer cases. Smith *et al.* examined the effects of three types of social support (Table 4) on self-reported feelings of isolation and loneliness in 357 women aged 20 to 54 years with breast, ovarian, and endometrial cancers (Table 5). They found that older, more educated women were less likely to feel isolated and lonely. The support network was not associated with feelings of loneliness except among married women where there was an inverse association between level of spousal support and loneliness.

Dunkel-Schetter studied the association between psychologic adjustment (Table 3) and social support (Table 4) in a sample of breast and colorectal cancer cases (Table 5). Although cases were interviewed from seven to 20 months after their diagnosis, analysis considering time since diagnosis showed no significant differences on any variables. Support was associated with adjustment, and the results were fairly consistent across three indicators of support; however, the effects differed by prognosis. In general, among those with a good prognosis, the greater the support the more positive their affect, but among those with a poor prognosis, that association did not hold. Because there were no differences between prognosis groups in mean levels of support, affect, or self-esteem, the author suggested that the link between support and well-being was attenuated under high stress conditions.

Only one study (Metzger *et al.*, 1983) looked at fear of recurrence, but marital status was the only indicator of social support. Marriage was found to provide only limited protection against this fear. Never married women were less likely than married women to worry about recurrence in all age groups.

Prospective (from diagnosis) studies

Dean (1987) interviewed 121 women prior to mastectomy in order to assess preoperative predictors of psychiatric morbidity, including social support, at three and 12 months post-surgery (Table 5). In contrast to the other studies which used measures of psychologic distress or adjustment, Dean interviewed study participants with a structured psychiatric interview. A comparison group of women participating in a community-based study were interviewed using the same instrument. At the three-month postoperative assessment, overall rates of psychiatric morbidity as well as rates for major and minor depression were higher for mastectomy patients than for controls. Preoperative variables which predicted psychiatric disorder at three months among mastectomy patients were preoperative psychiatric status, having a bad marital relationship, and treatment protocol (those receiving mastectomy alone did better than those receiving mastectomy plus adjuvant therapy). Although the baseline psychiatric assessments were made prior to surgery, women knew the results of their biopsy, and so these assessments probably did not accurately reflect prior psychiatric status. At 12 months, the mastectomy cases continued to show higher rates overall and for minor depressive disorder compared with the controls. The predictors of psychiatric status at 12 months were preoperative psychiatric status, lower social class, and menopausal status (perimenopausal patients did the worst). No multivariate analysis was performed that included all of the preoperative variables.

Hughes *et al.* (1986) and Morris *et al.* (1977) used a design in which initial measurements were made prior to final diagnosis among women undergoing evaluation of breast symptoms. Hughes *et al.* interviewed 140 women after referral to a breast clinic but before their appointment, and Morris *et al.* interviewed 160 women prior to biopsy. In the Morris *et al.* study, women also were interviewed at three, 12 and 24 months after diagnosis while the study by Hughes *et al.* provided only pre-diagnostic information. The design of these studies had the advantage that knowledge of diagnosis did not confound assessment, although it is possible that some women's symptoms were more indicative of a probable breast cancer diagnosis.

In the Hughes *et al.* study, anxiety and depression were the outcomes measured, and comparisons were made between women who were subsequently diagnosed as having breast cancer and women whose diagnosis was benign breast disease (BBD). Although not statistically significant, women diagnosed as having breast cancer were less likely to be depressed using DSM III (American Psychiatric Association, 1980) criteria for major depression or using the high cut-off score on a depression scale (Table 3); however, they were more likely to have a diagnosis of minor depression using DSM III criteria and to score high on anxiety. When major and minor depression were combined and a less stringent cut-off score on the depression and anxiety scale was used, there was little difference in the psychiatric status of these two groups. Moreover, depression at interview was associated with a past history of psychiatric disorder in both groups, and there was no association between depression and type of breast pathology in the BBD group. In both groups of women depression at interview was associated with the experience of life events in the prior year: 77% of the depressed women in the BBD group and 75% in the breast cancer group had experienced an 'extreme or severe' stress in the past year. The BBD group reported slightly more life events than the cancer group, and this difference persisted when a subsample of BBD patients matched for age was compared with the cancer patients. Limitations of this study were that no multivariate analysis was performed, that the only indicator of social support was marital status, and that marital status was not considered in relation to depression or life events.

Morris *et al.* (1977) also studied women prior to biopsy for a breast lump and followed them at periodic intervals over the next two years. Although not statistically significant, women diagnosed as having breast cancer were rated preoperatively as more depressed than women with BBD; this pattern held over the follow-up intervals, and at two years the difference was statistically significant. For women undergoing mastectomy, a high depression score and a high neuroticism score were associated with adjustment at two years. There also was a tendency for patients who were not married or cohabitating at the time of mastectomy to adjust better than those who were.

Summary

A number of studies found a positive relationship between various manifestations of psychologic or psychiatric status and perceived social support. Bloom (1982b) found that the effects of support on distress were mediated through coping, and this finding was consistent with the differential pattern between support and adjustment for self-reliant versus other-reliant women reported by Funch and Marshall (1984). A number of other studies found positive, direct effects between various measures of perceived support from family and friends and various measures of psychologic status or adjustment (Bloom and Spiegel, 1984; Dunkel-Schetter, 1984; Funch and Mettlin, 1982; Jamison *et al.*, 1978; Spiegel *et al.*, 1983). In contrast, Funch and Mettlin (1982) found no association between perceived financial support and psychologic adjustment, Bloom (1982b) found no association between perception of leisure activities and distress, and Spiegel *et al.* (1983) found a positive association between mood disturbance and a moral – religious orientation. Smith *et al.* (1985) found no association between perceived support and loneliness with the exception of married women.

The findings for marital status or having a confidant were less consistent and frequently were not in the expected direction. Metzger *et al.* (1983) found that the effect of marital status on psychologic distress was mediated by age. Two studies reported that single women did better than married women at 12 (Dean, 1987) and 24 months (Morris *et al.*, 1977) of follow-up, while Bloom (1982b) found no association between the presence of a confidant and psychologic distress.

Self-concept

Only four studies included measures of self-concept (Bloom, 1982b; Dunkel-Schetter, 1984; Metzger *et al.*, 1983; Penman *et al.*, 1987). Penman *et al.* recently reported the results of a multicenter collaborative study which examined the effects of mastectomy on self-concept and social functioning and which included measures of social support. The study design is noteworthy in that it included multiple cross-sectional evaluations of different samples of women at different points in time post-mastectomy as well as a longitudinal assessment of the baseline cross-sectional sample over a 15-month period. A number of other important factors were taken into consideration in the design of this study including (1) the inclusion of a number of comparison groups—healthy women, women undergoing biopsy for BBD, and women undergoing surgery for gall bladder disease—in order to distinguish the impact of surgery for breast cancer from surgery for other conditions and from no surgery, (2) the comparison of women who were treated only by mastectomy with those treated by mastectomy plus some adjuvant therapy, (3) the exclusion of women with preexisting mental or physical illness, and (4) the stratification of the sample by age for four decades (30−39, 40−49, 50−59, 60−69 years). The overall sample included 1715 women, and 412 of them participated in the longitudinal component of the study.

Four self-concept outcomes (Table 3) were studied in relation to four measures of social support (Table 4). The most striking finding of their study was the relative absence of measurable differences for the outcomes studied between the two mastectomy groups and the comparison groups. As might be expected, there were some differences in the two outcomes related to self-image (body image dissatisfaction and feminine self-image concerns). Regarding feminine self-image concerns, the mastectomy plus adjuvant therapy group (but not the mastectomy-only group) expressed greater self-image concerns compared with the no surgery group, and these differences were observed in both the cross-sectional and the longitudinal data. The amount of variance explained, however, was only about one percent. For the outcome measure of dissatisfaction with body image, differences were again observed only for the mastectomy plus adjuvant therapy group and only in the cross-sectional analysis, particularly in the first post-surgical time period; again, the amount of explained variance was very small. There were no differences among the study groups for intimacy concerns, but the mastectomy plus adjuvant therapy group showed a consistent rise in those concerns over time.

Because there was no differential effect of treatment group, analysis of social support was done across groups. The measure of social contacts was not associated with any of the self-concept outcomes in the cross-sectional analysis. Group participation also was not associated with three of the four self-concept outcomes in the cross-sectional analysis; there was a modest negative association between feminine self-image concerns and group participation. (Social contacts and group participation were not included in the longitudinal analysis.) Marital status was not associated with any of the self-concept outcomes. In contrast, perceived lack of supports, i.e. the anticipation of fewer social supports being available, was associated with all four outcomes in both cross-sectional and longitudinal analyses. Likewise, the magnitude of life change stress during the preceding three-month interval was inversely associated with all self-concept outcomes except body image dissatisfaction. It should be noted that although neither of the mastectomy groups reported lower self-esteem in the year post-surgery than any of the comparison groups, there was a decrease over time in the self-esteem of the mastectomy plus adjuvant therapy group.

Although the report by Penman *et al.* is by far the strongest study in terms of its design and breadth of variables examined, three other studies (Bloom, 1982b; Dunkel-Schetter, 1984; Metzger *et al.*, 1983) included measures of self-concept (Table 3). As with the findings reported for psychologic distress, Bloom found that two of five measures of social support—perceived social support and family cohesiveness—were indirectly associated through coping with self-concept and sense of power among nonmetastatic breast cancer patients. In a similar vein, Dunkel-Schetter found that among breast and colon cancer cases with a good prognosis, the greater the social support, the higher their self-esteem, but among those with a poor prognosis, this association did not hold. Metzger *et al.* found no consistent pattern of association between marital status and concern about disfigurement. Younger divorced women experienced more concern about disfigurement than did married women of the same age, but their never married counterparts did not. Among older women, the married were more concerned about disfigurement than the never married.

Summary

Few studies examined the effects of mastectomy on measures of self-concept. Based on the report by Penman *et al.* (1987), there was little evidence that mastectomy affected self-concept when those women were compared with women undergoing other surgical procedures or with asymptomatic, healthy women. Perceived social support was associated with the measures of self-concept studied by Penman *et al.* (1987), by Bloom (1982b), and by Dunkel-Schetter (1984). There was, however, no differential pattern of association between social support and self-concept by treatment group in the Penman *et al.* study. In contrast to the positive findings for perceived social support, Penman *et al.* found that the measure of social contacts was not associated with any of the self-concept measures, and group participation showed only a modest association with one of the outcomes in the cross-sectional component of this study. Marital status was not associated with any of the outcomes analyzed by Penman *et al.*, and it showed an inconsistent pattern by age in the Metzger *et al.* (1983) study.

Social, marital, sexual, and physical functioning

A number of studies have included various measures of functioning (Bloom and Spiegel, 1984; Dunkel-Schetter, 1984; Funch and Mettlin, 1982; Jamison *et al.*, 1978; Morris, *et al.*, 1977; Penman *et al.*, 1987; Woods and Earp, 1978), although Penman *et al.* was the most comprehensive. Most of the others were cross-sectional (Bloom and Spiegel, 1984; Dunkel-Schetter, 1984; Funch and Mettlin, 1982; Smith *et al.*, 1985; Woods and Earp, 1978), but two were prospective from diagnosis (Dean, 1987; Morris *et al.*, 1977). Four of the investigators developed their own measures while three modified existing instruments (Table 3).

Penman *et al.* studied six social function outcomes: social health, dysfunctional interaction with family, personal and social life events stress, workplace life events stress, social role function impairment, and daily life activities impairment (Table 3). In contrast to their findings on self-concept, the mastectomy-only group as well as the other surgical comparison groups, i.e. BBD patients and cholecystectomy patients, but not the mastectomy plus adjuvant therapy group showed a difference on the social health outcome measure (a measure of social ties and frequency of interaction with relatives, friends, and social groups) when compared with the no surgery group. These findings obtained in the cross-sectional but not in the longitudinal component of the study. (The measure of social health, or at least some of the subscales, also appear to have been used as measures of social support in other analyses.) The only other evidence of a differential effect of mastectomy on functioning was that both mastectomy groups had more difficulty carrying out expected social role functions in the first three-month time period than the nonsurgical comparison group. The difference in function was small, however, and was similar to the cholecystectomy group; moreover, there was no difference at 12 months. (Analysis of social role function impairment was done only on the longitudinal data.

As with the analysis of self-concept measures, analysis of social support was done across treatment groups. Perceived lack of support was associated with three of the four social function outcomes in the cross-sectional component of the study (the exception being workplace life events stress) and with four of the six social function outcomes in the longitudinal component (the exceptions were workplace life events stress and personal and social life events stress). Marital status was associated with two of the social function outcomes. Married women were less likely to report personal and social life events stresses and were less likely to report workplace change in both the cross-sectional and longitudinal analyses. As with self-concept, when age differences were observed in this study, they showed uniformly more favorable psychosocial outcomes with increasing age.

Cross-sectional studies

Bloom and Spiegel (1984) found that social activity, an indicator of social support (Table 4), as well as outlook on life, self-concept, and coping response, was associated with social functioning. Their other measure of social support, family support, was not associated with social functioning directly but did affect it indirectly through its influence on outlook on life. Marital status was not associated with functioning.

Funch and Mettlin (1982) examined the effects of three indicators of social support (Table 4) on five indicators of physical recovery (Table 3) as well as on an overall index in multivariate analysis which controlled for demographic and health status variables. They found that financial support was consistently associated with the overall index and four indicators of physical recovery (the exception was perceived recovery). The other two measures of support, perceived support and professional support, were not associated with any of the indicators of physical recovery. Time since surgery was associated with only one indicator of physical recovery—restricted mobility. Life stress since surgery (but unrelated to it) also was associated with restricted mobility and with the overall physical recovery index.

In contrast to expectation, Dunkel-Schetter (1984) found that support, as rated by the interviewer, was inversely associated with functioning but only for poor prognosis patients, i.e. more support was associated with more problems in functioning. A likely explanation for this finding is that these patients experienced more problems in functioning which elicited more support. Also in contrast to expectation, poorer prognosis patients' estimates of number of close family members were associated positively with problems in functioning. Again, the explanation could be that the patient's perceptions of closeness in the family increased as problems in functioning increased, or the perception may have reflected greater attention paid to the patient because of her condition. These findings emphasize the need to control for stage of disease in examining associations between psychosocial factors and prognosis outcomes.

Smith *et al*. (1985) compared women who reported marital problems to those who reported no marital problems. Age was inversely associated with reporting marital problems. Women who said their husbands provided 'a high or moderate amount of support were significantly less likely to report marital problems related to the cancer ($p < 0.02$) and were more likely to say they received an adequate amount of understanding ($p < 0.001$) and the desired amount of affection ($p < 0.001$)' (p. 75). The authors suggested that because time since diagnosis was short, it may have been too soon for the marital relationship to reflect adjustment to sexual and other changes caused by cancer. An alternative explanation is that perceived support may be confounded with their measure of marital adjustment or satisfaction in that it may be a component of it.

Although Jamison *et al*. (1978) inquired about sexual adjustment, they did not analyze their data quantitatively. Woods and Earp (1978) also studied sexual adjustment by asking women about frequency of intercourse and satisfaction with their sexual relationships four years after surgery. Women who reported decreased frequency were more likely than those who reported no change to be less satisfied with their current sexual relationships and to be less satisfied with their husband's companionship. Satisfaction with one's sexual relationship was correlated with whether the husband was perceived as understanding, whether a woman felt able to confide in her husband, and her age (being older). Unexpectedly, satisfaction with the sexual relationship was not correlated with the extent of surgery or the level of physical symptoms persisting four years after surgery, but these factors were inversely correlated with frequency.

Prospective (from diagnosis) studies

Dean (1987) analyzed marital, social, and sexual functioning at three months post-surgery, but only bivariate analysis was performed. No measures of social support were included, but there was a significant association between neuroticism scores as assessed preoperatively and deterioration of the marital relationship at three months post-surgery, and there was a significant relationship between preoperative psychologic status and sexual deterioration at three months.

Morris *et al*. (1977) compared the marital, sexual, interpersonal, and work adjustment of breast cancer cases to women with BBD. Marital adjustment and interpersonal relationships did not appear to be negatively affected by mastectomy. At three months, work adjustment and ability to carry out household tasks deteriorated among the cancer patients but improved by the two-year follow-up. Sexual adjustment deteriorated at three months in both the breast cancer cases and the women with BBD and did not improve over the follow-up period. The effect of social support on functioning was not discussed.

Summary

Similar to the findings for self-concept, Penman *et al*. (1987) found little evidence of a differential effect for measures of functioning in breast cancer patients compared with other groups. Of six measures of functioning studied, only one showed a differential effect for mastectomy patients. Perceived support was associated with three of four functioning outcomes in the cross-sectional analysis, but the other two measures of support were not. Perceived support also was associated with four of the six outcomes in the longitudinal analysis; the other two measures of support were not included in this analysis. There was no differential effect of social support by treatment group.

The findings of Morris *et al*. (1977) were consistent with those of Penman *et al*. in that there was virtually no difference in changes over time between women with breast cancer and those with BBD for marital and interpersonal functioning. Dean (1987) also found few changes over time on three measures of functioning among breast cancer cases.

Although Bloom and Spiegel (1984) found no direct association between family support and social functioning, there was an indirect association through outlook on life, and there was a direct association between functioning and social activities. Funch and Mettlin (1982) found no association between indicators of physical recovery and perceived support or professional support, but there was an association with financial support. Dunkel-Schetter (1984) found an inverse association between support and functioning, but this anomalous finding held only for patients with a poor prognosis.

Marital status was not consistently associated with functioning. Penman *et al*. (1987) found that being married was associated with two of six functioning measures; married women reported fewer personal and social life stresses and fewer workplace changes than their unmarried counterparts. In contrast, Bloom and Spiegel (1984) found no association between functioning and marital status.

DISCUSSION

As summarized throughout this chapter, the findings from studies of the associations between social support and prognosis and adjustment were characterized by inconsistency. Of the six studies of prognosis, only four included measures of social support other than marital status. The effects on survival of marital status and of other indicators of social support were inconsistent as summarized above. The strongest study of adjustment both from a conceptual and a methodologic standpoint was the study by Penman *et al.* (1987). Overall, the findings from that study suggested that there were very few differences in outcomes—as measured by four indices of self-concept and six indices of functioning—between women undergoing mastectomy, women undergoing other surgical procedures, and healthy women. Morris *et al.* (1977) also found few differences in functioning between breast cancer cases and women with BBD over two years of follow-up. Two other studies (Craig, Comstock and Seiser, 1974; Worden and Weisman, 1977) also reported few differences for a number of measures of adjustment between breast cancer cases and population-based and neighborhood controls (Craig *et al.*, 1974) and women with other types of cancer (Worden and Weisman, 1977), but those studies did not examine measures of social support.

Perceived social support was fairly consistently related to self-concept and to functioning regardless of treatment group in both the cross-sectional and longitudinal components of the Penman *et al.* (1987) study. Findings on social support from other studies of self-concept which did not include comparison groups are consistent with those results (Bloom, 1982b; Dunkel-Schetter, 1984) as are most of the findings reported for functioning (Bloom and Spiegel, 1984; Smith *et al.*, 1985; Woods and Earp, 1978). In contrast, Funch and Mettlin (1982) found no association between physical recovery and perceived support among nonmetastatic breast cancer cases, although there was an association with financial support. From the available evidence it appears that social support, as well as life stress, are not associated with functioning or self-concept differentially for women with breast cancer compared with women who had other health problems and with healthy women.

Another recent report from the data source analyzed by Penman *et al.* examined the psychologic responses of this study population; however, social support was not analyzed (Bloom *et al.*, 1987). In general, they found that women who had had a mastectomy experienced more psychologic distress and disruption for a year post-mastectomy than women undergoing other surgical procedures or than healthy women, but the risk of developing severe reactive anxiety or depression after mastectomy was low. Those findings are in general agreement with results from the three studies reviewed in this chapter that included comparison groups (Dean, 1987; Hughes *et al.*, 1986; Morris *et al.*, 1977). They also are in agreement with those reported by Maguire *et al.* (1978) who compared selected psychiatric symptoms over the course of one year in women newly diagnosed with breast cancer to women with BBD. In contrast, Worden and Weisman (1977) found no difference in depression scores over a six-month period for women with breast cancer compared with women who were newly diagnosed with other cancers. Craig *et al.* (1974) also found no difference in symptoms of depression between breast cancer cases (diagnosed at least ten months prior to the study) and population-based controls. Several recent studies examined psychologic outcomes (but not social support) associated with different types of treatment for breast cancer and reported inconsistent findings (de Haes, van Dostrom and Welvaart, 1986; Fallowfield, Baum and Maguire, 1986; Hughson *et al.*, 1980, 1986, 1987; Lasry *et al.*, 1987; Steinberg, Juliano and Wise, 1985).

Most studies that included social support found a positive association between perceived support and psychologic or psychiatric status (Bloom 1982b; Bloom and Spiegel, 1984; Dunkel-Schetter, 1984; Funch and Mettlin, 1982; Jamison *et al.*, 1978; Spiegel *et al.*, 1983), and Hughes *et al.* (1986) found a similar pattern of association between life events and depression among breast cancer cases and women with BBD. Marital status showed an inconsistent pattern of association with psychologic status, and in one study (Metzger *et al.*, 1983) the association was mediated by age.

Penman *et al.* (1987) noted that one year may not be sufficient for differences in outcomes to become apparent. Although not statistically different from the other groups, Penman *et al.* (1987) found that the mastectomy plus adjuvant therapy group showed a decrease in self-esteem and an increase in intimacy concerns over time. The relatively short follow-up period also might explain Penman *et al.*'s findings on self-image concerns; i.e. there was a weak association between expressed self-image concerns for the mastectomy plus adjuvant therapy group (but not the mastectomy-only group) compared with the no surgery group. Polivy (1977) also found that self-image concerns of mastectomy patients increased over pre-surgical measurements during a follow-up period of about one year, as did the concerns of women who were biopsied or who had other surgeries. The self-image concerns of mastectomy patients appeared to be greater than those of the other two groups, but no test of significance was done. These trends were consistent with the findings of Morris *et al.* (1977) for depression in that although breast cancer cases were more depressed than women with BBD at all follow-up assessments, the difference was not statistically significant until two years.

Because there is a paucity of information on long-term adjustment and because most of the available data come primarily from cross-sectional studies which used retrospective measurements, extending the follow-up period of studies would provide useful information. It is likely that the disease process affects one's psychologic responses and social networks and support systems. Thus, limiting the initital assessments to early stage cancer, as was done in the Penman *et al.* report, provides the opportunity to study the effects of changes over time in disease status on social support as well as on other behavioral and psychologic factors.

There were very few reports in the literature of intervention programs designed to provide support to breast cancer cases (Bloom, Ross and Burnell, 1978; Morgenstern *et al.*, 1984; Orr, 1986; Rogers, Bauman and Metzger, 1985; Spiegel, Bloom and Yalom, 1981; Winick and Robbins, 1977). Only three of these (Bloom *et al.*, 1978; Morgenstern *et al.*, 1984; Spiegel *et al.*, 1981) were designed to systematically evaluate the effects on survival or adjustment of providing social support to women with breast cancer. Morgenstern *et al.* (1984) conducted a retrospective follow-up study to assess the impact on survival of a psychosocial support program. What appeared to be a beneficial effect of the program in their initial analyses was due to selection bias resulting from failure to match cases and comparison subjects on duration of lag time between cancer diagnosis and program entry. Although it is important to study endpoints other than survival, i.e. adjustment, the need to consider methodologic problems, particularly selection bias, in the conduct of these studies remains a salient concern. Indirect support for this point comes from a study of factors that led cancer patients to join support groups (Taylor, Falke, Shoptaw and Lichtman, 1986). Attenders and nonattenders differed on a number of factors: attenders were more likely to be female, to be of higher socioeconomic status, to have received their diagnosis less recently, to feel that family members did not understand what they were going through and expected too much of them, to have used more social support resources of all kinds, and to have consulted with mental health professionals about both cancer-related and non-cancer-related problems.

Very few studies examined age in a systematic way. Because half of all breast cancer cases are over age 65 (Horm, Asire, Young and Pollack, 1984), it would be advisable to include older women in future studies of adjustment. Although Penman *et al.* (1987) reported that age was positively associated with favorable outcomes, the age cut-off for their sample was 70 years. The authors noted that 'The concerns of older women may be tempered by experience and perspective and their concerns may also be different from those of younger women. On the other hand, the increased physical frailty and greater likelihood of more concurrent medical conditions may render some aspects of adaptation more difficult for individuals more elderly than we studied' (p. 127). Holland and Mastrovito (1980) reiterated the point that the psychologic impact of a diagnosis of breast cancer will be influenced by the point in the life cycle at which it occurs and by what social tasks are interrupted. Older women are likely to be experiencing other losses which affect their social network and support system, and those additional losses may have consequences for adjustment to breast cancer. Those ideas have yet to be tested empirically.

Two recent studies (Chu *et al.*, 1987; Greenfield, Blanco, Elashoff and Ganz, 1987) found that older breast cancer cases were managed differently from younger cases. Chu *et al.* (1987) reported that older women received fewer services including diagnostic biopsies, number of lymph nodes examined, chemotherapy, and radiation therapy. They also were less likely to receive consultations with medical specialists and to be referred to a mastectomy group. Although the reasons for those differences are not well understood, the findings have potential implications not only for survival and adjustment but also for sources of social support, particularly from medical professionals and patient support groups.

In terms of the methodologic requirements of future studies of adjustment, the inclusion of multiple comparison groups is strongly recommended. Studies which include only breast cancer cases may yield prevalence estimates of adjustment at specified time points pre- and post-treatment or tell us whether or not there is an association between social support and other psychosocial variables and adjustment, but they do not inform us as to whether or not the direction and magnitude of the associations are similar to those found in other groups. Moreover, cross-sectional studies which ascertain measures of adjustment and support months or years after diagnosis and treatment should, at the minimum, control for time since diagnosis. Because there are serious methodologic problems associated with the cross-sectional study design in which measures of adjustment are ascertained retrospectively (in particular, recall bias and differential survival), it is preferable to study associations using cross-sectional or longitudinal designs in newly diagnosed patients.

With respect to the conceptualization and measurement of social support, many of the studies of survival did not make explicit their conceptual definition or operational measure of social support; in fact, in two studies (Goodwin *et al.*, 1987; Neale *et al.*, 1986) the only measure of social support was marital status. Although studies of adjustment were, in general, clearer about the measures of social support, most measures were of self-reported frequency and quality of social contacts, primarily perceived emotional support from family and friends. As mentioned, several writers (Lindsey *et al.*, 1981; Satariano and Eckert, 1983; Wortman, 1984) have considered the conceptualization and measurement of social support in the context of studies of cancer patients, and one study compared perceptions of social support in a group of breast cancer cases with support which healthy persons predicted they would receive were they to be diagnosed with cancer (Peters-Golden, 1982). Wortman (1984) suggested a number of approaches to measuring social support in cancer patients, including a discussion of the assets and limitations of specific instruments with respect to their use in this group. Because these and other conceptual and methodologic issues have been discussed by others (Caplan, 1974; Caplan, 1979; Cobb, 1976; Cobb, 1979; Thoits, 1982; Weiss, 1974; Wortman, 1984; Wortman and Dunkel-Schetter, 1987), we have not reiterated them here. We strongly believe, however, that the suggestions made by other reviewers should be incorporated into future studies of social support and cancer, in this case breast cancer. In particular, it would be useful to measure a number of components of social support. Most studies reviewed here measured perceived emotional support from relatives and friends, and findings were fairly consistent using various operational definitions of perceived support and most indicators of adjustment. Findings from the few studies which included other components of social support tended to show different patterns of association between these components of support and indicators of adjustment.

Measures of adjustment also suffer from lack of conceptual clarity. Frequently, researchers have not measured the same underlying construct (Temoshok and Heller, 1984), and even when they have, the operational measure or the method of measurement (e.g. interview versus self-report) differed. Although they did not address the broader issue of conceptualization, Clark and Fallowfield (1986) recommended a number of standardized instruments that clinicians could use to assess adjustment, or in their words 'quality of life,' in cancer patients. As more life-extending treatments are introduced, many of which have toxic side effects, adjustment or quality of life may be a preferred endpoint to survival. Steinberg *et al.* (1985) suggested that behavioral and functional changes might even be more useful as indicators of long-term adjustment than psychiatric outcomes; however, at this time, the best approach would seem to be one that included a variety of adjustment measures.

Another unresolved issue meriting attention is the underlying mechanisms or mediating processes through which social support affects health outcomes or host vulnerability (Levy, 1986; Wortman, 1984). Much attention has been focused on whether social support is a protective factor which interacts with stressors or whether it has direct effects (Thoits, 1982). Wortman (1984) noted that less attention has been given to whether it operates through other intervening processes such as an individual's initial appraisal of a stressor, coping strategies, or self-esteem. Although these may be intervening variables, they still do not tell us about the biologic processes through which social support might bring about its effects. Fox (1983) emphasized that studies are needed which include measures of immune function and hormonal levels in addition to simply measuring attitudinal and behavioral factors. Very few of the studies discussed above addressed the issue of intervening factors, and many of them did not perform multivariate analysis to control for clinical and biologic factors that affect the course of breast cancer. As Levy (1986, p. 291) noted 'the major determinant of cancer outcome is the biology of the tumor and its host organism—constitutional host vulnerability, cell histopathology, genetic factors and so on.' She also noted, however, that for tumors which have a relatively indolent course, a reasonably wide interindividual variation in tumor course, and some evidence of hormonal and/or immunologic reactivity, there is the opportunity for cognitive, emotional, and behavioral responses of the host to play a contributing role in disease progression. This is the case for breast cancer because many of the identified risk factors (being female, young age at menarche, age at menopause over 55, late age at first birth, and obesity) have a final common endocrine pathway (Levy, 1986).

The recent work of Levy and her colleagues (Levy, 1986; Levy *et al.*, 1985, 1987) addresses possible mediating biologic pathways, although they have not yet looked at prognosis outcomes. The general hypothesis being tested in their work is that effects of the central nervous system influence malignant cell growth via hormonal and immunologic pathways (Levy, 1986). More specifically, emotional, cognitive, and behavioral responses of the organism are hypothesized to be biologic response modifiers relevant to cancer risk and progression of disease. To test this hypothesis, they have looked at the relationships among psychologic and behavioral variables, including social support, suppression of lymphocyte function, in particular natural cytotoxic action by natural killer (NK) cells, and axillary nodal status in breast cancer patients.

Levy *et al.* (1985) found that peripheral NK activity was associated with axillary nodal status in a sample of 75 stages 1 and 2 breast cancer patients; lower levels of NK activity at the time of primary treatment were associated with greater number of axillary lymph nodes positive for cancer. Although none of the psychosocial factors was independently associated with nodal status when NK activity was included in the model, three psychosocial factors accounted for 51% of the variance in NK activity, and one of those factors was social support. Patients who complained about lack of social support, as measured by communication with spouse, quality of spousal relationship, and general adequacy of the family as a support system, tended to have lower levels of NK activity. A later report (Levy *et al*, 1987) tested the hypothesis that variation in NK activity over a three-month period could be predicted on the basis of psychosocial factors that had been significant in the baseline study. Although the most important predictive factor in the follow-up study was baseline NK activity, a trend was seen for patients who reported little in the way of social support at baseline to show a decrease in NK activity levels at follow-up. In addition, the results of the baseline analysis were replicated at three months. The ultimate aim of their research is to assess whether or not psychosocial factors independently predict time to recurrence in breast cancer patients.

Many gaps in our knowledge still exist, and many questions remain unanswered. In comparing the state of affairs in psychosocial research on cancer to that on cardiovascular disease, Temoshok and Heller (1984, p. 231) noted that 'no psychosocial construct has emerged for cancer with the coordinated and systematic investigation, nor with the strength and weight of empirical evidence as has the Type A Behavior pattern for coronary heart disease...' They added, however, that the subject of cancer probably is more complex than the area of cardiovascular disease because there are numerous types of cancer that vary with regard to incidence, etiology, risk factors, course, and mortality. It would be useful, therefore, for future studies to evaluate the associations between psychosocial factors and prognosis and adjustment separately for each type of cancer.

ACKNOWLEDGEMENTS

This work was partially supported by a grant from the Pennzoil Company through the Kelsey-Seybold Foundation's Cancer Prevention Center.

REFERENCES

American Psychiatric Association (1980). *Diagnostic and Statistical Manual of Mental Disorders*, American Psychiatric Association, Washington, DC.

Baltrusch, H.J.F. and Waltz, M. (1985). Cancer from a biobehavioural and social epidemiological perspective. *Social Science and Medicine*, **20**, 789−94.

Berkman, L.F. and Syme, S.L. (1979). Social networks, host resistance, and mortality: a nine-year follow-up study of Alameda County residents. *American Journal of Epidemiology*, **109**, 186−204.

Berscheid, E., Walster, E. and Bohrnstedt, G. (1972). Body image: a Psychology Today questionnaire. *Psychology Today*, **6**, 58−66.

Bloom, J.R. (1982a). Social support systems and cancer: a conceptual view. In J. Cohen *et al.* (eds.) *Psychosocial Aspects of Cancer*, Raven Press, New York, pp. 129−49.

Bloom, J.R. (1982b). Social support, accommodation to stress and adjustment to breast cancer. *Social Science and Medicine*, **16**, 1229−38.

Bloom, J.R. (1986). Social support and adjustment to breast cancer. In B.L. Andersen (ed.) *Women and Cancer: Psychological Perspectives*, Springer-Verlag, New York, pp. 204−29.

Bloom, J.R., Ross, R.D. and Burnell, G. (1978). The effect of social support on patient adjustment after breast surgery. *Patient Counselling and Health Education*, **1**, 50−9.

Bloom, J.R. and Spiegel, D. (1984). The relationship of two dimensions of social support to the psychological well-being and social functioning of women with advanced breast cancer. *Social Science and Medicine*, **19**, 831−7.

Bloom, J.R. *et al.* (1987). Psychological response to mastectomy: a prospective comparison study. *Cancer*, **59**, 189−96.

Bradburn, N. (1969). *The Structure of Psychological Well-Being*, Aldine, Chicago.

Caplan, G. (1974). *Support Systems and Community Mental Health*, Behavioral Publications, New York.

Caplan, R.D. (1979). Social support, person−environment fit and loving. In L.A. Ferman and J.P. Gordus (eds.) *Mental Health and the Economy*, Upjohn Institute, Kalamazoo, MI.

Cassileth, B.R., Lusk, E.J., Miller, D.S., Brown, L.L. and Miller, C. (1985a). Psychosocial correlates of survival in advanced malignant disease? *New England Journal of Medicine*, **312**, 1551−5.

Cassileth, B.R., Miller, D.S., Miller, C., Lusk, E.J. and Brown, L. (1985b). Letter to the Editor. *New England Journal of Medicine*, **313**, 1356.

Chu, J., Diehr, P., Feigl, P., Glaefke, G., Begg, C., Glicksman, A. and Ford, L. (1987). The effect of age on the care of women with breast cancer in community hospitals. *Journal of Gerontology*, **42**, 185−90.

Clark, A. and Fallowfield, L.J. (1986). Quality of life measurements in patients with malignant disease. *Journal of the Royal Society of Medicine*, **76**, 165−9.

Cobb, S. (1976). Social support as a moderator of life stress. *Psychosomatic Medicine*, **38**, 300−14.

Cobb, S. (1979). Social support and health through the life course. In M.W. Riley (ed.) *Aging from Birth to Death: Interdisciplinary Perspectives*, Westview Press, Boulder, Colorado.

Cobb, S. and Erbe, C. (1978). Social support for the cancer patient. *Forum on Medicine*, **1**, 24−9.

Craig, T.J., Comstock, G.W. and Geiser P.B. (1974). The quality of survival in breast cancer: a case-control comparison. *Cancer*, **33**, 1450−7.

Dean, C. (1987). Psychiatric morbidity following mastectomy: preoperative predictors and types of illness. *Journal of Psychosomatic Research*, **31**, 385−91.

de Haes, J.C.J.M., van Oostrom, M.A. and Welvaart, K. (1986). The effect of radical and conserving surgery on the quality of life of early breast cancer patients. *European Journal of Surgical Oncology*, **12**, 337 – 42.

Derogatis, L. (1975). *The Affect Balance Scale*, Clinical Psychometric Research, Baltimore.

Donald, C.A. and Ware, J.E. (1982). *Quantification of Social Contacts and Resources* (Publication No. R-2937-HHS), Rand Corporation, Santa Monica, California.

Dunkel-Schetter, C. (1984). Social support and cancer: findings based on patient interviews and their implications. *Journal of Social Issues*, **40**, 77 – 98.

Fallowfield, L.J., Baum, M. and Maguire, G.P. (1986). Effects of breast conservation on psychological morbidity associated with diagnosis and treatment of early breast cancer. *British Medical Journal*, **293**, 1331 – 4.

Feighner, J.P., Robins, E., Guze, S.B., Woodruff, R.A., Winokur, G. and Munoz, R. (1972). Diagnostic Criteria for use in psychiatric research. *Archives of General Psychiatry*, **26**, 57 – 63.

Flamer, D. (1977). *Perception of Social Support*. Unpublished manuscript (available from the author, Shaklee Corp., 444 Market St, San Francisco, California).

Fox, B.H. (1983). Current theory of psychogenic effects on cancer incidence and prognosis. *Journal of Psychosocial Oncology*, **1**, 17 – 31.

Funch, D.P. and Marshall, J.R. (1983). The role of stress, social support and age in survival from breast cancer. *Journal of Psychosomatic Research*, **27**, 77 – 83.

Funch, D.P. and Marshall, J.R. (1984). Self-reliance as a modifier of the effects of life stress and social support. *Journal of Psychosomatic Research*, **28**, 9 – 15.

Funch, D.P. and Mettlin, C. (1982). The role of support in relation to recovery from breast surgery. *Social Science and Medicine*, **16**, 91 – 8.

Gilson, B.S., Gilson, J.S., Bergner, M., Bobbitt, R.A., Kressel, S., Pollard, W.E. and Vesselago, M. (1975). The sickness impact profile, development of an outcome measure of health. *American Journal of Public Health*, **65**, 1304 – 10.

Goodwin, J.S., Hunt, W.C., Key, C.R. and Samet, J.M. (1987). The effect of marital status on stage, treatment, and survival of cancer patients. *Journal of the American Medical Association*, **258**, 3125 – 30.

Greenfield, S., Blanco, D.M., Elashoff, R.M. and Ganz, P.A. (1987). Patterns of care related to age of breast cancer patients. *Journal of the American Medical Association*, **257**, 2766 – 70.

Greer, S., Morris, T. and Pettingale, K.W. (1979). Psychological response to breast cancer: effect on outcome. *Lancet*, **ii**, 785 – 7.

Greer, S. and Watson, M. (1985). Towards a psychobiological model of cancer: psychological considerations. *Social Science and Medicine*, **20**, 773 – 7.

Hamilton, M. (1967). Development of a rating scale for primary depressive illness. *British Journal of Social and Clinical Psychology*, **6**, 278 – 96.

Heimler, E. (1965). *Survival in Society*, Halsted Press, New York.

Henry, J.P. (1982). The relation of social to biological processes in disease. *Social Science and Medicine*, **16**, 369 – 80.

Hislop, T.G., Waxler, N.E., Coldman, A.J., Elwood, J.M. and Kan, L. (1987). The prognostic significance of psychosocial factors in women with breast cancer. *Journal of Chronic Diseases*, **40**, 729 – 35.

Holland, J.C. and Mastrovito, R. (1980). Psychologic adaptation to breast cancer. *Cancer*, **46**, 1045 – 52.

Holmes, T.H. and Rahe, R.H. (1967). The social readjustment rating scale. *Journal of Psychosomatic Research*, **11**, 213 – 18.

Horm, J.W., Asire, A.J., Young, J.L., Jr and Pollack, E.S. (1984). SEER Program: Cancer Incidence and Mortality in the United States, 1973 – 81. USDHHS,

PHS, NIH, National Cancer Institute (NIH Publication No. 85-1837), Bethesda, Maryland.

Hughes, J.E., Royle, G.T., Buchanan, R. and Taylor, I. (1986). Depression and social stress among patients with benign breast disease. *British Journal of Surgery*, **73**, 997 – 9.

Hughson, A.V.M., Cooper, A.F., McArdle, C.S., Russell, A.R. and Smith, D.C. (1980). Psychiatric morbidity in disease-free survivors following radiotherapy and adjuvant chemotherapy for breast cancer: a 2-year follow-up study. *British Journal of Surgery*, **67**, 370.

Hughson, A.V.M., Cooper, A.F., McArdle, C.S. and Smith, D.C. (1986). Psychological impact of adjuvant chemotherapy in the first two years after mastectomy. *British Medical Journal*, **293**, 1268 – 71.

Hughson, A.V.M., Cooper, A.F., McArdle, C.S. and Smith, D.C. (1987). Psychosocial effects of radiotherapy after mastectomy. *British Medical Journal*, **294**, 1515 – 18.

Jamison, K.R., Wellisch, D.K. and Pasnau, R.O. (1978). Psychosocial aspects of mastectomy: 1. The woman's perspective. *American Journal of Psychiatry*, **135**, 432 – 6.

Janis, I.L. (1958). *Psychological Stress*, John Wiley & Sons, New York.

Lasry, J.C.M., Margolese, R.G., Poisson, R., Shibata, H., Fleischer, D., LaFleur, D., Legault, S. and Taillefer, S. (1987). Depression and body image following mastectomy and lumpectomy. *Journal of Chronic Diseases*, **40**, 529 – 34.

Levy, S.M. (1986). Behavior as a biological response modifier: psychological variables and cancer prognosis. In B.L. Andersen (ed.) *Women and Cancer: Psychological Perspectives*, Springer-Verlag, New York, pp. 289 – 306.

Levy, S., Herberman, R., Lippman, M. and d'Angelo, T. (1987). Correlation of stress factors with sustained depression of natural killer cell activity and predicted prognosis in patients with breast cancer. *Journal of Clinical Oncology*, **5**, 348 – 53.

Levy, S., Herberman, R.B., Maluish, A.M., Schlien, B. and Lippman, M. (1985). Prognostic risk assessment in primary breast cancer by behavioral and immunological parameters. *Health Psychology*, **4**, 99 – 113.

Lindsey, A.M., Norbeck, J.S., Carrieri, V.L. and Perry, E. (1981). Social support and health outcomes in postmastectomy women: a review. *Cancer Nursing*, **4**, 377 – 84.

McNair, P.M., Lorr, M. and Droppelman, L. (1971). *POMS Manual*, Education and Industrial Testing Service, San Diego, California, pp. 24 – 5.

McQueen, D.V. and Siegrist, J. (1982). Social factors in the etiology of chronic disease: an overview. *Social Science and Medicine*, **16**, 353 – 67.

Maguire, G.P., Lee, E.G., Bevington, D.J., Küchemann, C.S., Crabtree, R.J. and Cornell, C.E. (1978). Psychiatric problems in the first year after mastectomy. *British Medical Journal*, **i**, 963 – 5.

Marshall, J.R. and Funch, D.P. (1983). Social environment and breast cancer: a cohort analysis of patient survival. *Cancer*, **52**, 1546 – 50.

Metzger, L.F., Rogers, T.F. and Bauman, L.J. (1983). Effects of age and marital status on emotional distress after a mastectomy. *Journal of Psychosocial Oncology*, **1**, 17 – 33.

Moos, R. (1974). *Family Environment Scale*, Consulting Psychological Press, Palo Alto, California.

Mortgenstern, H., Gellert, G.A., Walter, S.D., Ostfeld, A.M. and Siegel, B.S. (1984). The impact of a psychosocial support program on survival with breast cancer: the importance of selection bias in program evaluation. *Journal of Chronic Diseases*, **37**, 273 – 82.

Morris, T., Greer, H.S. and White, P. (1977). Psychological and social adjustment to mastectomy: a two-year follow-up study. *Cancer*, **40**, 2381 – 7.

Neale, A.V., Tilley, B.C. and Vernon, S.W. (1986). Marital status, delay in seeking treatment and survival from breast cancer. *Social Science and Medicine*, **23**, 305 – 12.

Orr, E. (1986). Open communication as an effective stress management method for breast cancer patients. *Journal of Human Stress*, **12**, 175–85.

Penman, D.T., Bloom, J.R., Fotopoulos, S., Cook, M.R., Holland, J.C., Gates, C., Flamer, D., Murawski, B., Ross, R., Brandt, U., Muenz, L.R. and Pee, D. (1987). The impact of mastectomy on self-concept and social function: a combined cross-sectional and longitudinal study with comparison groups. In S.D. Stellman (ed.) *Women and Cancer*, Haworth Press, New York, pp. 101–29.

Peteet, J.R. (1986). Psychological factors in the causation and course of cancer. In S.B. Day (ed.) *Cancer, Stress, and Death*, 2nd edn, Plenum Medical Book Co., New York, pp. 63–77.

Peters-Golden, H. (1982). Breast cancer: varied perceptions of social support in the illness experience. *Social Science and Medicine*, **16** 483–91.

Pettingale, K.W. (1985). Towards a psychobiological model of cancer: biological considerations. *Social Science and Medicine*, **20**, 779–87.

Pettingale, K.W., Morris, T., Greer, S. and Haybittle, J.L. (1985). Mental attitudes to cancer: an additional prognostic factor. *Lancet*, **i**, 750.

Polivy, J. (1977). Psychological effects of mastectomy on a woman's feminine self concept. *Journal of Nervous and Mental Disease*, **164**, 77–86.

Radloff, L.S. (1977). The CES-D Scale: A self-report depression scale for research in the general population. *Applied Psychological Measurement*, **1**, 385–401.

Rogers, T., Bauman, L. and Metzger, L. (1985). An assessment of the Reach to Recovery Program. *CA—A Cancer Journal for Clinicians*, **36**, 116–24.

Rosenberg, M. (1965). *Society and the Adolescent Self-Image*, Princeton University Press, Princeton.

Satariano, W.A. and Eckert, D. (1983). Social ties and functional adjustment following mastectomy: criteria for research. In P.F. Engstrom, P.N. Anderson and L.E. Mortenson (eds.) *Advances in Cancer Control: Research and Development*, Alan R. Liss, New York, pp. 387–94.

Schain, W. (1977). Personal Problem Checklist. Unpublished manuscript (available from the author, 5335 Strathmore Ave., Kensington, MD).

Smith, E.M., Redman, R., Burns, T.L. and Sagert, K.M. (1985). Perceptions of social support among patients with recently diagnosed breast, endometrial, and ovarian cancer: an exploratory study. *Journal of Psychosocial Oncology*, **3**, 65–81.

Spiegel, D., Bloom, J.R. and Gottheil, E. (1983). Family environment as a predictor of adjustment to metastatic breast carcinoma. *Journal of Psychosocial Oncology*, **1**, 33–44.

Spiegel, D., Bloom, J.R. and Yalom, I. (1981). Group supports for patients with metastatic cancer. *Archives of General Psychiatry*, **38**, 527–33.

Spitzer, R.L., Endicott, J. and Robins, E. (1978). Research diagnostic criteria: rationale and reliability. *Archives of General Psychiatry*, **35**, 773–82.

Steinberg, M.D., Juliano, M.A. and Wise, L. (1985). Psychological outcome of lumpectomy versus mastectomy in the treatment of breast cancer. *American Journal of Psychiatry*, **142**, 34–9.

Stewart, A.L., Ware, J.E., Brook, R.H. and Davies-Avery, A. (1978). *Conceptualization and Measurement of Health for Adults in the Health Insurance Study. Vol. II, Physical Health in Terms of Functioning*, Rand Corporation, Santa Monica, California.

Taylor, S.E., Falke, R.L., Shoptaw, S.J. and Lichtman, R.R. (1986). Social support, support groups, and the cancer patient. *Journal of Consulting and Clinical Psychology*, **54**, 608–15.

Temoshok, L. and Heller, B.W. (1984). On comparing apples, oranges and fruit salad: a methodological overview of medical outcome studies in psychosocial oncology.

In C. L. Cooper (ed.) *Psychosocial Stress and Cancer*, John Wiley & Sons, New York, pp. 231—60.

Thoits, P.A. (1982). Conceptual, methodological, and theoretical problems in studying social support as a buffer against life stress. *Journal of Health and Social Behavior*, **23**, 145—59.

Wallston, B.S., Wallston, K.A., Kaplan, G.D. and Maides, S.A. (1976). Development and validation of the health locus of control (HLC) Scale. *Journal of Consulting and Clinical Psychology*, **44**, 580—5.

Weisman, A.D. and Worden, J.W. (1975). Psychosocial analysis of cancer deaths. *Omega*, **6**, 61—75.

Weiss, R. (1974). The provisions of social relationships. In Z. Rubin (ed.) *Doing Unto Others*, Prentice Hall, Englewood Cliffs.

Wing, J.K., Cooper, J.E. and Sartorius, N. (1974). *The Measurement and Classification of Psychiatric Systems*, Cambridge University Press, Cambridge.

Winick, L. and Robbins, G.F. (1977). Physical and psychological readjustment after mastectomy: an evaluation of Memorial Hospital's PMRG Program. *Cancer*, **39**, 478—86.

Woods, N.F. and Earp, J.A.L. (1978). Women with cured breast cancer: a study of mastectomy patients in North Carolina. *Nursing Research*, **27**, 279—85.

Worden, J.W. and Weisman, A.D. (1977). The fallacy of postmastectomy depression. *American Journal of Medical Science*, **273**, 169—75.

Wortman, C.B. (1984). Social support and the cancer patient: conceptual and methodologic issues. *Cancer*, **53**, 2339—60.

Wortman, C.B. and Dunkel-Schetter, C. (1979). Interpersonal relationships and cancer: a theoretical analysis. *Journal of Social Issues*, **35**, 120—55.

Wortman, C.B. and Dunkel-Schetter, C. (1987). Conceptual and methodological issues in the study of social support. In A. Baum and J.E. Singer (eds.) *Handbook of Psychology and Health, Vol.V, Stress*, Lawrence Erlbaum Associates, Hillsdale, NJ, pp. 63—108.

Wright, B. (1960). *Physical Disability: A Psychological Approach*, Harper, New York.

Zigmond, A.S. and Snaith, R.P. (1983). The Hospital Anxiety and Depression Scale. *Acta Psychiatrica Scandinavica*, **67**, 361—70.

Informal and Formal Supports

Chapter 9

Investigating Caregiver Burden

Rhonda J.V. Montgomery

Over the past decade there has been an exponential growth in studies undertaken to investigate the role of the family in the long-term care delivery system for impaired older adults. As the prevalence and importance of family members as providers of care became common knowledge, numerous research efforts have been undertaken to gain a better understanding of the caregiving experience. Central to much of the research is the concept of caregiver burden.

To a large degree, interest in the family member as a caregiver grew from a social problems approach as clinicians and practitioners attempted to meet real and anticipated needs of families contending with a difficult situation. Because much of the research developed in association with intervention programs, the work in this area has been conducted with little theoretical guidance and a lack of consensus as to the meaning of the key terminology (Zarit, Todd and Zarit, 1986). Of particular interest here is the concept of caregiver burden which has been widely but not uniformly used to refer to the impact and/or stress that a family member incurs when assuming the caregiver role (Horowitz, 1985a; Montgomery, Stull and Borgatta, 1985a; Zarit, Reever and Bach-Peterson, 1980; Zarit, Todd and Zarit, 1986). A lack of consistency in conceptualization and operational measurement of the concept combined with methodological limitations has resulted in findings that are conflicting at best and more often disappointing. Few consistent patterns have emerged between caregiver burden and plausible predictor or outcome variables. This situation has prompted at least one research team (George and Gwyther, 1986) to abandon the concept of caregiver burden and has certainly raised questions in the minds of other researchers about the utility of the concept for advancing our knowledge about caregiver situations.

The intent of this chapter is to bring clarity to the concept of caregiver burden by reviewing the literature and noting both discrepancies and consistencies among findings. Issues to be addressed include the definition, measurement and use of burden as an independent, dependent and descriptive variable. Ultimately the chapter is aimed at providing a context within which the utility of the concept of caregiver burden can be judged in terms of its potential for aiding

Aging, Stress and Health Edited by K.S. Markides and C.L. Cooper researchers in their quest to explain or understand the caregiving experience or situation.

DEFINING BURDEN

According to the dictionary (Merriam-Webster, 1975), burden can mean the 'load or responsibilities' to be carried, or burden can mean 'something oppressive'. While it is possible that one's responsibilities can be defined as a burden using both definitions, it is not necessarily true. Not all loads are oppressive. Furthermore, a subjective judgement is involved in the determination as to whether a load or responsibility is oppressive.

To a large degree, the inconsistencies in the use of the concept of caregiver burden and in findings reported concerning correlates of burden stem from the fact that both definitions have been used by investigators with little if any attention being given to the distinction between the two meanings. This failure to distinguish between the 'load' borne and 'extent to which that load is oppressive' has not only prevented conceptual clarity but has led to great variety in measurement and in the statement of research questions and hypotheses concerned with caregiver burden.

The concept of caregiver burden was first introduced into the health care literature by investigators concerned with the consequences for families of their mentally ill members being discharged from institutions. In the earliest of these studies it was assumed that the presence and or behavior of these individuals was oppressive or burdensome and therefore costly to family members (Thompson and Doll, 1982). These early investigations did not measure burden in terms of actual responsibilities or tasks nor in terms of subjective judgements about the difficulty or imposition that these responsibilities created. Rather, it was assumed that these caregivers paid costs and the costs were inferred from attitudinal measures of social distance and stigma (Kelley, 1964; Cumming and Cumming, 1965; Thompson and Doll, 1982).

The work of Grad and Sainsbury (1963) represents the first effort to clarify and measure the costs of caring for a mentally ill individual rather than simply assuming these costs. In their work family burden was conceptualized as 'any costs to the family', a definition more in keeping with the notion of burden as oppressive. This conceptualization of burden as costs that are associated with the responsibilities of caring for a dependent individual was further refined by the work of Hertz, Endicott and Spritzer (1976), Hoenig and Hamilton (1967), Platt and Hirsch (1981), and Thompson and Doll (1982). These more recent investigations not only measured the costs but made a distinction between those costs that could be objectively observed (e.g. financial costs, disruption to routines, costs in time) and those costs that were subjectively felt such as feelings of embarrassment, overload or resentment. This distinction between 'objective burden' and 'subjective burden' contributed to the literature by adding clarity to the concept but at the same time introduced yet another dimension to the meaning of burden. As found in the mental health literature, burden can mean the actual responsibilities, observable costs that are perceived to be a consequence of responsibilities (objective burden) or felt impositions that are not observable to the outsider but require the subjective judgement of the caregiver (subjective burden).

The concept of caregiver burden is still quite new to the gerontological field. While some investigations concerned with the consequences for families of providing care for impaired elderly members have benefited from the work of their colleagues concerned with the mentally ill, much of the work has been done without reference to the earlier literature. Hence, there has been a delayed yet parallel development in the conceptualization and measurement of burden. Burden is but one of a myriad of concepts used to refer to the consequences or effects of caregiving. Other terms used in the literature include caregiver strain, costs of care, family inconveniences, caregiving consequences, personal strains, stress effects and caregiving impact, and caregiver well-being (Cantor, 1983; Cicirelli, 1981; George and Gwyther, 1986; Horowitz, 1985a; Kosberg, 1983; Morycz, 1985; Robinson, 1983; Teresi, Bennett and Wilder, 1978). This variation in terminology not only underscores the lack of consistency in terminology but also attests to some uniformity in conceptualization of the issue. Essentially all of the studies concerned with the effect of, consequence of, or impact of caregiving assume that the responsibilities of caregiving are causally related to some type of negative effect or oppression. This negative effect or oppression is the central concept of concern here and in the interest of simplicity, will be termed caregiver burden for the duration of this chapter.

Differences that exist in the literature in the conceptualization and measurement of caregiver burden stem from different views as to the appropriate levels of specification and measurement of these effects (Horowitz, 1985a). The earliest work tended to assume that a single unidimensional measure could be used to obtain a summary measure of the effect of caregiving on the life of the caregiver. Whether referred to as caregiver strain (Robinson, 1983), consequences (Horowitz, 1985b), cost (Kosberg and Cairl, 1986) or burden (Zarit and Zarit, 1982) such summary measures are treated as a measure of the degree of oppression imposed upon a caregiver by the caregiving responsibilities. Horowitz (1985a) notes that researchers in this tradition have made the implicit assumption that all experience will affect the evaluation of objective problems and the degree to which lifestyles are perceived to be altered.

More recently there has been a trend to distinguish between different dimensions of burden. In keeping with the earlier work that focused on the impacts of deinstitutionalization of the mentally ill some investigators have distinguished between impositions that can be objectively quantified such as infringement on time, money and activities, and impositions on more subjective dimensions of people's lives, such as relationships and feelings (Circirelli, 1981; Hooyman, Gonyea and Montgomery 1985; Montgomery, Gonyea and Hooyman,

1985b). It has been argued that this distinction provides for more clarity in understanding the issues since the causes and consequences of the two types of burden may be very different. It is also possible that the two types of burden interact to influence the level of each other. Regardless of the measure used in the works to this point, there appears to be an implicit agreement as to the meaning of burden. Caregiver burden is conceptualized as: 'the extent to which the caregiving role is judged to infringe upon an individual's life space and be oppressive'. Differences in measurement have centered on differences in the aspect of the caregivers' life space that are measured and how they are summed to arrive at a score.

In their 1984 article Poulschock and Deimling introduced yet another meaning for the term burden. These authors assert that the term 'caregiver impact' is a better term for the outcome measure of interest than is objective burden. Burden, they argue, is better viewed as the subjective judgement that a caregiver makes about the extent to which a patient's behavior or impairments translate into responsibilities that are troublesome, difficult or upsetting. From their perspective this subjective judgement of burden serves as an intervening variable between the level of impairment and different types of caregiver impact. In general they argue for more specification and measurement of the concepts involved. Not only is there a different burden score for different types of impairment or behavior but there can be multiple caregiver impacts. In particular, their work identifies two types of impact, i.e. effects of elder caregiver—family relations (EFC) and restrictions on caregiver activities. For the most part, the items that compose the EFC scale parallel those used by other researchers to construct subjective burden and the items that make up the restriction of caregiver activities parallel those used in other scales to construct objective burden. Hence, the work of Poulshock and Deimling introduces a new definition of burden but does not dispense with the concept of burden as used by others; it simply renames it caregiver impacts.

ASSESSING THE UTILITY OF THE CONCEPT

Consensus on the definition of caregiver burden is only beneficial to the extent that the concept adds significantly to an understanding of the caregiving situation. That is, the utility of caregiver burden as a concept must be judged against the criteria that the concept increases understanding, enables explanation of the caregiving experience and/or facilitates prediction of future outcomes of interest. This judgement will involve two levels of consideration. First, it must be determined that the concept is unique from other concepts that are more widely used in the social science literature. For if another concept is synonymous with or can be substituted for burden in a theoretical or empirical model then caregiver burden would be a superfluous concept. Second, it must be determined whether the concept serves as a parsimonious descriptor of the situation or as a predictor of other outcome variables of interest.

An underlying framework

To assess the merits of the concept against these two criteria it is first necessary to identify the framework that has been used by investigators concerned with caregiver burden and the way in which the concept has been placed within this framework. Regardless of the definition or the measurement used, virtually all of the research concerned with caregiver burden is premised on the notion that an understanding of correlates, predictor variables or consequences will lead to a better understanding of the caregiver situation and/or directions for interventions.

While few studies have begun with an explicitly stated theoretical or conceptual framework, an implicit model appears to have guided the majority of research. Much of the work to date has treated burden as a dependent variable using a model that, at minimum, assumes that characteristics of the elder (e.g. age, health status, activities of daily living, income etc.), characteristics of the caregiver (e.g. relationship to elder, age, sex, income, health status), and/or characteristics of caregiving responsibilities (type of task, amount of time, length of time in role) are in some manner associated with the level of burden (George and Gwyther, 1986; Montgomery, Stull and Borgatta, 1985a; Poulshock and Deimling, 1984; Zarit and Zarit, 1982). Depending upon the definition of burden used, this model may hypothesize direct relationships between burden and the three sets of antecedent variables, or the model may depict the variables in a series with caregiving tasks treated as intervening variables as shown in Figure 1. In either case, when burden is approached with this framework, it is viewed as intrinsically of interest not because it leads to other consequences nor to specific behaviors but because burden is by definition viewed as bad. When investigated from this perspective, burden appears to be viewed as a specific type of stress or strain and interest in antecedents or correlates stems from the desire to identify factors that can be altered to minimize or reduce this stress (e.g. Drinka, Smith and Drinka, 1987; Haley, 1987; Pratt, Schmall, Wright and Cleland, 1985; Scott, Roberto and Hutton, 1986).

Although the truncated model shown in Figure 1 appears to have guided much of the existing research, the expanded model in Figure 2 is probably more representative of the conceptual framework that has served as an impetus to more recent work concerned with caregiver burden (e.g. Colerick and George, 1986; Montgomery and Borgatta, 1987; Montgomery and Hatch, 1987; Morycz, 1985; Noelker and Townsend, 1987). It is also the model that underlies legislation aimed at creating services to support families. Here, caregiver burden is seen as an intervening variable that is not only a consequence of various elder and caregiver characteristics but is a predictor of future caregiver behavior, and ultimately the living arrangement of the elder. The assumptions underlying this model are that increased burden will reduce the willingness or ability of a caregiver to provide care and thereby contribute to the decision to institutionalize an elder. Again, the model is premised on the assumption that knowledge of predictors of burden and thereby predictors of other outcome variables will help in the identification and development of intervention procedures that can be used to influence caregivers' behavior.

Having established the way in which caregiver burden has been approached by investigators, both as an independent and a dependent variable, it is now possible to assess the utility of the concept against the criteria of uniqueness. This notion

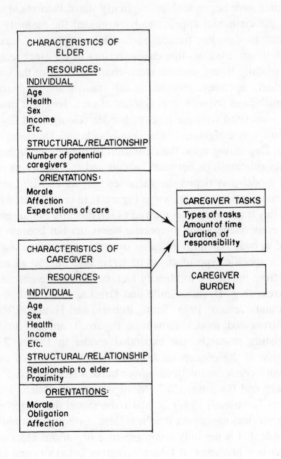

Figure 1 Model of Caregiver Burden

of uniqueness has been addressed by George and Gwyther (1986) who suggest that 'caregiver burden' and 'caregiver well-being' are opposite sides of the same coin. Specifically, they write (George and Gwyther, 1986, p.253):

> To anticipate caregiver burden among family members caring for an impaired relative is synonymous with the expectation that caregivers will experience decrements in selected dimensions of well-being relative to their age peers who do not have caregiving responsibilities.

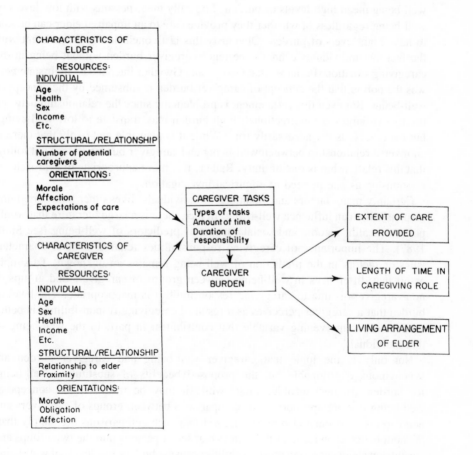

Figure 2 Expanded model of Caregiver Burden

In short, George and Gwyther argue against the uniqueness of burden as a social science concept, given the concept of well-being. They offer three methodological benefits to be gained by substituting the concept of well-being for caregiver burden. These include (1) the ability to compare distributions for caregivers with those for other relevant comparison groups; (2) conceptual and empirical freedom from a specific situation, e.g. caregiving; and (3) the ability to measure dimensions of well-being rather than being confined to a more global concept.

Although the work of George and Gwyther is persuasive, there are several aspects of their stance that deserve examination. First, the logic that leads to the assertion that caregiver burden is synonymous with caregiver well-being is questionable. For if burden is simply the opposite of well-being, it should follow that high levels of burden necessarily mean low levels of well-being and conversely low levels of well-being mean high levels of burden. Logically then, persons with low levels of well-being regardless of whether they provide care to an impaired elder can be said to have high levels of burden. Obviously this last conclusion is inconsistent with the fact that individuals cannot experience caregiver burden without being in the caregiving situation. Perhaps what George and Gwyther intended by their statement was the notion that the concept of caregiver burden is subsumed by the concept of well-being. But even this restatement is problematic since the relationship between the two variables is unidirectional: high burden may translate to low well-being, but the reverse is not necessarily true. While it is plausible and likely that there is an inverse relationship between well-being and caregiver burden it does not follow that this relationship is one of unity. Rather, it is more appropriate to approach the relationship as one in need of empirical investigation.

Certainly many factors and situations in individuals' lives other than caregiving responsibility can influence well-being. In fact, there is a large literature that would point to health, income and social support as predictors of well-being (see Stull, 1987). The importance of caregiving responsibilities relative to other characteristics or factors in the prediction of well-being remains an unknown. To simply assert that differences in well-being between groups of caregivers and groups of non-caregivers is due to caregiving responsibilities is inappropriate. The level of burden that a caregiver perceives as a result of caregiving responsibilities is better viewed as an intervening variable that contributes, in part, to the well-being of that individual.

Not only is the logic that caregiver well-being and caregiver burden are synonymous questionable but the proposed benefits of substituting well-being for burden are questionable. First, while it may be true that the concept of well-being is more appropriate for comparisons between groups of caregivers and non-caregivers it must also be recognized that such comparisons are simply that. Without better knowledge of the factors that select persons into the two groups any conclusion about caregiving responsibilities causing high or low levels of well-being are unjustified. It may well be that persons with low levels of well-being opt to assume caregiving roles or, conversely, those with high levels of well-being choose not to assume caregiving responsibilities. The influence of personality as a factor in measures of well-being may be indicative of such a process (see, for example, Costa *et al.*, 1987).

The second proclaimed benefit of using caregiver well-being rather than burden is that well-being is conceptually and empirically distinct from the specific situation. This separation of the concept from the situation could be viewed as a disadvantage of the variable if the research questions of interest are focused on differences among caregivers rather than differences between caregivers and non-caregivers. If the questions of interest concern predictors of variation in the impact of caregiving on caregivers, a concept grounded in the situation would seem more useful. Certainly, many factors other than the caregiving responsibility could contribute to variances in well-being among individuals and therefore numerous controls would be necessary before assertions of causal order could be made between caregiving and well-being. Moreover, the influence of caregiving responsibilities on an individual's well-being could be masked or overpowered by other factors in caregivers' lives if the more global concept of well-being is used as an outcome variable.

Finally, there is nothing inherent about the concept of caregiver burden that prevents it from being measured along several dimensions. Indeed the previous discussion of objective and subjective burden would suggest that caregiver burden, like well-being, can be and should be measured along multiple dimensions.

To summarize then, caregiver burden differs from well-being in that it is a concept that has a specific referent, i.e. the caregiving role. As such, it is likely to be a more sensitive measure of the effects of caregiving than is well-being. It is the variation in this burden and the antecedents and consequences of this variation that are of most interest as researchers investigate the caregiving experience, especially as they seek appropriate measures for intervention or identification of vulnerable individuals. Without knowledge of the specific cause and effect relationship it is impossible to identify plausible solutions. The more generic concept of well-being may be appropriate for studies comparing caregivers and non-caregivers but is less useful as a tool for understanding differences among caregivers in their experience.

A second concept that should be considered as the uniqueness of caregiver burden is evaluated is that of stress. Indeed many investigators of the effects of caregiving have conceptualized caregiver burden as a type of stress or strain and used the terms caregiver burden and caregiver stress interchangeably. Certainly, the definition of caregiver burden offered earlier is in keeping with the following definition of stress given by Lazarus and Folkman (1984, p. 19):

> psychological stress is a particular relationship between the person and the environment that is appraised by the person as taxing or exceeding his or her resources and endangering his or her well-being.

The only point at issue here is that of using the qualifying term 'caregiver' with the term 'stress' or 'burden'. Again the issue is one of specification. While stress is a generic term that has been defined in a number of ways, 'caregiver burden' or 'caregiver stress' is defined with reference to the caregiving responsibilities. Therefore, caregiver burden would be a more sensitive measure of the effects of caregiving then would the more global concept of stress which could be influenced by a multitude of other factors. The point at issue is not whether stress is a better concept than burden but whether the research questions of interest are those focused on overall stress in an individual's life or those focused on stress related to the caregiving role. For the most part, researchers and practitioners have been interested in the specific consequences of caregiving rather than in the overall level of stress within caregivers' lives since they are seeking knowledge to facilitate the design and targeting of interventions. Given this interest, it is important to use the qualifier 'caregiver' when using the term stress. However, there is probably not an imperative reason to use the term burden rather than stress. This choice is simply one of preference although large variations of definitions and measures of stress that already exist in the literature might prompt the use of burden in the interest of clarity.

Methodological limitations

Before summarizing the findings in the literature concerned with antecendents and predictors of burden, it is important to recognize several methodological limitations that pervade the literature in addition to the problems of conceptual clarity. Most problematic is the predominant use of cross-sectional designs. Although the implicit model that has guided research in the area is one of causal order that requires a longitudinal design, with few exceptions (George and Gwyther, 1986; Montgomery and Borgatta, 1987; Zarit *et al.*, 1986) cross-sectional designs have been used. Hence, analyses have been restricted to correlations between variables measured at a single point in time or in those studies looking at comparison groups to test for differences. Any conclusion drawn from these studies about causal order should necessarily be treated as speculative, if not inappropriate.

Even when researchers have carefully acknowledged the limitations of their findings to relationships of correlation rather than causation they have not been equally careful to raise questions about relationships that may be artifacts of measurement. For example, one might question whether there is sufficient independence in the measurement of burden and EFC, in the study conducted by Poulshock and Deimling (1984), to merit a discussion of causal order. If a respondent is asked, in a single interview, to judge the level of difficulty or strain of a set of particular tasks or impairments and in the same interview asked to make more global judgements about the impact of the caregiver role (the culminations of these specific tasks or impairments) on various aspects of his/her life, it could be argued that the two sets of questions are separate measures of the same concept. The difference is in level of specificity. Both questions require a judgement on the part of respondents about the extent to which an activity or a group of activities (i.e. the caregiver role) infringe upon their life in some manner. The intent here is not to critique any particular work but to illustrate a potentially problematic procedure that has been widely used (see, for example, Scott *et al.*, 1986; Zarit and Zarit, 1982; Zarit *et al.*, 1986). Caregivers have been regularly asked for their subjective judgements about their role and many other aspects of their lives at a single point in time. Given the subjective nature of their responses and the practice of using the caregiving role as a referent, it would be surprising if correlations were not found among the variables measured. However, any conclusions about causal order should be suspect. In many cases the basis of correlation may be an artifact of common measurement procedures or it may be that the variables are not tapping unique domains but, instead, are tapping different aspects of the same domain. In short, it may be that the factors that have been found to be related to burden are not predictors of burden but rather alternative measures of burden.

Finally, much of the work on caregiver burden has been done using small clinical or volunteer samples. The small sample sizes often preclude the use of multivariate analyses while at the same time the select nature of the samples introduces variables that co-vary with the critical independent and/or dependent variable. Hence, even correlations among variables must be cautiously interpreted since they may be spurious. An example of this is the confounding of the variables 'relationship to elder' and 'living arrangements'. Since spouses are more likely to be living with an elder than are adult children, it has not been always clear whether the greater burden reported for spouses is due to the relationship or to the living arrangement. Without sufficient samples sizes and multivariate analyses, such questions cannot be addressed.

Burden as a dependent variable

Despite these methodological limitations several consistent findings have emerged from the literature concerned with predictors of caregiver burden or strain. Among these consistent findings has been the frequent report that a substantial number of caregivers experience no or very low levels of burden even when dealing with apparently difficult circumstances (Cicirelli, 1981; Noelker and Poulshock, 1982; Zarit *et al.*, 1980). While practitioners and researchers continue to postulate a strong relationship between caregiving tasks and burden many caregivers view their situation far more positively than do these outside observers. It is clear from the consistency of the empirical findings that the act of providing care for an elderly individual cannot be intrinsically defined as a burden. Rather, it is important to measure the tasks associated with caregiving separately from the perceptions of burden associated with the caregiving tasks. Moreover, even when caregivers assert a relationship between their role and diminished personal resources it does not follow that caregivers will see these diminished resources oppressive or a burden. Indeed the findings of low levels of burden serve to underscore the need to specify the conditions or factors that contribute to burden or mediate between the absolute costs in terms of physical, emotional and financial resources and the level of felt imposition.

This leads to the second consistent finding. Despite common sense beliefs, little evidence has been found to support the notion that characteristics of the elder are associated with the caregiver's level of burden. Studies have repeatedly reported that neither background characteristics such as elder's age, sex, and income nor measures of the elder's health including level of disability, diagnosis or symptoms are associated with the level of burden or stress (Fitting, Rabins, Lucas and Eastman, 1986; George and Gwyther, 1986; Montgomery *et al.*, 1985b; Montgomery and Borgatta, 1987; Scott *et al.*, 1986; Zarit *et al.*, 1980, 1986). Although numerous studies have shown that as the older person's level of functional or mental impairment increases the amount of assistance provided by the caregiver also increases, there is insufficient evidence to conclude that there is a corresponding increase in the level of burden. Furthermore, there is little empirical data to support the notion that persons caring for elders with greater levels of mental impairment experience higher levels of burden although this belief is widely stated within the clinical literature (Drinka *et al.*, 1987; Montgomery and Kosloski, 1988; Scott *et al.*, 1986).

Findings regarding the relationship of caregiver characteristics to caregiver burden have been more promising although patterns have still been fragmented and inconsistent. For example, several studies have reported higher levels of burden or stress for women (Cantor, 1983; Horowitz, 1982; Noelker and Poulshock, 1984; Robinson and Thurner, 1979; Select Committee on Aging, 1987; Zarit, 1980) but this pattern has not always been replicated (Fitting *et al.*, 1986; Montgomery and Kamo, 1987; Pratt *et al.*, 1985; Zarit *et al.*, 1986). Similarly, George and Gwyther (1986) reported higher levels of burden among spouse caregivers than among adult children while others have reported no differences in the level of burden between spouses and adult children (Montgomery and Borgatta, 1985; 1987) or greater strain for adult children (Johnson, 1983). A plausible explanation for these inconsistencies rests in the covariance of key independent variables and the predominance of univariate analyses within the literature. Most studies have investigated the effects of the sex of the caregiver on burden without controlling for the relationship of the caregiver to the elder. Therefore, findings of differences or similarities between males and females may be confounded with the effects of the relationship of the caregiver to the elder (i.e. spouse versus child).

The literature clearly documents differences between children and spouses in the types of caregiving tasks performed, the extent of care provided and the duration of the caregiving role (Colerick and George, 1986; Horowitz, 1985a; Montgomery and Borgatta, 1987; Select Committee on Aging, 1987). As a rule, spouses tend to provide more extensive and more personal care for a longer period of time than do children. At the same time there is evidence that women provide more personal care than do men and women do so with less help from formal care providers (Horowitz, 1985b; Stalle , 1983; Stone, 1987). What is not known is whether the relationship of the caregiver to the elder or the sex of the caregiver is more important in defining the caregiver role. That is, how do daughters differ from husbands in their caregiving experience? The issue becomes even more complex when the living arrangement of the elder is introduced as a variable. Again the literature suggests that caregivers who reside with the elder experience more stress or burden (Horowitz, 1985a). However, the living arrangement of the elder is often confounded with the relationship of the caregiver to the elder since spouses are more likely to be living with an elder than are children. Hence the relative importance of the living arrangement, the caregiver relationship, and the sex of the caregiver in determining the level of burden becomes an important question. Other variables that add to this complexity include income and age of the caregiver, which have been found to be related to burden in some studies (Cicirelli, 1981; Horowitz, 1982; Montgomery *et al.*, 1985b). Again, these variables are correlated with the relationship of the caregiver to elder. Obviously children are younger and generally have higher incomes.

The result of this confounding of independent variables is that it is almost impossible to summarize the relationships between caregiver characteristics of burden with any definitive statement. However, when considered together the scattered and conflicting results do point to the caregiver context or situation as the critical element determining burden. For all of these variables, i.e. age, income, sex, relationship to the elder and living arrangement, combine to determine the resources of a caregiver, the expectations of the elder for help and, to a large degree, the type and extent of care provided by a given family member. It is within this context that a caregiver makes a subjective judgement about the extent to which his or her caregiving activities are an infringement that is oppressive. Rather than the absolute level of care or the level of impairment determining burden, it appears that burden is a function of the level and type of care provided along with the expectations and resources available. What is needed to clarify the issues are larger studies that will allow for multivariate analyses to untangle the effects of highly correlated independent variables. In addition, attention needs to be given to identifying and measuring the domain of variables that are critical elements of the caregiver context. These might include such elements as elders' and caregivers' expectations for care, financial resources, and competing demands for time, energy and money.

Some work has been done in this direction that does lend support to the notion that the caregiver context is the important determinant of burden. This work has focused on the social support available to caregivers. While the number of persons available to assist the caregiver has not been found to be consistently related to burden there is some notion that the perceived adequacy of available support is related to burden. Scott and her colleagues (1986) found that those persons who judged their support to be adequate reported lower levels of burden than did those who judged it to be less than adequate or more than adequate. Similarly, George and Gwyther (1986) report that the perceptions of need for more assistance from friends and relatives was strongly associated with four dimensions of well-being. While the cross-sectional nature of both of these studies creates methodological and interpretation problems, the findings are noteworthy in that they point to caregivers' perceptions of adequacy of resources as critical factors influencing the level of burden.

Burden as a predictor variable

As an independent variable caregiver burden has been put forth as a probable predictor of caregiver well-being, elder abuse (Beck and Phillips, 1983) and institutionalization of elderly relatives (Montgomery *et al.*, 1985b; Morycz, 1985; Zarit *et al.*, 1986). To date, however, empirical investigations have been limited to the study of the impact of caregiver burden on nursing home placement. Given the neonatal nature of the work in this area and the methodological limitations of much of the research, it is encouraging to find consistency in findings reported by the small number of researchers who have completed studies. In a 1985 study, Morycz found a positive and significant relationship between family strain and the desire of family caregivers to institutionalize patients. This relationship was retained when multivariate analyses were used although the study indicated that strain was not an adequate predictor for males or blacks. The study did not look at actual nursing home placement but a follow-up interview did show that the desire to institutionalize was significantly associated with actual institutionalization.

Similar results were reported by Zarit *et al.* (1986) and Colerick and George (1986) using longitudinal data sets. The small sample size prevented Zarit and his colleagues from using multivariate analysis, but tests for differences in the level of burden reported at Time 1 between caregivers who placed their elder at Time 2 and caregivers who continued to care for their elders at Time 2 indicated significantly higher levels of burden for the group who placed their elder. Although Colerick and George emphasize the importance of the relationship of the caregiver to the elder (i.e. spouse versus adult child) to the decision to institutionalize, they also report higher levels of stress and more dissatisfaction with time spent in recreational pursuits at Time 1 among caregivers who chose to place their elder at Time 2.

Most recently, Kosloski, Montgomery and Borgatta (1988) reported that caregivers who placed their elder in a nursing home at Time 2 had higher levels of subjective burden at Time 1. This pattern was most notable for those caregivers who were adult children. While there is need for more longitudinal studies and multivariate analyses to further specify the extent to which caregiver burden or stress contributes to the decision to institutionalize an elder, these early findings clearly point to the importance of the variable in understanding caregivers' behaviors.

CONCLUSION

Perhaps the most significant conclusion that can be drawn from this discussion of the concept of burden is the fact that the work in this area is in its infancy and any movement to abandon the concept as redundant, superfluous or uninformative is highly premature. The more appropriate direction to be taken is to intensify the work in this area by introducing more adequate theoretical frameworks and research designs that will allow the study of a situation that is clearly more complex than most investigations to date have allowed.

The absence of definitive patterns of direct relationships between either elder characteristics and burden or caregiver characteristics and burden underscore the complex way in which the caregiver situation is experienced. Caregiver burden, if measured appropriately, is likely to serve as a very good descriptor of a caregiver's situation. In a sense, it is a barometer that can be more sensitive than either physical aspects of the elder or more direct measures of caregiver resources because it is a function of both. While useful as a descriptor of the situation, a barometer reading can also be useful in predicting future events. In the case of burden, there is some evidence in the literature to suggest that it can help to predict future caregiving behaviors and institutionalization. As a consequence, greater knowledge of predictors of burden is likely to lead to more efficient and effectual means of helping families to cope with this difficult role.

Certainly, this review of the literature affirms the potential of the caregiver burden as a useful concept in the study of the caregiving role. There are, however, numerous directions that future investigations can take to improve both the measurement of burden and its use as a concept to facilitate an understanding of caregiving as a phenomenon. Attention needs to be given to the refinement of measures used and the delineation of different types of burden. Just as well-being can be subdivided into physical, emotional and financial well-being, burden can be conceived of as physical, emotional, social or financial. While some attention has been given to this division, much of the work has relied upon global measures. All of the work in this area could benefit from attention to issues of validity and reliability.

For those researchers and practitioners interested in the development of interventions, considerably more knowledge needs to be gained about the domain of variables that define the boundaries of caregivers' resources and living space. Equally important, multivariate analysis techniques need to be employed so that the relative importance of independent variables can be assessed and interaction effects can be investigated.

Finally, more studies employing longitudinal designs with sufficient sample sizes need to be conducted to investigate the consequences of burden. These studies need to focus on the long-term and short-term effects of burden on caregivers' lives as well as elders' lives. Furthermore, work needs to be done to specify the types of burden that impact future behaviors and conditions under which burden leads to alternative behaviors.

REFERENCES

Beck, C.M. and Phillips, L.R. (1983). Abuse of the elderly. *Journal of Gerontological Nursing*, **9** (2), 97–101, 122.

Cantor, M.H., (1983). Strain among caregivers: A study of experience in the United States. *The Gerontologist*, **23**, 597–604.

Cicirelli, V.G., (1981). *Helping Elderly Parents: The Role of Adult Children*, Auburn House, Boston.

Colerick, E.J. and George, L.K. (1986). Predictors of institutionalization among caregivers of patients with Alzheimer's disease. *Journal of the American Geriatrics Society*, **34** 493–8.

Costa, P.T. Jr, Zonderman, A.B., McCrae, R.R., Cornoni-Huntley, J., Locke, B.Z. and Barbano, H.E. (1987). Longitudinal analyses of psychological well-being in a national sample: Stability of mean levels. *Journal of Gerontology*, **42**, 50–5.

Cumming, J. and Cumming, E. (1965). On the stigma of mental illness. *Community Mental Health Journal*, **1**, 135–43.

Drinka, T.J., Smith, J.C. and Drinka, P.J. (1987). Correlates of depression and burden for informal caregivers of patients in a geriatrics referral clinic. *Journal of the American Geriatrics Society*, **35**, 522–5.

Fitting, M., Rabins, P., Lucas, M.J. and Eastman, J. (1986). Caregivers for dementia patients: A comparison of husbands and wives. *The Gerontologist*, **26**, 248–52.

George, L.K. and Gwyther, L.P. (1986). Caregiver well-being: A multidimensional examination of family caregivers of demented adults. *The Gerontologist*, **26** 253–9.

Grad, J., and Sainsbury, P. (1986). Mental illness and the family. *Lancet*, 544–7.

Haley, W.E., Levine, E.G., Brown, S.L., Berry, J.W. and Hughes, G.H. (1987). Psychological, social, and health consequences of caring for a relative with senile dementia. *Journal of the American Geriatrics Society*, **35**, 405–11.

Hertz, M.I., Endicott, J. and Spritzer, R.L. (1976). Brief versus standard hospitalizations: The families. *American Journal of Psychiatry*, **133**, 795–801.

Hoenig, J. and M.W. Hamilton (1967). The burden on the household in an extramural psychiatric service. In H. Freeman, (ed.) *New Aspects of the Mental Health Service*, Pergamon Press, London, pp. 612–635.

Hooyman, N., Gonyea, J. and Montgomery, R. (1985). The impact of in-home services termination on family caregivers. *The Gerontologist*, **25**, 141–5.

Horowitz, A. (1982). The impact of caregiving on children of the frail elderly. Paper presented at the Annual Meeting of the American Orthopsychiatric Association, San Francisco.

Horowitz, A. (1985a). Family caregiving to the frail elderly. *Annual Review of Gerontology and Geriatrics*, Vol. 5. Spring, New York, pp. 199–246.

Horowitz, A. (1985b). Sons and daughters as caregivers to older parents: Differences in role performance and consequences. *The Gerontologist*, **25**, 612–17.

Johnson, C.L. (1983). Dyadic family relations and social support. *The Gerontologist*, **23**, 377–83.

Johnson, C.L. and Catalano, D.J. (1983). A longitudinal study of family supports to impaired elderly. *The Gerontologist*, **23**, 612–18.

Kelley, F. (1964). Relatives' attitudes and outcome of schizophrenia. *Archives of General Psychiatry*, **10**, 389–94.

Kosberg, J.I. (1983). The cost of care index: A case management tool for predicting family abuse of the aged. Paper presented at the Annual Scientific Meeting of the Gerontological Society of America, San Francisco.

Kosberg, J.I. and Cairl, R.E. (1986). The cost of care index: A case management tool for screening informal care providers. *The Gerontologist*, **26**, 273–8.

Kosloski, K.D., Montgomery, R. and Borgatta, E. (1988). Factors influencing the nursing home of the elderly. Paper submitted to be presented at the 41st Annual Meeting of the Gerontological Society of America. San Francisco, November, 1988.

Lazarus, R.S. and Fokman, S. (1984). *Stress, Appraisal, and Coping*, Springer, New York.

Montgomery, R.J.V. and Borgatta, E. (1985). Family support project. Final Report to the Administration on Aging.

Montgomery, R.J.V. and Borgotta, E.F. (1987). Effects of alternative family support strategies. Final report to the Health Care Financing Administration.

Montgomery, R.J.V., Stull, D.E. and Borgatta, E.F. (1985a). Measurement and the analysis of burden. *Research on Aging*, **7**, 137–52.

Montgomery, R.J.V., Gonyea, J.G. and Hooyman, N.R. (1985b). Caregiving and the experience of subjective and objective burden. *Family Relations*, **34**, 19–26.

Montgomery, R.J.V. and Kamo, Y. (in press) Parent Care by Sons and Daughters. In J. Mancini, (ed.) *Parent Child Relationships and the Life Course*, D.C. Heath, Lexington.

Montgomery, R.J.V. and Kosloski, K.D. (1988). Type of impairment, service use, and caregiver response: Does Alzheimer's make a difference? *North Central Sociological Association*, Pittsburgh, April 15–17.

Morycz, R.K. (1985). Caregiving strain and the desire to institutionalize family members with Alzheimer's disease. *Research on Aging*, **7**, 329–61.

Noelker, L.S. and Poulshock, S.W. (1982). The effects on families of caring for impaired elderly in residence. Final report submitted to the Administration on Aging. The Margaret Blenkner Research Center for Family Studies. The Benjamin Rose Institute, Cleveland, OH.

Noelker, L.S. and Townsend, A.L. (1987). Perceived caregiving effectiveness: The impact of parental impairment, community resources, and caregiver characteristics. *Aging, Health and Family*, Sage Publications, Newbury Park, CA., pp. 58–99.

Poulshock, S.W. and Deimling, G.T. (1984). Families caring for elders in residence: Issues in the measurement of burden. *Journal of Gerontology*, **39** (2), 230–9.

Platt, S. and Hirsch, S. (1981). The effects of brief hospitalization upon the psychiatric patient's household. *Acta Psychiatrica Scandinavica*, **64**, 199–216.

Robinson, B. (1983). Validation of a caregiver strain index. *Journal of Gerontology*, **38**, 344–8.

Robinson, B. and Thurnher, M. (1979). Taking care of aged parents: A family cycle transition. *The Gerontologist*, **19**, 586–93.

Scott, J.P., Roberto, K.A. and Hutton, J.T. (1986). Families of Alzheimer's victims: Family support to the caregivers. *Journal of the American Geriatrics Society*, **34**, 348–54.

Select Committee on Aging, House of Representatives. (1987). *Exploding the myths: Caregiving in America. A Study by the Subcommittee on Human Services*, Comm. Pub. No. 99-611, Government Printing Office, Washington, DC.

Stoller, E.P. (1983). Parent caregiving by adult children. *Journal of Marriage and the Family*, **45**, 851–8.

Stone, R., Cafferata, G.L. and Sangl, J. (1987). Caregivers of the Frail Elderly: A National Profile. *The Gerontologist*, **27**, 617–626.

Teresi, J.A., Bennett, R.G., and Wilder, D.E. (1978). Personal time dependency and family attitudes. In *Dependency in the Elderly in New York City*, Community Council of Greater New York, New York.

Thompson, E.H. Jr and Doll, W. (1982). The burden of families coping with the mentally ill: An invisible crisis. *Family Relations*, **31**, 379–88.

Zarit, S.H., Reever, K.E. and Bach-Peterson, J. (1980). Relatives of the impaired elderly: Correlates of feelings of burden. *The Gerontologist*, **20**, 649–55.

Zarit, S.H., Todd, P.A. and Zarit, J.M. (1986). Subjective burden of husbands and wives as caregivers: A longitudinal study. *The Gerontologist*, **26**, 260–6.

Zarit, J.M. and Zarit, S.H. (1982). Measuring burden and support in families with Alzheimer's disease elders. Paper presented at the Annual Scientific Meeting of the Gerontological Society of America, Boston.

Chapter 10

Linkages Between Informal and Formal Support

Neena L. Chappell
and Lorna W. Guse

INTRODUCTION

This chapter deals with informal and formal support, with a focus on what is known about linkages between them. Despite the fact that interest in both informal and formal care derives largely from a concern with quality of life, stress, and psychological well-being, surprisingly little research has addressed the interrelationship between these three important areas. There is a longstanding interest in the area of stress and the role of informal support in minimizing stress in the lives of elderly individuals. There is a fair literature on utilization of formal services, interested primarily in the factors which predict who uses expensive physician and hospital services. There is an extensive literature on informal exchanges and support for the elderly. Much of this literature focuses on the family, in particular on spouses and children, with a growing literature on other relatives such as siblings, peer friendships, and neighbours. A relatively small but growing literature deals with the interrelationship between informal support and receipt of care from formal services. This paper discusses linkages between these two areas.

INFORMAL SUPPORT

Many studies examine interaction with and assistance to the elderly, assuming beneficial outcomes but not explicitly examining them. This literature has documented the strength of family ties with the elderly. Older people turn first to family members for assistance, for emotional and social support, for crisis intervention, and bureaucratic linkages (Shanas, 1979; Shanas and Maddox, 1985). Most elderly live close to at least one child (Hanson and Sauer, 1985) and the elderly prefer intimacy-at-a-distance. It is well-documented that the elderly today are not alienated from their families. As Brody (1981) has summarized so well, research demonstrates the strength of intergenerational ties, the continuity of filial responsibility, the frequency of contacts between the generations, the

Aging, Stress and Health Edited by K.S. Markides and C.L. Cooper
© 1989 John Wiley & Sons Ltd

predominance of families rather than professionals in the care of the elderly and the strenuous efforts by the family to avoid institutional placement of the old.

Approximately 80% of all assistance provided to the elderly comes from family members and from friends. Family support usually is provided by one or two members rather than the familial network as a whole. These primary caregivers traditionally have been women—wives, daughters, and daughters-in-law. Elderly individuals receive assistance first from the spouse, if one exists, and then from children, notably from daughters. Daughters tend to provide direct services, i.e. physical maintenance and emotional support. Sons play a more substantial role in decision-making or with financial assistance. However, when no female is available (there is none or she is geographically distant), sons do provide such care. The sexual division of labour is also evident in the contributions of the children's spouses (the elderly person's children-in-law). If a daughter is providing care her husband tends to accept her role but does not assist. If a son is providing care, his wife also assists (Treas, 1977; Horowitz, 1981).

Who helps after children is more open to debate. The literature frequently assumes that assistance is then provided by other relatives, followed by friends, and finally formal services (Cantor, 1975). However, recent Winnipeg data (Chappell, 1987) suggest that after children, assistance is received specifically from siblings and then from friends. That is, grandchildren seldom provide assistance and extended kin (nieces, nephews, cousins, in-laws, etc.) tend to be bypassed beyond siblings. After siblings, the elderly in modern day society turn to non-kin ties, to peer friendships.

Little research, however, has been conducted on family members other than spouses and children or on friendships and neighbouring relationships. Cicirelli (1985) maintains elderly people feel closer to siblings than to any other relative except their own children and perhaps their spouses. The closest bond among siblings is the sister–sister bond, highlighting the female–female relationship also reported in the strength of mother–daugher ties. Both role congruence and the socio-emotional involvement characteristic of women (Adams, 1986) are thought to account for these female–female relationships. Research on grandparents and grandchildren is sparse although increasing. Hagestad (1985) reports that the instrumental/emotional-expressive distinction between men and women holds at least for this cohort of grandparents. The same-sex bond emerges once again, with the grandmother–granddaughter tie the strongest. The quality of the bond is mediated through the kinkeeper work of the middle generation—the mother.

As Peters and Kaiser (1985) note, if friendship is studied at all, it tends to be treated as a residual category, included to assist in the understanding of other social roles such as kinship. Most frequently friendship ties are contrasted with kinship ties where friendship is characterized by voluntary involvement, affective bonds and consensus. While friendships can involve strong and long-term commitment, they are based less on obligation than kinship ties. Most elderly have friends, many of whom are long-term. There is some suggestion that women have more friends or at least more intimate friends. Women are more likely to have confidant relationships with friends than are men, who tend to confine such relationships to their spouses (Strain and Chappell, 1982; Heinemann, 1985).

Until recently, this body of literature generally has not distinguished between different types of support (informational, associational, functional, appraisal, etc.). By and large the informal network provides socio-emotional support (confidants and companions) and assistance in areas of the instrumental activities of daily living. It is frequently more difficult to provide assistance with the basic activities of daily living (walking, going to the bathroom, eating, etc.). Only recently have studies of informational links been the focus of research.

There are, furthermore, those who caution against unwarranted conclusions regarding intergenerational solidarity and support. Orbach (1983) notes that the family is frequently treated as a sacred institution, with the negative aspects of interaction overlooked. Nydegger (1983) argues that the tendency to idealize family ties stems from an emphasis on personal affective ties rather than formal relations which form the bases of kinship. Support for a less idealized view of family relations comes from both conceptual and empirical work. According to Dowd (1986) the elderly are disadvantaged in their intergenerational relations. Arguing from the principles of exchange theory, Dowd notes that age relations are power relations involving the exchange of power resources. Lacking access to such resources (including money, personal characteristics, personal social worth, and social attractiveness), elderly persons often are without the ability to maintain equity within their relationships. This includes primary relationships even within the family. For Dowd, the elderly are left with nothing to exchange but compliance in order to maintain their involvement within the interaction.

Dowd's work points to the importance of power and dependency issues for understanding the qualitative aspects of relationships. From this perspective, the receipt of substantial and unreciprocated support which is provided out of a sense of obligation can erode self-esteem. Krause (1987) has demonstrated empirically that emotional support beyond the average can lead to lowered feelings of control. Cohler and Lieberman (1980) studied the negative consequences of 'supportive' relations among three European ethnic groups. Findings reported by Johnson and Catalano (1983) reveal that over time, if dependency is prolonged, various social factors may undermine the caregiving dyad resulting in attempts by children to create physical and psychological distance between themselves and frail elderly parents, while continuing to meet their instrumental needs. The negative consequences of supportive relations require much more research, especially through studies which focus on both the positive `d negative dimensions, since most interactions no doubt contain elements

of each. Under what circumstances is interaction with others stress producing?

A related area in which there is a little information is the reciprocity of some
relationships. Hess and Waring (1980) argue that, when all forms of assistance are
considered, reciprocity characterizes parent–child relations. The most frequently
reported types of assistance given by children include companionship, emotional
support, living nearby, providing care when ill, and household management. Less
is known about the types of support which elderly persons provide to their
children. An exchange view of social support which focuses on the balance of
personal or social costs and benefits involved in the interaction between those
providing and those receiving support, suggest that unbalanced support within
the exchange is negatively related to well-being (Froland, Pancoast, Chapman
and Kimboko, 1981). Studies of elderly persons receiving care, usually from
family members, indicate that elders' ability to reciprocate is associated with
lower levels of depression (Dunkle, 1985) and with higher levels of self-esteem
(Stein, Linn and Stein, 1982). Supportive relationships characterized by excessive
giving appear to have a negative effect on the helped recipient while relationships
which are reciprocal do not (Ingersoll and Antonucci, 1983).

One reason why investigators have not looked more often at reciprocity
as a variable is because of the measurement difficulties. Reciprocity can be
conceptualized in a number of ways, and presently there are no answers
concerning the best way to measure this construct. There are measurement
issues of under-reporting and over-reporting when help is given or received and
these discrepancies appear to be rooted in individual appraisal. For example, one
study reported that those visiting a sick friend recognized this as 'giving' help
while conversely, those being visited perceived this as 'friendliness' (Jonas and
Wellin, 1980). In addition, discrepancies were often found between spouses,
likely based on differential role expectations. Husbands more often reported
giving help for the same tasks that wives seemed to consider part of household
duties. Similarly, elderly parents may be more aware of the help they receive
than are their adult children of the help that they give (Marshall, Rosenthal
and Synge, 1981). Such findings suggest important implications for individual
perception of support that have not been addressed to a large degree in
the literature.

In other words, despite the multidimensionality of the concept of social
support, existing research has tended to restrict the focus to specific dimensions, generally associational solidarity (frequency of interaction, types of
activities engaged in) and functional solidarity (type of assistance) to the
exclusion of other dimensions. In addition, the vast majority of research
focuses on and assumes the supportive nature of social relationships neglecting
important negative aspects. There is as well a tendency to focus on family
relations, particularly parent-child relations, to the neglect of other types of
relationships such as grandparenting and friendships. Analyses of relations

with children compared with siblings, and compared with friends, for example, are infrequent.

INFORMAL SUPPORT AND QUALITY OF LIFE

There is literature on the relationship between informal support and quality of life or well-being. The findings, however, are inconsistent. Some report a positive relationship between social support and well-being. For example, Badura and Waltz (1984) explored the relationship between serious illness, quality of interpersonal relationships, and socio-emotional support, and psychological well-being. They concluded that a supportive social environment was a key determinant of the positive dimensions of well-being. Porritt (1979) examined quality versus quantity of social support and found that quality of reactions to a person in crisis was more important to outcome than quantity. Thomas, Garry, Goodwin and Goodwin (1985) found a positive association between good health, longevity, and social support among the elderly. However, Andrews and associates (1978) found that neither coping style nor social support showed a mediating effect on the relationship between life event stress and psychological impairment. However, crisis support did exert an independent effect on psychological impairment. Similarly, Lin, Simeone, Ensel and Kuo (1979) found very weak support for a relationship between social support and well-being. These contradictory findings between social interaction and well-being are evident in the literature on life satisfaction as well (Graney, 1975; Bultena and Olyer, 1971; Mancini, Quinn, Gavigan and Franklin, 1980).

Generally, as Horowitz and Shindelman (1981) point out, a relationship between emotional closeness and interaction frequency has not been established. Furthermore, quantity of interaction does not seem to be central to adaptation in later life. Quality of interaction is more likely to be important. Even the importance of relations with children for the elderly's well-being is inconclusive. Some research shows no relationship between interaction with children and well-being or morale of the elderly (Conner, Powers and Bultena, 1979; Lee and Ellithorpe, 1982). Kendig (1986) reports that the strength of expressive bonds with children bears little or no relationship to the amount of instrumental support received from them. In other words, the relationships even between elderly members and their children are little understood.

Much of the basis for current attention directed to informal support was developed in the 1970s. Cassel (1976) argued that social support was a buffer or a cushion to the harmful effects of environmental stressors. In the same decade, Cobb (1976) argued that social support was information leading the person to believe that he or she is cared for and loved, esteemed and valued, and a member of a network of communication and mutual obligation. This definition emphasized the socio-emotional aspect of support. Subjective perception was highlighted.

Today social support is commonly viewed as a buffer to stress, i.e. having an indirect effect on stress. The buffer view argues that a lack of social support during stressful times results in somatic and psychiatric illnesses (Rook and Dooley, 1985; Dean and Lin, 1977). Frequently stressful life events (e.g. widowhood) are considered the stressors within this research. Broad measures of psychological well-being are the outcome measures. Usually formal support is not taken into account. This may be because the focus is on basic needs, such as feeling cared for, loved, and valued, rather than on material or instrumental support. Such emotional gratification is generally believed to come from informal interactions rather than from the formal support system. Formal support is primarily associated with instrumental interaction, i.e. the carrying out of tasks which are aimed at partial support or replacement of declining functional abilities. Informal support comes from those who are significant in emotional and social senses so the primacy of emotional support is assumed. Even task specific support from significant others is believed to imply emotional support which is not assumed of the formal care system.

Social support is also considered an ongoing part of everyday life, not only as a buffer mobilized primarily during stress periods. That is, social support is frequently viewed as having a direct effect on stress. In this approach, social support is also conceptualized as gratifying needs but these needs require fulfilment on a daily basis regardless of stressful life events. This literature frequently does not measure stress but looks at the relationship between support and various measures of well-being or health (Liang, Dvorkin, Kahana and Mazian, 1980; Lee, 1985). Some argue that the objective aspect of support or integration and its relationship with well-being is mediated by the subjective dimension, i.e. the individual's perception (Lowenthal and Haven, 1968; Ward, Sherman and LaGory, 1984).

Research findings are contradictory but nevertheless we have learned much over the past couple of decades. There is general agreement that social support is an important dimension. The specific details on how it works and under what circumstances are still open to question. Some recent work provides an indication of directions future research is likely to take. Krause (1987) hypothesized a non-linear relationship between social support and well-being. Specifically, he hypothesized that when older adults become overly dependent on significant others, the social support they receive tends to diminish rather than increase their feelings of control. That is, social support may generally serve to bolster feelings of control but there is a threshold point beyond which continued support may lead to dependence.

Studying informational support, tangible assistance, emotional help and integration (support provided by the respondent to others), it was concluded that initially emotional support tends to be associated with moderate feelings of personal control but when approximately average levels of emotional support are approached, the positive influence decreases and additional emotional support is related with decreased feelings of control. Similar findings are reported for integration but not for tangible assistance or informational support. This study indicates new directions for future research both in distinguishing between types of support and in examining curvilinear relationships.

Also in a recent study, Linn (1986) reports that social support has both a direct affect on health, those with more social support having more positive health, and a buffering effect when stress is high. Those with high stress report better evaluations of their health and self-esteem when they have more social support. The effects of stress and social support were greater in areas of psychological than in physical health.

Generally speaking, there is evidence in favour of the possible beneficial effects of social interaction. There is support for both direct and indirect effects. There is also sufficient evidence to indicate that there are negative dimensions to supportive interactions. However, details are lacking on which types of interactions, with whom, and under what circumstances interaction is most beneficial.

FORMAL CARE

The formal care system is established to provide care which, for whatever reason, individuals themselves or the informal support system are unable to provide. Despite current concerns over rising costs of formal health care services, the most prevalent form of care is self-care and informal assistance from others. It has long been known that the majority of illnesses are taken care of without professional consultation (Pratt, 1973). It is estimated that between 70% and 90% of all illness episodes are treated without recourse to expert knowledge (Helman, 1978; Blumhagen, 1980). Lay treatment includes the use of folk remedies, patent medicines, and prescribed medications.

As just discussed, assistance from family and friends is also prevalent. It is estimated that approximately 80% of the care to the elderly comes from this source, with only about 20% coming from the formal care system. It is still largely unknown who seeks assistance from the formal care system and why. Nevertheless, few argue that where symptoms are severe some kind of formal help is usually requested. McKinlay (1980) argues that interference with everyday activities is one of the major criteria laymen use to define illness. Generally, socially disruptive symptoms are more likely to be defined as requiring some kind of attention.

Not only is utilization of the formal care system the least prevalent form of health care in society, it is usually accessed after self-care and after assistance from the informal network. That is, people turn to their informal network initially, to family and friends, and contact relief agencies, professional service organizations only as a last resort. Evans and Northwood (1979) and Schmidt (1981) confirm this finding among the elderly. The sole use of formal services is found much less frequently than exclusive reliance on informal helpers or helpseeking from both sources. Furthermore, those who seek help within the social network represent a cross-section of the general population while those who eventually utilize formal health care services tend to be those who are young, white, educated, middle class, and female. This varies somewhat depending on the health care system in place.

For example, the formal health care system in Canada is more likely to be universal, to be based on need rather than on age, and to be uniform rather than based on past income differences when compared with the United States. In the United States it is more likely to be tied to age (Medicare is for the elderly) and to income (Medicaid is provided for the poor). Evans (1984) provides evidence demonstrating that universal access to health care does not lead to abuses of the system but rather those who are poor are more likely to receive formal health care services. User fees or spend down policies tend to exclude the poor from receiving such services. The health care systems in both countries tend to be patient initiated but doctor driven. That is, it is usually the individual who decides to access the system, to make an appointment, and to maintain that appointment. However, it is the physician who recommends a return visit, who recommends specialty care, who recommends hospitalization, and who has responsibility for ordering tests, etc.

It is not uncommon to hear that elderly individuals are the heaviest adult users of the health care system. In reality a small minority (approximately 20%) are very heavy users and the majority of elderly use no more formal services than do younger adults (Kane and Kane, 1978; Roos, Shapiro and Roos, 1984). The utilization by the elderly of formal health care services reflects the types of services which are available to them. Fully 85% of the elderly in Canada and 79% of those in the United States (Health and Welfare Canada and Statistics Canada, 1981; Kovar, 1977) in 1980 made at least one visit to a physician. Only 18% spent at least one night in hospital in Canada in 1984 (Statistics Canada, 1985). Figures from the United States are not strictly comparable—29% of all discharges from hospital in 1983 were accounted for by the elderly. The higher figure is at least partially due to the fact that one person can have more than one discharge (US, Bureau of the Census, 1986).

Figures for community care are difficult to obtain but are instructive. National statistics for community care are not collected for the United States. In Canada it is estimated that 0.8% of elderly persons received meals-on-wheels, 3.5% transportation services, 4.3% homemaker or home help services, 4.3% assistance with shopping and baking, and 3.7% nursing or other medical calls at home in 1981 (Statistics Canada, 1983). The higher utilization figures for physician services partially, at least, reflect the predominance of physicians within the health care systems of these two countries. Both systems offer primarily medical care. Only recently has the need among the elderly for community social services been recognized. The recognition, however, came after a large, complex, and powerful medical-industrial complex was well established.

Although over three decades have passed since Freidson (1960) coined the now well-known phrase 'the lay referral system' to refer to the role of family and friends in influencing an individual's decision to utilize or not utilize formal services, surprisingly little research has been done in this area. As McKinlay (1972) stated over a decade ago, studies on the utilization behaviour of individuals tend to isolate and assess differences between users and non-users. Seldom do studies examine how individuals or groups make the decision, what factors or individuals are influential in making that decision, or why one form of behavior is selected over another. This criticism is still valid today.

One suggestion is that the informal network provides a link into formal services. For example, McKinlay (1973) studied users of a maternity clinic and concluded the under-ultilizers relied more on a variety of readily available relatives and friends as lay consultants which represented one large interlocking network upon which advice was drawn and was probably relatively consistent. The utilizers, however, tended to have kin and friendship networks which were differentiated and separated from one another. This group frequently did not seek advice from members of their lay network or consulted only their husbands.

Starrett, Mindel and Wright (1983) found that those who utilized social as opposed to more traditional medical services in the United States tended to be those who were more involved with kin, with friends and neighbours, and in informal organized activities. This finding is confirmed by some network analysts studying strong versus weak ties in reference to what is known as the broker role (also discussed as the instrumental relationship by others). Lin (1982), for example, argues that there are advantages to weak ties (which are characterized by infrequent interactions and peripheral relationships among dissimilar individuals as opposed to strong ties which are characterized by an intimate social circle of individuals with similar characteristics) because weak ties can provide possible linkages with individuals who are dissimilar to one another. In other words, weak ties outside of one's own intimate social circle can provide access to information or influence not otherwise available.

Wellman (1981) argues that the large-scale nature of our social system means that much social support is intercorporate rather than interpersonal, so that personal networks spend much time helping an individual deal with corporate bureaucracy as well as directly providing assistance. In other words, people need brokers as much as supporters. On the other hand, Wagner and Keast (1981) studied medication among the elderly and reported that self-referral or referral from a formal source predominated in the use of formal services. That is, in the case of complex services, their data do not point to informal groups assisting the elderly in negotiating the complexity of help-seeking behaviour in a bureaucratic society. The informal group, rather, is more likely to function as a buffer than as a link between formal groups and the elderly.

This is an area in which much more research is required. Under what circumstances do what types of groups serve as linkages to which formal services? Are there differences between individuals in this regard? The relationships between informal and formal support networks are not well understood.

Increasingly studies of the Andersen–Newman (1973) model for predicting utilization of formal services are taking the informal network into account.

This adds to our knowledge of how the lay referral system works. Andersen and Newman outlined three main determinants of health utilization behaviour under general headings of predisposing factors, enabling factors, and need factors. Predisposing are those characteristics that exist prior to one's illness and which may affect need for services but not necessarily be the cause of utilization. They include such things as age, sex, ethnicity, education, and attitudinal factors. Enabling factors are conceptualized as those circumstances or individual characteristics which can either hinder or facilitate the use of appropriate services once the need has been recognized. These include, for example, financial resources and the availability of informal support. The third category is need, generally measured in terms of physical health. In the past, much of the literature focusing on utilization of formal health care services has been concerned with the extent to which need (disease, chronic conditions, and functional disability) is a good correlate of utilization.

There has been relative consistency in the finding that need is the single most important predictor of physician and hospital utilization among the elderly (Wolinsky, 1983; Wan and Arling, 1983). This, however, does not hold for dental services. Other factors in addition to need have also emerged in the few studies of social service utilization that are available. It is frequently unclear from these studies which type of need is the best predictor e.g. whether it is disability or illness. There is some indication that functional disability is a major predictor of home care services (Chappell and Blandford, 1987).

Despite the appeal of conceptualizing the role of social support within the Andersen–Newman model, it has not emerged as a major determinant in these utilization studies. However, it has not received a major focus when testing the Andersen–Newman model either. Sometimes social support measures are not included at all and when they are it is frequently one or two measures which look at the number of or frequency of contact with family members only. In other words, the fact that it has not emerged should not be interpreted, yet, as a sign that it is unimportant. More sophisticated measures of social support are necessary to test its relationship within this model.

Consistent with the conceptualization of social support as an enabling factor are those studies which examine the role of informal support as sources of knowledge about the formal care system. For example, Silverstein (1984) reports that informal sources and the media are better sources of overall knowledge than formal sources (but formal sources are better predictors of utilization). Ward *et al.* (1984) find that knowledge of services comes best from informal networks with weak ties. Confidants, friends, and instrumental helpers can actually reduce awareness of formal services. In other words, there are particular types of relationships which are more likely to lead to increased knowledge of formal services. Rundall and Evashwick (1982) report that it is the relative network rather than the friendship network which is significantly related to the use of health and social services. Those engaged with their families are more likely to use health and social services.

Evident within the foregoing is the suggestion that involvement with family and friends can in fact hinder utilization of formal services, at least in some circumstances. This view has been formulated explicitly in the so-called substitution model of assistance. This view argues that patterns of assistance follow an orderly hierarchical selection process determined by the primacy of the relationship between giver and recipient.

INFORMAL AND FORMAL SUPPORT

The substitution model of assistance is consistent with Cantor's (1979) hierarchical compensatory model of social supports. It argues for the primary importance of the family in old age. This normative pattern sees kin as responding first to the needs of the elderly, followed in order by friends, neighbours, and finally formal organizations, each successively providing assistance which compensates when aid from more preferred sources becomes unavailable or insufficient to meet needs (Cantor and Little, 1985). Within this model, formal services, and particularly formal home care services, are used when informal sources are exhausted. Use of the formal care system is determined not by health needs alone but by health needs combined with the unavailability of informal social supports.

Research to date demonstrates the prevalence of informal support, even among those receiving formal care (Chappell and Havens, 1985). Horowitz, Dono and Brill (1983) report the continuation of informal support with the provision of formal home care. Such data suggest that formal services could be used as a last resort, but if they are they do not substitute for informal care. Rather, they become utilized in addition to informal care, perhaps when informal care alone is no longer sufficient.

Such studies suggest informal and formal care are complementary to one another rather than substitutes for one another, except in the absence of informal support. Elderly people with few or limited family relationships are prime candidates for institutionalization when they become sick (Shanas, 1979). Coe, Wolinsky, Miller and Prendergast (1985) report elderly persons without access to a family support network have high rates of utilization of emergency room services but not physician or hospital in-patient services. Conversely, Wan and Weissert (1981) report that social networks have a positive effect on a patient's physical and mental functioning in a day care and homemaker experiment. Pilisuk and associates (1982) find that a supportive network is critical for maintenance of health.

Of more concern than evidence that those without extensive social ties are the ones who tend to utilize formal services, is the argument that formal services (especially community social services) will replace informal care if they are established. This assumes that certain services should be provided by the informal network and furthermore that families will not provide such services if they can be obtained elsewhere. However, it is also possible that the two systems are complementary. They could be complementary if some services are provided by family and friends but some by the formal system, i.e. there is a division of labour. It could also be complementary if initially informal sources provided care while they could but when they could no longer provide them the formal care system stepped in.

In one of the few longitudinal studies in this area, Horowitz and associates (1983) examined the question of short-term substitution in relation to a home care programme. Their study showed that those caregivers not assisting initially with basic activities of daily living were not assisting at follow-up. However, those providing a moderate level of assistance initially, then receiving assistance from the formal home care programme, increased their support over time compared to the control group. Caregivers providing maximum informal assistance initially and who then received formal assistance from the programme showed no reduction in the provision of informal care at the time of follow-up. The control group, however, providing maximum care initially and receiving no formal support showed a reduction in care over the six month period. In other words, the provision of formal services can affect the provision of informal care differentially depending on the circumstances. However, the evidence does not suggest a substitution and certainly does not suggest that informal caregivers relinquish the responsibility because there is a formal source of home care. In some instances the provision of formal care can increase the provision of informal support.

Studying family caregiving, Noelker and Poulshock (1982) report that, among the impaired elderly, families in their sample have been providing care on average for six years and were the major source of assistance. They assist with three personal tasks three hours a day on average. In addition, 60% of the elderly people receiving personal care also receive formal services, generally consisting of in-home health care. Two-thirds receive formal services on a weekly basis and one-fifth receive one to four hours of formal services per week. That is, formal services totalled a fraction of the hours per week when compared to the care provided from informal sources.

Chappell (1987) examined the relationship between informal and formal care systems among the elderly in Winnipeg, Canada. The results point to a relative separateness between these systems of care. Use of the two care systems was not correlated with one another. Furthermore, social network variables were significantly related to informal care (they have to be available in order to provide it) but health belief variables were significantly correlated with utilization of the formal care system. Given the self-initiated nature of contact with formal services, it was not surprising that locus of control, with those highly sceptical of medical doctors less likely to engage in formal care, is related. Given that the Canadian medical care system (like that in the United States) is primarily oriented around acute and institutional services, it is not surprising that the two systems are uncorrelated with one another. Informal care is oriented much more around functional disability.

There has been little attention devoted to possible harmful (stressful) effects of utilization of formal services. This no doubt is due to the focus on utilization patterns and the assumption that health care services assist individuals with illness episodes. However, the broader medical sociology literature does give attention to possible iatrogenic effects of medicine (Illich, 1977; Evans, 1984). Especially given the fact that the medical care systems in the United States and Canada tend to be oriented towards medical intervention and acute care rather than towards chronic conditions and maintenance of the elderly in the community, there is reason to believe that harmful or at least a lack of beneficial effects of utilization of this system could be apparent.

Furthermore, society has not yet come to grips with the following question: given an aging population and medical intervention which cannot prevent death but can in many instances have important side effects in decreasing quality of life, when is it appropriate for medicine not to intervene? It can be argued that when medicine is not able to provide a successful intervention (such as old age) that these circumstances lend themselves to the use of more self-care practices or to adherence to an alternative health belief model. Research is only beginning to examine the interplay between formal health care practices and folk health care systems. To date they have tended to be studied as separate systems and indeed much of the research has studied formal services to the exclusion of other types of remedies. It is, however, an area receiving increasing attention from researchers. It is clear that a simple relationship does not characterize these systems. It would appear that informal support is the norm with the utilization of formal services much less prevalent. Furthermore, formal services intervene by and large after informal sources.

As noted earlier, there are surprisingly few studies that relate informal and formal care explicitly to stress among the elderly. In a recent study Wan (1987) did examine the functionally disabled elderly. This author studied use of formal services, social support, and a health functioning measure referred to as psychological health (self-reported health and functionally assessed health). The findings suggest that social support is an enabling factor for the use of services but also a buffering factor between poor health functioning and use of services. That is, social support has both a direct and indirect effect on use of services. It has a direct effect on both use of services and on psychological health which could be interpreted as either a measure of stress or an outcome of stress.

A relatively recent development in gerontology which does deal explicitly with stress and informal and formal care is the burden literature. Much of this literature focuses on attempts to devise measures of strain or burden and to examine its correlates (Zarit, Reever and Bach-Peterson, 1980; Montgomery, Gonyea and Hooyman 1985). Generally the focus is on strain of the informal caregiver rather than on the strain of the care recipient. Most of this research has been conducted on families with elderly members experiencing some form of dementia, frequently Alzheimer's disease, so we know much less about stress experienced by individuals caring for elderly members who are non-demented. Research which is available indicates that the provision of formal support does not necessarily decrease caregiver burden or strain, and furthermore that informal support continues even after the establishment of formal support. Some new developments in this area are identifying different types of burden with the expectation that different types of burden require different types of intervention in order to result in alleviation (Novak and Guest, 1987; Hooyman, Gonyea and Montgomery, 1985; Gwyther and George, 1986).

This research has tended not to examine gender differences although we do know that women are the traditional caregivers and that they are more likely to provide hands-on assistance than men (Springer and Brubaker, 1984). Furthermore, women appear to handle stress differently than do men, and as caregivers seem to suffer from greater stress than men (Robinson and Thurnher, 1979; Cantor, 1983). Finally, most of this research is on elderly persons who are identified through agencies or institutions, i.e. families who are already in contact with formal support services. We know little about the strain experienced by families in the community without or before formal support interventions.

There has also been an explicit focus on stress in the gerontological literature on relocation. The vast majority of these studies examine institution to institution moves and examine mortality as the outcome. As noted by Grant (1985), few studies examine community to institution moves. In addition, few studies examine relocation stress rather than mortality. This author argues that relocation stress may be tied to loss of independence as a key factor and the outcome may be psychological distress and not necessarily death. This author presents data supporting this interpretation and calling for more research which examines relocation stress.

CONCLUSIONS

This paper has summarized and highlighted the general trends in research on informal and formal support of the elderly. There is much literature on informal support which generally documents the supportive nature of family ties during old age. This literature, however, has an emphasis on the family and on the supportiveness of ties to the neglect of negative or stressful aspects of these interactions. Furthermore, studies of relatives other than spouses and children and of friendships or instrumental relationships tend to be lacking. Comparative studies which include different types of relationships are also lacking. Frequently, this literature has examined whether interaction exists and then assumed it is necessarily beneficial but without explicitly examining the consequences of such interaction.

There is other literature which assesses directly the relationship between quality of life and well-being. The two general perspectives are that which views support as having an indirect or buffering effect during stressful situations and that which views social support as having a general direct effect on overall well-being. Despite the wealth of literature in this area, the findings are contradictory. The general conclusion is that social support is good but it is no panacea. Furthermore, we do not have sufficient understanding of the details of how it operates, in which circumstances, and for whom.

The literature on informal and formal supports tends to focus on whether the two are a substitution for one another or are complementary. Existing research demonstrates the prevalence of informal support and of informal support as the first choice before formal support. However, once formal support is called into play it does not substitute for the informal but rather is complementary to it. The two systems are somewhat separate from one another rather than enhancing the tasks of each. This no doubt at least partially results from the fact that the formal care system has an emphasis on task orientation toward acute care and institutional care whereas the informal network is more oriented towards social care and is better equipped to handle chronic care. None of the literature, whether it is on informal care, formal care, or the interaction between them, focuses on the possible stressful aspects of utilization or receipt of assistance. The fact that the receipt of informal assistance or the utilization of formal services can be stress producing for the individual recipient is an area which is in need of study. The growing literature in this area attests to the recognition of its importance. However, many questions remain fruitful areas for research in the future.

REFERENCES

Adams, B.N. (1986). *The Family, A Sociological Interpretation*, 4th edn,. Harcourt, Brace, Jovanovich, New York.

Andersen, R. and Newman, J.F. (1973). Societal and individual determinants of medical care utilization in the United States. *Milbank Memorial Fund Quarterly*, **51**, 95–124.

Andrews, G., Tennant, G., Hewson, D. and Vaillant, G. (1978). Life event stress, social support, coping style, and risk of psychological impairment. *Journal of Nervous and Mental Disease*, **166**, 307–16.

Badura, B. and Waltz, M. (1984). Social support and quality of life following myocardial infarction. *Social Indicators Research*, **14**, 295–311.

Blumhagen, D. (1980). Hyper-tension: a folk illness with a medical name. *Culture, Medicine and Psychiatry*, **1**, 197–227.

Brody, E.M. (1981). Women in the middle and family help to older people. *The Gerontologist*, **21**, 470–80.

Bultena, G. and Olyer, R. (1971). Effects of health on disengagement and morale. *Aging Human Development*, **2**, 142–8.

Cantor, M.H. (1975). Life space and the social support system of the inner city elderly of New York. *The Gerontologist*, **15**, 23–7.

Cantor, M.H. (1979). Neighbours and friends: an overlooked resource in the informal support system. *Research on Aging*, **1**, 434–63.

Cantor, M.H. (1983). Strain among caregivers: a study of experience in the United States. *The Gerontologist*, **23**, 597–604.

Cantor, M.H. and Little, V. (1985). Aging and social care. In R.H. Binstock and E. Shanas (eds.) *Handbook of Aging and the Social Sciences*, 2nd edn, Van Nostrand Reinhold, New York, pp. 745–81.

Cassel, J. (1976). The contribution of the social environment to host resistance. *American Journal of Epidemiology*, **104**, 108–23.

Chappell, N.L. (1987). Intergenerational Helping Patterns. Paper presented at the annual meeting of the Canadian Sociology and Anthropology Association, Hamilton, Ontario.

Chappell, N.L. and Blandford, A.A. (1987). Health service utilization by elderly persons. *Canadian Journal of Sociology*, **12**, 195–215.

Chappell, N.L. and Havens, B. (1985). Who helps the elderly person: discussion of informal and formal care. In W. Peterson and J. Quadagno (eds.) *Social Bonds in Later Life*, Sage, Beverly Hills, pp. 211–27.

Cicirelli, V.G. (1985). The role of siblings as family caregivers. In W.J. Sauer and R.T. Coward (eds.) *Social Support Networks and the Care of the Elderly*, Springer, New York, pp. 93–107.

Cobb, S. (1976). Social support as a moderator of life stress, presidential address. *Psychosomatic Medicine*, **38**, 300–14.

Coe, R.M., Wolinsky, F.D., Miller, D.K. and Prendergast, J.M. (1985). Elderly persons without family support networks and use of health services: a follow-up report on social network relationships. *Research on Aging*, **7**, 617–22.

Cohler, B.J. and Lieberman, M.A. (1980). Social relations and mental health: middle-aged and older men and women from three European ethnic groups. *Research on Aging*, **2**, 445–69.

Conner, K.A., Powers, E.A. and Bultena, G.L. (1979). Social interaction and life satisfaction: an empirical assessment of late-life patterns. *Journal of Gerontology*, **34**, 116–21.

Dean, A. and Lin, N. (1977). The stress-buffering role of social support. *Journal of Nervous and Mental Disease*, **165**, 403–17.

Dowd, J.J. (1986). The old person as stranger. In V.W. Marshall (ed.) *Later Life: The Social Psychology of Aging*, Sage, Beverly Hills, pp. 147–89.

Dunkle, R. E. (1985). Comparing the depression of elders in two types of caregiving arrangements. *Family Relations*, **34**, 235–40.

Evans, R.G. (1984). *Strained Mercy: The Economics of Canadian Health Care*, Butterworths, Toronto.

Evans, R.L. and Northwood, L.K. (1979). The utility of natural help relationships. *Social Science and Medicine*, **13A**, 789–95.

Freidson, E. (1960). Client control and medical practice. *American Journal of Sociology*, **65**, 374–82.

Froland, C., Pancoast, D.L., Chapman, N.J. and Kimboko, P.J. (1981). Informal helping networks. In C. Froland *et al.* (eds.) *Helping Networks and Human Services*, Sage, Beverly Hills, pp. 31–54.

Graney, M.J. (1975). Happiness and social participation in aging. *Journal of Gerontology*, **30**, 701–6.

Grant, P.R. (1985). Who experiences the move into a nursing home as stressful? Examination of the relocation stress hypothesis using archival, time-series data. *Canadian Journal on Aging*, **4**, 87–99.

Gwyther, L.P. and George L.K. (1986). Caregivers for dementia patients: complex determinants of well-being and burden. *The Gerontologist*, **26**, 245–7.

Hagestad, G.O. (1985). Continuity and connectedness. In V.L. Bengtson and J.F. Robertson (eds.) *Grandparenthood*, Sage, Beverly Hills, pp. 31–48.

Hanson, S.M. and Sauer, W.J. (1985). Children and their elderly parents. In W.J. Sauer and R.T. Coward (eds.) *Social Support Networks and the Care of the Elderly*, Springer, New York, pp. 41–66.

Health and Welfare Canada and Statistics Canada (1981). *Canada Health Survey*, Minister of Supply and Services, Ottawa.

Heinemann, G.D. (1985). Interdependence in informal support systems: the case of elderly, urban widows. In W.A. Peterson and J. Quadagno (eds.) *Social Bonds in Later Life*, Sage, Beverly Hills, pp. 165–86.

Helman, C.G. (1978). Feed a cold, starve a fever—folk models of infection in an English surburban community, and their relation to medical treatment. *Culture, Medicine and Psychiatry*, **2**, 107–37.

Hess, B.B. and Waring, J.M. (1980). Changing patterns of aging and family bonds in later life. In. A. Skolnick and J.H. Skolnick (eds.) *Family in Transition*, Little Brown, Boston.

Hooyman, N., Gonyea, J.G. and Montgomery, R.J.V. (1985). The impact of in-home service termination on family caregivers. *The Gerontologist*, **25**, 141–5.

Horowitz, A. (1981). Sons and Daughters as Caregivers to Older Parents: Differences in Role Performance and Consequences. Paper presented at the annual meeting of the Gerontological Society of America, Toronto, Ontario.

Horowitz, A., Dono, J.E. and Brill, R. (1983). Continuity of Changes in Informal Support? The Impact of an Expanded Home Care Program. Paper presented at the annual meeting of the Gerontological Society of America, San Francisco, California.

Horowitz, A. and Shindelman, L.W. (1981). Reciprocity and Affection: Past Influence on Current Caregiving. Paper presented at the 34th annual meeting of the Gerontological Society of America, Toronto, Ontario.

Illich, I. (1977). *Medical Nemesis*, Bantam Books, New York.

Ingersoll, B. and Antonucci, T. (1983). Non-Reciprocal Social Support: Another Side of Intimate Relationships. Papers presented at the annual meeting of the Gerontological Society of America, San Francisco, California.

Johnson, C.L. and Catalano, D.J. (1983). A longitudinal study of family supports to the impaired elderly. *The Gerontologist*, **23**, 612–18.

Jonas, K. and Wellin, E. (1980). Dependency and reciprocity: home health aid in an elderly population. In C.L. Fry (ed.) *Aging in Culture and Society*, Bergin & Garvey, South Hadley, pp. 217–38.

Kane, R.L. and Kane, R.A. (1978). Care of the aged. Old problems in need of new solutions. *Science*, **200**, 913–19.

Kendig, H. (ed.) (1986) Intergenerational exchange. In *Aging and Families: A Social Networks Perspective*, Allen & Unwin, Boston, pp. 85–109.

Kovar, M.G. (1977). Health of the elderly and use of health services. *Public Health Research*, **92**, 9–19.

Krause, N. (1987). Understanding the stress process: linking social support with locus of control beliefs. *Journal of Gerontology*, **42**, 589–93.

Lee, G.R. (1985). Kinship and social support of the elderly: the case of the United States. *Aging and Society*, **5**, 19–38.

Lee, G.R. and Ellithorpe, E. (1982). Intergenerational exchange and subjective well-being among the elderly. *Journal of Marriage and the Family*, **44**, 217–24.

Liang, J., Dvorkin, L., Kahana, E. and Mazian, F. (1980). Social integration and morale: a re-examination. *Journal of Gerontology*, **35**, 746–57.

Lin, N. (1982). Social resources and instrumental action. In P.V. Marsden and N. Lin (eds.) *Social Structure and Network Analysis*, Sage, Beverly Hills, pp. 131–45.

Lin, N., Simeone, R.S., Ensel, W.M. and Kuo, W. (1979). Social support, stressful life events, and illness: a model and empirical test. *Journal of Health and Social Behavior*, **20**, 108–19.

Linn, M.W. (1986). Elderly women's health and psychological adjustment: life stressors and social support. In S.E. Hobfoll (ed.) *Stress, Social Support, and Women*, Hemisphere, Washington, pp. 223–35.

Lowenthal, M.F. and Haven, C. (1968). Interaction and adaptation: intimacy as a critical variable. In B. Neugarten (ed.) *Middle Age and Aging*, University of Chicago Press, Chicago, pp. 390–400.

Mancini, J.A., Quinn, W., Gavigan, M.A. and Franklin, H. (1980). Social network interaction among older adults: implications for life satisfaction. *Human Relations*, **33**, 543–54.

Marshall, V.W., Rosenthal, C.J. and Synge, J. (1981). The Family as a Service Organization for the Elderly. Paper presented at the annual meeting of the Society for the Study of Social Problems, Toronto, Ontario.

McKinlay, J.B. (1972). Some approaches and problems in the study of the use of services—an overview. *Journal of Health and Social Behavior*, **13**, 115–52.

McKinlay, J.B. (1973). Social networks, lay consultation and help-seeking behavior. *Social Forces*, **51**, 275–92.

McKinlay, J.B. (1980). Social network influences on morbid episodes and the career of help seeking. In L. Eisenberg and A. Kleinman (eds.) *The Relevance of Social Science for Medicine*, D. Reidel, Boston, pp. 77–107.

Montgomery, R.J.V., Gonyea, J.G. and Hooyman, N.R. (1985). Caregiving and the experience of subjective and objective burden. *Family Relations*, **34**, 19–25.

Noelker, L.S. and Poulshock, S.W. (1982). *The Effects on Families of Caring for Impaired Elderly in Residence*, Final report, US Department of Health and Human Services, Administration on Aging, Washington.

Novak, M.W. and Guest, C. (1987). Application of the Caregiver Burden Inventory. Paper presented at the annual meeting of the International Psychogeriatric Association, Chicago, Illinois.

Nydegger, C.N. (1983). Family ties of the aged in cross-cultural perspective. *The Gerontologist*, **23**, 26–32.

Orbach, H.L. (1983). Symposium: Aging, Families, and Family Relations: Behavioral and Social Science Perspectives on Our Knowledge, Our Myths, and Our Research. *The Gerontologist*, **23**, 24–5.

Peters, G.R. and Kaiser, M.A. (1985). The role of friends and neighbors in providing social support. In W.J. Sauer and R.T. Coward (eds.) *Social Support Networks and the Care of the Elderly*, Springer, New York, pp. 123–58.

Pilisuk, M., Heller, S., Kelly, J. and Turner, E. (1982). The helping network approach: community promotion of mental health. *Journal of Primary Prevention*, **3**, 116–32.

Porritt, D. (1979). Social support in crisis: quantity or quality? *Social Science and Medicine*, **13A**, 715–21.

Pratt, L. (1973). The significance of the family in medication. *Journal of Comparative Family Studies*, **4**, 13–35.

Robinson, B. and Thurnher, M. (1979). Taking care of patients: a family cycle transition. *The Gerontologist*, **19**, 586–93.

Rook, K.S. and Dooley, D. (1985). Applying social support research: theoretical problems and future directions. *Journal of Social Issues*, **41**, 5–28.

Roos, N.P., Shapiro, E. and Roos, L.L. (1984). Aging and the demand for health services: which aged and whose demand. *The Gerontologist*, **24**, 31–6.

Rundall, T.G. and Evashwick, C. (1982). Social networks and help-seeking among the elderly. *Research on Aging*, **4**, 205–26.

Schmidt, M.G. (1981). Personal networks: assessment, care and repair. *Journal of Gerontological Social Work*, **3**, 65–76.

Shanas, E. (1979). The family as a support system in old age. *The Gerontologist*, **19**, 169–74.

Shanas, E. and Maddox, G.L. (1985). Health, health resources, and the utilization of care. In R.H. Binstock and E. Shanas (eds.) *Handbook of Aging and the Social Sciences*, Van Nostrand Reinhold, New York, pp. 697−726.

Silverstein, N.M. (1984). Informing the elderly about public services: the relationship between sources of knowledge and service utilization. *The Gerontologist*, **24**, 37−40.

Springer, D. and Brubaker, T.H. (1984). *Family Caregivers and Dependent Elderly*, Sage, Beverly Hills.

Starrett, R.A., Mindel, C.H. and Wright Jr., R. (1983). The role of the Kinship and Quasi-Formal Support Systems in Predicting the Use of Formal Social Services by the Hispanic Elderly. Paper presented at the annual meeting of the Midwest Sociological Society.

Statistics Canada (1983). *Fact Book on Aging in Canada*, Minister of Supply and Services, Ottawa.

Statistics Canada (1985). *General Social Survey*. (This analysis is based on Statistics Canada microdata tape, Health and Social Support, which contains data collected in the 1985 General Social Survey. All computations on these microdata were prepared by the Centre on Aging, University of Manitoba, and the responsibility for the use and interpretation of these data is entirely that of the authors.)

Stein, S., Linn, M.W. and Stein, E.M. (1982). The Relationship of self-help networks to physical and psycho-social functioning. *Journal of the American Geriatrics Society*, **30**, 764−68.

Strain, L.A. and Chappell, N.L. (1982). Confidants—Do They Make a Difference in Quality of Life? *Research on Aging*, **4**, 479−502.

Thomas, P.D., Garry, P.J., Goodwin, J.M. and Goodwin, J.S. (1985). Social bonds in a healthy elderly sample: characteristics and associated variables. *Social Science and Medicine*, **20**, 365−9.

Treas, J. (1977). Family support systems for the aged: some social and demographic considerations. *The Gerontologist*, **17**, 486−91.

US Bureau of the Census (1986). *Statistical Abstract of the United States: 1986*, 106th edn, Table No. 175, Washington.

Wagner, D.L. and Keast, F. (1981). Informal groups and the elderly: A preliminary examination of the mediation function. *Research on Aging*, **3**, 325−31.

Wan, T.T.H. (1987). Functionally disabled elderly: health status, social support, and use of health services. *Research on Aging*, **9**, 61−78.

Wan, T. and Arling, G. (1983). Differential use of health services among disabled elderly. *Research on Aging*, **5**, 411−31.

Wan, T.T.H. and Weissert, W.G. (1981). Social support networks patient status and institutionalization. *Research on Aging*, **3**, 240−56.

Ward, R.A., Sherman, S.R. and LaGory, M. (1984). Subjective network assessments and subjective well-being. *Journal of Gerontology*, **39**, 93−101.

Wellman, B. (1981). Applying network analysis to the study of support. In B.H. Gottlieb (ed.) *Social Network and Social Support*, Sage, Beverly Hills, pp. 171−200.

Wolinsky, F.D. (1983). Health Care Policy and the Elderly: Short-Term Cures and Long-Term Catastrophies. Paper presented at the annual meeting of the Society for the Study of Social Problems, Detroit, Michigan.

Zarit, S.H., Reever, K.E. and Bach-Peterson, J. (1980). Relatives of impaired elderly: correlates of feelings of burden. *The Gerontologist*, **20**, 649−55.

Psychological Factors and Outcomes

Chapter 11

Stress, Social Support, and Depression over the Life-Course

Linda K. George

An adequate consideration of stress and social support as health-related phenomena must examine psychiatric as well as physical health outcomes. Indeed, research examining mental health outcomes provides some of the strongest evidence available documenting the importance of stress and social support for personal well-being. This chapter focuses specifically on the relationships between stress, social support, and depression.

Stress and social support have been linked to a variety of psychiatric outcomes in previous research. Nonetheless, this chapter is largely restricted to a review of the importance of stress and social support for depression—both depressive symptomatology and depressive disorder as clinically defined. The decision to focus on a single psychiatric disorder rests on the fact that the effects of stress and social support vary to some degree for different psychiatric conditions (Wheaton, 1983; Cronkite and Moos, 1984). Depression is the specific psychiatric outcome of choice for both pragmatic and scientific reasons. Pragmatically, a majority of previous studies based on specific psychiatric conditions focused on depression—especially studies based on samples of older adults. More importantly, the effects of stress and social support appear to be stronger for depression that for other kinds of psychiatric disorders (Wheaton, 1983; Cronkite and Moos, 1984; Kessler and McLeod, 1985). Stress may be especially relevant to depression because of the losses and deprivations often involved in life events and chronic stressors. Social support may be particularly important for depression because of its power to promote feelings of control and self-worth—psychological states closely related to depressed mood.

During the past twenty-five years, investigations of the relationships between stress, social support, and health/mental health outcomes have increased in complexity and sophistication. This increasing complexity can be documented in several ways, including the movement from bivariate to multivariate models, the recognition that these phenomena are multidimensional, and awareness of the need for longitudinal data to trace the dynamics of personal well-being. Most important, perhaps, questions currently being asked about the relationships

Aging, Stress and Health Edited by K.S. Markides and C.L. Cooper
© 1989 John Wiley & Sons Ltd

between stress, social support, and health are different than they were two decades ago. Investigators no longer question whether these phenomena are interrelated. Current issues of study are considerably more complex. For example, researchers now are identifying (a) the conditions under which stress has negative implications for health and the conditions under which social support has beneficial health implications; (b) the degree to which effects vary across types of stressors, dimensions of social support, and specific health/mental health outcomes; and (c) the mechanisms by which stress and social support affect health/mental health outcomes. The increasing complexity of this research field will be highlighted in this chapter.

Congruent with the focus of this volume, age differences in the distributions of and relationships between stress, social support, and depression will be highlighted in this chapter. In some cases, previous research has focused specifically upon the degree to which the relationships among these phenomena are age or cohort specific. More frequently, however, conclusions must be based on comparisons across studies—and these conclusions clearly are more speculative than those based on empirical tests of age differences.

This chapter is organized in four major sections. The first section provides conceptual and operational definitions of stress, social support, and depression, as well as describing their distributions across age groups. The second section comprises a review of main effects models of the effects of stress and social support on depression. Both robustness of findings and mediating effects are discussed. In the third section, interactive models are reviewed. The chapter ends with a discussion of the degree to which the stress process varies across adulthood.

As well as describing what this chapter includes, it also is prudent to note what is not covered. First, a major concern in any review of previous research is the methodological adequacy of extant findings. To the extent possible, methodological issues will be highlighted in this chapter. Nonetheless, space limitations preclude a thorough methodological critique of this research field. Second, stress and social support do not operate upon depression in a vacuum—a variety of other personal and social factors are related to the experience of stress, the availability and use of social support, and the risk of depression. Consequently, to the extent possible given space limitations, attention is paid to the complex web of personal and social factors that underpin personal well-being. Nonetheless, other factors predicting depression are necessarily underemphasized.

DEFINITIONS AND DISTRIBUTIONS

In this section, stress, social support, and depression are examined individually. Each concept is defined both conceptually and in terms of its standard operationalizations. In addition, distributions of these variables are examined in terms of their stability over time and across age groups.

Stress

In broadest terms, stress is a condition that challenges or threatens personal well-being (e.g. George, 1980; House and Robbins, 1983). Review of available research suggests three important and distinct types of stress: life events, chronic stress, and daily hassles. These three types of stress differ in duration and intensity or importance.

Life events typically are defined as identifiable, discrete changes in life patterns that disrupt usual behaviors and can threaten or challenge personal well-being. There are several well-known life event measures (e.g. the Schedule of Recent Events, Holmes and Rahe, 1967; the Geriatric Social Readjustment Rating Scale, Amster and Krauss, 1974). Most life event measures inquire about events experienced during the recent past both because recent stress is expected to be most relevant to current well-being and because memory problems threaten the reliability of reports of more distant events (e.g. Brown and Harris, 1982; Funch and Marshall, 1984). Because of their discrete nature, it is assumed that life events can be clearly dated in terms of onset. Available literature is vague with regard to the expected duration of life events, though the common assumption is that their effects are bounded. Life events are expected to vary widely in intensity or importance.

Chronic stress refers to long-term conditions that challenge or threaten personal well-being. Examples of chronic stress examined in previous research include work stress (e.g. House, 1981), financial deprivations (e.g. Krause, 1987a; Ross and Huber, 1985), and interpersonal and role strains (e.g. Pearlin and Schooler, 1978). Chronic stress is distinguished from life events primarily by its longer duration. Interestingly, however, available literature provides no guidelines concerning the length of time required for a stress to qualify as chronic. It appears that chronic stressors also are assumed to vary in intensity—though, again, extant literature reveals no efforts to quantify the intensity of various chronic stressors.

Hassles refer to ordinary, but stressful transactions encountered in daily living (Lazarus and Folkman, 1984; Folkman, Lazarus, Pimley and Novacek 1987). The Hassles Scale, developed by Lazarus and associates, is the major tool available for measuring the experience of hassles (DeLongis *et al.*, 1982). Hassles are expected to reflect relatively long-term or ongoing sources of stress (DeLongis *et al.*, 1982; Folkman *et al.*, 1987), but lack the intensity characteristic of life events and chronic stressors. Hassles are not expected to vary widely in intensity—by definition they represent relatively low-intensity transactions with the environment.

In addition to distinctions among types of stress, a variety of other issues cross-cut the assessment of stressful experiences. Two are particularly important to the research to be reviewed and will be briefly described: objective versus subjective assessments and aggregate versus single-stressor approaches.

Objective versus subjective assessment of stress

Investigators differ in the extent to which stress is viewed as an objective condition external to the individual versus the degree to which it is conceptualized as a subjective evaluation of life circumstances (e.g. George, 1980; House, 1981). Some investigators view stress as an external condition; as a life situation that is, by definition, stressful. This perspective has been particularly characteristic of traditional life event checklists. For these investigators, the essence of stress is the disruption of usual behavior patterns—and it does not matter whether that change is perceived as desirable or undesirable (e.g. Holmes and Rahe, 1967; Dohrenwend, 1973). Other investigators believe that stress is a subjective state and that the same life event may or may not be stressful depending upon its meaning for the individual. From this perspective, subjective evaluations are a necessary component of stress assessment; examples of the kinds of subjective assessments obtained include ratings of the desirability (i.e. positive versus negative), importance, and predictability of the stressful experiences (George, 1980; House, 1981; Hughes, George and Blazer, 1988b; Lowenthal, Thurnher and Chiriboga, 1975).

Evidence for these competing perspectives has been mixed. Nonetheless, a majority of evidence supports the subjective approach. That is, it appears that subjective assessment of stress—especially the degree to which life circumstances are viewed as desirable or undesirable—is more predictive of health and mental health outcomes than is the simple occurrence of experiences defined as stressful by external observers (e.g. George, 1980).

Objective versus subjectives stress measures are relevant to all three types of stress. At this point, however, comparisons of these approaches have been restricted to the measurement of life events. It appears that virtually all studies of chronic stress have focused on perceptions of long-term deprivation (e.g. Pearlin and Schooler, 1978; Pearlin, Lieberman, Menaghan and Mullan, 1981; Krause, 1987a; 1987b; House, 1981) rather than objective assessments of long-term problems. The limited research based on measures of daily hassles reveals no attention to the issue of objective versus subjective assessment. It appears that hassles are intended, by definition, to represent a subjective assessment of daily frustrations.

Aggregate versus single-stressor approaches

Investigators also differ in the extent to which they focus upon aggregate levels of stress versus the effects of single, specific stressful experiences. At one extreme are studies based on summary scores of the numbers of life events or other stressors experienced by respondents in the recent past. At the other extreme are studies that examine the effects of one specific type of stressor (e.g. widowhood, divorce). There is considerable debate in the literature concerning the advisability of these approaches (e.g. Kessler and McLeod, 1985). To pose the issue as an either/or one, however, is to miss the point: aggregate and single-stressor studies are designed to answer distinct and equally meaningful questions. Studies using aggregate stress measures are designed to investigate the effects of cumulative stress—the degree to which the sheer amount of stress experienced by individuals affects personal well-being. Studies based on examination of a single stressor are designed to depict the consequences of a specific kind of stressful experience.

Although both aggregate stress and single-stressor approaches can generate important information about the consequences of stress, the two approaches also lead to different methodological concerns. Investigators using aggregate stress measures must be aware that ignoring the nature of the specific stresses experienced by individuals may mask or blur underlying patterns. For example, some of the stresses that have been aggregated may be important for physical health outcomes and others may be relevant only to mental health outcomes. Or, some of the stresses that have been aggregated may be ameliorated by social support and others may not. A single-stressor approach avoids the lack of specificity associated with aggregation. On the other hand, however, single-stressor studies should take into account other sources of stress that are not of immediate interest to the investigator. For example, studies of widowhood should include measures of other sources of stress so that the effects of widowhood are distinguished from those of other stressors. Unfortunately, single-stressor studies seldom include information about other stressors.

In the life events arena, some recent research has attempted a middle-ground that involves limited aggregation of stressors. In a number of studies, life events have been classified into categories such as family events, work events, and loss events (e.g. Krause, 1986a; Thoits, 1987). The obvious hope for the limited aggregation approach is that an economy can be realized such that events need not be examined in a purely individual manner but that the aggregation will not be so great as to mask the distinctive relationships between stressors and their outcomes.

The aggregate versus single-stressor approach is relevant to all three types of stressors. Exploration of the implications of aggregated versus single-stressor approaches, however, has taken place primarily in the context of life events. Most literature on chronic stressors has examined them individually and with-out controlling on other potential sources of stress. In theory, individuals may experience multiple chronic stressors—nonetheless, the impact of cumulative chronic stressors has not been examined in previous studies. As Folkman *et al.* (1987) point out, it would be virtually impossible to examine the impact of individual hassles on personal well-being—moreover, because hassles are, by definition, of relatively low intensity, it is not clear that there would be any rationale for doing so. Nonetheless, the limited research available reveals alternate aggregation strategies for analyzing the effects of daily hassles. Some investigators sum across all hassles to generate a single summary score (e.g. Burks and Martin, 1985; Holahan, Holahan and Belk, 1984; Monroe, 1983; Zarski, 1984). More recently, however, investigators have used measures based on clusters of similar hassles (e.g. Folkman *et al.*, 1987).

The aggregate versus single-stressor issue applies across as well as within types of stress. That is, in theory, an investigation of any type of stress should take into account the effects of other kinds of stress. For example, life event studies should take respondents' levels of chronic stress and daily hassles into account. Similarly, studies of chronic stress should control upon levels of recent life events and daily hassles. Unfortunately, the field has not yet reached this level of sophistication.

Age differences in stress exposure

There is strong and consistent evidence that, in terms of the life events included in most standardized measures, older adults experience fewer events than younger and middle-aged adults (Chiriboga and Dean, 1978; Dekker and Webb, 1974; Goldberg and Comstock, 1980; Lazarus and DeLongis 1983; Hughes, Blazer and George, 1988a; Lowenthal *et al.*, 1975; Uhlenhuth, Lipman, Balter and Stern, 1974). Age groups also differ in the types of events experienced. Compared to younger adults, older people are more likely to report health events, retirement, and loss of family and friends (e.g. Goldberg and Comstock, 1980; Hughes *et al.*, 1988a, Lowenthal *et al.*, 1975). Only two studies have systematically examined age differences in the subjective ratings assigned to specific life events. Chiriboga and Dean (1978) report that, though they report fewer life events than their younger couterparts, older adults experience greater unhappiness and more intrusion on their lives as a result of life events. In a more recent study, Hughes *et al.* (1988b) examined age differences (age range = 18−96) in the ratings of valence (i.e. positive versus negative), expectedness, and importance of 19 life events, using data from a representative community sample. Only three significant age differences emerged from the 57 comparisons: compared to younger adults, older adults reported that (a) family illness was more expected, (b) personal hospitalization was more negative, and (c) retirement was less negative.

To my knowledge, no studies have examined age differences in chronic stress. It seems clear that some stressors—particularly chronic illness and perhaps financial deprivation—are more common among older than younger adults. But a systematic comparison of age difference in chronic stress has not been performed. Age differences in subjective assessments of chronic stressors also have not been systematically investigated. Again, however, tentative conclusions can be made in limited areas based on reseach performed for other purposes. For example, it appears that older adults view chronic illness as less unexpected and less negative than younger adults (e.g. Shanas and Maddox, 1985) and that older people are substantially more satisfied with their incomes—even when those incomes are of questionable adequacy—than younger persons (e.g. Streib, 1985; Vaughan and Lancaster, 1981).

Limited information is available concerning age differences in the experience of daily hassles. Folkman *et al.* (1987) compared older and younger adults on the frequency of experiencing daily hassles in eight areas. Younger adults reported significantly more total hassles than older persons. The most dramatic differences, however, were in the types of hassles experienced by the two age groups. Older adults reported significantly more hassles in the areas of health, social and environmental issues, and home maintenance. Younger adults reported significantly more hassles in household responsibilities, finances, and work. There were no age differences in personal hassles or hassles with family and friends.

Social support

Broadly speaking, social support refers to the provision and receipt of tangible and intangible goods, services, and benefits in the context of informal relationships (e.g. family and friends) (e.g. Blazer, 1982; Weiss, 1974). Examples of tangible (or instrumental) services include transportation, help when sick, and household repairs. More intangible forms of social support include advice, companionship, and feedback promoting feelings of self-worth.

Conceptualization and measurement of social support has advanced considerably during the past decades. There is general agreement that social support is multidimensional and substantial consensus that different dimensions of support vary in importance for different outcomes. The simplest and most common distinction is between objective and subjective dimensions of social support (e.g. George, 1987; Wethington and Kessler, 1986; Cohen and Wills, 1985). Objective social support typically refers to reports of the frequency of specific supportive transactions. Subjective support typically refers to perceptions of the adequacy of or satisfaction with the amount and/or quality of support received from significant others. Interestingly, there is consistent evidence that objective and subjective measures of social support are not significantly correlated (e.g. George, 1987; Wethington and Kessler, 1986; Ward, Sherman and LaGory, 1984). At this point, it is unclear whether this pattern reflects individual differences in the need or desire for affiliation (e.g. Henderson, Bryne and Duncan-Jones, 1981) or differences in the need for assistance (e.g. George, 1987; Krause, 1987c).

Other investigators have used more complex classifications of social support. For example, the Social Provisions Scale (Cutrona, Russell and Rose, 1986) measures the six supportive transactions identified by Weiss (1974): attachment, social integration, reassurance of worth, reliable alliance, guidance, and opportunity for nurturance. The Duke Social Support Index measures four dimensions of supportive relationships: network size, interaction frequency, instrumental support, and subjective support (George, Hughes, Blazer and Fowler, (in press). The Inventory of

Socially Supportive Behaviors (Barrera, Sandler and Ramsey, 1981) assesses emotional support, tangible help, and informational support. Krause (1987a) modified the latter instrument by adding a dimension measuring the support that respondents provide to others.

Most measures of social support focus on the support received by respondents from significant others. As Krause (1987e) points out, however, it also is important to examine respondents as support providers. The major importance of support provision is that individuals often profit from the help-giving role (Krause, 1987e; Reissman, 1965). In addition, given strong cultural norms favoring reciprocity (e.g. Gouldner, 1960), an appropriate ratio of help-giving to help-receiving may foster both satisfaction with social support and personal well-being (George, 1986). Krause (1987e) also points out, however, that the relationship between help-giving and well-being is likely to be curvilinear because the social costs of excessive help-giving are likely to be high.

Social support often is assumed to be an unqualified benefit—and, as documented below, most research substantiates the benefits of social support for personal well-being. A more balanced view of social support, however, may be needed. Not all transactions with significant others are positive or satisfying, and dissatisfying transactions may have more negative implications for well-being than the absence of transactions (e.g. Rook, 1984; Stephens, Kinney, Norris and Ritchie, 1987). Moreover, excessive support may have unintended negative consequences in terms of lowering autonomy, self-reliance, or feelings of personal control (e.g. Krause, 1987e, Lee, 1985). More balanced investigations of the benefits *and* liabilities of supportive transactions are an important area for future research.

Age differences in social support

There is considerable evidence that most older adults are enmeshed in reasonably extensive and reliable networks of significant others and are satisfied with the support available to them (e.g. Shanas, 1979a, 1979b; Ward *et al.*, 1984; Markides, Boldt and Ray, 1986). A number of studies also focus on variability in social support among older adults (e.g. Strain and Chappell, 1982; Mindel, Wright and Starrett, 1986). Relatively few studies, however, focus specifically on age differences in the scope of, functions provided by, or satisfaction with social support.

Several studies have examined age differences in social support within relatively narrow age ranges. Cantor (1975) reported that both young-old and old-old typically report extensive support networks and that network size is not significantly related to age. Stephens, Blau, Oser and Miller (1978) reported that persons aged 70 and older are more likely than their younger peers (age 55–69) to report lacking helpers to perform specific supportive functions; otherwise, however, social networks did not vary by age. Babchuk (1978–79), using data from a sample aged 45 and older, found no age differences in network size or the availability of confidants. Fischer

(1982) reports that persons under 40 report a greater proportion of non-kin in their support networks than persons 40 and older; otherwise, support networks did not vary by age. Perhaps the major study of this kind was conducted by Antonucci and associates (Antonucci, 1985; Antonucci and Akiyama, 1987). This study, based on a national sample of noninstitutionalized adults aged 50 and older, indicated no age differences in network size or in amount of received support. Two major age differences did emerge, however. First, age was negatively related to the amount of support provided to other network members. Second, older respondents were more satisfied with their support networks and rated them as more dependable than younger sample members.

Depression

Depression has been conceptualized and operationalized in two ways in previous research: as depressed mood (as evinced by a large number of depressive symptoms) and as a psychiatric disorder that meets conventional diagnostic criteria (e.g. major depressive disorder) (American Psychiatric Association, 1980). The implications of these two measurement strategies are quite consequential.

Most studies by social scientists focus on depressed mood and use measures of depressive symptomatology. Among the measures most commonly used are the CES-D (Center for Epidemiologic Studies—Depression Scale; Radloff, 1977), the Depression Scale from the Health and Daily Living Form (Moos, Cronkite, Billings and Finney, 1983), and the Zung Self-Rating Depression Scale (Zung, 1965). The advantages of these symptom scales are: (1) the entire range of depressive symptomatology is examined and (2) the measures are based on a continuous metric, appropriate for use with a broad range of statistical techniques. Use of such measures also involves disadvantages, however: (1) no effort is made to measure depression in ways compatible with conventional diagnostic criteria and (2) the validity of the symptom scale remains unclear. Several symptom scales, especially the CES-D, have established cut-points designed to identify clinical depression—and, yet, these cut-points have been largely ignored by social scientists.

Studies performed by clinicians and epidemiologists are more likely to focus on depressive disorder(s) (usually major depression, but sometimes dysthymia or other depressive diagnoses) and to rely upon measures that have been validated against diagnoses made by mental health professionals. Examples of standardized diagnostic tools include the Beck Depression Inventory (Beck *et al.*, 1961), the Schedule for Affective Disorders and Schizophrenia (SADS) (Endicott and Spitzer, 1978), and the Depressive Disorders section of the Diagnostic Interview Schedule (DIS) (Robins, Helzer, Croughan and Ratcliff, 1981). These diagnostic tools measure more than number of depressive symptoms; in line with diagnostic criteria, additional information is obtained about duration, severity, and concurrence of symptoms. The relative advantages and disadvantages of diagnostic instruments are exactly the opposite of those for symptom scales. On the positive side, diagnostic tools have typically been validated against psychiatrists' diagnoses. On the negative side, diagnostic tools ignore mild symptomatology (which is quite common among representative community samples) and generate dichotomous measures (i.e. depressed versus non-depressed) which are more limited in terms of applicable statistical techniques.

Most of the research reviewed in this chapter is based on symptom scales. Considerably more effort is needed to examine the effects of stress and social support on depressive disorders.

Age differences in depression

Age has a fascinating and rather paradoxical association with depression. For all adults, many more individuals report depressive symptoms than qualify for a diagnosis depressive disorder. This discrepancy is especially large for older adults, however. In brief, older adults report, on average, more symptoms of depression than do younger adults—and, yet, older adults are less likely than their younger counterparts to experience depressive disorders (Gurland, 1976; Gurland, Dean, Cross and Golden, 1980; Blazer and Williams, 1980). The recent Epidemiologic Catchment Area (ECA) studies indicate especially low prevalences of major depressive disorder among community-residing adults age 65 and older. In four ECA sites, the six-month prevalence of major depressive disorder for older adults ranged from 0.5% to 0.9%, whereas the prevalences for persons age 64 and younger ranged from 1.5% to 3.1% (Myers *et al.*, 1984; Blazer *et al.*, 1985; George *et al.*, 1988). It also should be noted, however, that a few studies have failed to find that older adults report significantly more depressive symptoms than their younger peers (e.g. Keith, 1987) and that other studies suggest that age differences disappear if somatic signs of depression are deleted from analysis (e.g. Zemore and Eames, 1979).

There are a number of reasons that older adults may report relatively high levels of depressive symptoms and yet be less likely than young adults to meet diagnostic criteria for depressive disorders. First, older adults may be more prone to mild dysphoria—but not full-blown clinical depression—than younger adults (Gurland, 1976; Blazer, Hughes and George, 1987). Second, elevated rates of physical illness among older adults may lead to higher reports of depressive symptoms. Such symptoms may not affect diagnostic prevalences, however, because clinicians discount symptoms that are related to physical health problems (Gurland, 1976; Zemore and Eames, 1979) and because diagnostic tools often include severity criteria that discount both mild dysphoric symptoms and symptoms experienced in conjunction with physical illness (e.g. Robins *et al.*, 1981). Third, and most complex, the diagnostic criteria for depressive disorder may not be 'age-fair.' That is, it may be that older adults present significant depressive disorders in ways that do not fit the guidelines of conventional psychiatric practice. For example, Blazer *et al.* (1987) recently assessed 1300 community-dwelling older adults, 27% of whom exhibited significant depressive symptomatology. Only 0.8% of the sample qualified for a diagnosis of major depressive disorder and 19% appeared to have relatively mild dysphoria. The remainder of the respondents with depressive symptoms appeared to be severely depressed, however. Blazer *et al.* suggest that conventional diagnostic criteria may 'miss' these severely depressed older adults.

MAIN EFFECTS MODELS

Given this background concerning the definitions of stress, social support, and depression, how are these phenomena interrelated? Hypotheses about the effects of stress and social support on depression typically take one of two forms. Some investigators focus on main effects; others hypothesize more complex, interactive effects. Nearly all investigators expect stress to have significant direct effects on depression—with higher levels of stress increasing the risk of depression. Complexities are introduced when investigators appropriately turn to the issue of depicting the circumstances under which stress does and does not lead to negative mental health outcomes. One strategy for revealing individual differences in responses to stress is to focus on offsetting and/or mediating effects. Using this strategy, some investigators have argued that social support can offset or counterbalance the effects of stress. Similarly, a variety of factors have been hypothesized to mediate the effects of stress on depression. Both offsetting and mediating effects are statistically estimated in main effects models. Other investigators view individual differences in responses to stress as interactive effects.

In this section, results of main effects models concerning the relationships between stress, social support, and depression are reviewed (results of studies based on interactive models are described in the next section). First, the robustness of the relationships between stress and depression and between social support and depression is examined. It is important to confirm that stress and social support have stable and robust effects on depression when other risk factors for depression have been statistically controlled. Second, evidence concerning the factors that mediate the relationship between stress and depression and that between social support and depression is reviewed. Mediating factors are important because they help us to understand the conditions under which and the mechanisms by which stress and social support affect depression.

Robustness of relationships

Stress and depression

Literally hundreds of studies have examined the effects of stress on depression in the context of multivariate models. Space limitations preclude a comprehensive review of all relevant studies. Nonetheless, the evidence is consistent: stress is robustly related to depression. This conclusion applies to studies based on samples of adults of all ages (e.g. Cronkite and Moos, 1984; Kessler, 1979; Wheaton, 1983; Dohrenwend, 1973; Turner, 1981, Lin, Woelfel and Light, 1985; Burks and Martin, 1985; DeLongis *et al.*, 1982; Kanner, Coyne, Schaefer and Lazarus, 1981; Monroe, 1983; Zarski, 1984). The relationship between stress and depression also is robust in studies based on samples of older adults (e.g. Krause, 1986b, 1987a, 1987b; Norris and Murrell, 1984; Holahan *et al.*, 1984).

The studies referenced above include all three types of stress: life events, chronic stress, and daily hassles. Thus, the relationship between stress and depression is robust across types of stress. Nonetheless, there is some evidence that the three types of stress differ in the size of their effects on depression. Several studies suggest that chronic stress has stronger effects on depression than life events. These studies are based both on samples of adults of all ages (e.g. Billings and Moos, 1984; Pearlin *et al.*, 1981; Dressler, 1985; Wheaton, 1983) and, to a lesser extent, on samples restricted to older adults (Krause, 1986b; Pearlin, 1980). Similarly, a number of studies suggest that daily hassles are more strongly related to depression than are life events. Most of these studies are based on samples of adults of all ages (e.g Burks and Martin, 1985; DeLongis *et al.*, 1982; Kanner *et al.*, 1981; Monroe, 1983; Zarski, 1984); one study based on a sample of older adults reached the same conclusion (Holahan *et al.*, 1984). These comparisons may not be totally accurate, however. Because life events are bounded in duration, they can be expected to have stronger or weaker effects on depression depending on the precise interval between occurrence of the event and measurement of depression. In contrast, chronic stressors and daily hassles (which are relatively stable) should not be subject to equally rigid requirements in terms of the timing of measurements.

Comparisons of the relative importance of particular kinds of stressors for depression also can be made *within* types of stress. Thus, some life events may be more closely related to depression than others and chronic stressors also may vary in their effects on depression. Evidence concerning this issue exists, but it is not easily summarized and this issue has not been examined in a systematic manner. An example of this kind of research, however, is Krause's report (1986b) that chronic financial deprivation is more strongly related to depression for older women than are chronic health problems.

Social support and depression

There is considerable evidence that social support has significant direct effects upon depression such that higher levels of social support are associated with lower levels of depression. This pattern has been observed both in studies based on samples of adults of all ages (e.g. Cronkite and Moos, 1984; Williams, Ware and Donald, 1981; Kaplan, Robins and Martin, 1983; Dressler, 1985; Lin, Simeone, Ensel and Kuo, 1979; Turner, 1981; Lin and Ensel, 1984) and in studies of older adults (e.g. Krause, 1987c; Holahan and Holahan, 1987; Norris and Murrell, 1984; Dimond, Lund and Caserta, 1987).

There is limited, but fairly consistent evidence that various dimensions of social support are differentially important as predictors of depression. In general, subjective assessments of social support are more strongly related to depression than are objective measures (e.g. network size) (e.g. Wethington and Kessler, 1986; Kessler and McLeod, 1985; Krause, 1987c). The reason for this pattern is unclear. Some investigators argue that perceptions of social support are 'colored' or 'contaminated' by depression and other psychological states (e.g. Henderson *et al.*, 1981). Others believe that the quality of one's supportive transactions is of primary importance in protecting against depression.

Relationships between social support and depression may be even more complex, however. First, it may be that the distinction between objective and subjective social support is overly simple. As noted previously, some investigators distinguish between multiple types of support (e.g. informational, instrumental, emotional)—each of which can be assessed in both objective and subjective terms. Only limited research is available concerning the differential effects of more detailed support types on depression. Krause (1987c) examined the effects of four types of social support—each of which was assessed both objectively and subjectively—on depressed affect in a sample of older adults. He found that (a) each type of support had significant main effects on depression, (b) emotional support was the strongest predictor of depression, and (c) subjective assessments of support adequacy were usually, but not always, more potent predictors of depressed affect than objective measures.

Second, various dimensions of social support may be differentially important, depending on the type of stress confronted. For example, instrumental assistance may be most important for coping with material deficits whereas emotional support is most important when coping with bereavement. This issue also has received only limited empirical attention. Krause (1986a) compared the effects of four dimensions of social support across four types of life events and an aggregate measure of life events. His results suggest that both type of support and type of event differ in relative impact on levels of depression.

Third, and perhaps most complex, different dimensions of support may be differentially important at different points in the stress process. Jacobsen (1986), for example, suggests that emotional, cognitive, and material (or instrumental) support are all important and that each is *most* important at a specific stage of the stress process. He suggests that future research examine specific support sequences and their relative effects. Of course, the efficacy of specific support sequences also may vary across stressors.

Stress and social support

Though it is less central to the theme of this chapter, a brief note about the relationship between stress and social support is in order. Thus far, evidence concerning the main effects of stress and support on depression has been examined. It also is important to know, however, whether stress and support are themselves causally linked. Does the experience of stress alter the nature of support networks and their transactions? Conversely, does the nature and quality of one's support network alter the likelihood of exposure to stress?

Two hypotheses have been advanced concerning the effects of stress on social support. One perspective suggest that stressful situations mobilize support networks; consequently, the occurrence of stress should be followed by increased supportive transactions (e.g. Wheaton, 1985; Krause, 1987b). An alternate, albeit less frequently endorsed perspective is that stress drives away supporters—perhaps because norms of reciprocity and equity cannot be met (e.g. George, 1986). With regard to the effects of social support on stress, the usual hypothesis is that supportive interpersonal relationships decrease the likelihood of subsequent stress—either because stressful situations are avoided or because potential challenges and threats are less likely to be appraised as stressful (e.g. George, 1980; Lazarus and Folkman, 1984).

Causal links between stress and support have received limited attention in previous research, in part because of the need for longitudinal data. Available results are inconsistent across studies. Atkinson, Liem and Liem (1986) examined the impact of unemployment on support provided by respondents' spouses and other support network members. They found that spousal support decreased over time—perhaps because, as unemployment continued, the financial deprivations associated with income loss became stressful for the spouses as well as for their unemployed mates. Support from other network members, however, remained stable over time. Mitchell and Moos (1984) examined the relationships between stress and social support over a one-year interval. They found that support, especially contributions from family members, increased over time—but this increase was unrelated to baseline levels of life events or chronic strains. Social support at baseline was unrelated to time-two life events (a pattern also reported by Lin and Ensel, 1984), but high levels of time-one support were associated with decreases in chronic stress.

Mediating factors

An important issue in research on the effects of stress and social support on depression is identification of mechanisms. We need to know why and how social support exerts a salubrious effect on mental health, why and how life events threaten psychiatric status, and what factors help some individuals to avoid psychological problems when confronting stress. One method of acquiring such knowledge is identification of mediating variables (i.e. intervening variables that can statistically explain the relationships between independent variables and outcomes). At this point, only limited information is available concerning mediators of stress and social support on depression.

Mediators of the effects of stress on depression

Several factors have been suggested as mediators of the effects of stress on depression. In general, life events have less negative consequences for depression if the individual (a) scores high on measures of mastery, self-efficacy, or internal locus of control (e.g. Thoits, 1987; Turner and Noh, 1983; Pearlin *et al.*, 1981); (b) has high self-esteem (e.g. Pearlin *et al.*, 1981; Krause, 1987b); (c) has a 'hardy' personality (e.g. Kobasa, Maddi and Courington, 1981); and/or (d) exhibits high levels of social integration (e.g. Myers, Lindenthal and Pepper, 1975). Pearlin *et al.* (1981) report that feelings of mastery/control and self-esteem also mediate the effects of chronic stress on depression. These potential mediating factors rarely have been tested in samples of older adults, however.

The researcher base is too small to permit confident conclusions about the robustness of these mediating factors. Moreover, the mediating factors identified in previous studies raise two concerns. First, some of the psychological factors observed to mediate the effects of stress on depression are so closely related to depression that their status as distinct variables is questionable (e.g. Lazarus, DeLongis, Folkman and Gruen, 1985). Both self-esteem and perceptions of control, for example, may be components of rather than antecedents of depression.

Second, the effects of mediating variables may not generalize across samples or situations. This possibility is raised by research on locus of control. There is a widely held assumption that internal locus of control is associated with reduced risk of depression. Substantial research supports this assumption (e.g. Johnson and Sarason, 1978; Lefcourt, Miller, Ware and Sherk, 1981; Wheaton, 1983). A variation of this perspective is that the relationship between locus of control and depression is curvilinear—with both extreme internal and external locus of control associated with higher levels of depression (Krause, 1986b). Other research based on institutional samples of older adults, however, suggests that external locus of control—especially external locus of control based on beliefs about the potency of powerful others—promotes better adjustment to institutional settings (e.g. Felton and Kahana, 1974; Wolk, 1976; Cicirelli, 1987). Thus, the degree to which internal versus external locus of control promotes adaptation (and, presumably, mental health) may depend upon the congruence between the individual's perceptions of control and the degree of constraint in the environment.

Mediators of the effects of social support on depression

Evidence concerning the mediators of social support on depression is even more scarce than that for the mediators of stress. A recent study by Krause (1987b) provides the major illustration of this line of research. In this study, based on a sample of older adults, Krause tested the hypothesis that social support helps to reduce the effects of life events on depression primarily by bolstering self-esteem. The results supported this hypothesis: once the effects of social support on self-esteem are taken into account, social support does not have a significant direct effect on depressive symptoms.

Accurately specifying the causal order among antecedent and intervening (or mediating) variables also is an issue of concern—especially when models are based on cross-sectional data. For example, in another recent study, Holahan and Holahan (1987) tested the hypothesis that social support mediates the relationship between self-efficacy and depression. Much the opposite of Krause, these authors argue that self-efficacy reduces depression because it is associated with the ability to develop and mobilize support networks. Thus, issues of causal order remain important considerations in distinguishing between antecedent variables and mediating factors.

INTERACTION MODELS

Hypotheses about interactions among the antecedents of depression focus on the conditions under which stress does and does not increase the risk of depression and suggest that stress and social support vary in importance for particular types of people. In this section, evidence concerning the interactive effects of stress and social support on depression is reviewed. First, the stress-buffering hypothesis, which has been the major forum for debate concerning the effects of stress and social support on depression, is examined. Second, age interactions are examined. Finally, other interactions involving the effects of stress and social support are examined.

A cautionary note is appropriate at this point. Evidence of buffering effects can be obtained in two ways. First, interactions can be formally tested as in regression and analysis of variance models. Formal interaction tests are the most rigorous because the statistical significance of the conditional effect is assessed. Second, evidence of interaction can be obtained from comparison of main effects models calculated for different subgroups. These comparisons can generate evidence supporting interactive effects, but the statistical significance of the difference across subgroups is not directly tested. In the interests of breadth of scope, evidence of conditional effects based on both formal tests of interaction and subgroup comparisons will be reviewed. Evidence based on formal interaction tests, however, should be viewed as more rigorous.

The stress-buffering hypothesis

Without question, the most commonly hypothesized interaction regarding the effects of stress and social support on depression is the stress-buffering hypothesis (e.g. Kessler and McLeod, 1985; Cohen and Wills, 1985). According to this hypothesis, the relationship between stress and depression is conditional upon level of social support. More specifically, the effects of stress on depression are expected to be stronger under conditions of low support. In its most stringent form, the stress-buffering hypothesis suggests that social support is irrelevant to depression under conditions of low stress.

A large number of studies support the stress-buffering hypothesis. Some of these studies are based on samples of adults of all ages and/or younger adults (e.g. Atkinson *et al.*, 1986; Dressler, 1985; Eaton, 1978; Parry, 1986; Turner, 1981; Wethington and Kessler, 1986; Gore, 1978). Evidence supporting the stress-buffering hypothesis also is observed in studies based on samples of older adults (e.g. Cutrona *et al.*, 1986; Krause, 1986a; 1987a). On the other hand, a number of studies also fail to support the stress-buffering hypothesis (e.g. Cronkite and Moos, 1984; Williams *et al.*, 1981; Lin *et al.*, 1979). All of these studies are based on formal tests of statistical interaction; therefore, inconsistency across studies is not due to differences in the methods used to test for interaction.

Inconsistencies across studies concerning the presence of stress-buffering may reflect the need to address additional complexities. For example, the stress-buffering hypothesis may be applicable to some kinds of stressors, but irrelevant to others. Similarly, some dimensions of social support may be important primarily because of their direct effects on mental health outcomes whereas other dimensions are important primarily because they buffer the effects of stress. The specificity of the stress-buffering hypothesis to particular stressors, support dimensions, of combinations of stressors and support dimensions has received little attention. Krause (1986a, 1987a), however, has explored this issue with data based on a sample of older adults. His results suggest that stress-buffering effects are observed (a) for some but not all dimensions of social support (Krause, 1987a), (b) for some but not all kinds of stressors (Krause, 1986a), and (c) for some but not all dimensions of depressed affect (Krause, 1986a, 1987a).

Before leaving the stress-buffering issue, a theoretical issue merits brief note. Much of the debate concerning the relationships between stress, social support, and depresion is framed in terms of the direct effects of support on depression *versus* their stress-buffering properties. This either/or approach is theoretically ill-advised. Social support may have direct effects on depression (e.g. by bolstering self-esteem or perceptions of control) *and* a buffering effect such that it is more important during times of high stress (Jacobsen, 1986; Norris and Murrell, 1984; Turner, 1981). Or, as just noted, some dimensions of social support may be important primarily because of their direct effects on mental health outcomes whereas other dimensions are important largely during times of crisis or stress.

Age interactions

If there are age differences in the effects of antecedent variables, especially stress and social support, on depression, age interactions are the best method of identifying those differences. Unfortunately, very little research has examined age interactions in the relationships between stress, social support, and depression.

One area that has received limited attention is age differences in the effects of specific life events on personal well-being. Chiriboga (1982a) compared younger and older persons in terms of adjustment to marital separation. His results suggest that marital dissolution has more negative effects for older than younger persons. Glick, Weiss and Parkes (1974) performed a longitudinal study of the effects of widowhood. They found that the experiences of younger and older widows differ significantly, though it cannot be concluded that one group fares better, overall, than the other. Younger widows typically exhibit higher levels of psychiatric symptoms than older widows during the first year of bereavement, including symptoms of depression. On the other hand, older widows appear to confront more difficult and permanent changes in identify because few older widows remarry whereas remarriage is typical for younger widows. Palmore *et al.*, (1985) compared the consequences of early versus 'on-time' retirement. Their results indicate that the psychosocial adjustment of on-time retirees is significantly better than that of early retirees. As a set, these studies suggest that issues of normativeness and being 'on-time' may explain age differences in reactions to specific life events, with adjustment proceeding more smoothly for events that are on-time and/or more prevalent in particular age groups.

Perhaps the most relevant study of the age-as-moderator hypothesis for the determinants of depression was conducted by George, Landerman and Blazer (1987). In this study, levels of depressive symptoms were viewed as a function of demographic variables (age, sex, race, marital status), socioeconomic status (SES), chronic stress (specifically, chronic physical illness), negative life events, and four dimensions of social support (network size, interaction frequency, instrumental assistance, and subjective perceptions of support adequacy). In addition to examining the main effects of these predictors, a series of interaction hypotheses were tested: (a) the traditional stress-buffering hypothesis (which was supported) and (b) interactions between age (based on three age groups representing young adulthood, middle age, and old age) and all of the other independent variables in the model. Five significant age interactions were observed. First, there was a significant age by sex interaction such that young women were more likely to exhibit depressive symptoms than other respondents. Second, there was a significant interaction between marital status and age. Young unmarried persons exhibited higher levels of depression than older unmarried persons and the married of all ages. Third, race interacted with age such that young non-white respondents had higher levels of depressive symptoms than young whites and middle-aged and older adults of both races. Fourth, a SES by age interaction indicated that the low SES is a significant predictor of depressive symptoms for younger adults but not for middle-aged and older persons. Finally, chronic disease was a risk factor for depression only among young adults. Neither life events nor any of the social support dimensions significantly interacted with age. All of these conditional effects were tested via formal tests of statistical interaction. These results were interpreted as indicating that a number of the typically examined antecedents of depression exhibit age-specific effects.

One additional study merits note. In a recent study, Keith (1987) examined depressive symptoms in younger versus older *couples*—an interesting, but neglected research topic. Her results suggested that life events exert stronger effects on depressive symptoms among younger than older couples.

Other interactions

The primary purpose of reviewing other interactions is to highlight potential complexities in the relationships between stress, social support, and depression. With one exception, these interactions have not been tested in replicated studies—consequently, their robustness is questionable.

The most robust of the other interactions observed in previous literature concerns gender and stress. Several studies suggest that stress has more deleterious effects for women than for men. Most of these studies are based on samples of adults of all ages (e.g. Kessler, 1979; Chiriboga, 1982b); though more limited evidence suggests that this pattern also characterizes older adults (Krause, 1986c).

Thoits (1987) suggests that gender differences in the effects of life events are more complex than a simple increased sensitivity by women. Her study examined interactions between life events and gender. The results suggest that some events have stronger effects on depression for women whereas other events have stronger effects for men. Though complex, these 'unique stressor' results are compatible with theories that emphasize sex differences in role allocation and socialization experiences.

Additional evidence suggests that the effects of life events may differ across other demographic subgroups. Kessler (1979) reports that life events have greater impact on depression and/or psychological distress for women than for men, for persons of lower socioeconomic status as compared to their more advantaged peers, and for the unmarried than for the married. He suggests that these 'vulnerability' differences may be explained by one or more of three explanatory variables: constitutional differences in vulnerability, differences in social resources (including social support), and/or differences in coping styles across demographic subgroups. More recently, Kessler and Neighbors (1986) noted that race and socioeconomic status may interact to produce even more complex patterns of differential vulnerability to life events. These authors report that the combination of being black and having low economic resources has especially negative consequences for psychological well-being. This finding was replicated, using depressive symptoms as the outcome measure, by George *et al.* (1987).

On theoretical grounds, coping characteristics might be expected to buffer the effects of stress on depression. Surprisingly, very little research is available to support or refute this hypothesis. In perhaps the strongest study to date, Pearlin *et al.* (1981) report that coping modes buffer the effects of life events (but not chronic stress) on depression. Another interesting hypothesis, related to coping, has been advanced by Neff and Husaini (1985). These authors suggest that alcohol consumption (especially in moderation) may buffer the effects of life events on depressive symptoms. Their results support this hypothesis, though only for rural white respondents.

Psychosocial characteristics also may moderate the effects of stress and/or social support on depression. Again, evidence is limited, but suggestive. Using data from a sample of adults of all ages, Wheaton (1983) examined interactions between (a) inflexibility and life events and (b) fatalism and life events in terms of their effects on depressive symptoms. He hypothesized that life events would be more strongly related to depression among persons with inflexible stances toward their environments and among persons with high levels of fatalism. Both interactions were statistically significant and large in magnitude. Krause (1987c), using data from a sample of older adults, hypothesized that locus of control would moderate the impact of chronic financial strain on depressive symptoms. His results indicated that chronic financial strain had much weaker effects on depression among persons with an internal locus of control than among those who viewed outcomes as contingent upon external sources of control. Norris and Murrell (1984) examined the interaction between perceptions of stress and social resources, using data from a sample of older adults. One component of their composite measure of social resources was social support. Their results were statistically significant, suggesting that perceptions of stress were less likely to lead to depression under conditions of high rather than low social resources. Conclusions from all three of these studies were based on formal tests of interaction. As a group, these studies suggest that the joint effects of stress and/or social support and psychosocial characteristics may be important factors in predicting levels of depression.

DISCUSSION AND IMPLICATIONS

The purpose of this chapter was to examine the relationships between stress, social support, and depression, with special attention to life course differences in those relationships. Current evidence clearly confirms that these phenomena are interrelated and that both stress and social support have substantial implications for the risk of depression. All three types of stress examined in previous literature—life events, chronic stressors, and daily hassles—are associated cross-sectionally and prospectively with increased risk of depression. Available evidence suggests that social support plays a dual role in the stress process. On the one hand, social support has a direct effect on depression, helping to offset or counterbalance the effects of stress. In addition, social support appears to buffer the effects of stress.

There are numerous complexities in the stress process that require additional research. Several areas are especially ripe for further effort. These include the specificity of stress and support relationships (i.e. the degree to which various types of stress and dimensions of social support have differential main and interactive effects on depression), identification of the mediators (or explanatory mechanisms) underlying the effects of stress and social support on depression, and increased emphasis on longitudinal studies of the stress process. With regard to the latter, the need for longitudinal studies has perhaps been underemphasized in previous sections of the chapter. But the need for prospective studies is, indeed, critical.

Evidence concerning the degree to which the relationships between stress, social support, and depression vary by age or life stage is somewhat fragmentary. Overall, major patterns seem to apply to both younger and older adults. More specifically, main effects of both stress and social support on depression and the stress-buffering hypothesis appear to apply to both younger and older persons. Major differences between older and younger adults in the stress process are best identified by age interactions—a topic that has received only limited attention. Based on the limited information available it appears that specific stressors may have different impacts on depression for younger and older persons because of differences in normativeness or age-specific prevalence (e.g. Chiriboga, 1982a; Glick *et al.*, 1974) and that demographic variables may be more strongly related to depression for younger than for older adults (e.g. George *et al.*, 1987). Considerably more effort is needed to examine potential age interactions among the determinants of depression. In addition, research is badly needed to determine whether the mediators of stress and social support on depression operate the same across age/life stage.

The limited information available on age differences in the effects of stress and social support on depression is based largely on cross-sectional data—and, at best, on short-term longitudinal studies. Consequently, these age differences may reflect cohort differences, age changes, or both. To this point, nothing has been said about the possible role of cohort differences in the relationships between stress, social support, and depression. And yet, cohort differences may affect the distributions of any and all of the variables examined in this chapter. Indeed, cohort differences in the prevalence and incidence of psychiatric disorders is a hypothesis currently receiving increased attention (e.g. Robins *et al.*, 1984). Cohorts also clearly differ in exposure to various kinds of stresses and in socialization experiences that transmit or develop coping skills (e.g. Elder, 1974; Folkman *et al.*, 1987). There also is evidence, based on data collected twenty years apart, that cohort (to a greater degree than age) is related to the propensity to seek formal services for personal problems in general and mental health problems in particular (Veroff, Kulka and Douvan, 1981). It is difficult to imagine that the data needed to make firm conclusions about the degree to which age differences reflect age versus cohort effects will be available in the near future. Nonetheless, it is important that attention be paid not only to the generalizability of the relationships between stress, social support, and depression across age groups but also to their generalizability across time.

ACKNOWLEDGEMENT

Support for preparations of this chapter was provided by two grants (MH35386 and MH40159) from the National Institute of Mental Health.

REFERENCES

American Psychiatric Association (1980). *Diagnostic and Statistical Manual of Mental Disorders*, Third Edition, American Psychiatric Association, Washington, DC.

Amster, L.E. and Krauss, H.H. (1974). The relationship between life crises, and mental deterioration in old age. *International Journal of Aging and Human Development*, **5**, 51−5.

Antonucci, T.C. (1985). Personal characteristics, social support, and social behavior. In R.H. Binstock and E. Shanas (eds.) *Handbook of Aging and the Social Sciences*, Van Nostrand Reinhold, New York, pp. 94−128.

Antonucci, T.C. and Akiyama, H. (1987). Social networks in adult life and a preliminary examination of the convoy model. *Journal of Gerontology*, **42**, 519−27.

Atkinson, T., Liem, R. and Liem, J.H. (1986). The social costs of unemployment: implications for social support. *Journal of Health and Social Behavior*, **27**, 317−31.

Babchuck, N. (1978−79). Aging and primary relations. *International Journal of Aging and Human Development*, **9**, 137−51.

Barrera, M., Sandler, I. and Ramsey, T. (1981). Preliminary development of a scale of social support: studies on college students. *American Journal of Community Psychology*, **9**, 435−47.

Beck, A.T., Ward, C., Mendelson, M., Mock, J. and Erbaugh, J. (1961). An inventory for measuring depression. *Archives of General Psychiatry*, **4**, 53−63.

Billings, A.G. and Moos, R.H. (1984). Coping, stress, and social resources among adults and unipolar depression. *Journal of Personality and Social Psychology*, **46**, 877−91.

Blazer, D.G. (1982). Social support and mortality in an elderly population. *American Journal of Epidemiology*, **115**, 684−94.

Blazer, D., George, L.K., Landerman, R., Pennybacker, M., Melville, M.L., Woodbury, M., Manton, K.G., Jordan, K. and Locke, B. (1985). Psychiatric disorders: a rural urban comparison. *Archives of General Psychiatry*, **42**, 651−6.

Blazer, D., Hughes, D.C. and George, L.K. (1987). The epidemiology of depression in an elderly community population. *The Gerontologist*, **27**, 281−7.

Blazer, D. and Williams, C.D. (1980). Epidemiology of dysphoria and depression in an elderly population. *American Journal of Psychiatry*, **137**, 439−44.

Brown, G.W. and Harris, T. (1982). Fall-off in the reporting of life events. *Social Psychiatry*, **17**, 23−8.

Burks, N. and Martin, B. (1985). Everyday problems and life change events: ongoing versus acute sources of stress. *Journal of Human Stress*, **11**, 27−35.

Cantor, M.H. (1975). Life space and the social support system of the inner city elderly of New York. *The Gerontologist*, **15**, 23−7.

Chiriboga, D.A. (1982a). Adaptation to marital separation in later and earlier life. *Journal of Gerontology*, **37**, 109−14.

Chiriboga, D.A. (1982b). An examination of life events as possible antecedents to change. *Journal of Gerontology*, **37**, 595−601.

Chiriboga, D.A. and Dean, H. (1978). Dimensions of stress: perspectives from a longitudinal study. *Journal of Psychosomatic Research*, **22**, 47−55.

Cicirelli, V.G. (1987). Locus of control and patient role adjustment of the elderly in acute-care hospitals. *Psychology and Aging*, **2**, 138−43.

Cohen, S. and Wills, T.A. (1985). Stress, social support, and the buffering hypothesis. *Psychological Bulletin*, **98**, 310–57.

Cronkite, R.C. and Moos, R.H. (1984). The role of predisposing and moderating factors in the stress-illness relationship. *Journal of Health and Social Behavior*, **25**, 372–93.

Cutrona, C., Russell, D. and Rose, J. (1986). Social support and adaptation to stress by the elderly. *Journal of Psychology and Aging*, **1**, 47–54.

Dekker, D. and Webb, J. (1974). Relationships of the social readjustment rating scale to psychiatric status, anxiety, and social desirability. *Journal of Psychosomatic Research*, **18**, 125–30.

DeLongis, A., Coyne, J., Dakof, G., Folkman, S. and Lazarus, R.S. (1982). Relationship of daily hassles, uplifts, and major life events to health status. *Health Psychology*, **1**, 119–36.

Dimond, M., Lund, D.A. and Caserta, M.S. (1987). The role of social support in the first two years of bereavement in an elderly sample. *The Gerontologist*, **27**, 599–604.

Dohrenwend, B.S. (1973). Life events as stressors: a methodological inquiry. *Journal of Health and Social Behavior*, **14**, 167–75.

Dressler, W.W. (1985). Extended family relationships, social support, and mental health in a southern black community. *Journal of Health and Social Behavior*, **26**, 39–48.

Eaton, W.W. (1978). Life events, social supports, and psychiatric symptoms; a reanalysis of the New Haven data. *Journal of Health and Social Behavior*, **19**, 230–4.

Elder, G.H. Jr (1974). *Children of the Great Depression*, University of Chicago Press, Chicago.

Endicott, J. and Spitzer, R.L. (1978). A diagnostic interview: the schedule for affective disorders and schizophrenia. *Archives of General Psychiatry*, **35**, 837–44.

Felton, B. and Kahana, E. (1974). Adjustment and situationally bound locus of control among institutionalized aged. *Journal of Gerontology*, **29**, 295–301.

Fischer, C.S. (1982). *To Dwell Among Friends, Personal Networks in Town and City*, University of Chicago Press, Chicago.

Folkman, S., Lazarus, R.S., Pimley, S. and Novacek, J. (1987). Age differences in stress and coping processes. *Psychology and Aging*, **2**, 171–84.

Funch, D. and Marshall, J. (1984). Measuring life stress: factors affecting fall-off in the reporting of life events. *Journal of Health and Social Behavior*, **25**, 453–64.

George, L.K. (1980). *Role Transitions in Later Life: A Social Stress Perspective*, Brooks/Cole, Monterey, CA.

George, L.K. (1986). Caregiver burden: conflict between norms of reciprocity and solidarity. In K. Pillemar and R. Wolf (eds.) *Conflict and Abuse in Families of the Elderly: Theory, Research, and Intervention*, Auburn House, Boston, pp. 67–92.

George, L.K. (1987). Easing caregiver burden: the role of informal and formal supports. In R.A. Ward and S.S. Tobin (eds.) *Health in Aging: Sociological Issues and Policy Directions*, Springer, New York, pp. 112–43.

George, L.K., Blazer, D.G., Winfield-Laird, I., Leaf, P.J. and Fischbach, R.L. (1988). Psychiatric disorders and mental health service use in later life: evidence from the epidemiologic catchment area program. In J. Brody and G.L. Maddox (eds.) *Epidemiology and Aging*, Springer, New York.

George, L.K., Hughes, D.C., Blazer, D.G. and Fowler, N. (in press). Social support and the outcome of major depression. *British Journal of Psychiatry*.

George, L.K., Landerman, R. and Blazer, D.G. (1987). Age differences in the antecedents of depression and anxiety: Evidence from the Duke Epidemiologic Catchment Area Program. Paper presented at annual meetings of the American Association for the Advancement of Science, Chicago.

Glick, I.O., Weiss, R.D. and Parkes, C.M. (1974). *The First Year of Bereavement*, Wiley, New York.

Goldberg, E.G. and Comstock, G.W. (1980). Epidemiology of life events: frequency in general populations. *American Journal of Epidemiology*, **111**, 736–52.

Gore, S. (1978). The effect of social support in moderating the health consequences of unemployment. *Journal of Health and Social Behavior*, **19**, 157–65.

Gouldner, A.W. (1960). The norm of reciprocity: a preliminary statement. *American Sociological Review*, **25**, 161–78.

Gurland, B.J. (1976). The comparative frequency of depression in various adult age groups. *Journal of Gerontology*, **31**, 283–92.

Gurland, B.J., Dean, L., Cross, P. and Golden, R. (1980). The epidemiology of depression and dementia in the elderly: the use of multiple indicators of these conditions. In J.O. Cole and J.E. Barrett (eds.) *Psychopathology of the Aged*, Raven Press, New York, pp.37–60.

Henderson, S., Bryne, D.G. and Duncan-Jones, P. (1981). *Neurosis and the Social Environment*, Academic, New York.

Holahan, C.K. and Holahan, C.J. (1987). Self-efficacy, social support, and depression in aging: a longitudinal analysis. *Journal of Gerontology*, **42**, 65–8.

Holahan, C.K., Holahan, C.J. and Belk, S.S. (1984). Adjustment in aging: the role of life stress, hassles, and self-efficacy. *Health Psychology*, **3**, 315–28.

Holmes, T.H. and Rahe, R.H. (1967). The Social Readjustment Rating Scale. *Journal of Psychosomatic Research*, **11**, 213–18.

House, J.S. (1981). *Work Stress and Social Support*, Addison-Wesley, Reading, MA.

House, J.S. and Robbins, C. (1983). Age, psychosocial stress, and health. In M.W. Riley, B.B. Hess and K. Bond (eds.) *Aging in Society: Selected Reviews of Recent Research*, Erlbaum, Hillsdale, NJ, pp. 175–97.

Hughes, D.C., Blazer, D.G. and George, L.K. (1988a). Age differences in life events: a multivariate controlled analysis. *Internation Journal of Aging and Human Development*, **27**, 207–20.

Hughes, D.C., George, L.K., and Blazer, D.G. (1988b). Age differences in life event qualities: multivariate controlled analyses. *Journal of Community Psychology*, **16**, 161–74.

Jacobsen, D.E. (1986). Types and timing of social support. *Journal of Health and Social Behavior*, **27**, 250–64.

Johnston, J. and Sarason, I. (1978). Life stress, depression, and anxiety: internal-external control as a modifier variable. *Journal of Psychosomatic Research*, **22**, 205–8.

Kanner, A.D., Coyne, J.C., Schaefer, C. and Lazarus, R.S. (1981). Comparisons of two modes of stress measurement: daily hassles and uplifts versus life events. *Journal of Behavioral Medicine*, **4**, 1–39.

Kaplan, H.B., Robins, C. and Martin, S.S. (1983). Antecedents of psychological distress in young adults: self-rejection, deprivation of social support, and life events. *Journal of Health and Social Behavior*, **24**, 230–43.

Keith, P. M. (1987). Depressive symptoms among younger and older couples. *The Gerontologist*, **27**, 605–10.

Kessler, R.C. (1979). Stress, social status, and psychological distress. *Journal of Health and Social Behavior*, **20**, 259–72.

Kessler, R.C. and McLeod, J.D. (1985). Social support and mental health in community samples. In S. Cohen and S.L. syme (eds.) *Social Support and Health*, Academic, New York, pp. 19–240.

Kessler, R.C. and Neighbors, H.W. (1986). A new perspective on the relationships among race, social class, and psychological distress. *Journal of Health and Social Behavior*, **27**, 107–15.

Kobasa, S.C., Maddi, S.R. and Courington, S. (1981). Personality and constitution as mediators in the stress-illness relationship. *Journal of Health and Social Behavior*, **22**, 368–78.

Krause, N. (1986a). Social support, stress and well-being among older adults. *Journal of Gerontology*, **41**, 512–19.

Krause, N. (1986b). Stress and coping: reconceptualizing the role of locus of control beliefs. *Journal of Gerontology*, **41**, 617–22.

Krause, N. (1986c). Stress and sex differences in depressive symptoms among older adults. *Journal of Gerontology*, **41**, 727–31.

Krause, N. (1987a). Chronic financial strain, social support, and depressive symptoms among older adults. *Psychology and Aging*, **2**, 185–92.

Krause, N. (1987b). Life stress, social support, and self-esteem in an elderly population. *Psychology and Aging*, **2**, 349–56.

Krause, N. (1987c). Chronic strain, locus of control, and distress in older adults. *Psychology and Aging*, **2**, 375–82.

Krause, N. (1987d). Satisfaction with social support and self-rated health in older adults. *The Gerontologist*, **27**, 301–8.

Krause, N. (1987e). Understanding the stress process: linking social support with locus of control beliefs. *Journal of Gerontology*, **42**, 589–93.

Lazarus, R.S. and DeLongis, A. (1983). Psychological stress and coping in aging. *American Psychologist*, **38**, 245–54.

Lazarus, R.S., DeLongis, A., Folkman, S. and Gruen, R. (1985). Stress and adaptational outcomes: the problem of confounded measures. *American Psychologist*, **40**, 770–9.

Lazarus, R.S. and Folkman, S. (1984). *Stress, Appraisal, and Coping*, Springer, New York.

Lee, G.R. (1985). Kinship and social support of the elderly: the case of the United States. *Aging and Society*, **5**, 19–38.

Lefcourt, H.M., Miller, R.S., Ware, E.E. and Sherk, D. (1981). Locus of control as a modifier of the relationship between stressors and moods. *Journal of Personality and Social Psychology*, **41**, 357–69.

Lin, N. and Ensel, W.M. (1984). Depression-mobility and its social etiology: the role of life events and social support. *Journal of Health and Social Behavior*, **25**, 176–88.

Lin, N., Simeone, R.S., Ensel, W.M. and Kuo, W. (1979). Social support, stressful life events, and illness: a model and an empirical test. *Journal of Health and Social Behavior*, **20**, 108–19.

Lin, N., Woelfel, M.W. and Light, S.C. (1985). The buffering effect of social support subsequent to an important life event. *Journal of Health and Social Behavior*, **26**, 247–63.

Lowenthal, M.F., Thurnher, M. and Chiriboga, D.A. (1975). *Four Stages of Life*. Jossey-Bass, San Francisco.

Markides, K.S., Boldt, J.S. and Ray, L.A. (1986). Sources of helping and intergenerational solidarity: a three-generations study of Mexican Americans. *Journal of Gerontology*, **41**, 506–11.

Mindel, C.H., Wright, R. Jr and Starrett, R.A. (1986). Informal and formal health and social support systems of black and white elderly: a comparative cost approach. *The Gerontologist*, **26**, 279–85.

Mitchell, R. E. and Moos, R.H. (1984). Deficiencies in social support among depressed patients: antecedents or consequences of stress? *Journal of Health and Social Behavior*, **25**, 438–52.

Monroe, S.M. (1983). Major and minor life events as predictors of psychological distress: further issues and findings. *Journal of Behavioral Medicine*, **6**, 189–205.

Moos, R. H., Cronkite, R.C., Billings, A.G. and Finney, J.W. (1983). *Health and Daily Living Form Manual*, Social Ecology Laboratory, Verterans Administration and Stanford University Medical Center, Palo Alto, CA.

Myers J.K., Lindenthal, J.J. and Pepper, M.P. (1975). Life events, social integration, and psychiatric symptomatology. *Journal of Health and Social Behavior*, **16**, 421−9.

Myers, J.K., Weissman, M.M., Tischler, G.L., Holzer, C.E., Leaf, P.J., Orvaschel, H., Anthony, J.C., Boyd, J.H., Burke, J.D., Kramer, M. and Stoltzman, R. (1984). Six-month prevalence of psychiatric disorders in three communities. *Archives of General Psychiatry*, **41**, 959−70.

Neff, J.A. and Husaini, B.A. (1985). Stress-buffer properties of alcohol consumption: the role of urbanicity and religious identification. *Journal of Health and Social Behavior*, **26**, 207−21.

Norris, F.H. and Murrell, S.A. (1984). Protective function of resources related to life events, global stress, and depression in older adults. *Journal of Health and Social Behavior*, **25**, 424−37.

Palmore, E., Burchett, B., Fillenbaum, G.G., George, L.K. and Wallman,L. (1985). *Retirement: Causes and Consequences*, Springer, New York.

Parry, G. (1986). Paid employment, life events, social support, and mental health in working class mothers. *Journal of Health and Social Behavior*, **27**, 193−208.

Pearlin, L.I. (1980). Life strains and psychological distress among adults. In N. Smelser and E. Erikson (eds.) *Themes of Work and Love in Adulthood*, Harvard University Press, Cambridge, MA., pp. 174−92.

Pearlin, L.I., Lieberman, M.A., Menaghan, E.G. and Mullan, J.T. (1981). The stress process. *Journal of Health and Social Behavior*, **19**, 2−21.

Pearlin, L.I. and Schooler, C. (1978). The structure of coping. *Journal of Health and Social Behavior*, **19**, 2−21.

Radloff, L.S. (1977). The CES-D Scale: a self-report depression scale for research in the general population. *Journal of Applied Psychological Measurement*, **1**, 385−94.

Reissman, F. (1965). The helper therapy principle. *Social Work*, **10**, 27−32.

Robins, L.N., Helzer, J.E., Croughan, J.L. and Ratcliff, K.S. (1981). The NIMH Diagnostic Interview Schedule: its history, characteristics, and validity. *Archives of General Psychiatry*, **38**, 381−9.

Robins, L.N., Helzer, J.E., Weissman, M.M., Orvaschel, H., Gruenberg, E., Burke, J.D. and Regier, D.A. (1984). Lifetime prevalence of specific psychiatric disorders in three sites. *Archives of General Psychiatry*, **41**, 949−58.

Rook, K.S. (1984). The negative side of social interaction: impact on psychological well-being. *Journal of Personality and Social Psychology*, **46**, 1097−108.

Ross, C.E. and Huber, J. (1985). Hardship and depression. *Journal of Health and Social Behavior*, **26**, 312−27.

Shanas, E. (1979a). Social myth as hypothesis: the case of the family relations of old people. *The Gerontologist*, **19**, 3−9.

Shanas, E. (1979b). The family as a social support system in old age. *The Gerontologist*, **19**, 169−74.

Shanas, E. and Maddox, G.L. (1985). Health, health resources, and the utilization of care. In R.H. Binstock and E. Shanas (eds.) *Handbook of Aging and the Social Sciences*, Van Nostrand Reinhold, New York, pp. 697−726.

Stephens, M.A.P., Kinney, J.M., Norris, V.K. and Ritchie, S.W. (1987). Social networks as assets and liabilities in recovery from stroke by geriatric patients. *Psychology and Aging*, **2**, 125−9.

Stephens, R.C., Blau, Z.S., Oser, G.T. and Miller, M.D. (1978). Aging, Social support systems, and social policy. *Journal of Gerontological Social Work*, **1**, 33−45.

Strain, L.A. and Chappell (1982). Confidants: do they make a difference in quality of life? *Research on Aging*, **4**, 479−502.

Streib, G.F. (1985). Social Stratification and aging. In R.H. Binstock and E. Shanas (eds.) *Handbook of Aging and the Social Sciences*, Van Nostrand Reinhold, New York, pp. 339−60.

Thoits, P.A. (1983). Dimensions of life stress that influence psychological distress: an evaluation and synthesis of the literature. In H.B. Kaplan (ed.) *Psychosocial Stress: Trends in Theory and Research*, Academic, New York, pp. 33−103.

Thoits, P.A. (1987). Gender and marital status differences in control and distress: common stress status versus unique stress explanations. *Journal of Health and Social Behavior*, **28**, 7−22.

Turner, R.J. (1981). Experienced social support as a contingency in emotional well-being. *Journal of Health and Social Behavior*, **22**, 357−67.

Turner, R.J. and Noh, S. (1983). Class and psychological vulnerability among women: the significance of social support and personal control. *Journal of Health and Social Behavior*, **24**, 2−15.

Uhlenhuth, E.H., Lipman, R.S., Balter, M.B. and Stern, M. (1974). Symptom intensity and life stress in the city. *Archives of General Psychiatry*, **31**, 759−64.

Vaughan, D.R. and Lancaster, C.G. (1981). Applying a cardinal measurement model to normative assessments of income: synopsis of a preliminary look. *The 1980 Proceedings of the American Statistical Association*, Washington, DC.

Veroff, J., Kulka, R.A. and Douvan, E. (1981). *Mental Health in America: Patterns of Help-Seeking from 1957 to 1976*, Basic Books, New York.

Ward, R.A., Sherman, S.R. and LaGory, M. (1984). Subjective network assessments and subjective well-being. *Journal of Gerontology*, **39**, 93−101.

Weiss, R.S. (1974). The provisions of social relationships. In Z. Rubin (ed.) *Doing Unto Others*, Prentice-Hall, Englewood Cliffs, NJ, pp. 17−26.

Wethington, E. and Kessler, R.C. (1986). Perceived support, received support, and adjustment to stressful life events. *Journal of Health and Social Behavior*, **27**, 78−89.

Wheaton, B. (1983). Stress, personal coping resources, and psychiatric symptoms: an investigation of interactive models. *Journal of Health and Social Behavior*, **24**, 208−29.

Wheaton, B. (1985). Models for the stress-buffering functions of coping resources. *Journal of Health and Social Behavior*, **26**, 352−64.

Williams, A.W., Ware, J.E. and Donald, C.A. (1981). A model of mental health, life events, and social supports applicable to general populations. *Journal of Health and Social Behavior*, **22**, 324−36.

Wolk, S. (1976). Situational constraint as a moderator of the locus of control-adjustment relationship. *Journal of Consulting and Clinical Psychology*, **44**, 420−7.

Zarski, J.J. (1984). Hassles and health: a replication. *Health Psychology*, **3**, 243−51.

Zemore, R. and Eames, N. (1979). Psychic and somatic symptoms of depression among young adults, institutionalized aged, and noninstitutionalized aged. *Journal of Gerontology*, **34**, 716−22.

Zung, W.W. (1965). A self-rating depression scale. *Archives of General Psychiatry*, **12**, 63−70.

Chapter 12

Personality, Stress, and Coping: Some Lessons from a Decade of Research

Paul T. Costa, Jr
and Robert R. McCrae

Research on stress has preoccupied social and medical scientists since Selye brought it to their attention in the 1950s. Coping, however, has a much shorter history, with its real beginnings in the 1970s (Coelho, Hamburg, and Adams, 1974; Haan, 1977; Moos, 1976; Pearling and Schooler, 1978; Vaillant, 1977). Although voluminous research had shown associations between life stress and subsequent negative outcomes, the associations were generally small and inconsistent. One missing element in the equation, it was felt, was coping—what the individual did in response to stressful situations. Some researchers (Benson, 1975) offered a single form of stress-management intended to handle all forms of stress; others (Lazarus and Folkman, 1984) were impressed by the wide variety of possible ways of coping, and sought to assess the utility of all of them. There was considerable optimism that an empirical approach to this topic would soon yield a scientific basis for interventions that would reduce distress and promote mental and physical health.

Ten years later a more cautious assessment is called for. Several studies have shown a role for coping processes in the explanation of responses to stress, but rarely a large one (Aldwin and Revenson, 1987). Felton, Revenson, and Hinrichsen (1984), for example concluded that in the case of chronic illnesses, 'the effects of individual coping efforts on emotional distress are rather modest' (p. 897). The greatest achievement of the past decade has been an increased appreciation of the complexity of the problem and the need to consider simultaneously personality dispositions, situational variables, coping efforts, and meaningful outcomes. The increasing conceptual sophistication should form the basis for steady empirical progress.

In this chapter we will outline some of the conceptual distinctions that need to be made, review some conclusions suggested by previous research, and present some new data. One point we wish to make is that one class of behaviors that have been considered coping mechanisms may not, in fact, be responses to stress at all; instead, they may be manifestations of neuroticism that are attributed (or misattributed) to an external stress. The present chapter is concerned with research

Aging, Stress and Health Edited by K.S. Markides and C.L. Cooper
© 1989 John Wiley & Sons Ltd

on coping as a general process. Readers chiefly interested in coping with specific illnesses should consult Moos (1977) and Burish and Bradley (1983).

CONCEPTUALIZATIONS, AMBIGUITIES, AND OPERATIONALIZATIONS

The terms *personality, stress*, and *coping* are often used in such vague ways that it is impossible to know where one ends and the next begins. Is stress a demand from the environment (like loss of a spouse or unemployment), or is it a characteristic of the individual, akin to anxiety? Or is stress best considered from a transactional perspective (Lazarus, Averill, and Opton, 1974) as some interaction of person and environment? Is repression a coping or defense mechanism, or a part of personality that can be measured by a questionnaire (Byrne, 1964)? Is venting frustration on others a sign of stress, or a form of coping, or a personality trait, or perhaps an outcome indicating a failure of coping? Until we can sort out these alternative meanings both conceptually and operationally, we cannot hope to answer questions about the relations between personality, stress, and coping. Fortunately, research in recent years has made it possible to adopt meaningful, if provisional, definitions.

Let us begin with personality. We define personality in terms of individual differences in enduring and characteristic ways of thinking, feeling, and acting. As Allport and Odbert (1936) showed, the English language has thousands of trait-names for these differences (e.g *insecure, fun-loving, imaginative, generous, hardworking*), and hundreds of scales and inventories have been developed by personality psychologists to measure proposed traits, types, needs, and temperaments. Although each of these may highlight a somewhat different aspect of personality, there is considerable redundancy among them, and a substantial body of literature (Digman and Inouye, 1986; McCrae and Costa, 1987; Norman, 1963) points to the conclusion that people can be broadly characterized in terms of only five major dimensions of personality that we call *neuroticism, extraversion, openness to experience, agreeableness*, and *conscientiousness*. The dimensions can be measured by self-reports or observer ratings using a variety of instruments and formats (McCrae and Costa, 1987), and, at least after about age 30, they are highly stable in adulthood (Costa and McCrae, 1988). Individuals bring these enduring dispositions with them in their encounters with stressful events, and it is possible to ask empirically whether and in what ways personality traits affect the kinds of stress encountered, the ways individuals use to cope, and the ultimate effectiveness of coping behavior.

Although *stress* sometimes means the physical or psychological condition elicited by a stressful situation, we will use it to refer to the external danger, deprivation, or opportunity that puts demands on the individual. The researcher is confronted with a dilemma here. Events have different meanings for different people, and what is stressful to one person may not be to the next. If stress is operationalized in terms of objective events such as loss of spouse or unemployment, individual differences in the interpretation of these events will be ignored. Conversely, if individuals are allowed to define stressful events subjectively and idiosyncratically, biases are likely to enter. In particular, individuals high in neuroticism are prone to interpret many events as being stressful, and a subjectively defined 'high stress' group would probably contain a disproportionate number of emotionally unstable individuals.

The life events approach of Holmes and Rahe (1967) was intended to avoid this bias by recording objective events, weighted according to consensually defined 'life change units.' In practice, this approach has encountered many difficulties (Schroeder and Costa, 1984), and life event approaches are best when confined to a single, objectively definable event. Bereavement is a particularly useful model, because it is objective, relatively common (at least among older people), and universally conceded to be a highly stressful event (McCrae and Costa, 1988; Stroebe and Stroebe, 1987).

Stress can be treated qualitatively as well as quantitatively, and both theory (Lazarus and Launier, 1978) and research (McCrae, 1984) have supported the division of stressful events into threats, losses, and challenges. Here, too, the problem of subjective versus objective interpretation arises. For one person, unemployment may represent a threat, for a second, a loss, and for yet another, a challenge. (Of course, the same individual may also interpret the event differently at different times.) In our earlier research (McCrae, 1982, 1984; McCrae and Costa, 1986) we addressed this problem by conducting parallel studies: in the first, we selected specific events and categorized them a priori as threats, losses, and challenges; in the second, we asked subjects to identify their own threats, losses, and challenges. In general, the same pattern of findings could be seen in both studies, and we interpreted only effects that were replicated across studies.

We define *coping* as a set of concrete responses to a stressful situation or event that are intended to resolve the problem or reduce distress. We operationalize coping in terms of answers to questions about what individuals did when facing a specific threat, loss, or challenge. Note that coping is not assessed as a characteristic style that describes how individuals usually or typically respond to stress, but as a discrete response to a particular stress (cf. Lazarus and Folkman, 1984). This approach allows individuals to report unusual and uncharacteristic ways of responding that may be a function of particular stressful situations. Note that it also makes it possible to determine empirically whether there are characteristic ways or styles of coping, by assessing coping efforts across a variety of stresses. By making a relatively clear operational distinction between personality and coping, it permits meaningful questions about their relations.

The questionnaire approach to the study of coping tacitly assumes that individuals are able to understand and willing to report their responses to stress, and it therefore diverges from classic views of defense, a process which is often thought to operate unconsciously. Some such defenses almost certainly exist and operate at least occasionally in most people; they have, however, proven to be extraordinarily difficult to assess reliably and validly, and recent research has focused attention on what individuals can report themselves. (We will mention briefly a recent attempt to examine age and the use of defense mechanisms; the results do not differ greatly from what has been reported with regard to age and coping mechanisms.)

One area in which there is very little consensus at present is in the number or nature of different ways of coping. The Ways of Coping questionnaire (Folkman and Lazarus, 1980) is the most widely used instrument for measuring coping; it consists of 68 items that address a large number of possible responses to stress. Unfortunately, there is no agreement about how the items are to be grouped to form scales. Most researchers rely on factor analyses of some sort, but published literature has reported two (Folkman and Lazarus, 1980), three (Parkes, 1986), six (Felton *et al.*, 1984), seven (Scheier, Weintraub, and Carver, 1986), eight (Folkman *et al.*, 1986) and 28 factors (McCrae, 1982). There are resemblances between these coping factors, but also differences, making any summary of the literature difficult.

Because so little is yet known about the determinants or effectiveness of different ways of coping, our strategy has been to examine a large number of coping mechanisms, on the assumption that important distinctions might be blurred if different mechanisms were prematurely collapsed into broader categories. For example, the effective strategy of positive thinking and the ineffective strategy of escapist fantasy could both be considered 'emotion focused', but to combine them into a single index would be counterproductive.

Similarly, in our earlier research we followed Lazarus and his colleagues (Lazarus *et al.*, 1974) in including responses that are not traditionally viewed as constructive ways of handling stress, such as hostile reaction toward others, self-blame, and wishful thinking. Their inclusion among coping questionnaire items makes it possible to determine empirically whether such responses serve some useful function. Later in this chapter we will propose a reconceptualization based in part on empirical results to be presented. As we now see it, the fundamental question is not whether hostile reactions, self-blame, and related behaviors are effective or ineffective ways of coping; the question is whether they are coping efforts at all. Are these behaviors responses to stress, or reflections of personality merely attributed to stress?

DETERMINANTS OF THE USE OF COPING MECHANISMS

It is clear that there are a large number of ways to respond to stress. One can take action to solve the problem, seek help and advice from others, make conforting comparisons with the troubles of others, become fatalistic, or simply ignore the problem in the hope that it will go away. Historically, coping and defense mechanisms have been classified according to their pathology or maturity (e.g. Freud, 1936), and some theorists continue to view them primarily in this way (Haan, 1977; Vaillant, 1977). More recently, it has been suggested that the value of any particular form of coping depends on the specifics of the situation (Lazarus and Folkman, 1984): Different individuals will find different strategies effective in dealing with different problems. In this approach, the interventionist is asked to consider which of a large number of ways of coping are best suited for a particular individual facing a particular problem. For example, how should an older Mexican-American woman who is introverted but open to experience best deal with the minor pain and severe functional limitations caused by arthritis?

There are, of course, any number of person variables and problem variables that might be relevant to such choices, and a systematic experimental analysis of several levels of each of these factors would constitute a program of research for several lifetimes. Correlational studies that examine the use of different coping methods in relation to person and situation variables can provide hypotheses, on the assumption that individuals (at least relatively well-adjusted individuals) will tend to learn and adopt coping strategies that work relatively well.

Age, coping, and defense

A decade ago virtually nothing was known about age differences in coping, and speculations followed preferred views of the aging process. Thus, the elderly were sometimes portrayed as rigid and unable to adapt, and prone to the use of primitive mechanisms of coping and defense (cf. Pfeiffer, 1977). Conversely, aging was seen by others as a process of attaining wisdom, and greater maturity of coping was also hypothesized (Vaillant, 1977). McCrae (1982) characterized these as *regression* and *growth* hypotheses, respectively. It would seem to be simple enough to obtain cross-sectional data to decide between these two hypotheses, but when researchers began to examine data, it quickly became clear that age differences were likely to be confounded with differences in the types of stress typically encountered by adults of different ages: young adults reported more family- and job-related challenges; older adults reported more health problems for themselves or their spouses.

After controlling for types of stress, initial reports suggested that there were few age differences in coping (Lazarus and DeLongis, 1983). McCrae (1982) examined 28 finely differentiated coping mechanisms (see Table 1 for a list of mechanisms) in two parallel studies of coping with a variety of stresses classified as threats, losses, and challenges; only two mechanisms showed replicated age differences. Younger adults (under age 50) more frequently reported hostile reaction and the use of escapist fantasy than did middle-aged or older adults. There were no significant age differences in either study for rational action, seeking help, perseverance, isolation of affect, expression of feelings, distraction, intellectual denial, self-blame, social comparison, substitution, drawing strength from adversity, avoidance, withdrawal, active forgetting, or passivity. In a study of coping with interpersonal conflicts, Quayhagen and Quayhagen (1982) found that older adults used less help seeking and problem solving, but more affectivity (emotional ventilation). They found no differences in existential growth, fantasy, or minimization of threat.

More recent studies have also reported occasional age differences. Folkman, Lazarus, Pimley, and Novacek (1987) found that, across a range of stressful situations, older respondents used less confrontive coping (e.g. 'stood my ground and fought') and were less likely to seek social support; they were more likely to use distancing and positive reappraisal. Irion and Blanchard-Fields (1987), using a smaller sample but similar coping scales, also found that older individuals used less confrontive coping in dealing with threat (but not challenge). They did not replicate any of the other findings of Folkman *et al.* (1987). Felton and Revenson (1987) examined age differences in coping with chronic illness in middle-aged and older adults; by restricting the stress to illness, they reduced the confounding of age with type of stress. They reported lower use of emotional expression, self-blame, and information-seeking in their older subjects, but no age differences in the use of cognitive restructuring, wish-fulfilling fantasy, or threat minimization.

Although comparison between studies is made difficult by the different concepts and labels used for different coping mechanisms, it appears that there is no consistent pattern of age differences across these studies. As Felton and Revenson (1987) conclude, 'at this point we can state with some certainty that age-related differences in coping do not clearly fit with a regression or with an opposing growth hypothesis' (p. 169). Where they occur, age differences appear to be small in magnitude and specific to the particular sample and stress examined. Pending the results of longitudinal studies, the findings on age and coping begin to resemble those for age and personality traits, where stability in adulthood, rather than growth or decline, is the rule (Costa and McCrae, 1988).

Research interest in defense mechanisms has lagged in recent years among psychologists, although psychiatrists like George Vaillant (1977) and his colleagues continue to work in this tradition. In a recent study (Costa, Zonderman, and McCrae, in press) we examined correlations of age with three instruments intended to measure defenses: the Haan (1965) MMPI defense scales, the Defense Mechanisms Inventory (Ihilevich and Gleser, 1986), and the Defense Style Questionnaire (Bond, Gardner, Christian, and Sigal, 1983). Most of the scales showed little or no relation to age across the range from 20 to 96. There was some evidence that older people were more prone to report the use of defenses that suggest altruism and socialization instead of confrontation, but it is not yet clear whether this is a generational or a maturational effect. Overall, older individuals appeared to be neither more nor less mature than younger adults in their use of defense mechanisms.

Situational determinants

It would seem obvious that coping efforts would be dictated at least in part by the demands of the situation. A burning house should, and usually will, provoke direct action rather than positive thinking; a suspicious lump should (though if often does not) lead to seeking medical advice rather than to denial. In many cases, however, the lines are not so clear cut. There are usually alternative ways of trying to solve problems, as there are of trying to relieve distress. Further, as Lazarus and Folkman (1984) have pointed out, coping is really a series of actions that occur over time, and many different efforts may be needed during the course of the event (cf. Horowitz, 1985). An individual who smells smoke may need to deny the possibility of fire long enough to control panic, then seek information on the source and extent of the fire, then leave the house, then call for help, then wait fatalistically as the firefighters work, then seek support from friends and relatives, then reappraise the situation as one that could have been much worse. Asking subjects how they coped with a fire might find all these methods mentioned.

It is perhaps for this reason that expected situational differences in coping are sometimes not clear cut. Felton *et al.* (1984), for example, compared subjects with four chronic diseases (hypertension, diabetes mellitus, cancer, and rheumatoid arthritis). They found that differences in coping behavior were generally not explained by diagnosis, despite the fact that the diseases differed in pain, seriousness, and controllability.

Perhaps, however, the questions asked about coping were not specific enough to detect distinctions among these chronic diseases. McCrae (1984) contrasted broader categories of stress—threat, loss, and challenge—and did find replicated effects. Regardless of the kind of stress, some ways of coping were more common than others. Rational action and expression of feelings were used by a majority of subjects, whereas only a small fraction reported the use of sedation or active forgetting. There were, however, also systematic differences among the three types of stress. Across a wide range of specific events, individuals facing threats used more wishful thinking, faith, and fatalism; individuals facing loss used more faith, fatalism, and expression of feelings; and individuals facing challenge used more rational action, perseverance, positive thinking, intellectual denial, restraint, self-adaptation, drawing strength from adversity, and humor. Threats and losses thus appear to constrain the range of coping responses more than do challenges.

Personality and coping

It is notable, however, that threats and losses did not lead to a regressive use of immature or neurotic ways of coping, such as hostile reaction toward others, escapist fantasy, or self-sedation and passivity. Instead, the use of these forms of coping appeared to be more a result of pervasive personality traits. We tested this hypothesis in another study by correlating coping scores with measures of three of the five broad domains of personality, neuroticism, extraversion, and openness (McCrae and Costa, 1986). In two studies, extraversion was associated with increased use of rational action, positive thinking, substitution, and restraint. Openness was positively associated with the use of humor, and negatively associated with the use of faith. Finally, several coping mechanisms were used more often by individuals who scored high in neuroticism, including hostile reaction, escapist fantasy, self-blame, sedation, withdrawal, wishful thinking, passivity, and indecisiveness. Similar findings have been reported by several other investigators. For example, Rim (1986) found that individuals high in neuroticism were more likely to use wishful thinking, self-blame, and tension reduction, and less likely to use problem focused coping; Parkes (1986) reported that direct coping was positively associated with extraversion and negatively associated with neuroticism.

Although the 28 coping mechanisms we measured were conceptually distinct, they were not empirically independent. When factored, two replicated factors emerged: mature coping, defined by rational action, perseverance, positive thinking, restraint, and self-adaptation; and neurotic coping, defined by hostile reaction, escapist fantasy, self-blame, sedation, withdrawal, passivity, and indecisiveness (McCrae and Costa, 1986). Mechanisms that define the mature coping factor are rated by subjects themselves as among the most effective in solving problems and reducing distress; mechanisms that define neurotic coping are rated as among the less effective. The definers of neurotic coping are each individually correlated with measures of neuroticism, but none of them is significantly related to type of stress. Whether faced by threats, losses, or challenges, individuals high in neuroticism are more likely than others to use ineffective and immature ways of coping.

RESPONSE TO STRESS OR REFLECTION OF PERSONALITY? COPING WITH THE INCIDENT AT THREE MILE ISLAND

The distinction between mature and neurotic coping can be seen clearly in data that come from a study of the nuclear accident at Three Mile Island (TMI) and its consequences. The accident and its aftermath provided an extraordinarily valuable research opportunity: an instance of a significant and prolonged stressful situation occurring to an unselected population. The original threat of nuclear catastrophe was followed by lingering questions about radiation exposure and long-term health consequences, and by related events such as marked loss in property values. Previous research (Baum, Gatchel, and Schaeffer, 1983) had documented emotional, behavioral, and physiological consequences of the event in comparisons with matched controls. Our interest was in examining personality and coping at TMI.

This research was done in collaboration with Dr Andrew Baum and his colleagues and students at the Uniformed Services University of the Health Sciences, and, as is often the case in collaborations at a distance, communication was not perfect. Our intent had been to administer our personality measure to TMI

Table 1 Mean levels of coping use for TMI residents and controls and correlations with neuroticism

| Mechanism | Mean | | Effect Size | Correlation with Neuroticism |
	TMI (44)	Control (31)		(74)
Hostile reaction	1.75	1.58	—	0.47***
Rational action	3.47	2.22***	0.34	−0.20
Seeking help	3.06	2.14***	0.18	0.00
Perseverance	3.36	2.19***	0.25	−0.16
Isolation of affect	2.19	2.84*	0.07	0.12
Fatalism	2.70	2.77	—	0.14
Expression of feelings	3.39	2.29***	0.20	−0.14
Positive thinking	3.09	2.51	0.11	−0.20
Distraction	2.91	2.48	—	0.16
Escapist fantasy	1.77	1.84	—	0.30**
Intellectual denial	2.15	2.17	—	0.02
Self-blame	1.52	1.65	—	0.36**
Social comparison	2.71	1.81***	0.17	0.11
Sedation	1.59	1.29	—	0.27*
Substitution	2.58	2.45	—	−0.03
Restraint	3.44	2.95*	0.07	−0.38***
Drawing strength from adversity	2.88	2.06**	0.11	−0.26*
Avoidance	2.70	2.44	—	0.08
Withdrawal	1.66	1.84	—	0.36**
Self-adaptation	3.06	2.21***	0.17	−0.24*
Wishful thinking	3.50	2.94	—	0.31**
Active forgetting	2.30	2.97*	0.08	0.09
Humor	2.23	2.13	—	−0.08
Passivity	2.18	1.77*	0.07	0.19
Indecisiveness	2.55	2.16	—	0.44***
Assessing blame	3.25	2.32**	0.12	−0.12
Faith	3.70	3.13	—	−0.31**
Mature coping factor	3.28	2.42***	0.26	−0.28*
Neurotic coping factor	1.86	1.73	—	0.49***

Note: Numbers are given in parentheses. One coping mechanism, taking one step at a time, was not measured in this study.
*p<0.05; **p<0.01; ***p<0.001.

residents and to controls who lived near non-nuclear power plants (see Baum *et al.*, 1983, for details); we planned to give the coping questionnaire only to the TMI subjects, and designed it to ask how they had dealt with the TMI accident. As it happened, the coping questionnaire was also administered to the control subjects. A few refused to respond, claiming that they had not coped with the accident at all, because it did not affect them. Many other control subjects, however, dutifully completed the form. This design serendipitously allowed us to examine the effects of personality and situation on coping in the most extreme case: The situation for the TMI subjects was a major technological disaster that profoundly affected their lives; the situation for the controls was a distant event they heard or read about. Situational effects should be unmistakable here.

Subjects were given two questionnaires: the NEO Inventory (NEO)—a precursor of the NEO Personality Inventory (Costa and McCrae, 1985)—and an adaptation of the Coping Questionnaire (McCrae, 1984). Both were administered in 1983, approximately 4 years after the TMI accident. The NEO Inventory is a 144-item questionnaire developed through factor analysis to fit a three-dimensional model of personality. Of particular interest here is the 48-item neuroticism domain scale, which assesses such traits as anxiety, anger, depression, and vulnerability to stress. The scales of the NEO Inventory show high reliability and stability (Costa and McCrae, 1988), and have been validated against other self-report instruments and peer, spouse, and interviewer ratings (Costa and McCrae, 1985).

Because of an extensive literature on the stability of personality (Costa and McCrae, 1988), we did not expect personality differences between the two groups. Theorists who view personality dispositions as more malleable might have anticipated that the prolonged stress at TMI would have increased the neuroticism of TMI residents. Of course, no pre-accident baseline measures were available to test this hypothesis directly, but a comparison of the TMI residents and controls showed that the TMI residents were slightly but significantly lower—not higher—in neuroticism than the controls. It would probably be a mistake to make too much of this finding; selective attrition might well account for it. However, it provides no support for the view that adverse events create lasting impairment in emotional stability. More important for the present purposes, it suggests that the measure of neuroticism reflects enduring personality traits rather than effects of stress in the TMI sample.

The revised Coping Questionnaire consisted of 50 items measuring strategies for coping identified through a review of the literature. On both empirical and theoretical grounds, the items were combined into 27 scales containing from one to five items each measuring a conceptually distinct coping mechanism (McCrae, 1982); two broader factors—mature coping and neurotic coping—were also scored (McCrae and Costa, 1986). In the present application both TMI and control subjects were asked to 'decide whether you never, rarely, sometimes, often, or always' responded as the items suggested 'in dealing with the Three Mile Island incident and its effects.'

TMI residents and controls are compared on their coping responses to the accident in Table 1. Not surprisingly, there are many significant differences. TMI residents responded to the crisis with more frequent use of rational action, seeking help, perseverance, expression of feelings, positive thinking, social comparison, restraint, drawing strength from adversity, self-adaptation, passivity, assessing blame, and total mature coping. TMI residents were less likely than controls to use isolation of affect or active forgetting. Clearly, these results show that the stress of the TMI accident provoked a wide range of coping responses, most of which would be considered mature and effective. Control subjects, who faced no real danger from the incident, were more likely to deal with the event by simply putting it out of their minds.

The last column of Table 1 gives correlations of each of these coping mechanisms with NEO neuroticism scores for the full sample. There are two notable sets of findings here. First, previous results were replicated with regard to coping and neuroticism. Six of the seven mechanisms that defined a neurotic coping factor in previous research (McCrae and Costa, 1986) are significantly related to neuroticism in the combined sample; when analyzed separately, significant correlations are seen in both the TMI and control samples for hostile reactions, wishful thinking, indecisiveness, and total neurotic coping. Second, neuroticism is inversely related to the use of total mature coping, and to restraint, drawing strength from adversity, self-adaptation, and faith. These relations were not seen in earlier studies using larger samples, so they might be regarded as chance. However, it is possible that the stress at TMI was more severe, and that under severe stress, neuroticism interferes with the use of adaptive coping mechanisms as well as promoting the use of ineffective ones.

One of the striking features of Table 1 is the failure of neuroticism-related coping mechanisms to distinguish between TMI and control groups. Of the mechanisms previously identified as being related to neuroticism only one—passivity—was used significantly more often by TMI residents. Controls were just as likely as TMI residents to respond with hostile reaction, escapist fantasy, self-blame, sedation, withdrawal, wishful thinking, and indecisiveness. This is an odd and troubling finding, because we would expect some proportionality between the degree or immediacy of the stress and responses to it. The fact that individuals high in neuroticism responded to the TMI incident with hostile reaction and self-blame *whether or not* they were present at TMI suggests that these responses have more to do with the individual's personality than with the stress.

It might by hypothesized that such behaviors are attributed by the subjects to the stress, although they are not causally related to it. Individuals high in neuroticism frequently experience negative emotions like irritability and depression; if asked why, they will probably seek an environmental rather than a dispositional explanation (cf. Costa, McCrae, and Zonderman, 1987). Had TMI never happened, they would have resorted as often to hostile reaction and self-blame, but would have attributed it to some other event.

Note that the misattribution hypothesis calls into question the dominant research paradigm of the past decade: the use of self-report coping questionnaires. Coping researchers have assumed that individuals would accurately depict not only what they did, but why they did it (i.e. that it was in response to stress). The TMI data point out that this may not always be a realistic assumption. Individuals may not be blind to irrational or undesirable behavior, as classic theories of defense assumed—but they may be too eager to attribute it to an external cause.

We do not advocate abandoning coping questionnaires: much useful information can be obtained from them. But we need to supplement them with other research methods; in particular, we need to design studies to test the misattribution hypothesis. Coping responses are supposed to be extraordinary measures called into action by situational demands. They should therefore occur more frequently during a time of crisis than a time of calm. Repeated measures on the same individuals before and after a threat, loss, or challenge could help establish this basic characteristic of coping responses.

COPING EFFECTIVENESS

Another reason to think that neuroticism-related mechanisms are not really coping efforts is that they are ineffective in solving problems or in reducing distress. Lazarus and his colleagues (e.g. Lazarus *et al.*, 1974; Lazarus and Folkman, 1984) have provided strong and sound arguments for not assuming that we can evaluate the effectiveness of coping efforts a priori. Self-blame, hostile reaction, and withdrawal do not appear to be healthy and mature reactions to a situation, but perhaps for some individuals they provide needed emotional release, or a defense against even more debilitating reactions. For Lazarus, this was an empirical question; several studies now offer an empirical answer.

In our earlier research (McCrae and Costa, 1986), we asked subjects to rate the effectiveness of various ways of coping in solving the problem and making them feel better. Somewhat surprisingly, we found that the same mechanisms were generally found to be effective for both purposes, and were equally effective in dealing with threats, losses, and challenges. The mechanisms deemed most effective by our subjects were also the ones most frequently used. The most effective mechanisms were precisely those considered a priori as most mature: rational action, seeking help, expression of feelings, restraint, drawing strength from adversity, self-adaptation, humor, and faith. And the least effective were almost invariably among the neuroticism-related: hostile reactions, isolation of affect, escapist fantasy, self-blame, withdrawal, wishful thinking, active forgetting, passivity, and indecisiveness.

We found that the neurotic coping factor was significantly related to poorer subsequent psychological well-being—a result that has been reported elsewhere (Felton *et al.*, 1984). However, when we partialled out the influence of neuroticism on both coping and well-being, we found no remaining association. Apparently there was not even a negative effect directly attributable to these behaviors—a further reason to regard them as epiphenomena of stress and coping.

With regard to the remaining coping mechanisms, there is far too little data at the present time to make conclusive statements. When an index was created in which coping use was weighted by coping effectiveness rank, the resulting Effectiveness Index was significantly associated with subsequent psychological well-being even after controlling for the effects of neuroticism and extraversion (McCrae and Costa, 1986). This suggests that doing the right things may in fact help. Assessing effectiveness in any more detailed fashion, however, poses a number of difficulties. It is convenient to use psychological well-being as the outcome criterion, since we have a number of validated measures of well-being. It can be argued, however, that other criteria are equally important. Individuals may have coped well if they have learned from the experience, or fulfilled their social obligations, or minimized the strain placed on loved ones. An assessment of the individual's goals and values may be necessary as a first step in evaluating coping effectiveness.

One obvious but hazardous criterion for coping effectiveness is provided by health outcomes. If meditation, rational planning, or active denial leads to longer and healthier lives, that is surely a demonstration of its value. But health outcomes are problematic when self-reports are used in place of objective diagnostic criteria, because somatic complaints are often contaminated by neuroticism (Costa and McCrae, 1987). When Felton *et al.* (1984) reported that avoidance, self-blame, and emotional ventilation were associated with poorer adjustment to illness, and when Holahan and Moos (1986) found associations between avoidance coping and psychosomatic symptoms, neuroticism must be suspected as the third variable that accounts for the correlations.

We must also be realistic in expectations, since, in most medical situations, coping is likely to play a relatively minor role in comparison with such factors as physical constitution and medical therapy. Extremely large samples might be needed to demonstrate a reliable effect in such cases. Perhaps a more profitable strategy would be to assess proximal rather than distal medical outcomes: A stress-management program to reduce smoking is better judged by numbers of cigarettes smoked than by the incidence of lung cancer.

FUTURE DIRECTIONS

So little is firmly established about the nature and effects of coping that almost any research could contribute to our understanding. Instead of singling out a few critical questions for future research, this chapter has attempted to provide some guidance by pointing to a set of putative coping mechanisms that can profitably be ignored. Neuroticism-related mechanisms like hostile reaction and self-blame do not seem to be related to the stressful situation, nor to make any independent contribution to long-term well-being, and research should probably be intensified on other forms of coping, such as seeking help and self-adaptation.

From among the many possible directions that might be pursued, we will be addressing several in studies currently in progress. A seven-year longitudinal analysis of coping among participants in the Baltimore Longitudinal Study of Aging will be used to check previous cross-sectional findings on age differences in the use of coping mechanisms. The same data can be analyzed to address the stability of individual differences in coping. Although coping efforts should be assessed as specific responses to particular stresses, the extent to which individuals will respond consistently across time and situations is an empirical one. Strong correlations would suggest that the traditional notion of a generalized coping style may have more utility than is currently supposed.

We have examined the relations between coping mechanisms and the personality dimensions of neuroticism, extraversion, and openness to experience. Two additional dimensions, agreeableness and conscientiousness, should also be considered as dispositional determinants of coping efforts. It is reasonable to hypothesize that agreeable people may make more use of social support, and that conscientious people will rely more on persistence and direct action, and there is some preliminary evidence that these hypotheses are tenable. R. Vickers (personal communication, February 16, 1988) has found striking associations between conscientiousness as measured by the NEO-PI and several forms of coping, especially active problem solving. Further systematic research is clearly indicated.

We hope all investigators will pay more attention to the choice of outcome criteria. Physical health and psychological well-being may be important endpoints, but they need not be the only ones. The alcoholic may be satisfied with his or her way of dealing with stress, and the health consequences of drinking may be years away—but family, friends, and job suffer. We should consider a variety of signs of successful adaptation and be prepared to consider the necessary trade-offs.

In addition, we should supplement self-reports with objective biomedical measurements or with spouse, peer, or observer ratings where appropriate. Although it was a great conceptual and methodological advance to assert that coping is not a defensive process to which the individual is inevitably blind, it remains the case that self-reports provide only one view of the process and outcome. Objective measurements avoid some of the biases inherent in self-reports, and the perspective of those close to the coping individual may also prove valuable.

Finally, we believe that more attention must be paid to the temporal element in describing coping and its outcomes. Folkman *et al.* (1986) have demonstrated that coping is a dynamic process which must be assessed repeatedly to be fully understood, and recent analyses suggest that, in the long run, most individuals adapt even to the gravest stresses (McCrae and Costa, 1988). The issue is not, in general, whether people will adapt, but how soon, and at what emotional, social, and economic cost. Since the pioneering work of Janis (1958), illness and medical treatment have provided a natural laboratory for the study of stress and coping processes, one that is often particularly suited to the study of coping as a dynamic process. With added attention to personality variables, such research can continue to provide both theoretical insights and practical medical applications.

ACKNOWLEDGEMENT

Thanks are due to Andrew Baum for providing data from his project at Three Mile Island; the authors retain full responsibility for the interpretation of the data.

REFERENCES

Aldwin, C.M. and Revenson, T.A. (1987). Does coping help? A reexamination of the relation between coping and mental health. *Journal of Personality and Social Psychology*, **53**, 337−48.

Allport, G.W. and Odbert, H.S. (1936). Trait names: a psycho-lexical study. *Psychological Monographs*, **47** (1, Whole No. 211).

Baum, A., Gatchel, R.J. and Schaeffer, M.A. (1983). Emotional, behavioral, and physiological effects of chronic stress at Three Mile Island. *Journal of Consulting and Clinical Psychology*, **51**, 565−72.

Benson, H. (1975). *The Relaxation Response*, Morrow, New York.

Bond, M., Gardner, S.T., Christian, J. and Sigal, J.J. (1983). Empirical study of self-rated defense styles. *Archives of General Psychiatry*, **40**, 333−38.

Burish, T.G. and Bradley, L.A. (eds.). *Coping with Chronic Disease: Research and Applications*, Academic Press, New York.

Byrne, D. (1964). Repression-sensitization as a dimension of personality. In B.A. Maher (ed.) *Progress in Experimental Personality Research*, Vol. 1, Academic Press, New York.

Coelho, G., Hamburg, D. and Adams, J. (eds.) (1974). *Coping and Adaptation*, Basic Books, New York.

Costa, P.T., Jr and McCrae, R.R. (1985). *The NEO Personality Inventory Manual*, Psychological Assessment Resources, Odessa, FL.

Costa, P.T., Jr and McCrae, R.R. (1987). Neuroticism, somatic complaints, and disease: is the bark worse than the bite? *Journal of Personality*, **55**, 299−316.

Costa, P.T., Jr and McCrae, R.R. (1988). Personality in adulthood: a six-year longitudinal study of self-reports and spouse ratings on the NEO personality Inventory. *Journal of Personality and Social Psychology*, **54**, 853−63.

Costa, P.T., Jr, McCrae, R.R. and Zonderman, A.B. (1987). Environmental and dispositional influences on well-being: longitudinal follow-up of an American national sample. *British Journal of Psychology*, **78**, 299−306.

Costa, P.T., Jr, Zonderman, A.B. and McCrae, R. R. (in press). Personality, stress, and coping in older adulthood. In E.M. Cummings, A.L. Greene and K.H. Karraker (eds.) *Life-Span Developmental Psychology, Vol. 11: Stress and Coping Across the Life Span*, Lawrence Erlbaum Associates, Hillsdale, NJ.

Digman, J.M. and Inouye, J. (1986). Further specification of the five robust factors of personality. *Journal of Personality and Social Psychology*, **50**, 116−23.

Felton, B.J. and Revenson, T.A. (1987). Age differences in coping with chronic illness. *Psychology and Aging*, **2**, 164−70.

Felton, B.J., Revenson, T.A. and Hinrichsen, G.A. (1984). Stress and coping in the explanation of psychological adjustment among chronically ill adults. *Social Science and Medicine*, **18**, 889−98.

Folkman, S. and Lazarus, R.S. (1980). An analysis of coping in a middle-aged community sample. *Journal of Health and Social Behavior*, **21**, 219−39.

Folkman, S., Lazarus, R.S., Dunkel-Schetter, C., DeLongis, A. and Gruen, R.J. (1986). Dynamics of a stressful encounter: cognitive appraisal, coping, and encounter outcomes. *Journal of Personality and Social Psychology*, **50**, 992−1003.

Folkman, S., Lazarus, R.S., Pimley, S. and Novacek, J. (1987). Age differences in stress and coping processes. *Psychology and Aging*, **2**, 171−84.

Freud, A. (1936). *The Ego and the Mechanisms of Defense*, International Universities Press, New York.

Haan, N. (1965). Coping and defense mechanisms related to personality inventories. *Journal of Consulting Psychology*, **29**, 373−8.

Haan, N. (1977). *Coping and Defending*, Academic Press, New York.

Holahan, C.J. and Moos, R.H. (1986). Personality, coping, and family resources in stress resistance: a longitudinal analysis. *Journal of Personality and Social Psychology*, **51**, 389−95.

Holmes, T.H. and Rahe, R.H. (1967). The social readjustment rating scale. *Journal of Psychosomatic Research*, **11**, 213−18.

Horowitz, M.J. (1985). Disasters and psychological responses to stress. *Psychiatric Annals*, **15**, 161−7.

Ihilevich, D. and Gleser, G.C. (1986). *Defense Mechanisms: Their Classification, Correlates, and Measurement with the Defense Mechanisms Inventory*, DMI Associates, Owosso, MI.

Irion, J.C. and Blanchard-Fields, F. (1987). A cross-sectional comparison of adaptive coping in adulthood. *Journal of Gerontology*, **42**, 502−4.

Janis, I.L. (1958). *Psychological Stress*, Wiley, New York.

Lazarus, R.S., Averill, J.R. and Opton, E.M., Jr (1974). The psychology of coping: issues of research and assessment. In G.V. Coelho, D.A. Hamburg and J.F. Adams (eds.) *Coping and Adaptation*, Basic Books, New York, pp. 249−315.

Lazarus, R.S. and DeLongis, A. (1983). Psychological stress and coping in aging. *American Psychologist*, **38**, 245−54.

Lazarus, R.S. and Folkman, S. (1984). *Stress, Appraisal, and Coping*, Springer, New York.

Lazarus, R.S. and Launier, R. (1978). Stress-related transactions between person and environment. In L.A. Pervin and M. Lewis (eds.) *Perspectives in Interactional Psychology*, Plenum, New York, pp. 287−327.

McCrae, R.R. (1982). Age differences in the use of coping mechanisms. *Journal of Gerontology*, **37**, 454−60.

McCrae, R.R. (1984). Situational determinants of coping responses: loss, threat, and challenge. *Journal of Personality and Social Psychology*, **46**, 919−28.

McCrae, R.R. and Costa, P.T., Jr (1986). Personality, coping, and coping effectiveness in an adult sample. *Journal of Personality*, **54**, 385−405.

McCrae, R.R. and Costa, P.T., Jr (1987). Validation of the five factor model of personality across instruments and observers. *Journal of Personality and Social Psychology*, **52**, 81−90.

McCrae, R.R. and Costa, P.T., Jr (1988). Psychological resilience among widowed men and women: A 10-year followup of a national survey. *Journal of Social Issues*, **44**, 129–42.

Moos, R.H. (ed.) (1976). *Human Adaptation: Coping with Life Crises*, Heath, Lexington, MA.

Moos, R.H. (ed.) (1977). *Coping with Physical Illness*, Plenum Medical Book Co., New York.

Norman, W.T. (1963). Toward an adequate taxonomy of personality attributes: replicated factor structure in peer nomination personality ratings. *Journal of Abnormal and Social Psychology*, **66**, 574–83.

Parkes, K.R. (1986). Coping in stressful episodes: the role of individual differences, environmental factors, and situational characteristics. *Journal of Personality and Social Psychology*, **51**, 1277–92.

Pearlin, L.I. and Schooler, C. (1978). The structure of coping. *The Journal of Health and Social Behavior*, **19**, 2–21.

Pfeiffer, E. (1977). Psychopathology and social pathology. In J.E. Birren and K.W. Schaie (eds.) *Handbook of the Psychology of Aging*, 1st edn, Van Nostrand Reinhold, New York, pp. 650–71.

Quayhagen, M.P. and Quayhagen, M. (1982). Coping with conflict: measurement of age-related patterns. *Research on Aging*, **4**, 364–77.

Rim, Y. (1986). Ways of coping, personality, age, sex and family structure variables. *Personality and Individual Differences*, **7**, 113–16.

Scheier, M.F., Weintraub, J.K. and Carver, C.S. (1986). Coping with stress: divergent strategies of optimists and pessimists. *Journal of Personality and Social Psychology*, **51**, 1257–64.

Schroeder, D.H. and Costa, P.T., Jr (1984). Influence of life event stress on physical illness: substantive effects or methodological flaws? *Journal of Personality and Social Psychology*, **46**, 853–63.

Stroebe, W. and Stroebe, M.S (1987). *Bereavement and Health*, Cambridge University Press, New York.

Vaillant, G.E. (1977). *Adaptation to Life*, Little, Brown, Boston.

Index

Negative life events, 15
 see also Life events
Nonnormative transitions, 14
 see also Life-course transitions
Normative transitions, 3
 see also Life-course transitions

PERI life events scale, 22, 25−26
Personality, 7−8
 definition of, 270
 stress and coping, 269−285
Physician visits
 frequency of, 228
 and widowhood, 76
 see also Formal care; Service use
Pleasant and unpleasant events schedules,
  32−33
Positive life events, 15
 see also Life events
Psychiatric disorders, *see* Depression;
  Mental health
Psychological adjustment to breast cancer,
  175−182

Race and depression, 259
 see also Status characteristics
Reciprocity, related to depression and
  self-esteem, 222
 and well-being, 248
Relocation, 4, 13, 119−137, 140, 232
 adjustment to, 125−133
 and aging, 119−137
 and health of the elderly, 119−137
 institutional, 120−125
 and mental health, 126−127
 of mental patients, 123
 and migration, 129−130
 and mortality, 126
 nonvoluntary, 125−127
 and social support, 126
 voluntary, 127−133
 see also Institutionalization
Retirement, 3, 6, 62
 adjustment to, 99−100
 attitudes toward, 104−106
 and coping mechanisms, 109−112
 as a crisis, 93−95
 and finances, 102−103, 106−108
 and health, 91−118
 and longevity, 96−97
 meaning of, 95−96
 and mental health, 99−100

 and mortality, 96−97
 and social support, 109−112
 and stress, 91−118
 voluntary and involuntary, 108−109

Schedule of recent events, 18, 22, 24−27,
  33, 36
Self-concept and adjustment to breast
  cancer, 182−184
 see also Self-esteem
Self-esteem and stress, 19
 see also Self-concept
Service use, 225−229
 and social support, 77−79
 and widowhood, 76−77
 see also Formal support
Sexual functioning, and breast cancer,
  184−187
Social embeddedness, 46−48
 and social network analysis, 47
 see also Social support
Social network analysis, 47
Social networks, structure of in widowhood, 78−79
Social problems scale, 34−35
Social readjustment rating scale, 94
Social support, 2, 41−66
 and aging, 5−8, 248−249
 and bereavement, 76−77
 and breast cancer, 6−7, 165−198
 data analytic problems in studies of,
  54−63
 definition of, 247−249
 and depression, 7, 241−267
 distress deterrent model of, 46
 enacted, 50−54
 and health, 5−8
 informational, 224−225
 measurement of, 46−54
 and mental health, 7
 moderator model of, 45
 and mortality, 6
 perceived availability of, 48−49
 and residential relocation, 126
 and retirement, 109−112
 satisfaction with, 49−50
 and stress 5−8, 224
 stress-buffering hypothesis, 6, 45−46,
  54−63, 224, 256−257
 suppressor model of, 45
 see also Formal support; Informal
  support